HISTORIC PHOTOS OF
PHOENIX

TEXT AND CAPTIONS BY EDUARDO OBREGÓN PAGÁN

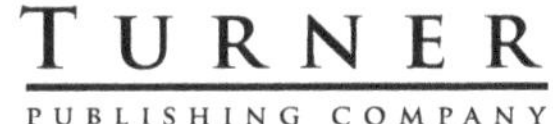

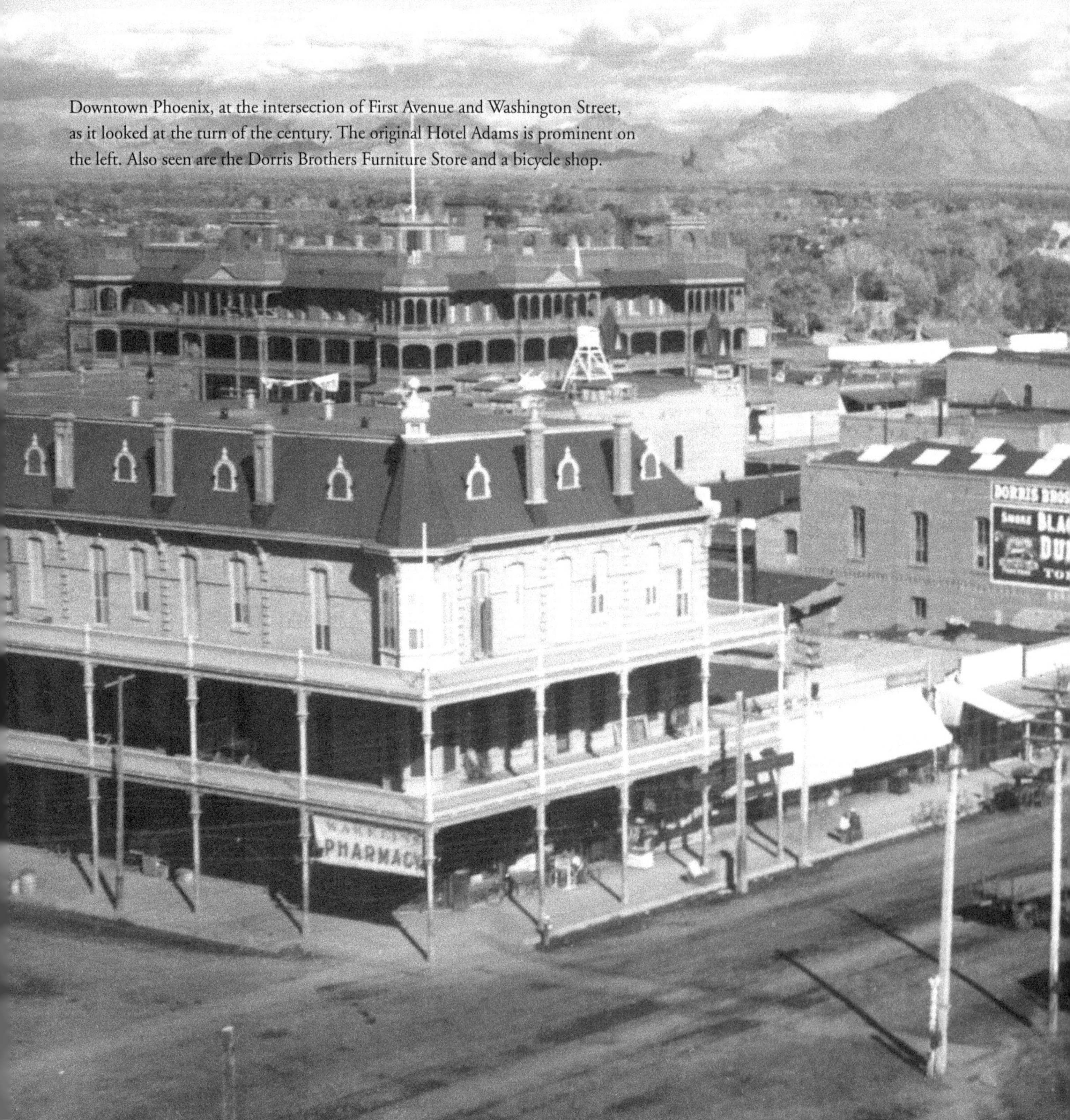

Downtown Phoenix, at the intersection of First Avenue and Washington Street, as it looked at the turn of the century. The original Hotel Adams is prominent on the left. Also seen are the Dorris Brothers Furniture Store and a bicycle shop.

HISTORIC PHOTOS OF PHOENIX

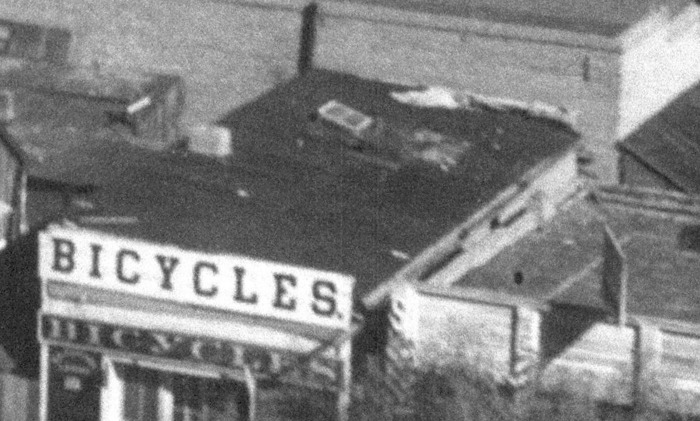

Turner Publishing Company
4507 Charlotte Avenue • Suite 100
Nashville, Tennessee 37209
(615) 255-2665

www.turnerpublishing.com

Historic Photos of Phoenix

Library of Congress Control Number: 2007929595

ISBN-13: 978-1-59652-375-3

ISBN-13: 978-1-68336-962-2 (hc)

Printed in the United States of America

09 10 11 12 13 14—0 9 8 7 6 5 4 3 2

Contents

Mulford Winsor, at right, poses with the staff of the Arizona State Library in Phoenix in 1950. Winsor served as the first territorial historian of Arizona and later as the director of the State Department of Library and Archives from 1932 to 1956. He was a key figure in lobbying the legislature for continued support of the archives.

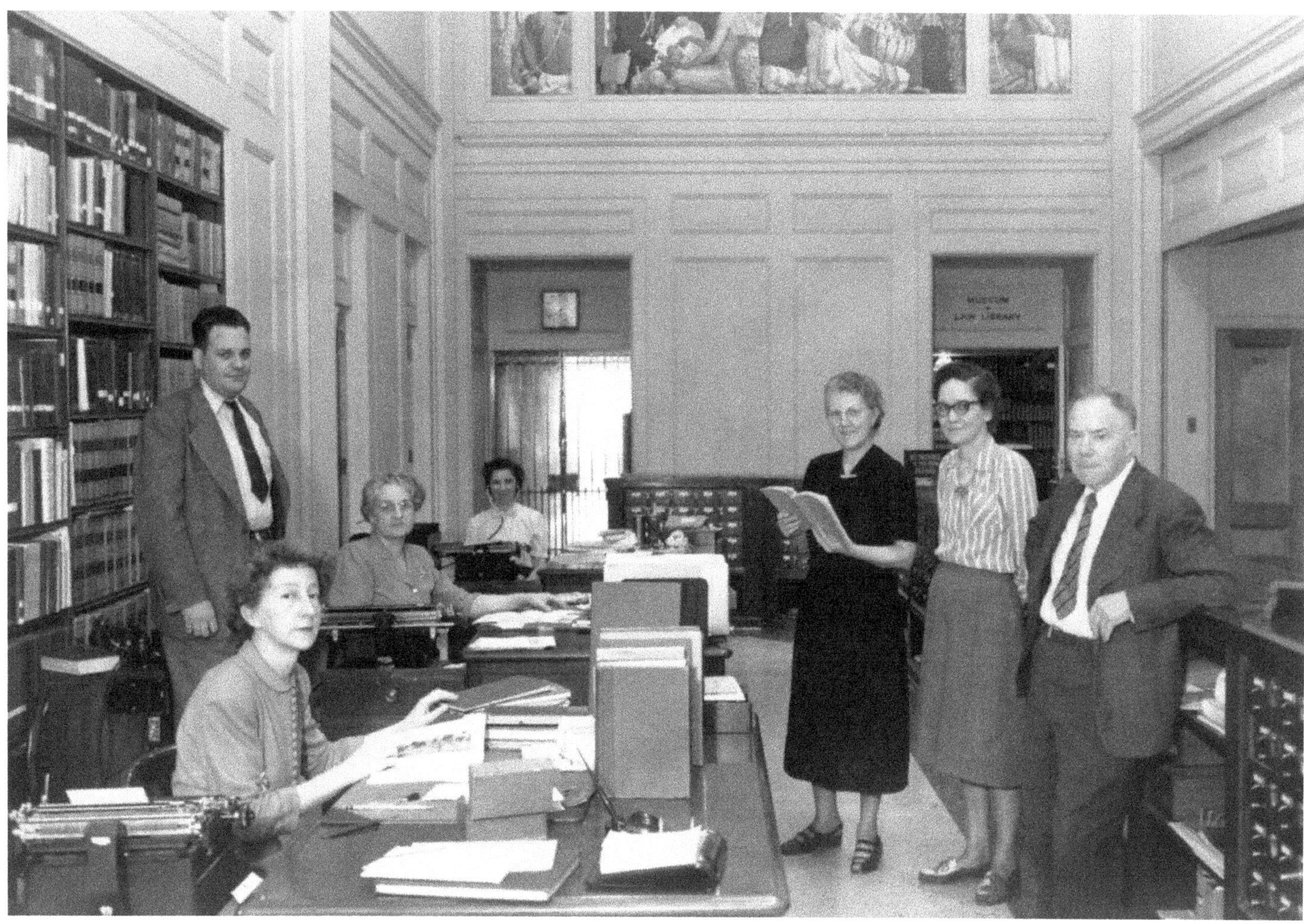

Acknowledgments

This volume, *Historic Photos of Phoenix,* is the result of the cooperation and efforts of many individuals and organizations. It is with great thanks that we acknowledge the valuable contribution of the following for their generous support:

Arizona State Library
the Library of Congress

The author would like to thank in particular Ruth Liljenquist, Stephanie Méndez, Sarah O'Neal, and the staff at the Arizona State Library, Arizona History and Archives Division, for valuable contributions and assistance in making this work possible.

PREFACE

The history of the Phoenix area has been captured in thousands of photographs that reside in archives, both locally and nationally. This book began with the observation that, while those photographs are of great interest to many, they are not easily accessible. The area today is growing and prosperous, with new residents arriving every day and prompting a demand for additional infrastructure and housing. Many residents, new and old, are curious about the local history, especially as the streetscapes and individual buildings associated with that history sometimes seem to be in the way of progress. Many people are asking how to treat these remnants of the past. The decisions made affect every aspect of the urban environment—architecture, public spaces, commerce, infrastructure—and these, in turn, affect the ways that people live their lives. This book seeks to provide decision makers—citizens and officials—a valuable, objective look into the history of Phoenix through photographs of the area.

The power of photographs is that they are less subjective than words in their treatment of history. Although the photographer can make subjective decisions regarding subject matter and how to capture and present it, photographs seldom interpret the past to the extent textual histories can. For this reason, photography is uniquely positioned to offer an original, untainted look at the past, allowing the viewer to learn for himself what the world was like a century or more ago.

This project represents countless hours of research. The editors and writer have reviewed thousands of photographs in numerous archives. We greatly appreciate the generous assistance of the organizations listed in the acknowledgments, without whom this project could not have been completed.

The goal in publishing this work is to provide broader access to these extraordinary images, to inspire, furnish perspective, and evoke insight that might assist those who are responsible for determining the future of Phoenix. In addition, we hope that the book will encourage the preservation of the past with adequate respect and reverence.

With the exception of cropping images where needed and touching up imperfections that have accrued over time, no other changes have been made. The caliber and clarity of many photographs are limited by the technology of the day and the ability of the photographer at the time they were made.

The book is divided into four eras. Beginning with some of the earliest-known photographs of Phoenix, the first section depicts early Phoenix up to the end of the nineteenth century. The second section spans the first decades of the twentieth century through the World War I era. Section Three covers the years between the wars and Section Four wraps up with a look at the city during the World War II era and beyond. In each of these sections we have made an effort to capture various aspects of life through our selection of photographs. People, commerce, industry, recreation, transportation, infrastructure, and religious and educational institutions have been included to provide a broad perspective.

We encourage readers to reflect as they drive or walk the streets of Phoenix, enjoy the beaches and parks, and experience the amenities of this bustling metropolitan area. It is the publisher's hope that in utilizing this work, longtime residents will learn something new and that new residents will gain a perspective on where the region has been, so that each can contribute effectively to its future.

—Todd Bottorff, Publisher

In 1871, only three years after Jack Swilling led a company to reconstruct the canals left by the Hohokam, John J. Gardner built the first hotel in Phoenix on the southwest corner of Washington Street and Pima Street (now Third Street). The Phoenix Hotel, pictured here, was a one-story square building made of adobe and constructed in the Mediterranean style with an interior courtyard.

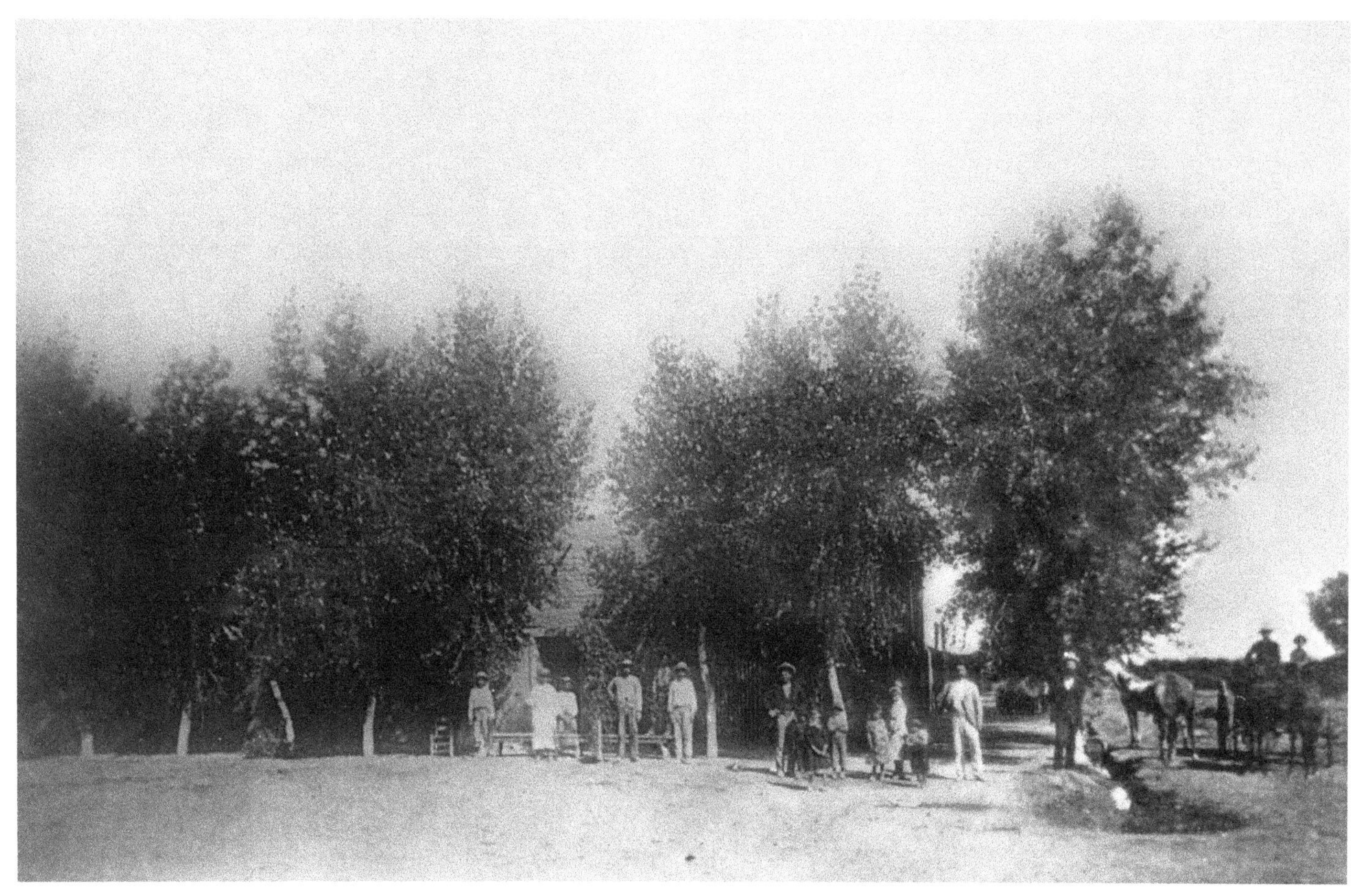

Phoenix Rising

(1869–1899)

It was during the 1850s that North Carolinian Jack Swilling moved to the Arizona territory to prospect for gold. As a scout during the Civil War, he explored the Hohokam ruins and their extensive canal network in the Salt River Valley and became convinced that the ancient canals could again be used for farming. After the war, Swilling arrived in the valley with 18 other members of the Swilling Canal Company, and within months of rebuilding the canals, they were joined by 50 more. John "Yours Truly" Smith, another Civil War veteran, had already started a small farm in the valley to sell grain to the newly established Fort McDowell. One of the settlers, Oxford-educated Darrell Duppa, proposed that the settlement be called Phoenix, after the mythical bird, to symbolize the rise of a new civilization from the ashes of an old one.

By 1870, about 240 people lived in Phoenix, and roughly half were from Mexico. In 1877, Latter-day Saint colonizer Brigham Young sent hundreds of followers to settle in the Salt River Valley. During the next decade, the territorial population doubled, aided in large part by the end of hostilities with Indians.

Yet life in a frontier town was still perilous. Fire destroyed almost the entire business district in 1886, prompting the creation of the first Volunteer Phoenix Engine Company. In 1891, the year that the first telephone system was installed in Phoenix, the river, swollen by the winter runoff, destroyed many of the homes and businesses along the banks.

Life rebounded and Phoenicians re-envisioned their community as they rebuilt. The arrival of the first train in Phoenix spurred a construction boom, as red brick and plumbing fixtures became available. Construction started on City Hall and the first public water system was installed. The Phoenix Indian School, filled with children removed from their families, opened to train them in the ways of the white man.

Phoenicians were eager to divest themselves of their past. They tore down Pueblo-style buildings made of adobe to erect Victorian-style homes and buildings, and changed the names of the streets that ran north and south from Indian names to numbers.

By 1893, paved sidewalks began to replace packed earth, and the city's mule-drawn streetcars were replaced by electric cars. By the time the Phoenix Rough Riders paraded down Central Avenue on their way to fight in the Spanish-American War, Phoenix had grown to almost 3,000 citizens.

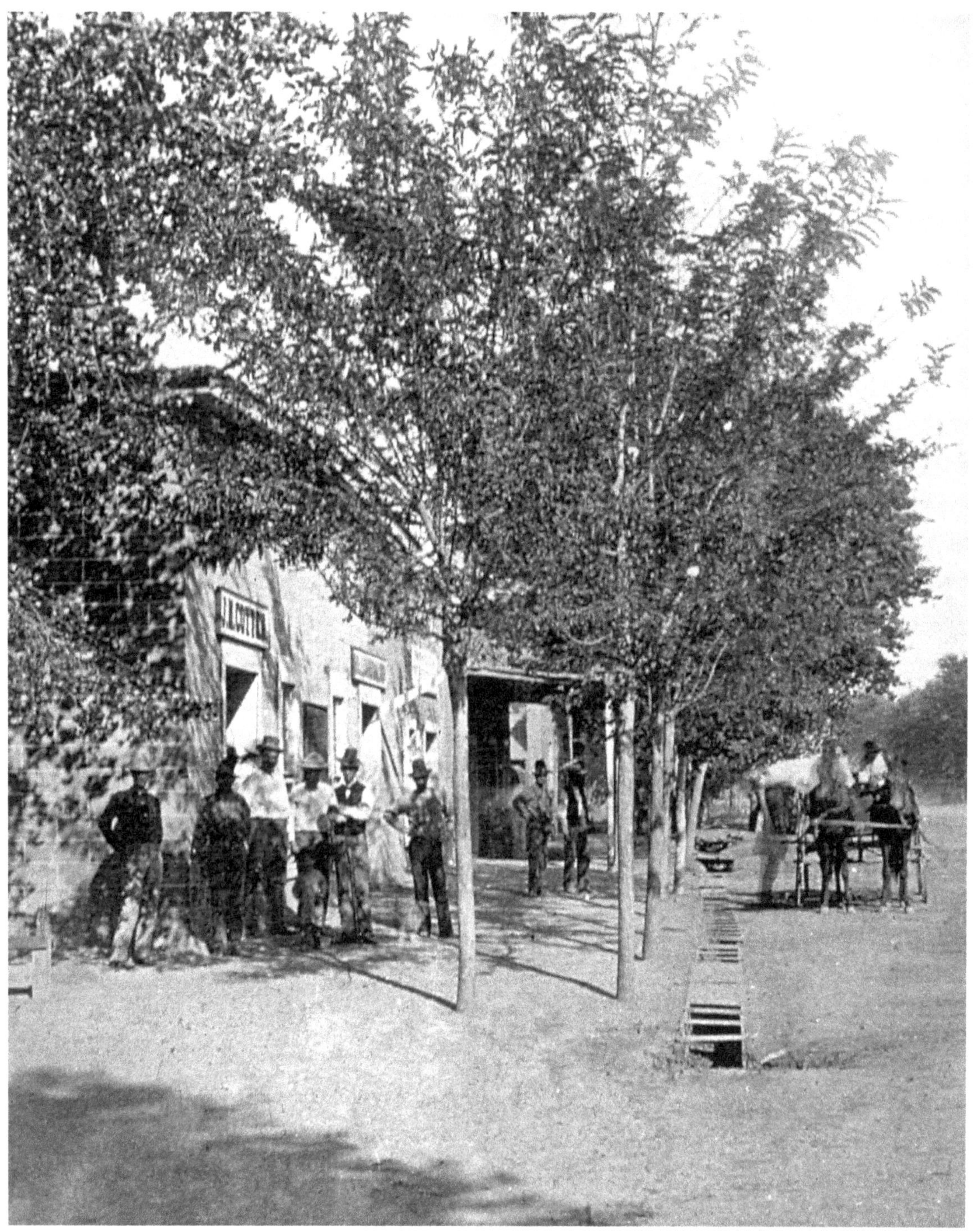

Early settlers immediately set about planting shade trees in Phoenix to line the dirt streets. Before the coming of trains to Phoenix, red bricks and other elements of what white Americans considered "civilized" were rare. Instead, early Phoenix looked very much like a Mexican settlement with half of the population being native-born Spanish speakers and almost every home and business made of sun-dried adobe bricks.

Slowly the appearance of Phoenix buildings began to favor the Victorian architecture of other American cities of the day, like the Goldman & Company building (1874) on the northeast corner of Centre Street (now Central Avenue) and Washington Street. Early Phoenix farmers, miners, and businessmen took their goods and services there to sell, trade, and pay bills.

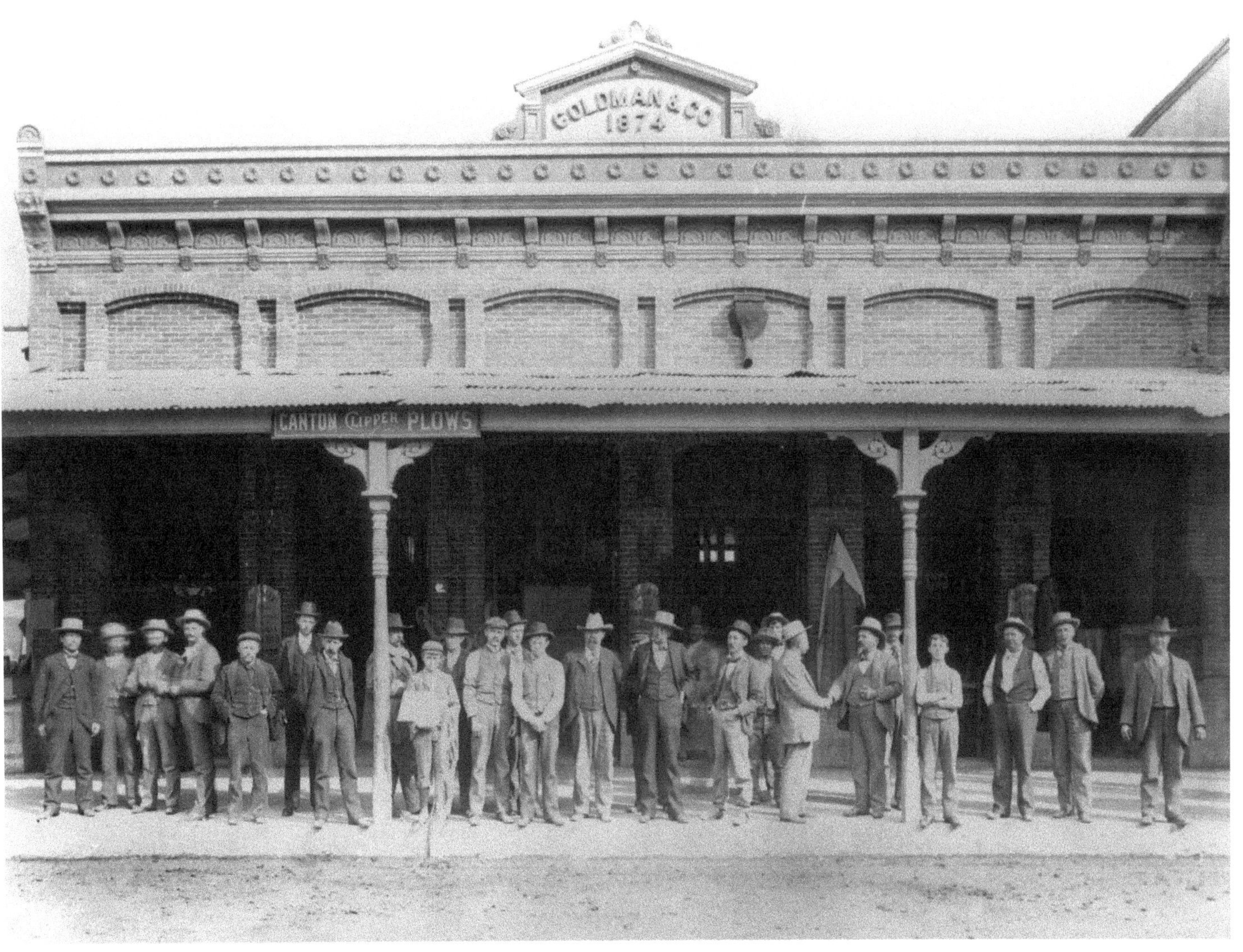

John Berger's blacksmith shop was a flat-roofed, open-air structure made of adobe. Berger was a native of Maryland and worked as a mine boss and a wainwright in Wickenburg before moving to Phoenix. For several years he operated the blacksmith and wagonmaking shop at First Avenue and Adams Street until he began to rent property and engage in mining and ranching, becoming one of the wealthier citizens in town.

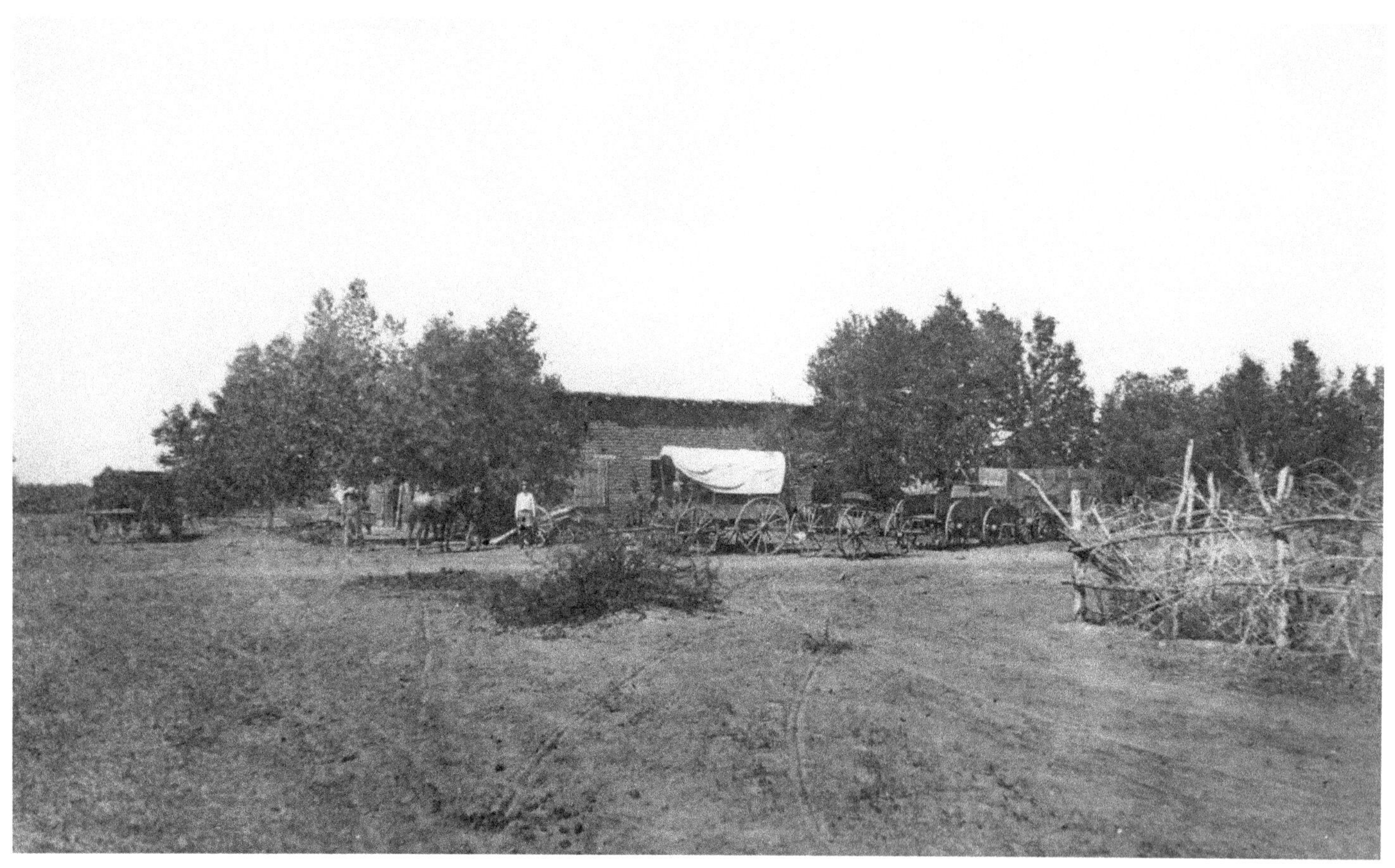

By 1881, Phoenix had outgrown its original form of government. The 11th Territorial Legislature passed the "Phoenix Charter Bill," which incorporated Phoenix and provided for a government consisting of a mayor and four council members. Blacksmith and wainwright John Berger, pictured here with two other blacksmiths, was elected to the first city council.

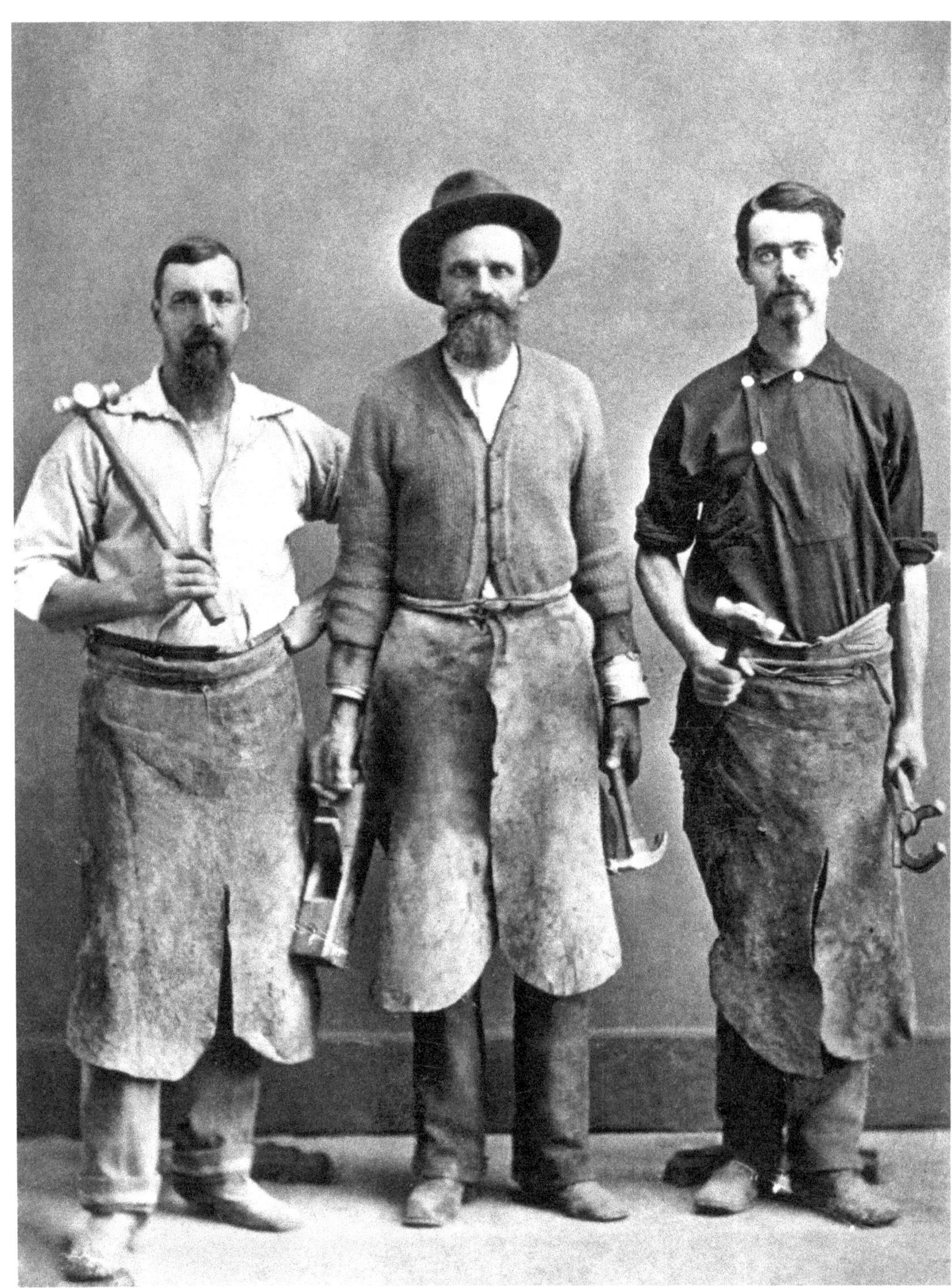

By 1880, the Phoenix population had reached almost 2,500. Phoenicians could also boast of having an ice factory and a brick sidewalk in front of Miguel Peralta's general goods store. That same year the first Phoenix newspaper, the bilingual *Salt River Valley Herald* (pictured here), changed its name to the *Phoenix Daily Herald* and went from a weekly to a semi-weekly publication.

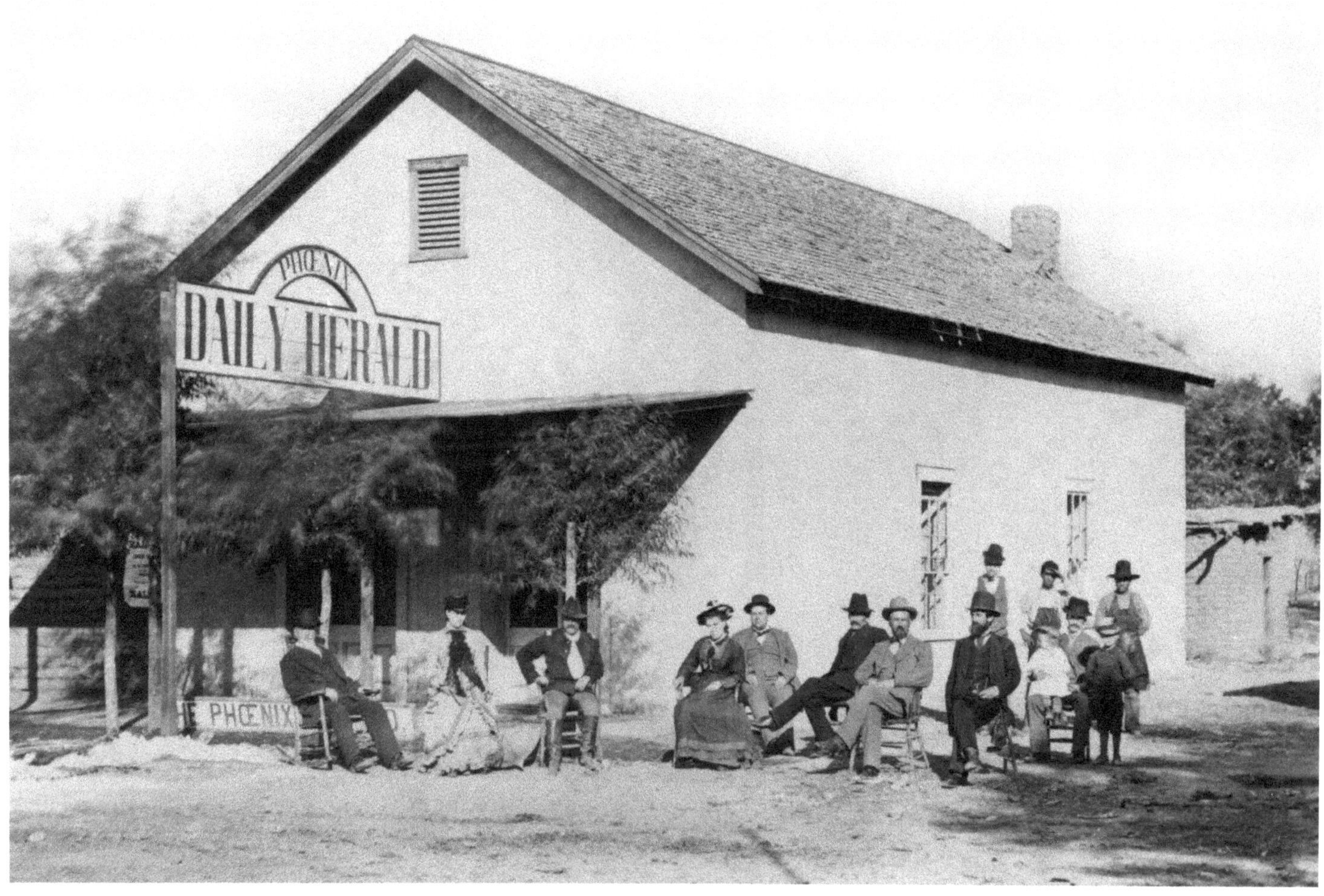

For many years, the intersection of Washington Street and Centre Street was the hub of the city. On the southeast corner, a plain adobe building owned by Jim Cotton was used as a drinking establishment and gathering place by lawyers and politicians. L. H. Goodrich, who came to Phoenix every winter to provide dental care for the residents, owned the Goodrich Building on the northwest corner.

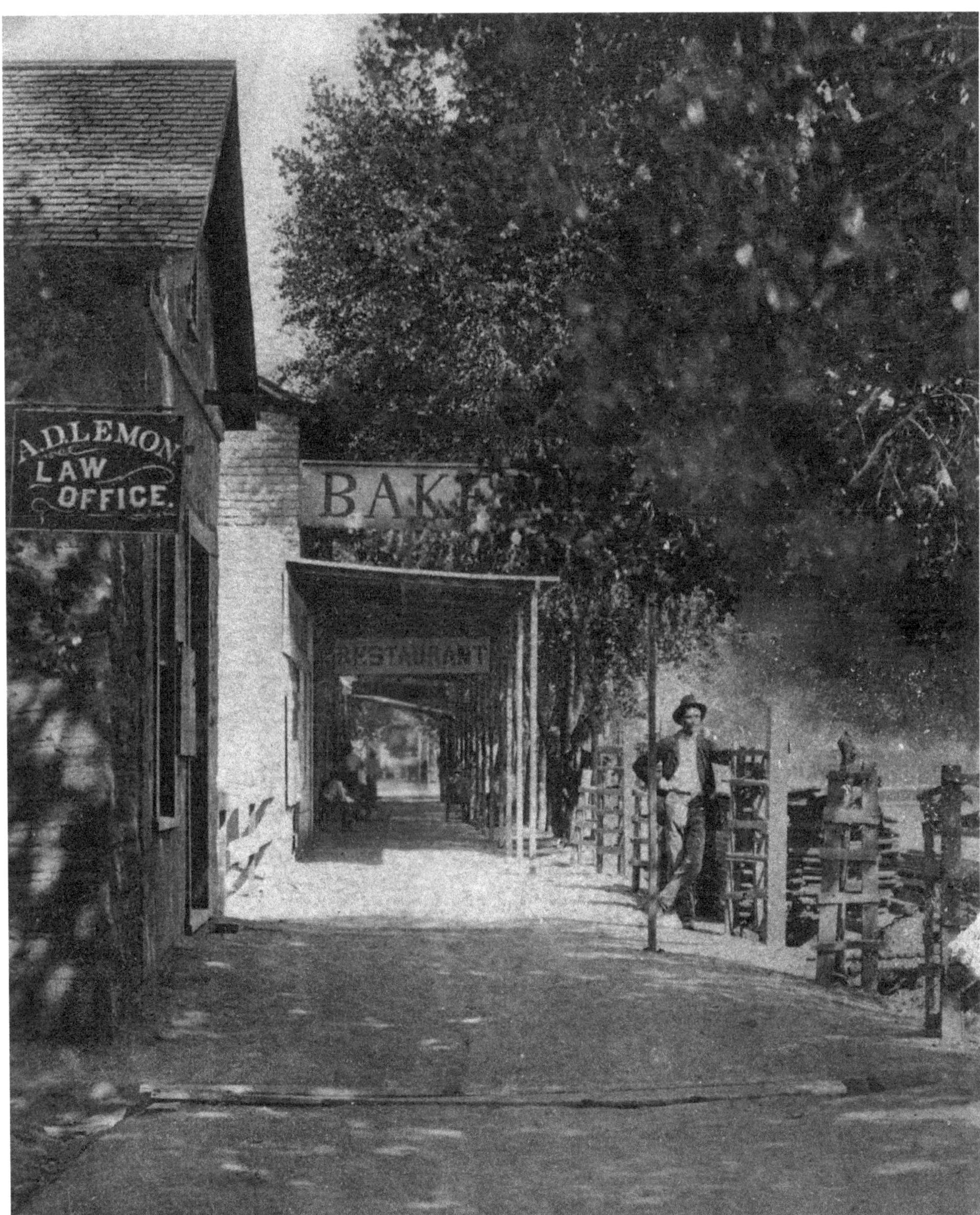

Emil Ganz, a Jewish German immigrant, arrived in Phoenix in 1879 after living in Prescott where he ran a saloon, rented rooms, and dabbled in gold and silver mining. Once in Phoenix, Ganz opened the Bank Exchange Hotel, with a bar and restaurant (pictured here). Three years later, he was considered a prominent citizen and business leader and became the city's first Jewish mayor.

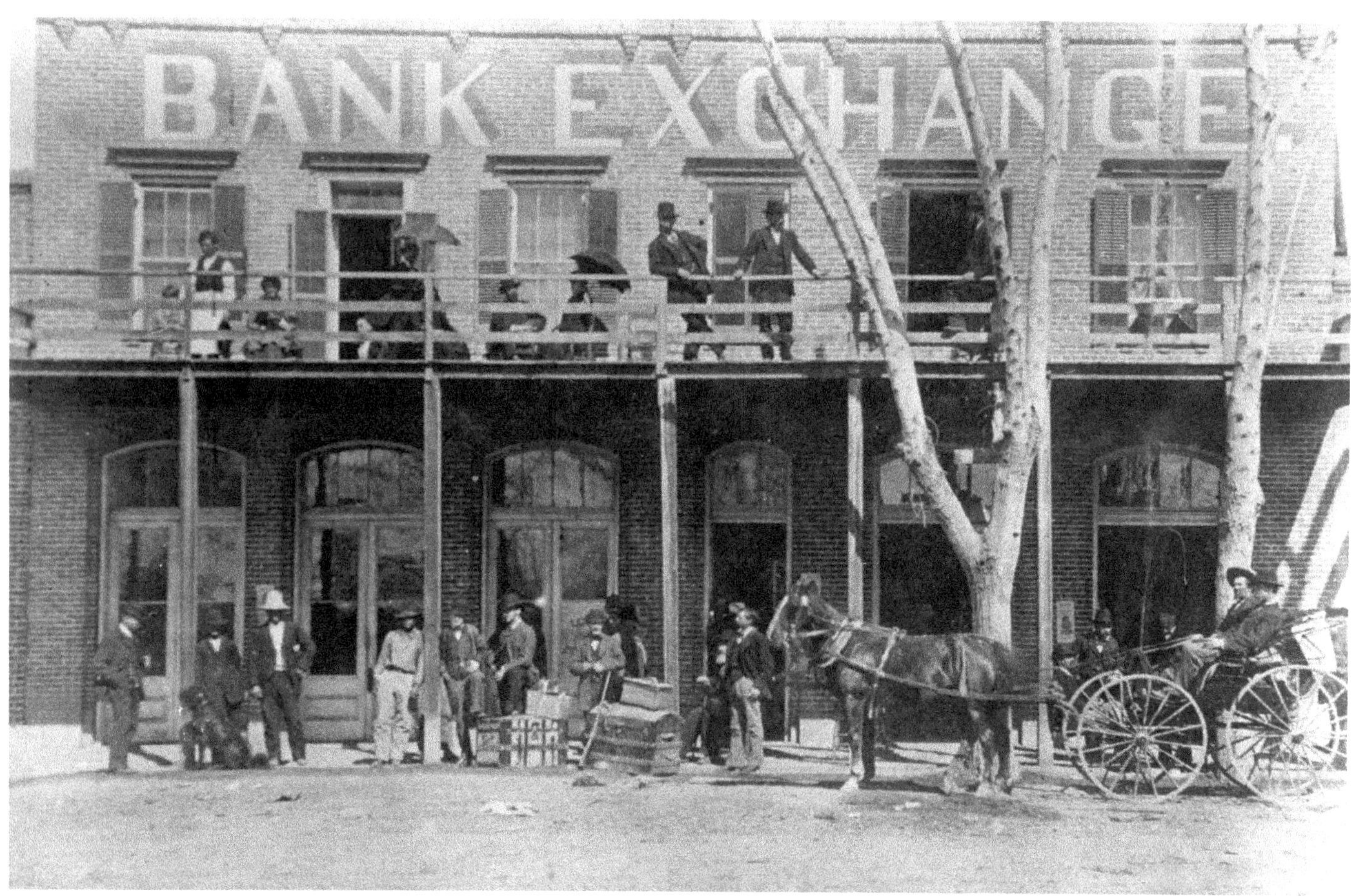

Although Phoenix was still very much a frontier town in 1885, Phoenicians were not without elements of refined culture, such as dress clothes for the formal occasion shown here.

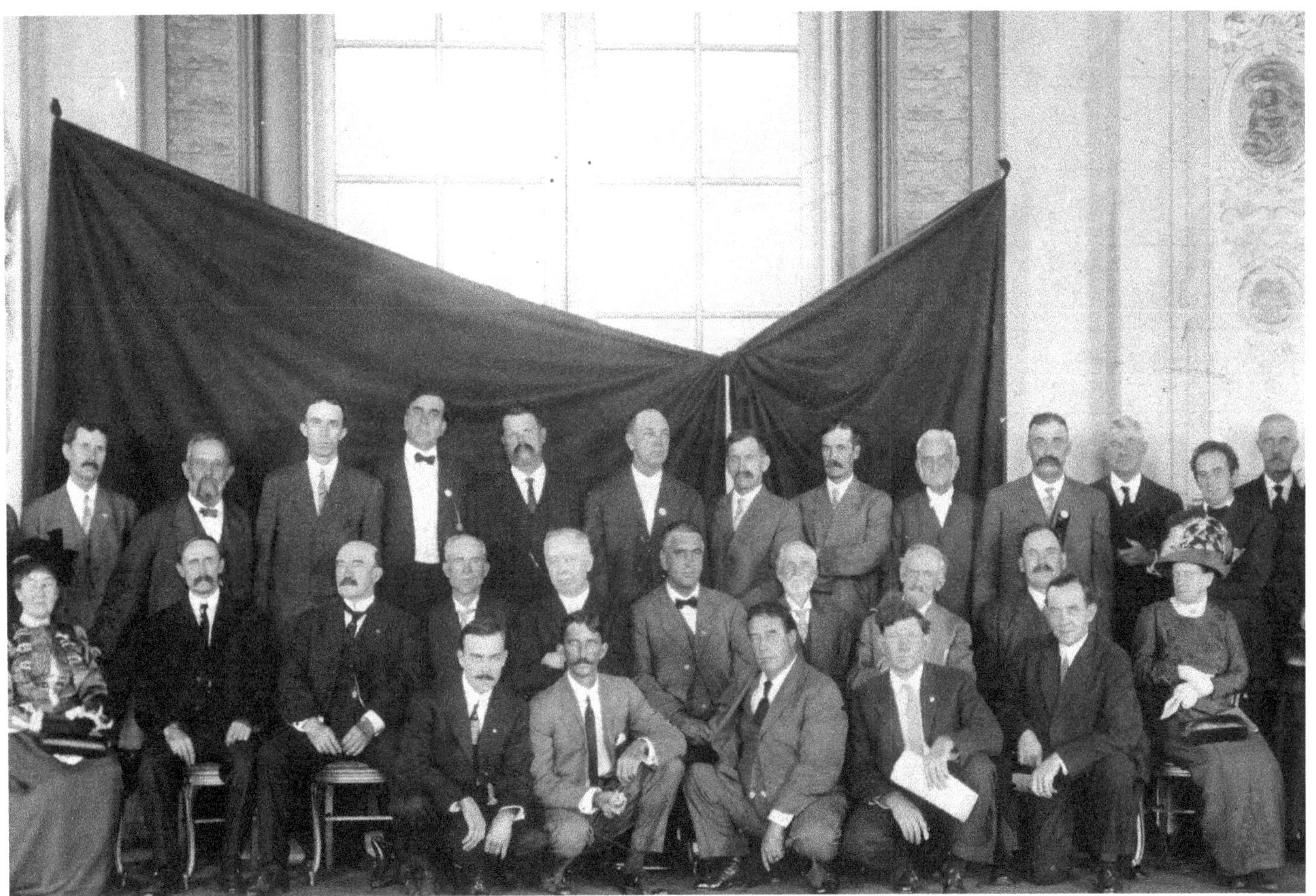

Construction began in 1887 on Phoenix's first City Hall, bounded by Jefferson, Washington, 1st, and 2nd streets. Mule-drawn streetcars began their service that same year.

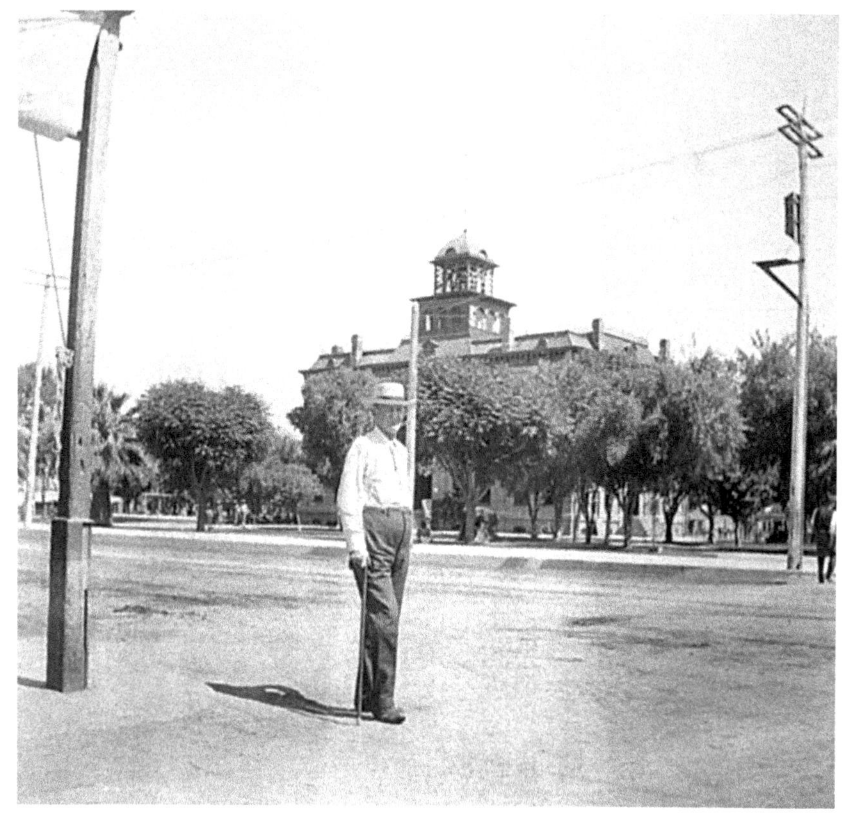

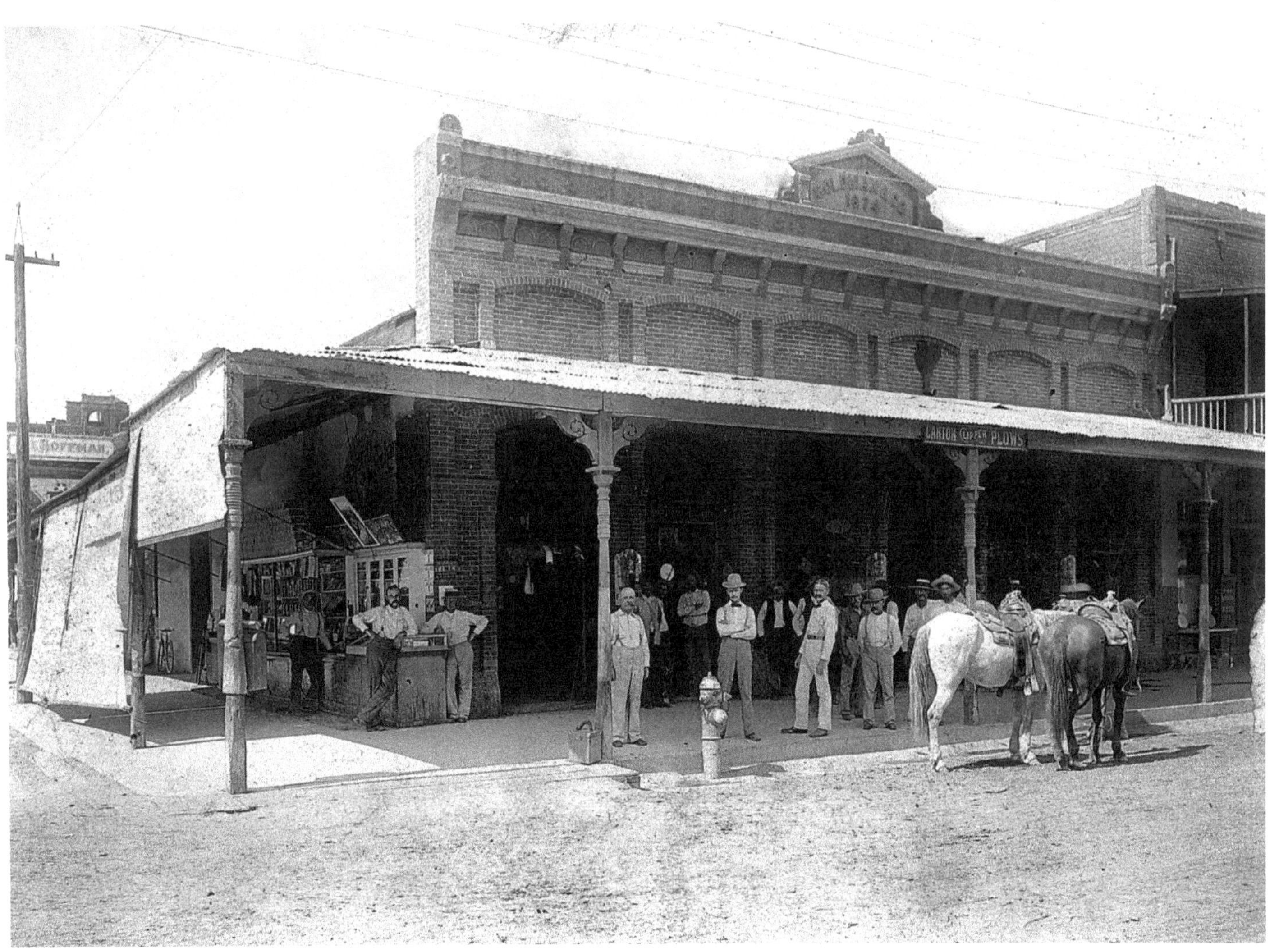

A view of Goldman & Company in 1885, on the northeast corner of Centre Street and Washington Street. That same year Phoenix resident Jim Cotton completed building a sidewalk made of beer bottles in front of his drinking establishment on Washington Street, and the Bank Exchange Hotel was destroyed by fire, as well as most of the businesses on Washington Street's north side.

Phoenix's first school began in the courtroom of the county building on September 5, 1872, with about 20 children under the tutelage of Jean Rudolph Derroche. By October the next year, a small adobe school building had been built on Centre Street. Miss Nellie Shaver from Wisconsin was appointed the first woman schoolteacher.

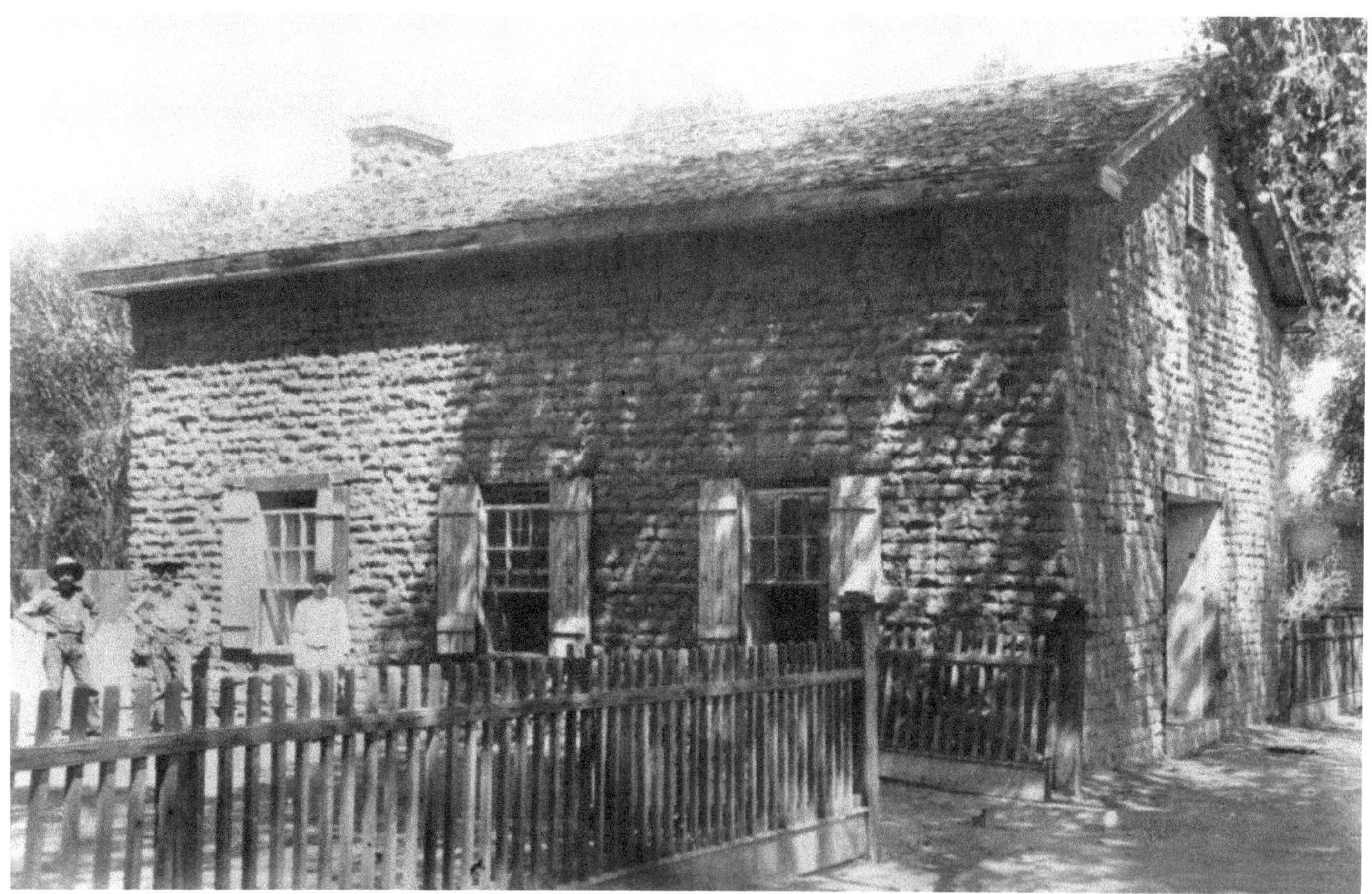

J. C. Adams built the Adams Hotel, pictured here, in 1896. The original wooden structure would burn down 14 years later in 1910. Adams immediately rebuilt it using the most fire-resistant materials available. The new Hotel Adams had 250 rooms and was considered the finest hotel in the Southwest.

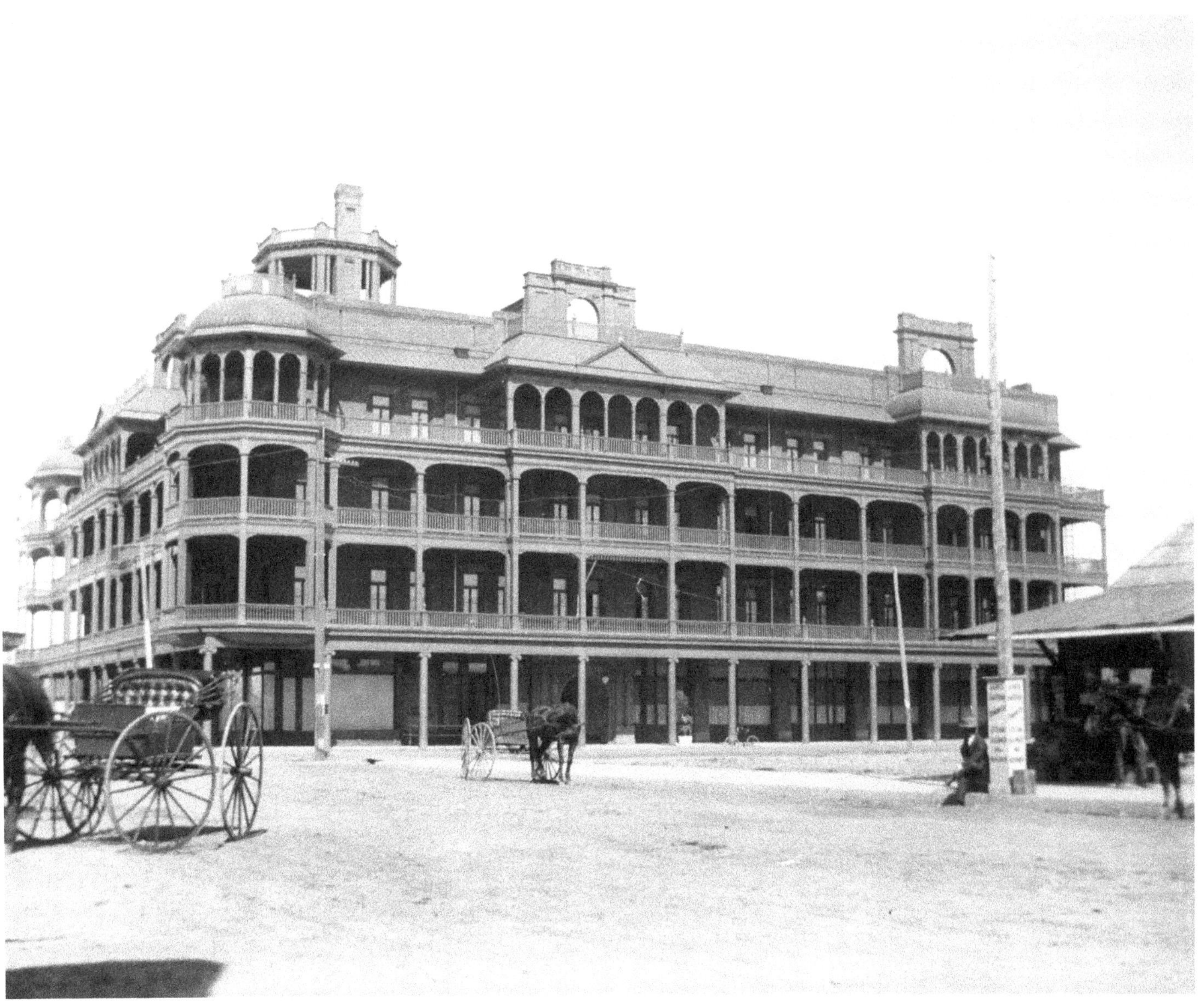

The Santa Fe Railroad Depot, around 1890. Phoenix remained an isolated outpost surrounded by hundreds of miles of inhospitable land until the railroads connected it to the rest of the nation. In 1888, the Arizona and Eastern Railroad came to Phoenix as a branch of the Southern Pacific Railroad. This provided easier and faster travel to Phoenix and allowed merchandise to flow to eastern and western markets by rail instead of wagon.

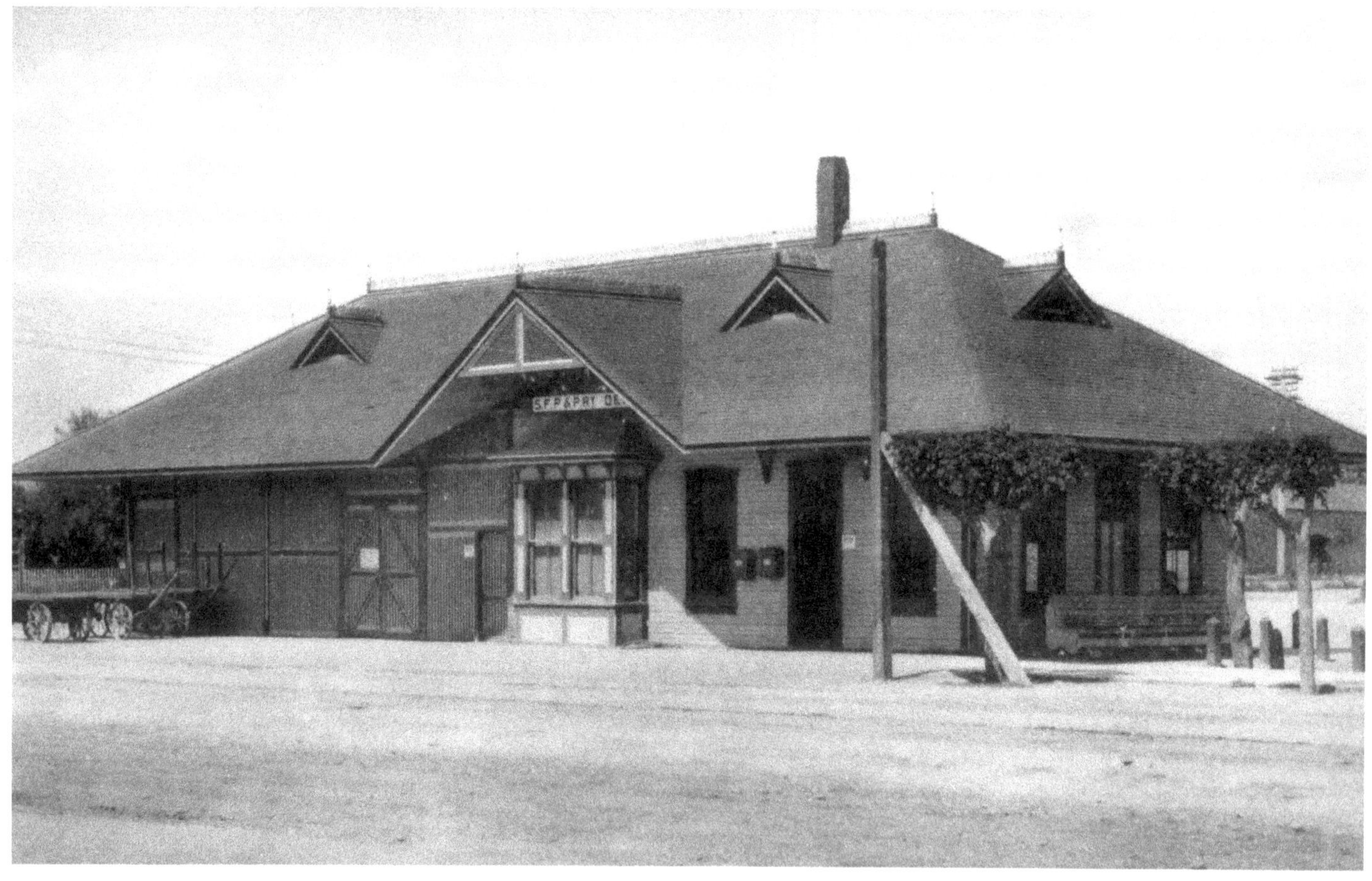

Clark Churchill, Arizona attorney general from 1884 to 1887, real estate investor, and president and executive officer of the Arizona Canal Company, built this mansion for his family in 1895. Two years later he sold the house to the city for $15,000 and it became the new Phoenix Union High School.

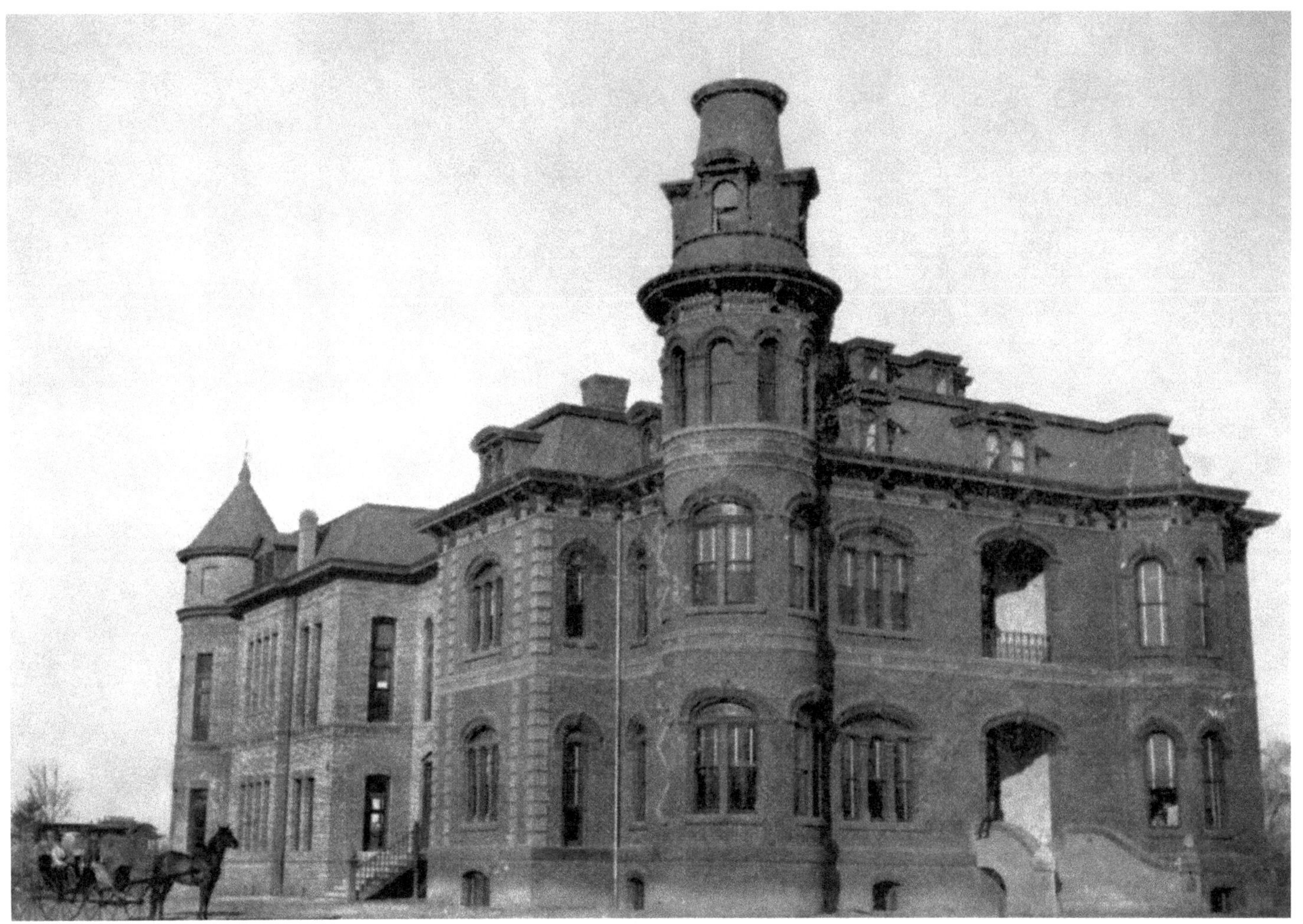

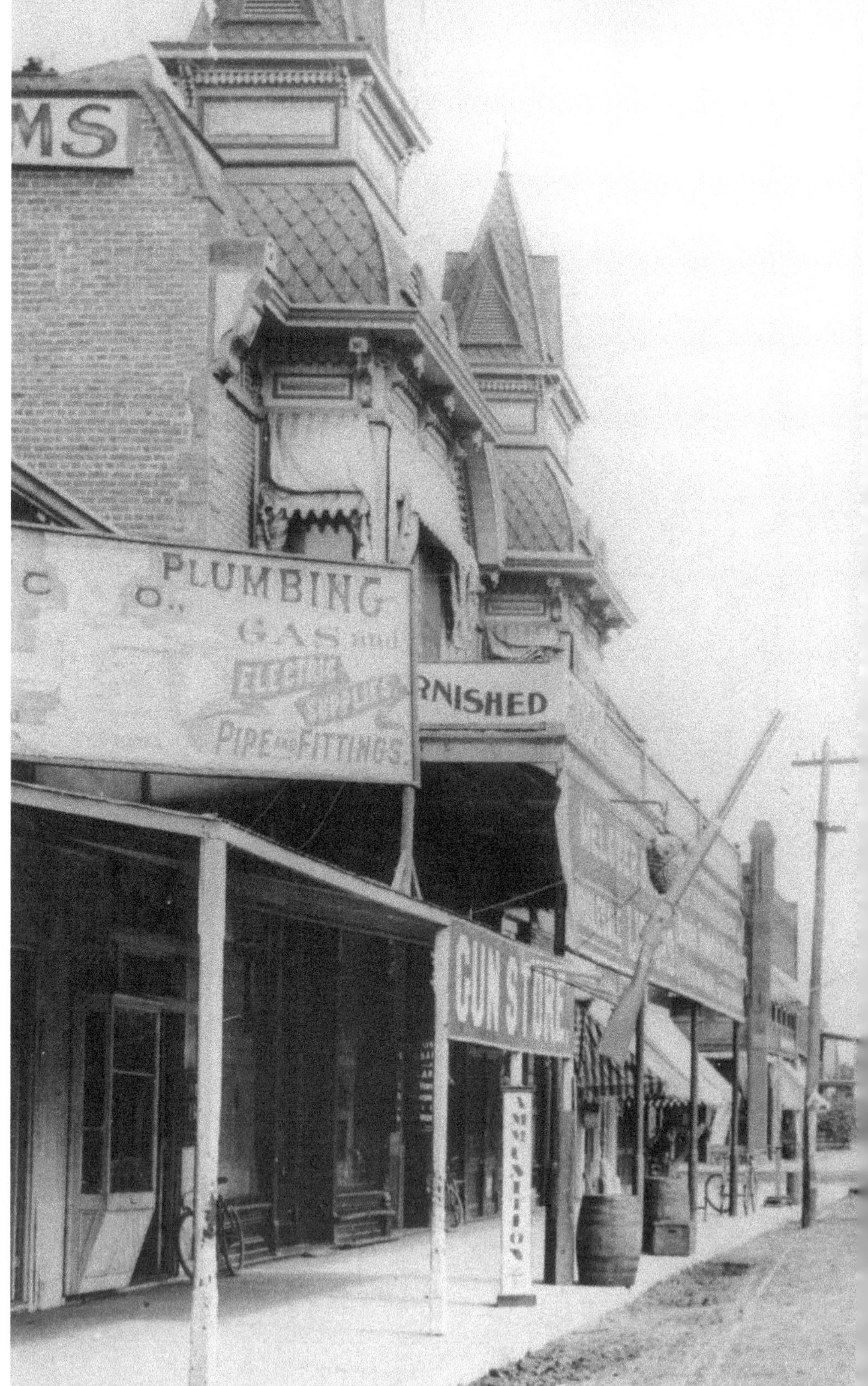
MS
PLUMBING
GAS
PIPE AND FITTINGS
RNISHED
GUN STORE
AMMUNITION

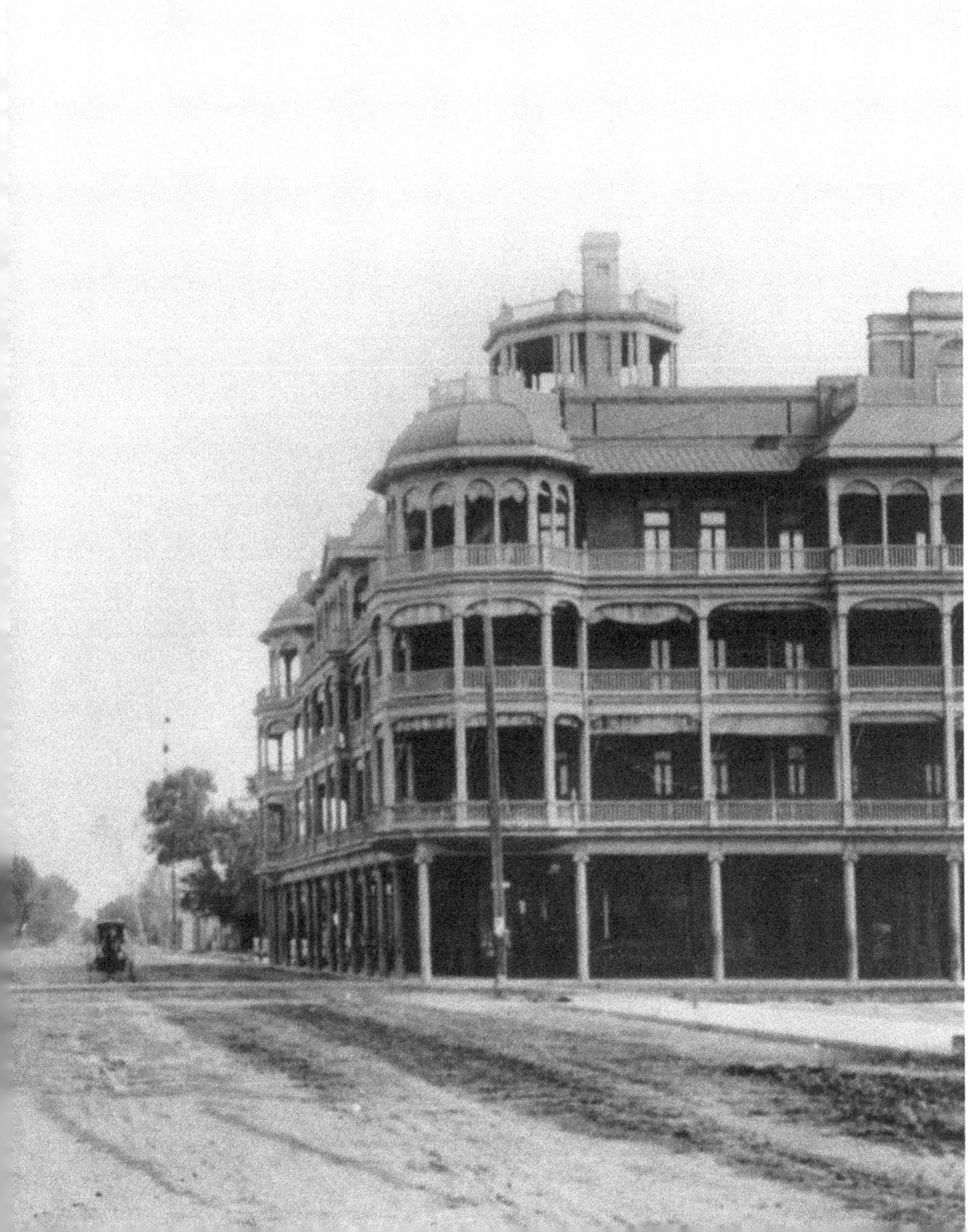

Phoenix was beginning to look more like a modern city when this 1890 photograph was taken at the intersection of Adams Street and Centre Street, with the Adams Hotel on the right. The first commercial orange grove had already been established, and with a population of 3,100, the city's Police Department had to employ two officers—one for the day and one for the night.

By the time this 1890s photograph was taken of a stagecoach in front of the Ford Hotel on Adams Street, stagecoaches were starting to become a relic of history. Trains and automobiles would soon replace them.

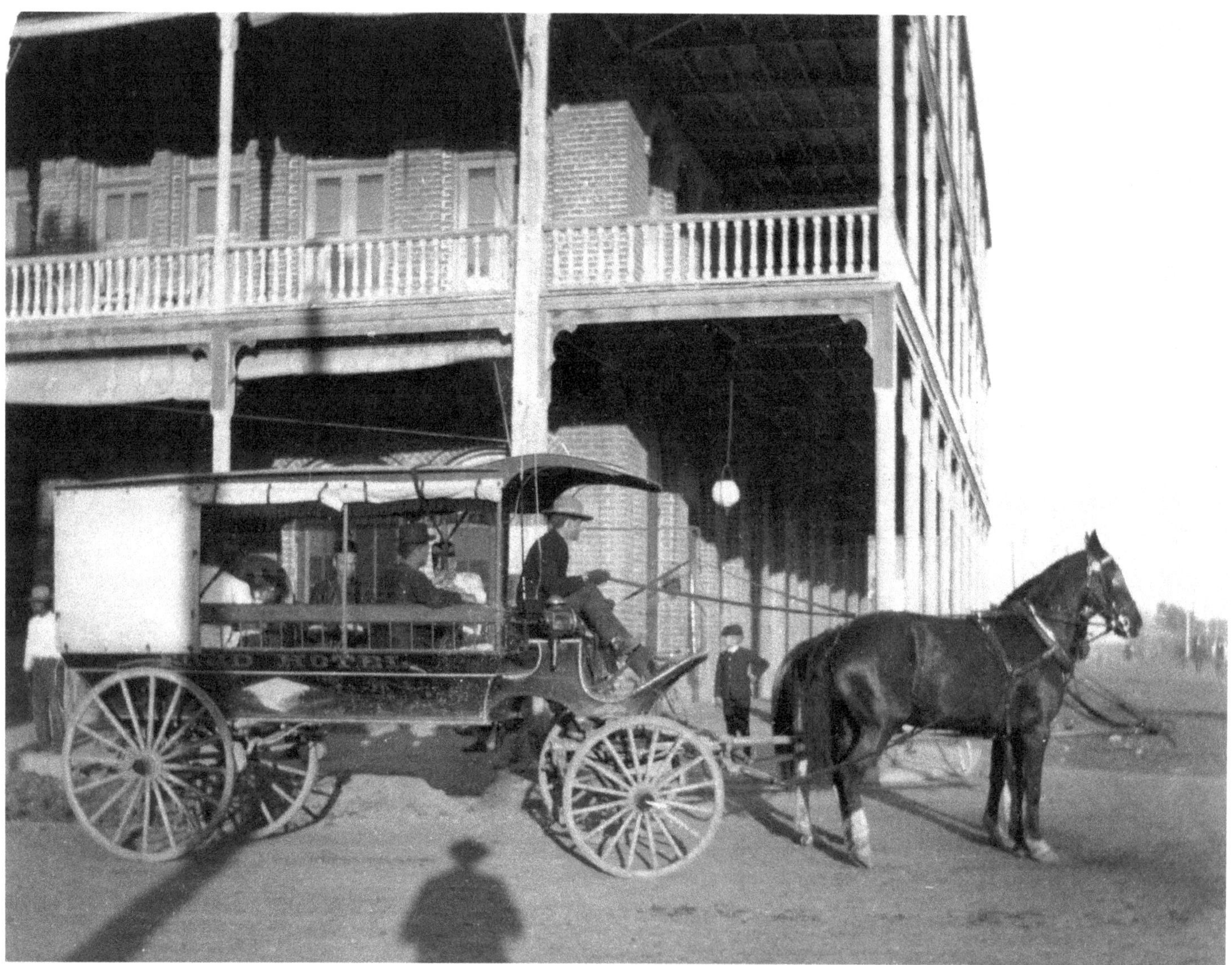

A parade passes the Ford Hotel, at upper-left, in 1890. The hotel's deep balcony and low-hanging shades provided relief from the Arizona sun.

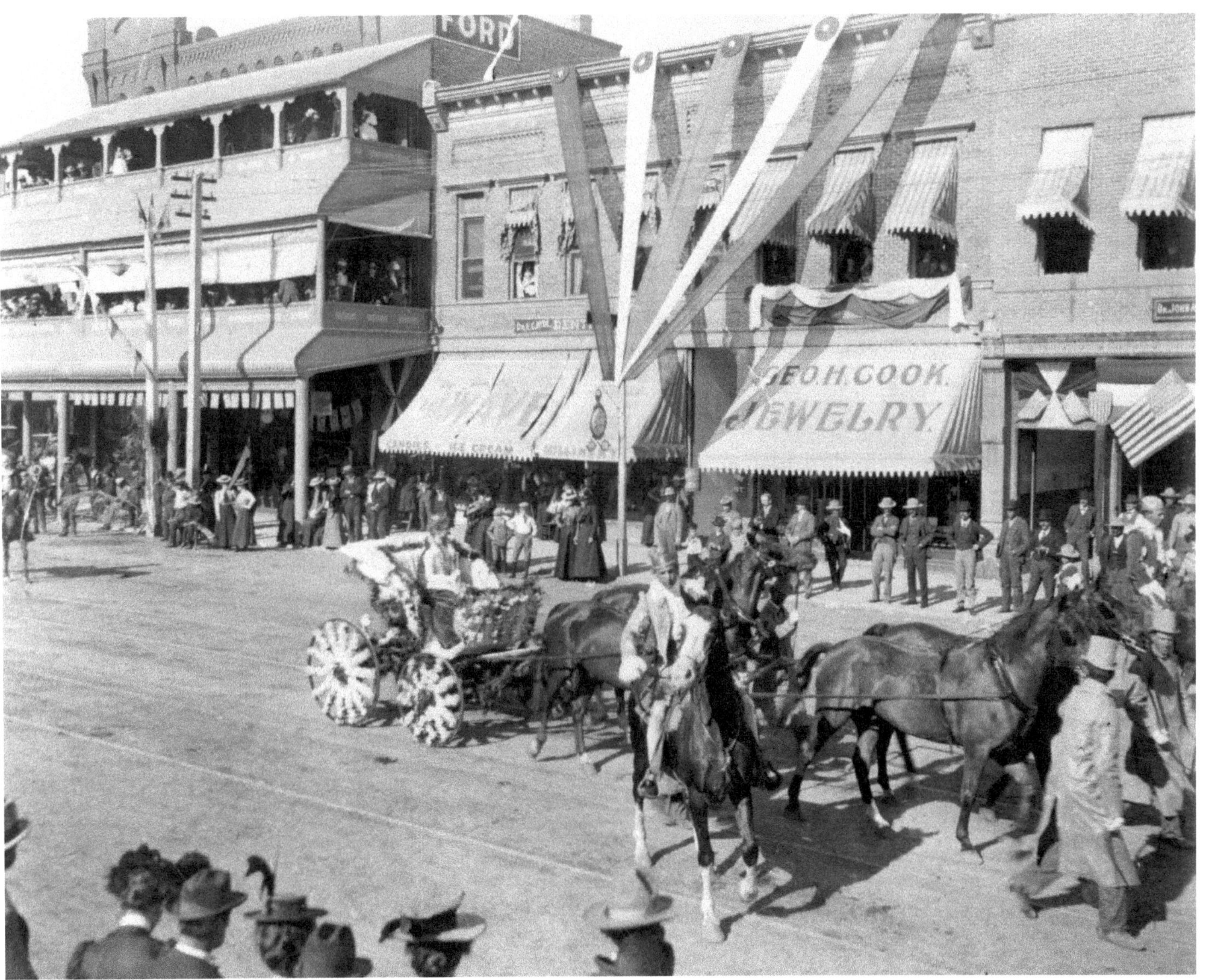

Beginning in 1891 Phoenix streets were lined with telephone poles, although the paving of streets was still a few years away. Pictured here is the Adams Hotel.

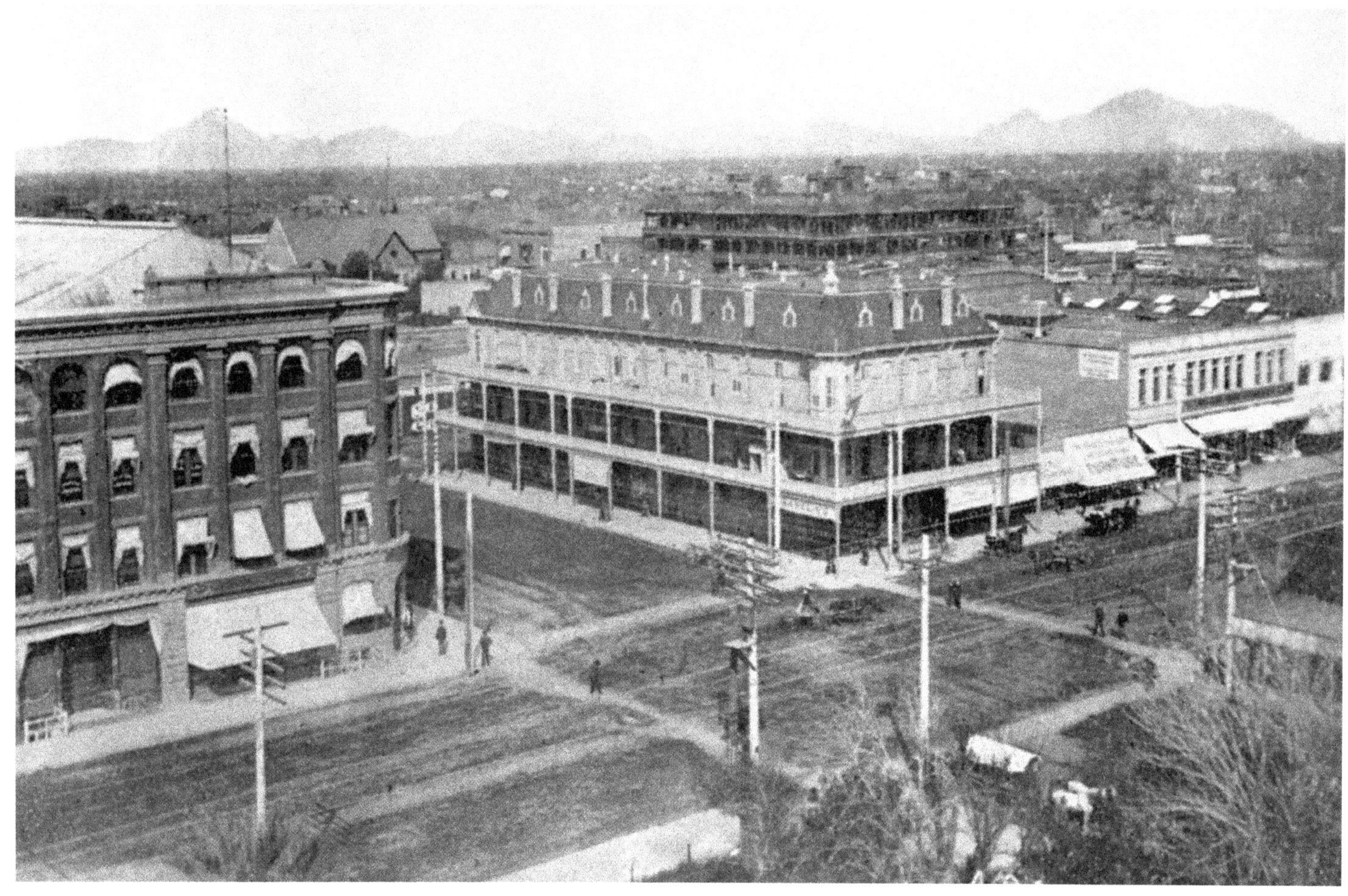

This 1890s photograph shows the intersection of Centre Street and Washington Street. Shaded sidewalks with awnings and curtains were common conveniences that Phoenix businesses offered their customers. Goodman's Pharmacy, the Western Union Telegraph Office, and the Adams Hotel were located on Centre Street (the hotel is in the background at right). In the middle of the street, a man on a stool appears to be working on a streetlamp.

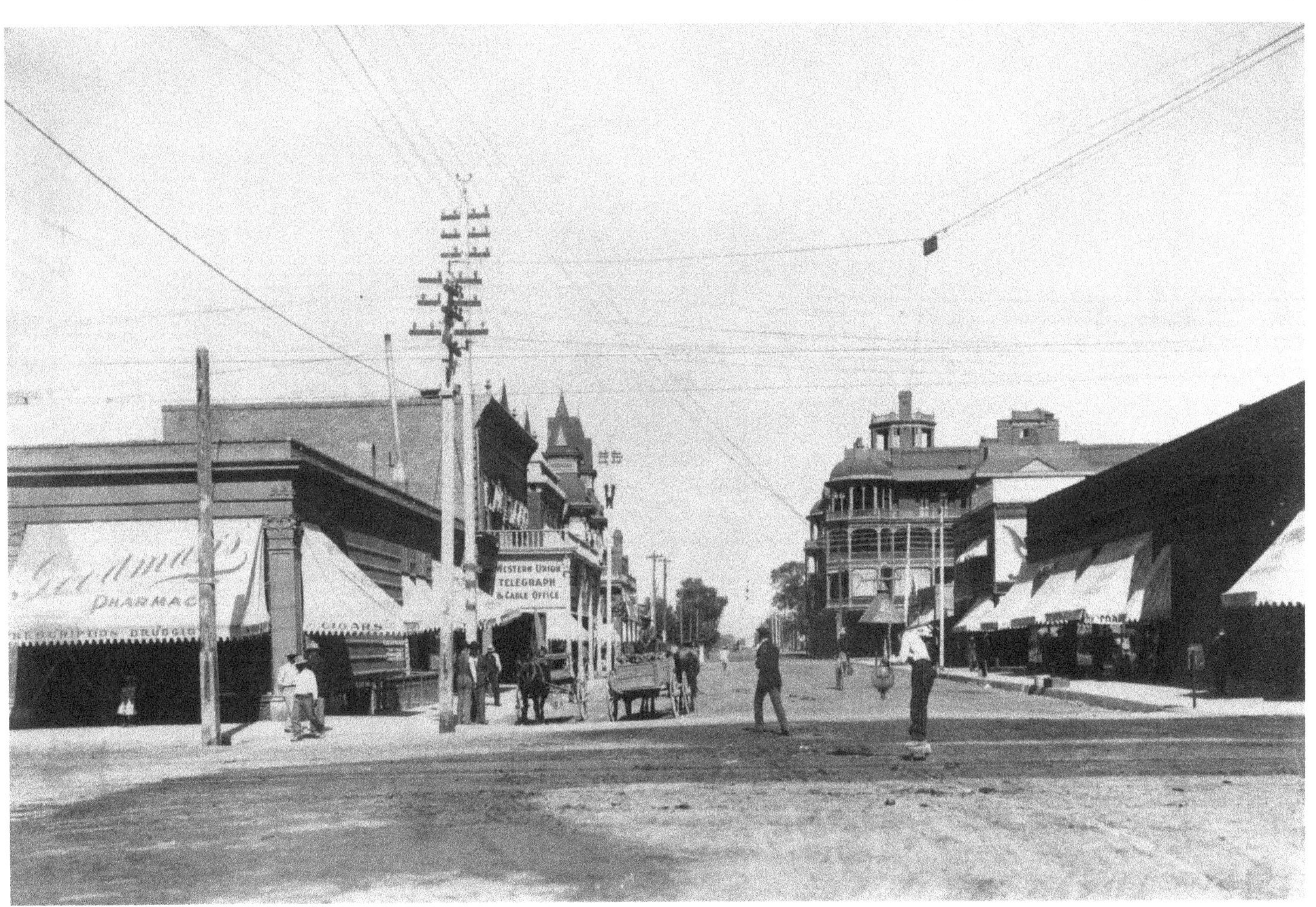

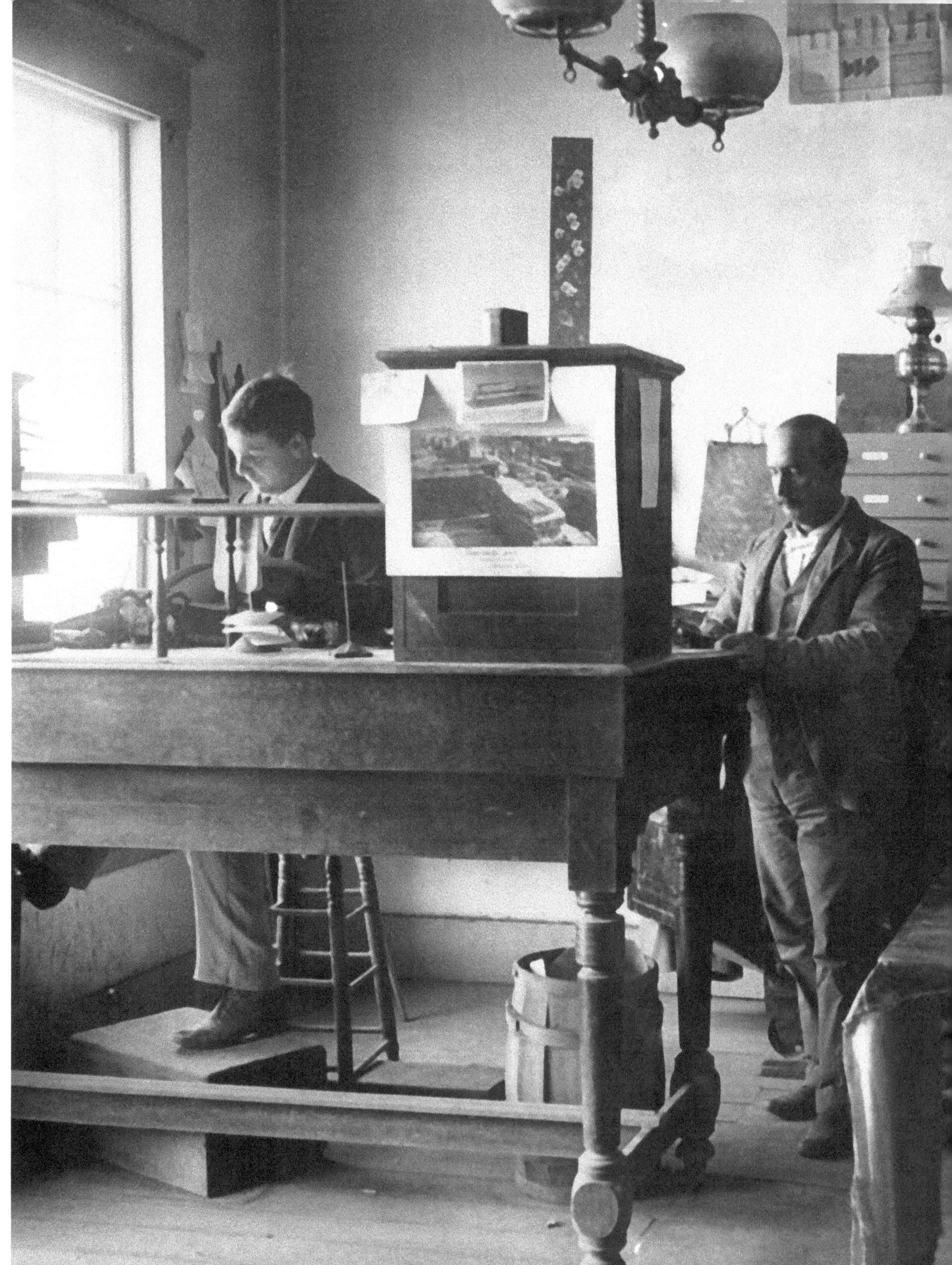

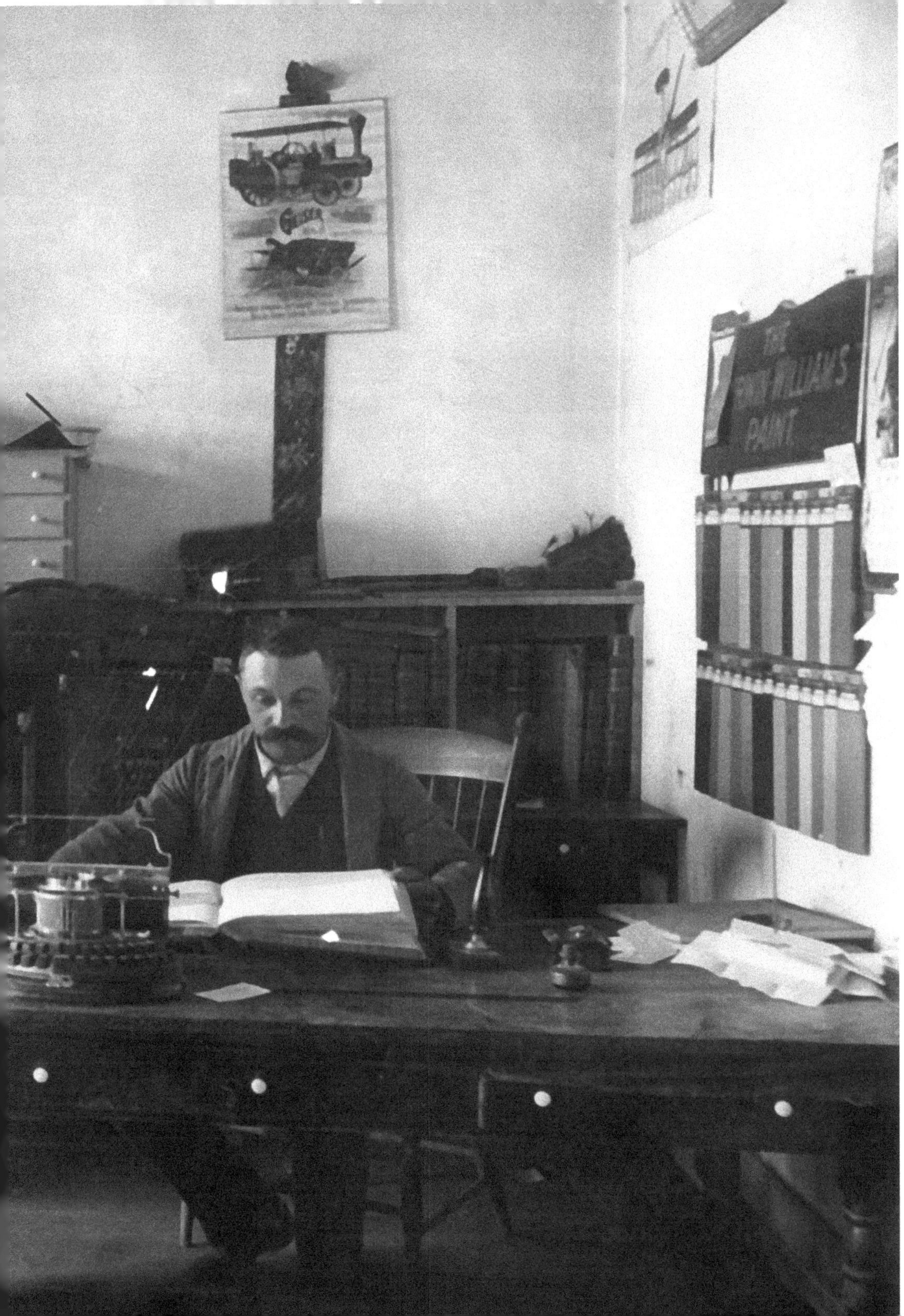

The office of the H. W. Ryder Lumber Company, around 1895, included contemporary office machinery and cabinets.

Phoenix's architecture began to conform to the dominant styles of the day as the city grew larger and its people more prosperous, although retractable awnings remained a unique feature of many Phoenix businesses. Pueblo-style buildings made of adobe brick were increasingly a thing of the past.

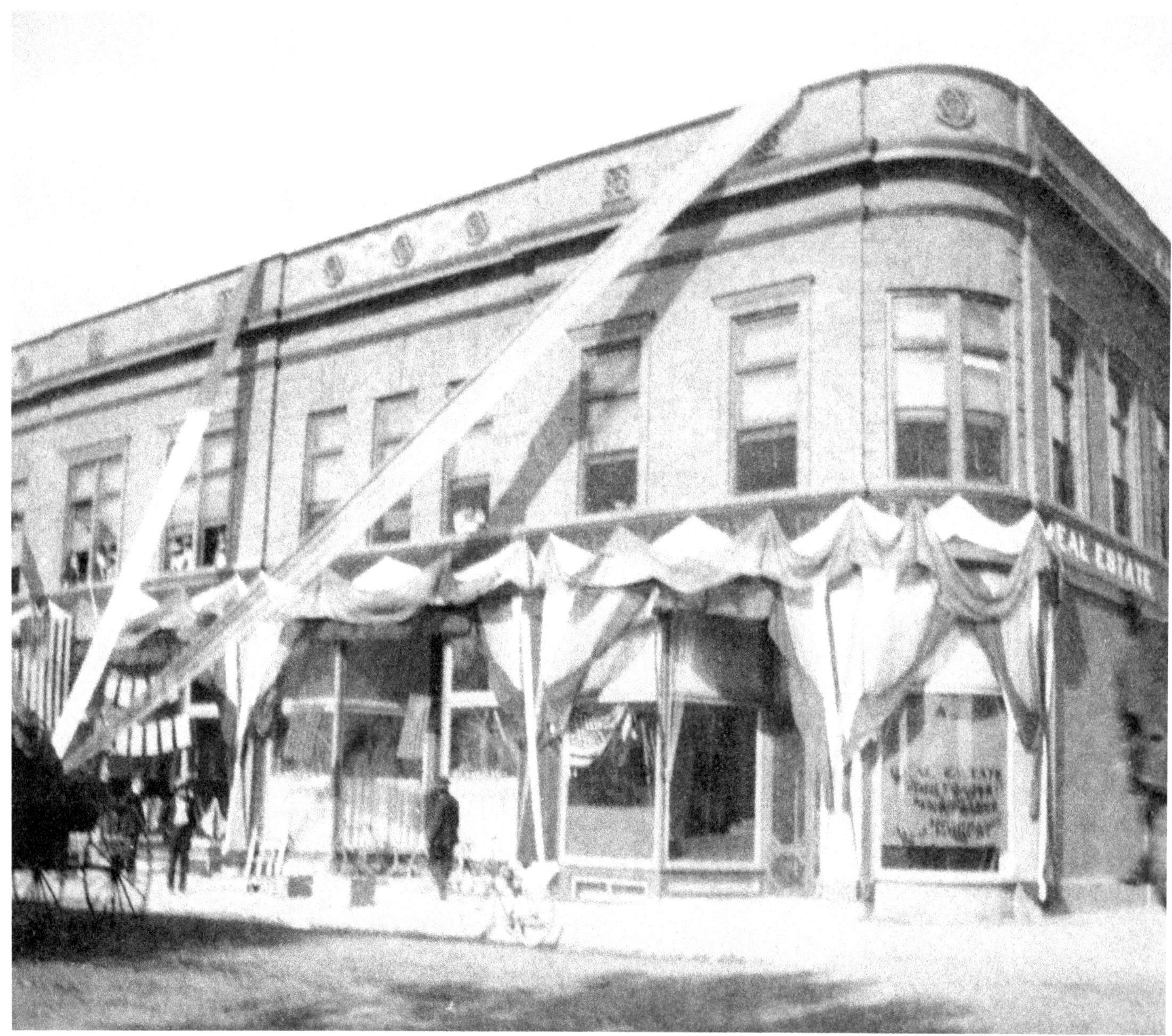

By 1899, with Phoenix connected to the rest of the nation by railroad, Phoenicians could enjoy goods that were available in most American cities.

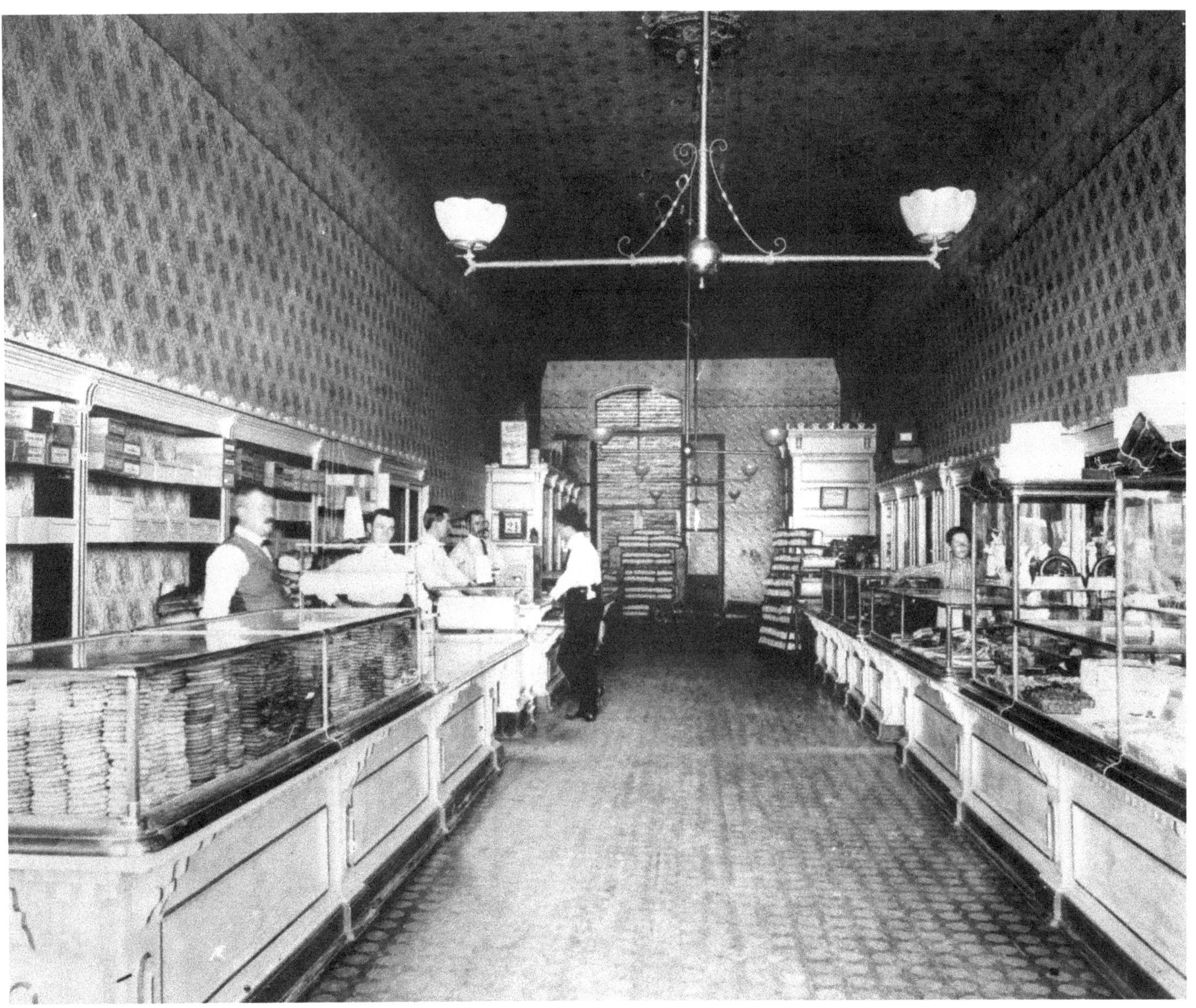

Farmers living outside the town still relied on mule-drawn carriages.

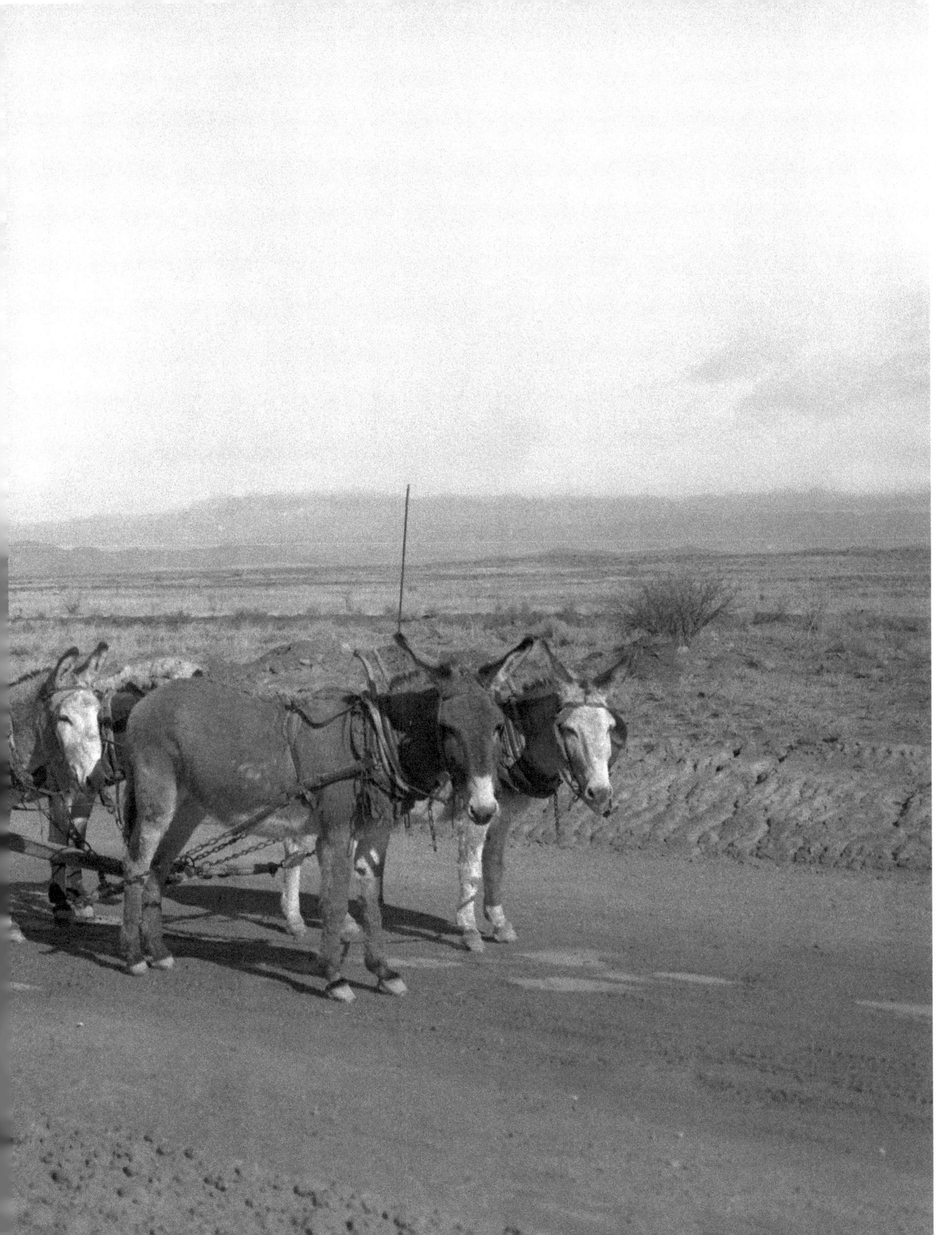

Members of the Phoenix Hunting Club proudly gather in front of their club headquarters in 1895.

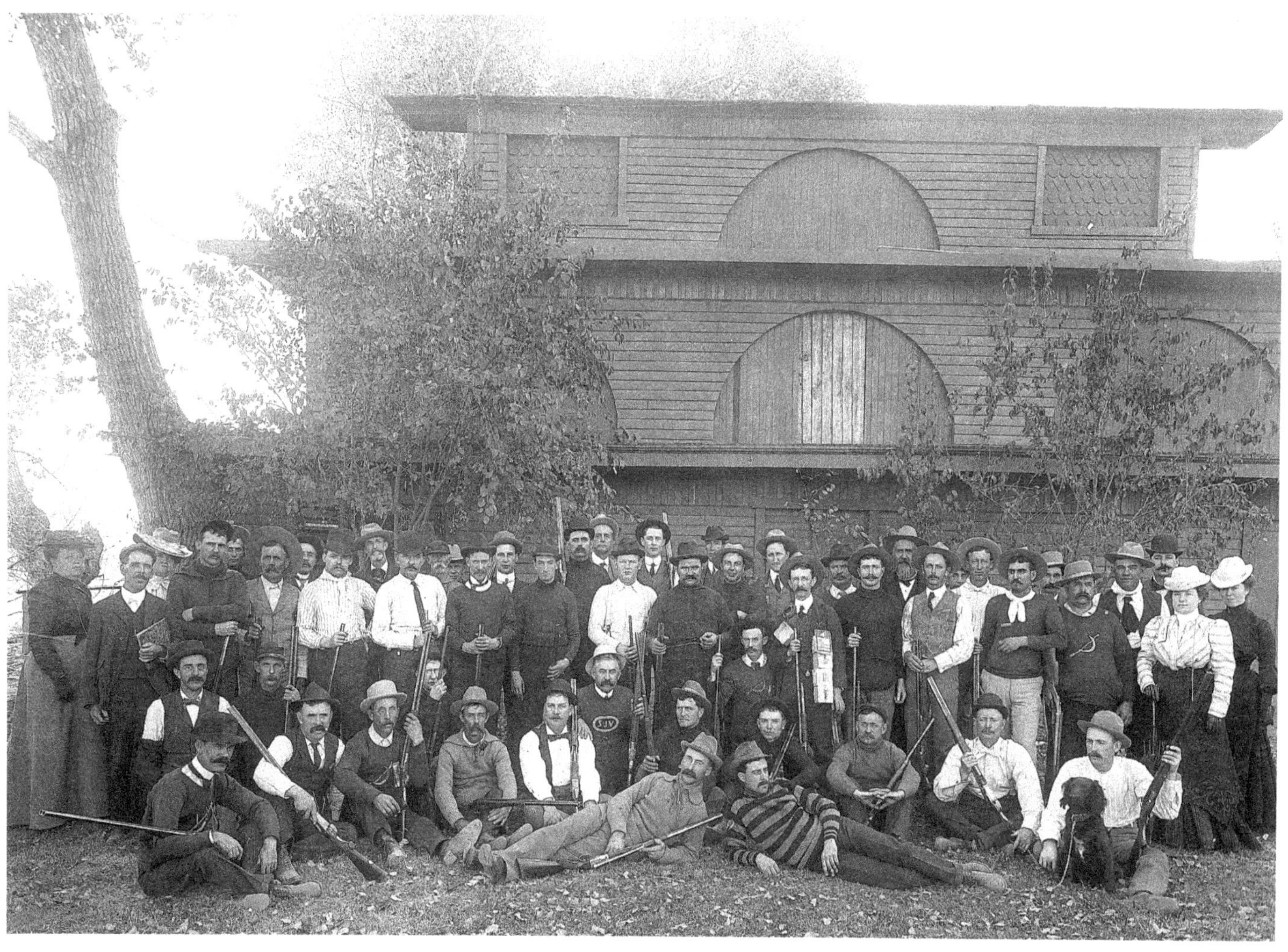

The all-volunteer Phoenix Fire Engine Company #1 was organized in 1881, but after two devastating fires that destroyed almost all of the business section in 1885 and 1886, the Phoenix city council authorized the formation of the Phoenix Fire Department, with Frank M. Czarnowsky, an immigrant from Poland, appointed as chief.

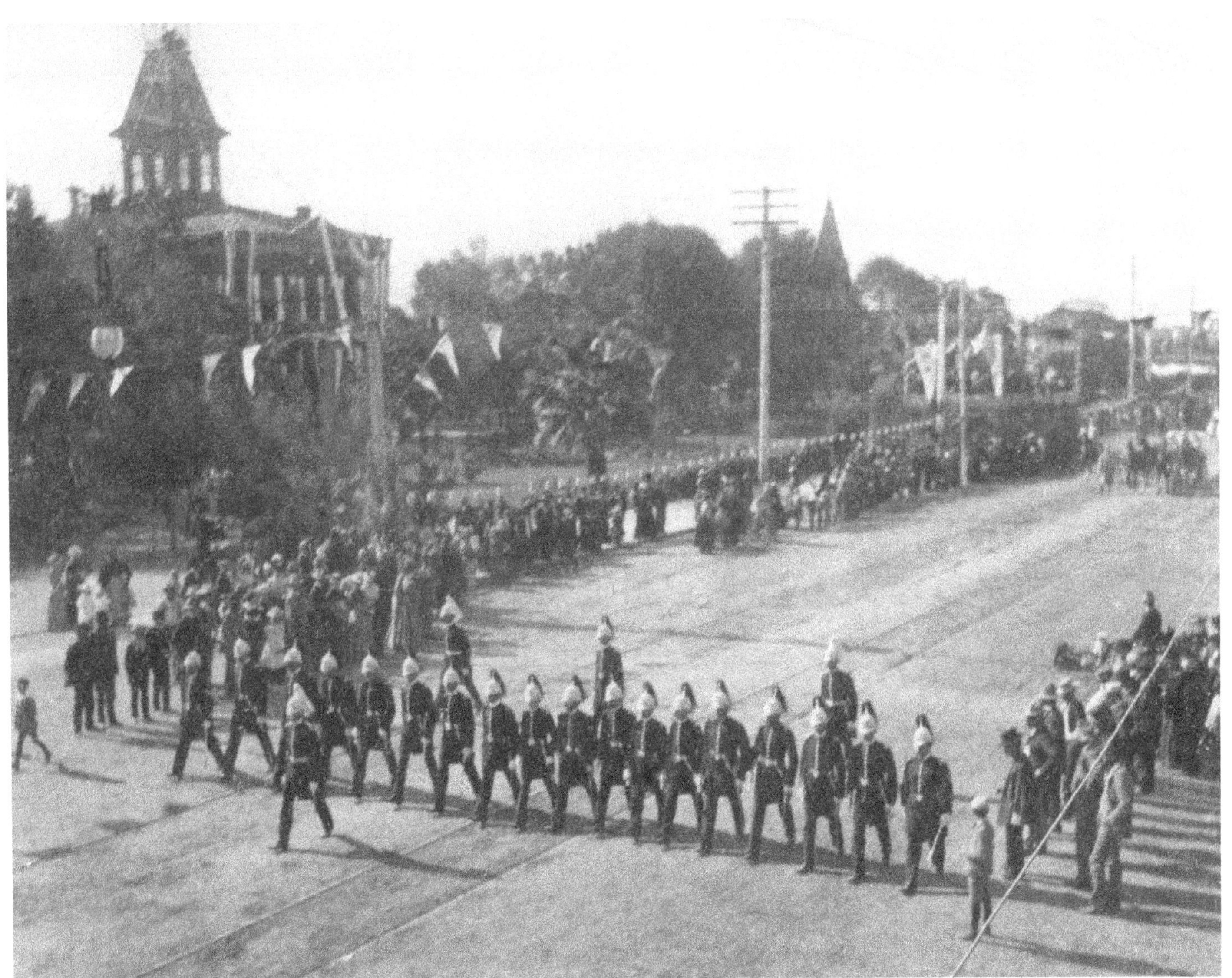

By the time this 1895 picture was taken, Phoenix had its first commercial telephones. The Farmer's Canal was completed, for a total of 131 miles of canals in the valley, the Phoenix Light and Power Company was operational, and the city had its first electric streetcars. Phoenix had grown large enough that the city council could authorize the hiring of four policemen, two of them on bicycle patrol.

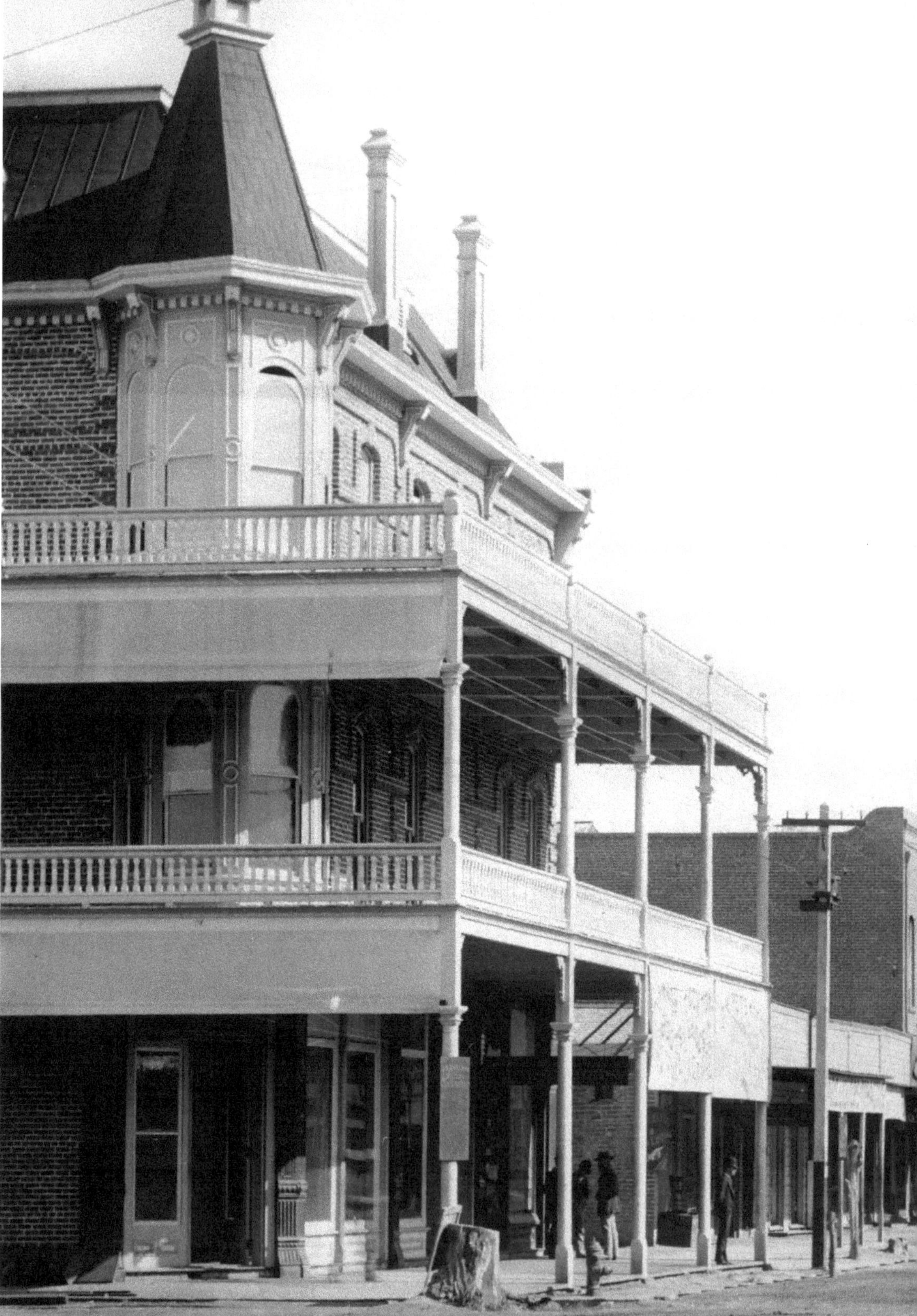

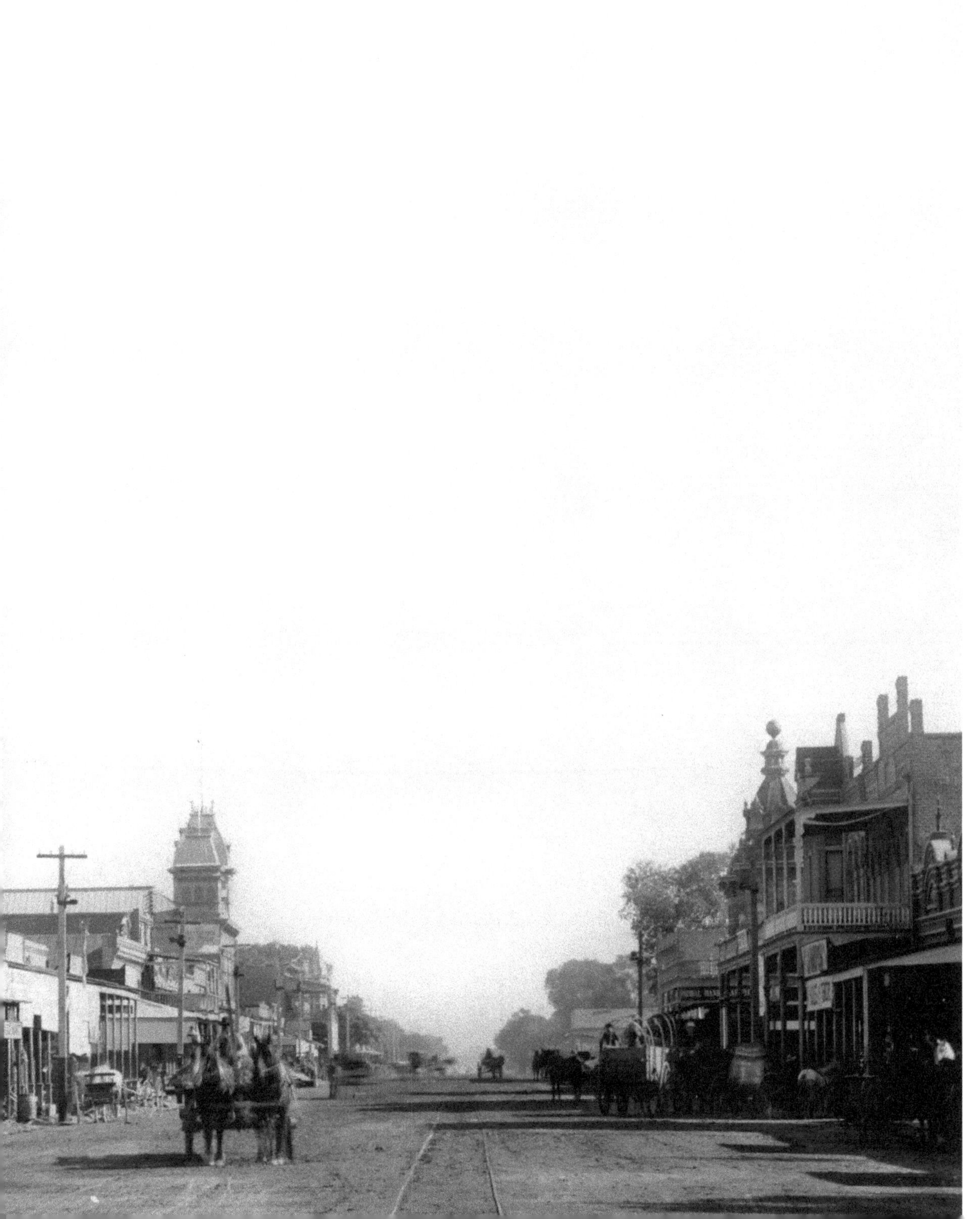

A group of Phoenicians gather to celebrate Thanksgiving Day 1899 with a picnic.

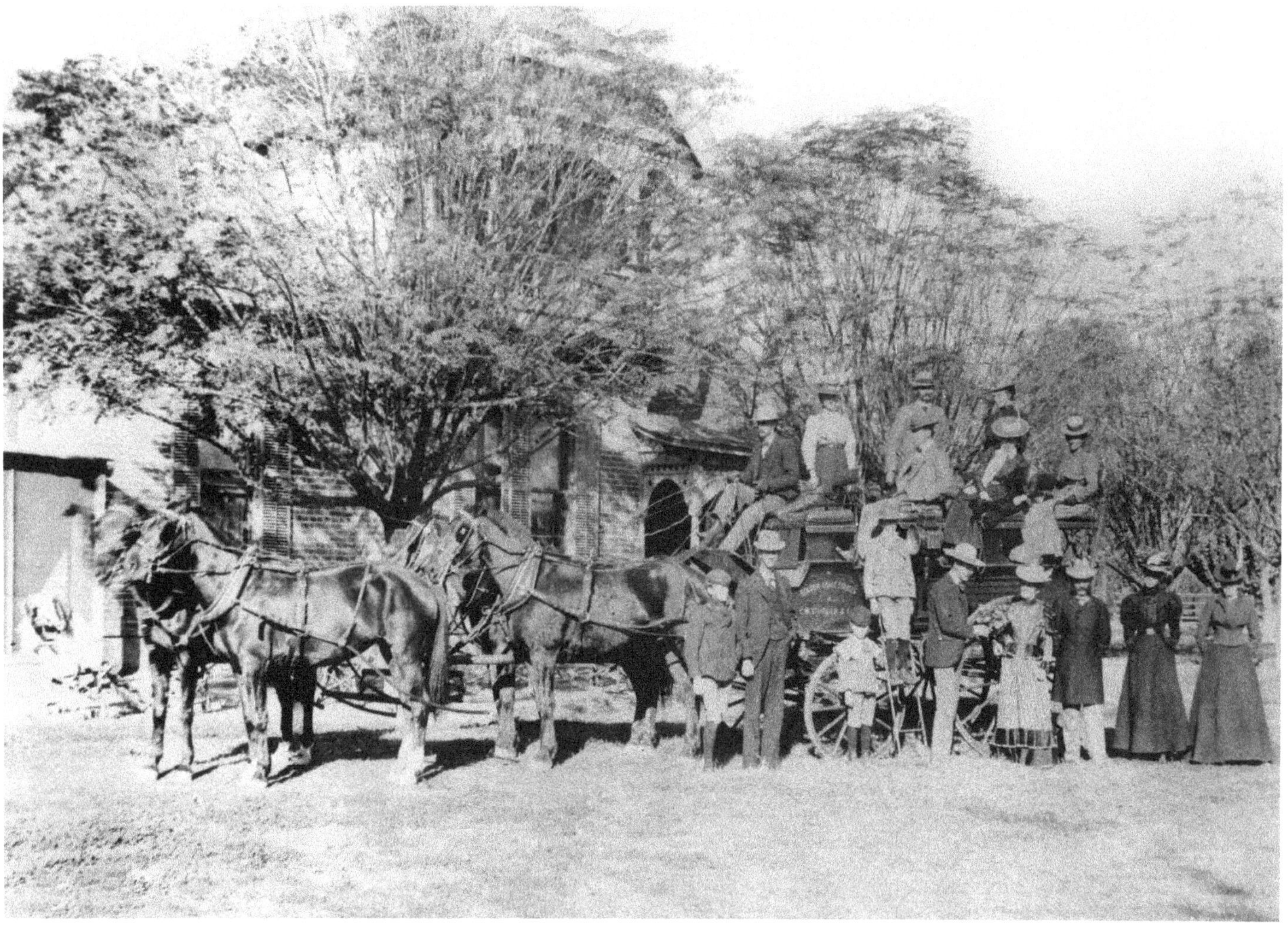

In November 1884, a group of Phoenix citizens organized the first Arizona Territorial Fair, held in late fall in Phoenix, near the Salt River west of Central Avenue. Fairgoers were treated to horse, pony, and mule races, along with exhibits of agriculture, home economics, and dairy and beef cattle. Fairs were then held annually at the location until 1891, when the Salt River flooded and destroyed the buildings and racetrack at the site.

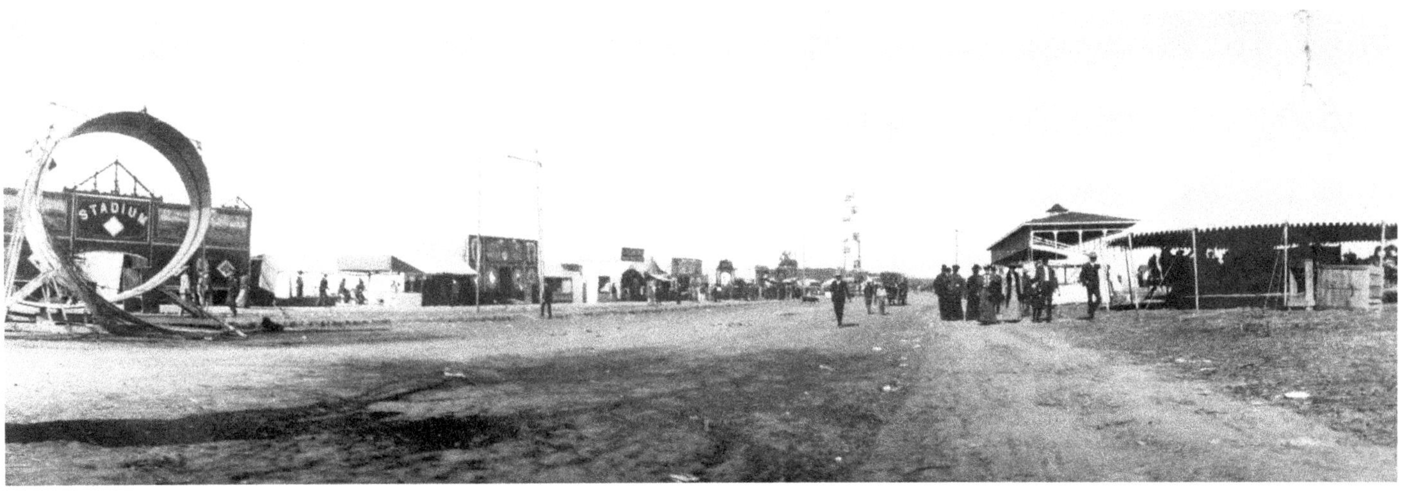

William J. Murphy was hired in 1883 to oversee the construction of the Arizona Canal that ran in a northwesterly direction from the Salt River. Murphy recruited Mexican laborers to survey and dig the nearly 50-mile-long canal, which became one of the major canals in the Salt River Valley. With a controlled and dependable supply of water available to valley farmers, several communities sprang up near Phoenix, including Scottsdale, Glendale, and Peoria.

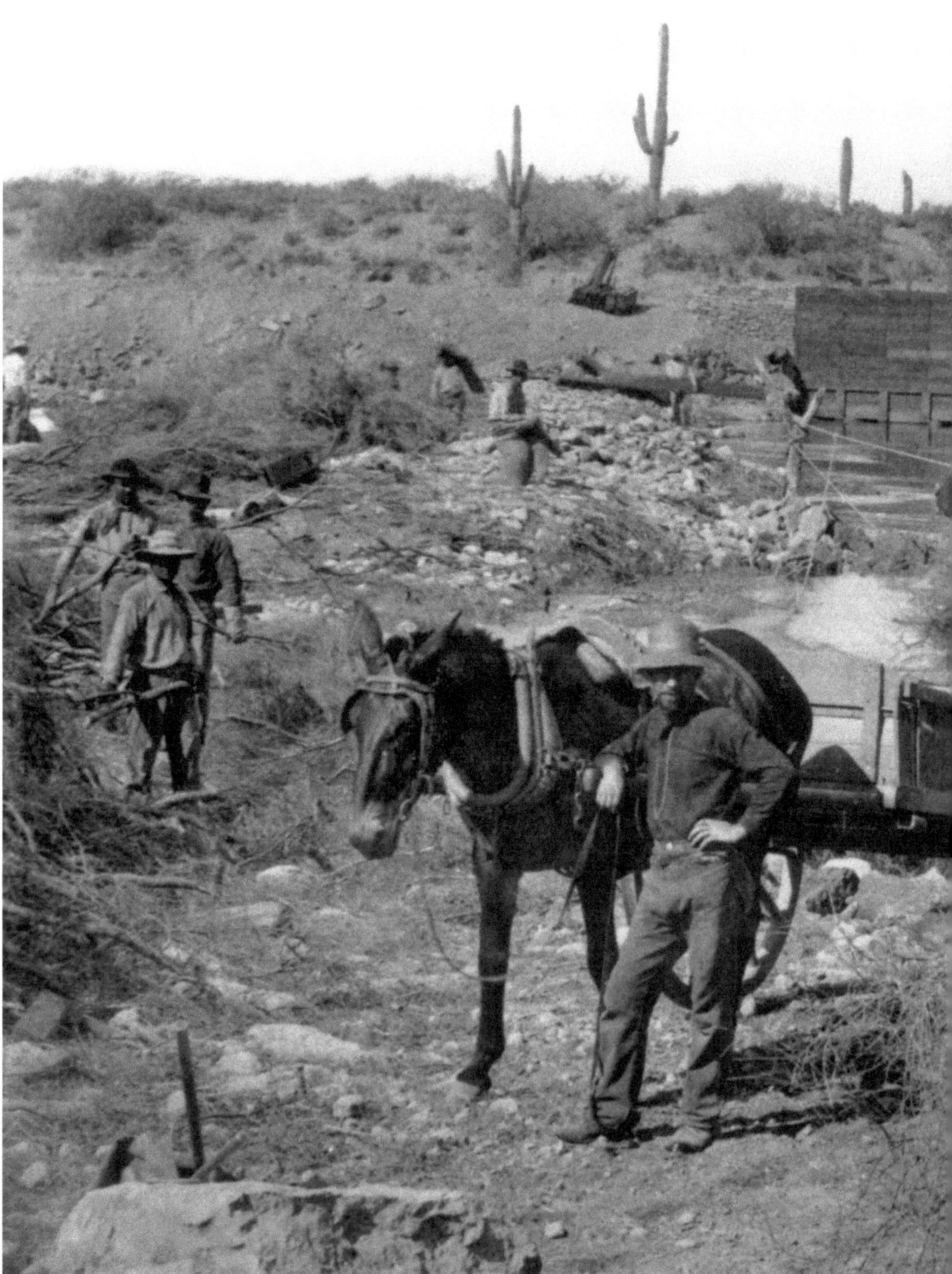

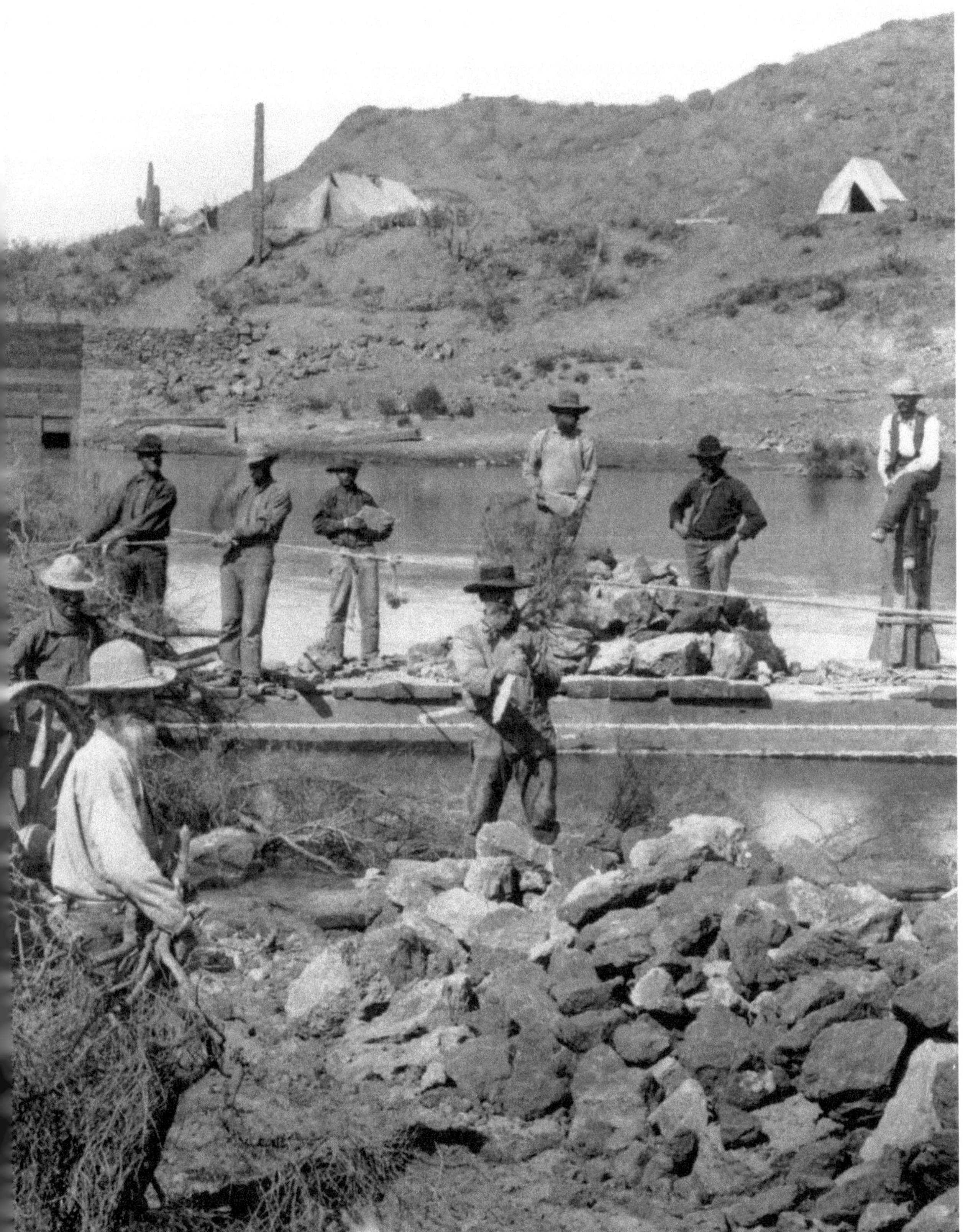

The territorial insane asylum was built in Phoenix on 24th and Van Buren streets. Construction began in 1885 and was completed in 1886.

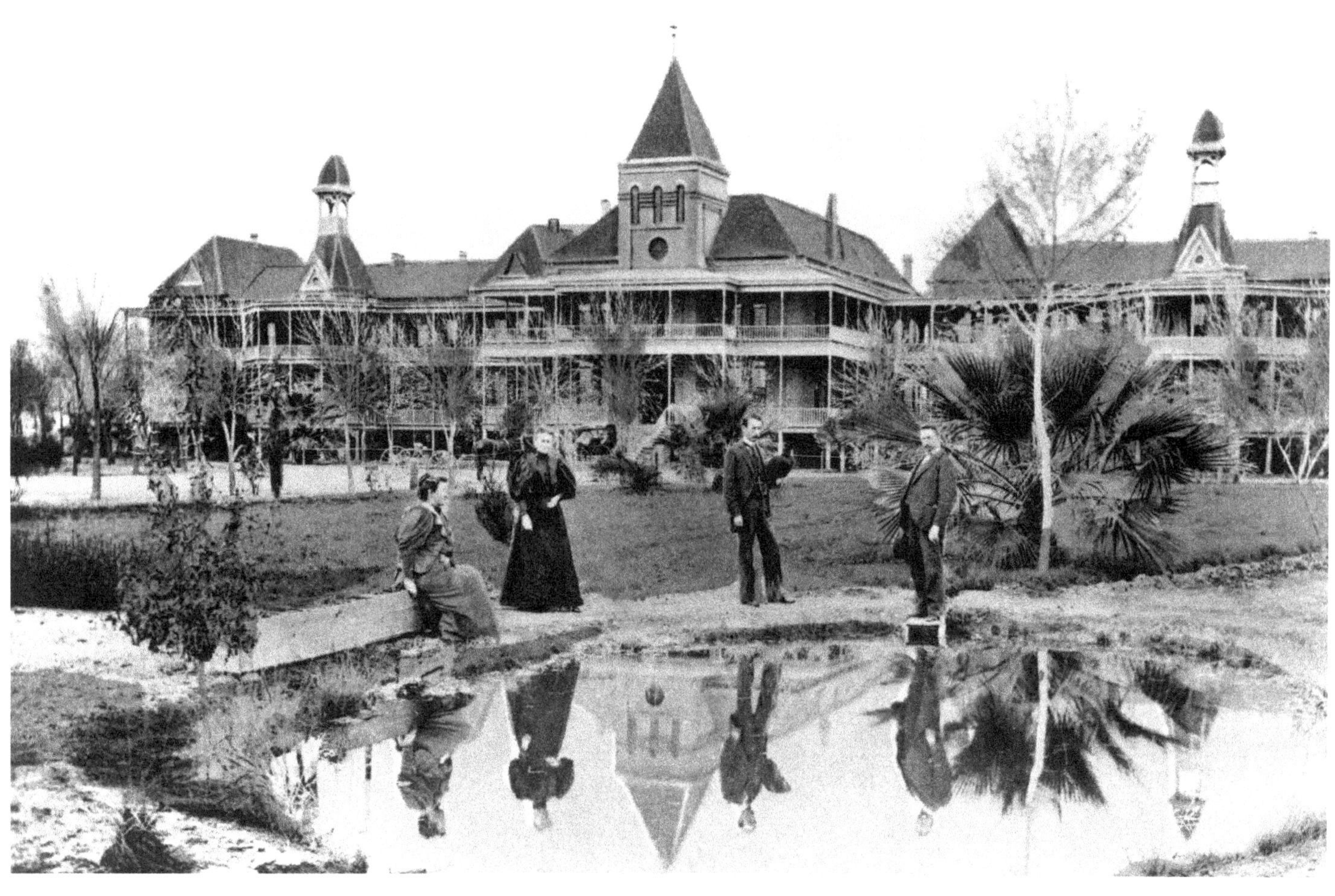

The first horse-drawn streetcar line ran along Washington Street in 1887 for 2 miles. Two years later an additional line was installed along Centre Street. By 1893 Phoenix had electric streetcars. The trolley system eventually became so extensive that tracks covered most of the city and extended north into the neighboring town of Glendale.

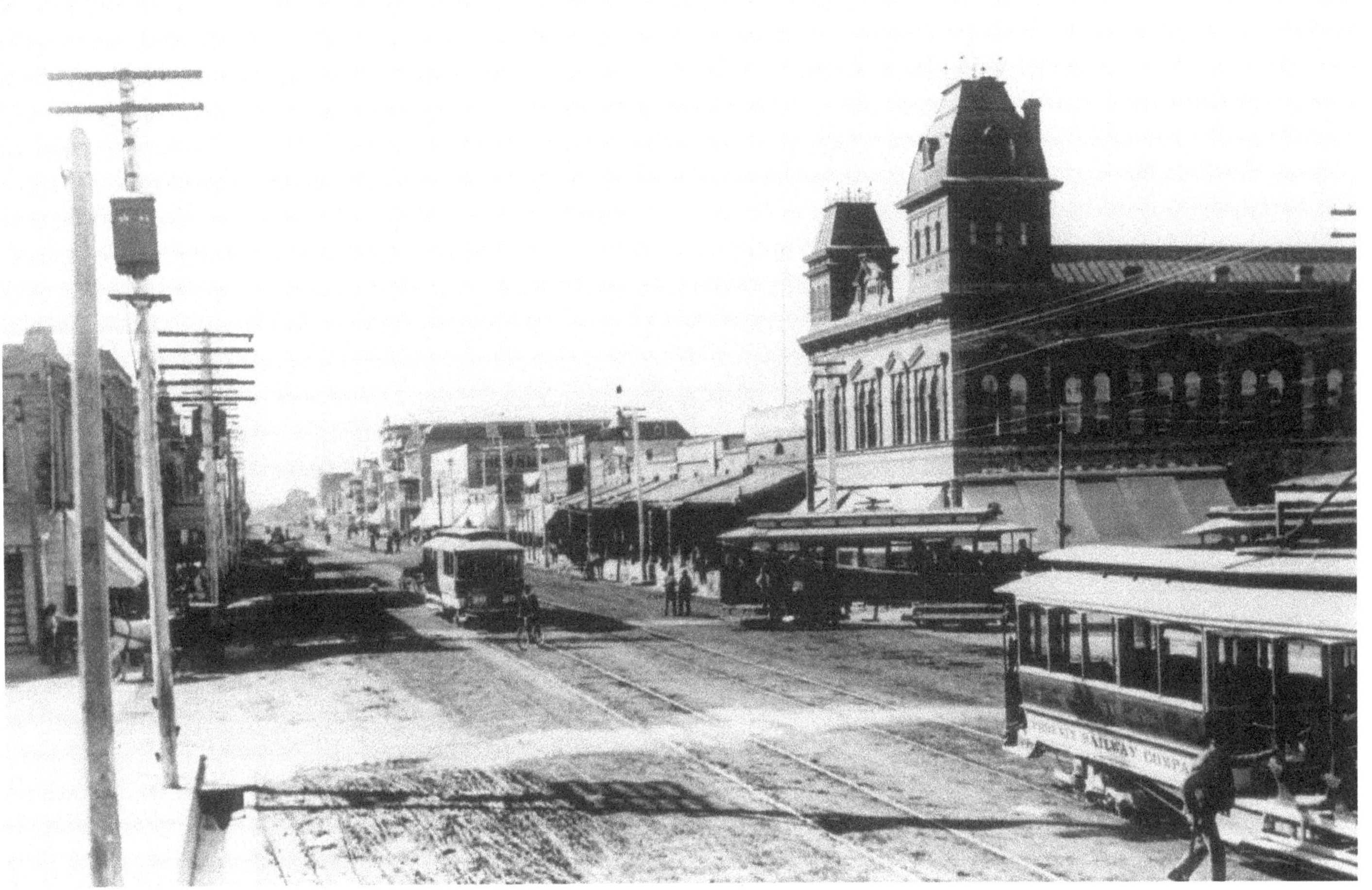

Teachers and students gather in front of the Phoenix Central School for this photograph, around 1890. The school was on Monroe Street, between Centre Street and First Avenue. School instruction was bilingual in Phoenix until 1893, when the railroads brought more and more English-speaking newcomers.

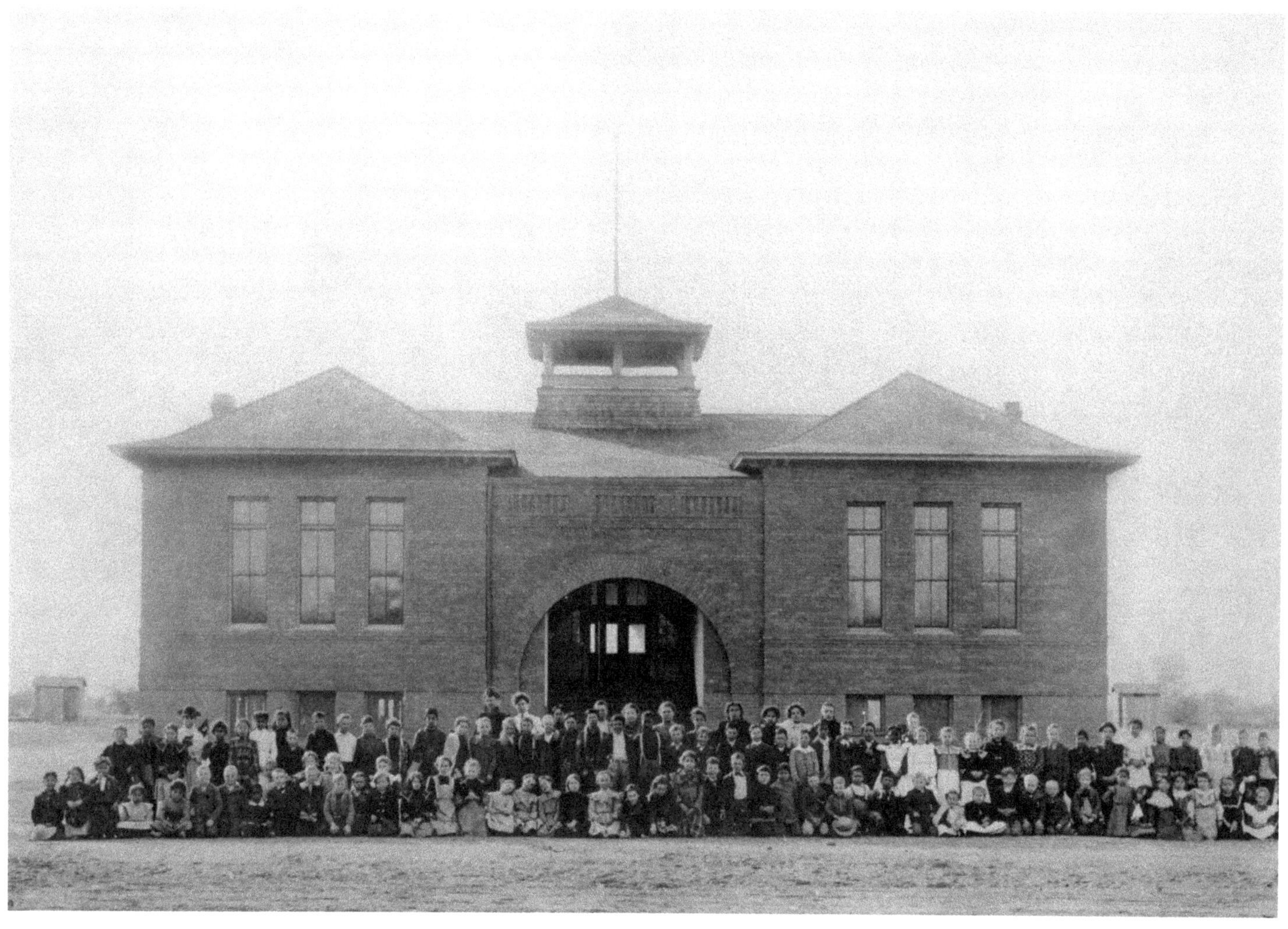

The first recognizably modern bicycle wasn't designed until 1885. This Phoenician proudly stands on a Phoenix street at the turn of the century with a thoroughly modern bike, complete with a diamond-shaped frame and chain-driven inflatable wheels. Phoenix became very quickly "a town full of bicycles" according to one report.

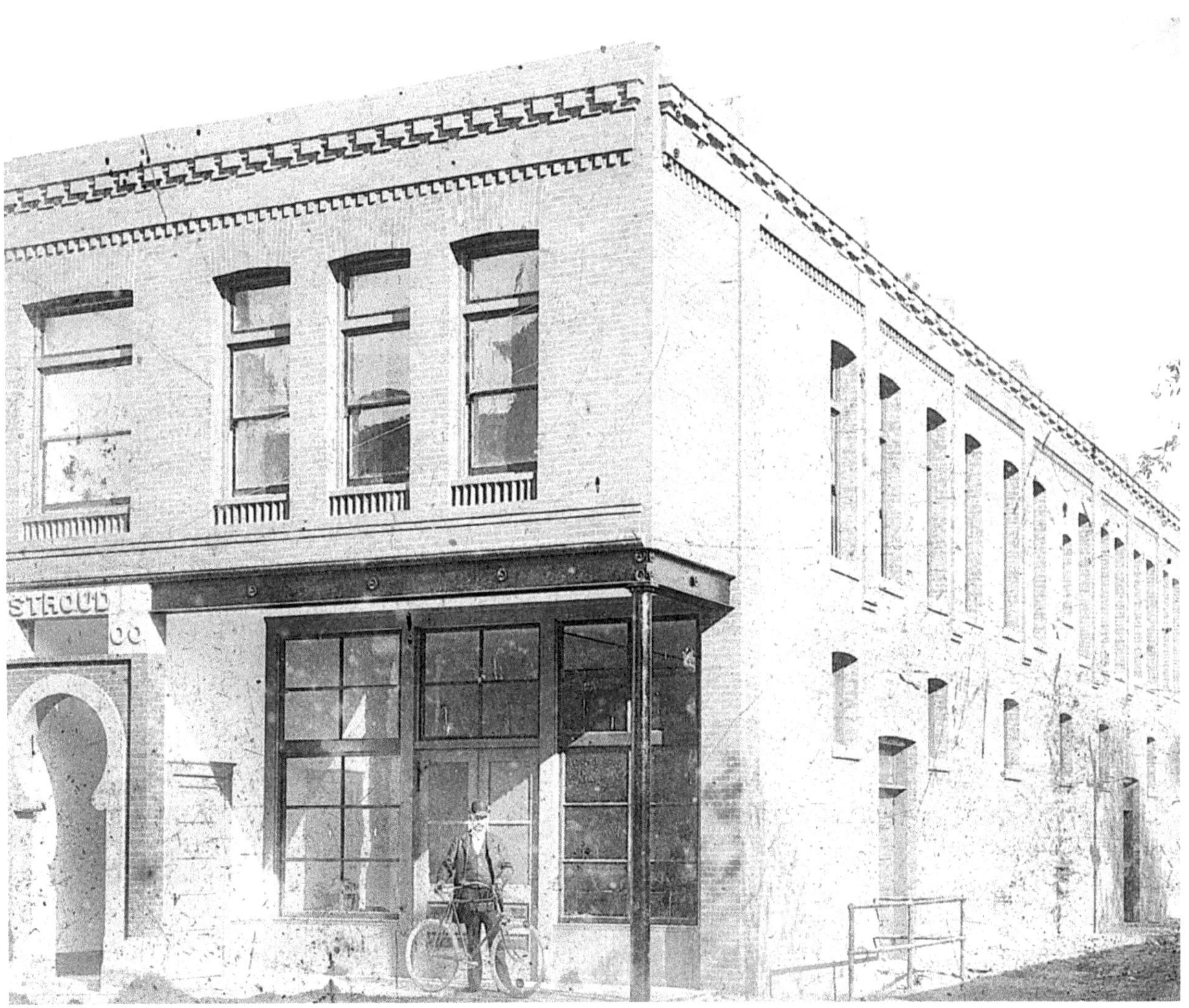

Phoenix City Hall housed the Arizona territorial government until the construction of the Capitol was completed. In 1889 city boosters and developers won a great victory for Phoenix when they persuaded the territorial legislature to move from Prescott to Phoenix. M. E. Collins and Moses H. Sherman donated ten acres for a capitol building and promised to extend city streetcar lines and provide stately landscaping for the grounds. The building was dedicated in 1901.

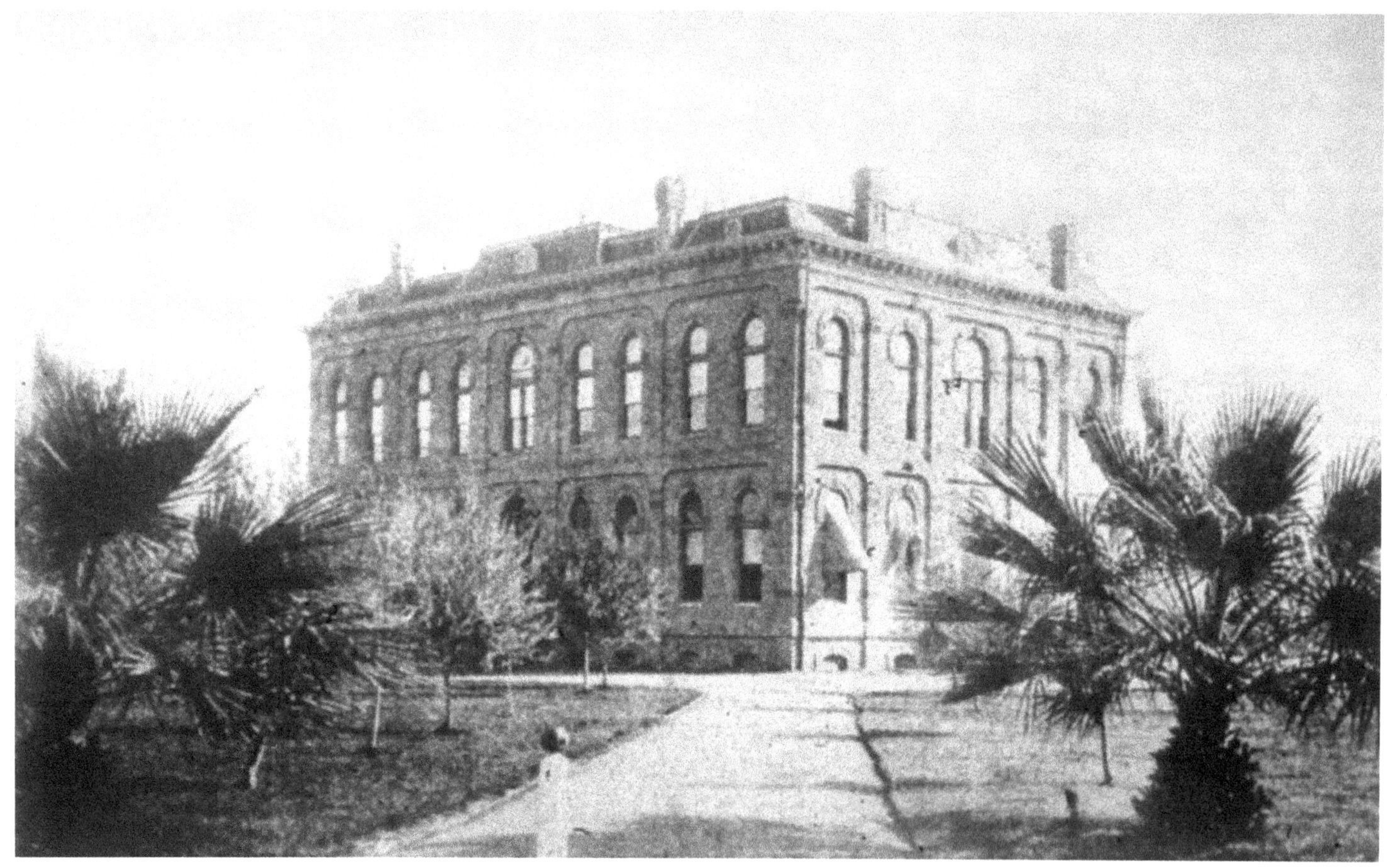

From Remote Settlement to State Capital (1900–1919)

Once isolated by a daunting landscape, Phoenix was now connected to the nation by railroad. City boosters convinced the territorial legislature to move the capital from Prescott to Phoenix, promising a modern building, landscaping, and streetcar lines. When the Capitol was completed in 1900, the population had grown to more than 5,000. That same year, the first automobile arrived in Phoenix. Within ten years the city had to assign a motorcycle patrolman to Central Avenue to catch motorists speeding over 10 miles an hour.

After a 20-year territory-wide effort, President William Taft signed the bill creating the State of Arizona in 1912. The Central Street Bridge, built over the Salt River to join the north and south portions of the city, symbolized Phoenix's growth in the new century. Activists succeeded at having the state constitution amended to give women the vote, and the city's police and fire departments became completely motorized.

Within a few short years, international events would influence the history of Phoenix. The assassination of the heir to the Austro-Hungarian Empire in Sarajevo touched off a terrible chain of events culminating in World War I. Between 1914 and 1918, more than nine million soldiers and civilians died in the Great War, Phoenicians among them. Nations devised technologies that could wreak destruction on an unprecedented scale. Old empires that had ruled for centuries fell and new nations rose.

Antagonized by the war and concerned about the influx of foreign ideologies like Bolshevism, Americans after the war supported tough anti-immigration legislation. The Spanish Influenza of 1918 killed an estimated 5 percent of the world's population. All public meeting places in Phoenix were closed for three months because of the epidemic.

The wartime demand for cotton proved to be an economic boon for Phoenix. Before the war the federal government began work on the Salt River Dam #1 (later renamed Roosevelt Dam) to control flooding along the river and provide irrigation for the valley, and by 1915 Phoenix's agricultural economy was growing. The wartime demand for cotton also reshaped the city's population as cotton growers actively recruited laborers from Mexico to work the fields.

Henrietta Hubbard Talbot stands in front of her ranch-style home in Phoenix. Talbot assisted Eliza Price Ainsworth in establishing the Territory's first chapter of the Daughters of the American Revolution. Henrietta and Eliza distributed applications and informational materials for two years before seeing their hopes realized on April 19, 1902, when under the shade of towering palm trees, a small group of women chartered the Arizona Society.

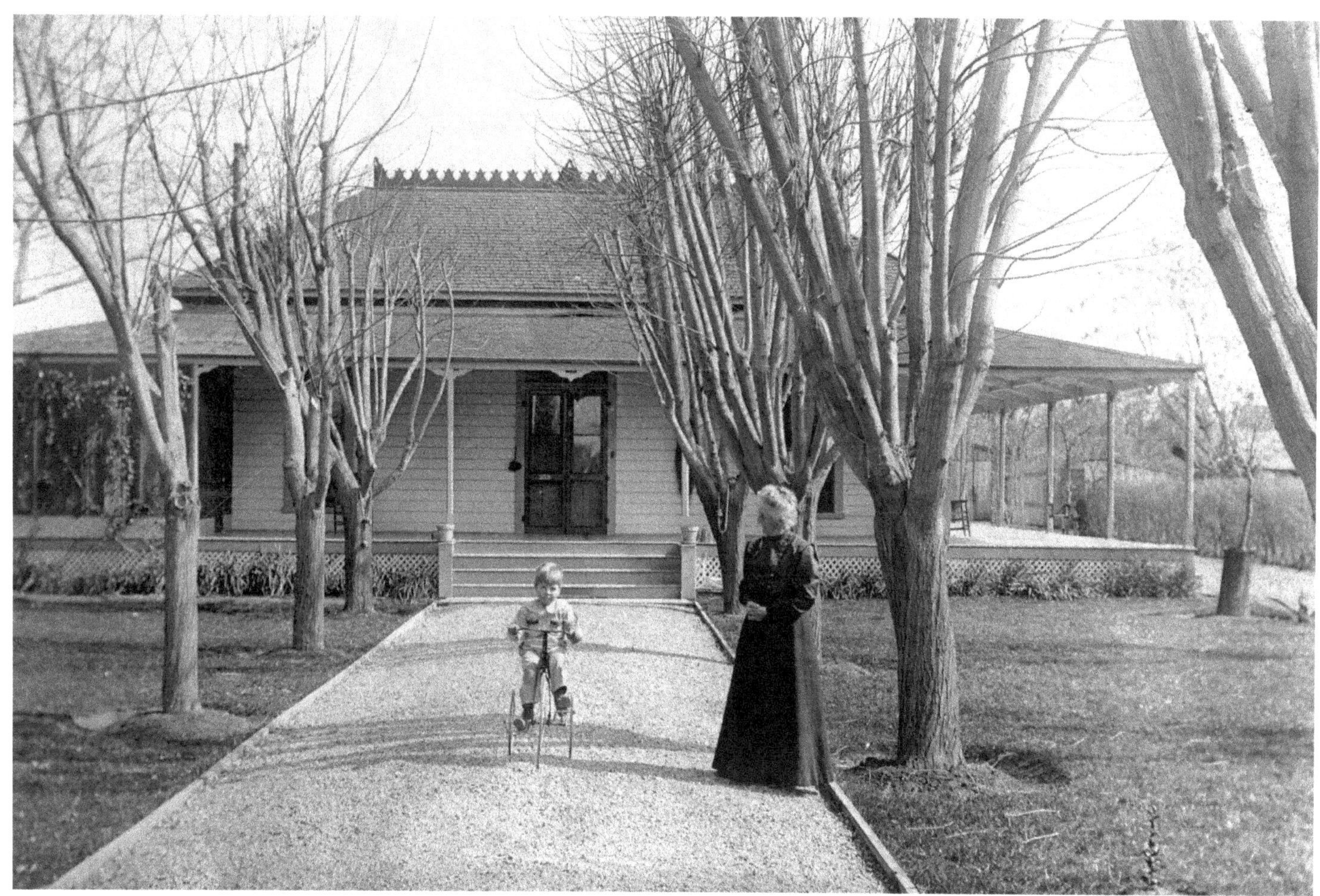

The Phoenix City Hall housed the Arizona Legislature until the completion of the Capitol in 1901. By that time, relations between English-speaking and Spanish-speaking Phoenicians had begun to deteriorate. Because the railroads made mutual dependency unnecessary, mixed marriages and inter-ethnic business partnerships became less common as white Phoenicians oriented their cultural focus to their east and west rather than to their south.

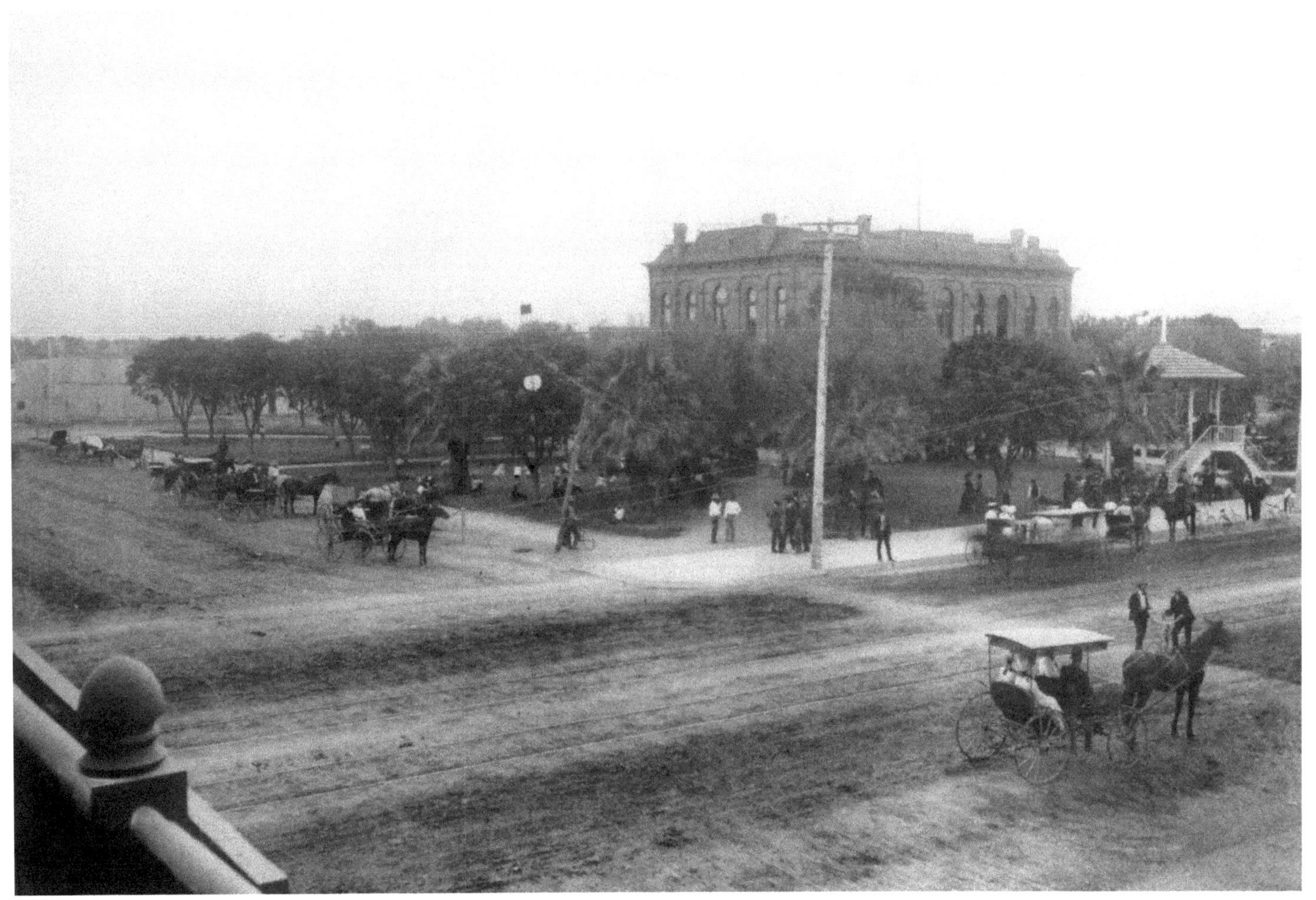

Gordon A. Wilson, an unmarried Virginian, was one of the valley's first settlers. He donated a small corner of his land for a new school, located near where Jack Swilling established his mill (around present-day 24th Street and Buckeye Road). The schoolchildren who attended the Wilson school were both Hispanic and white. Teacher Ruth Sullivan and her students pose outside the Wilson School in Phoenix in 1900.

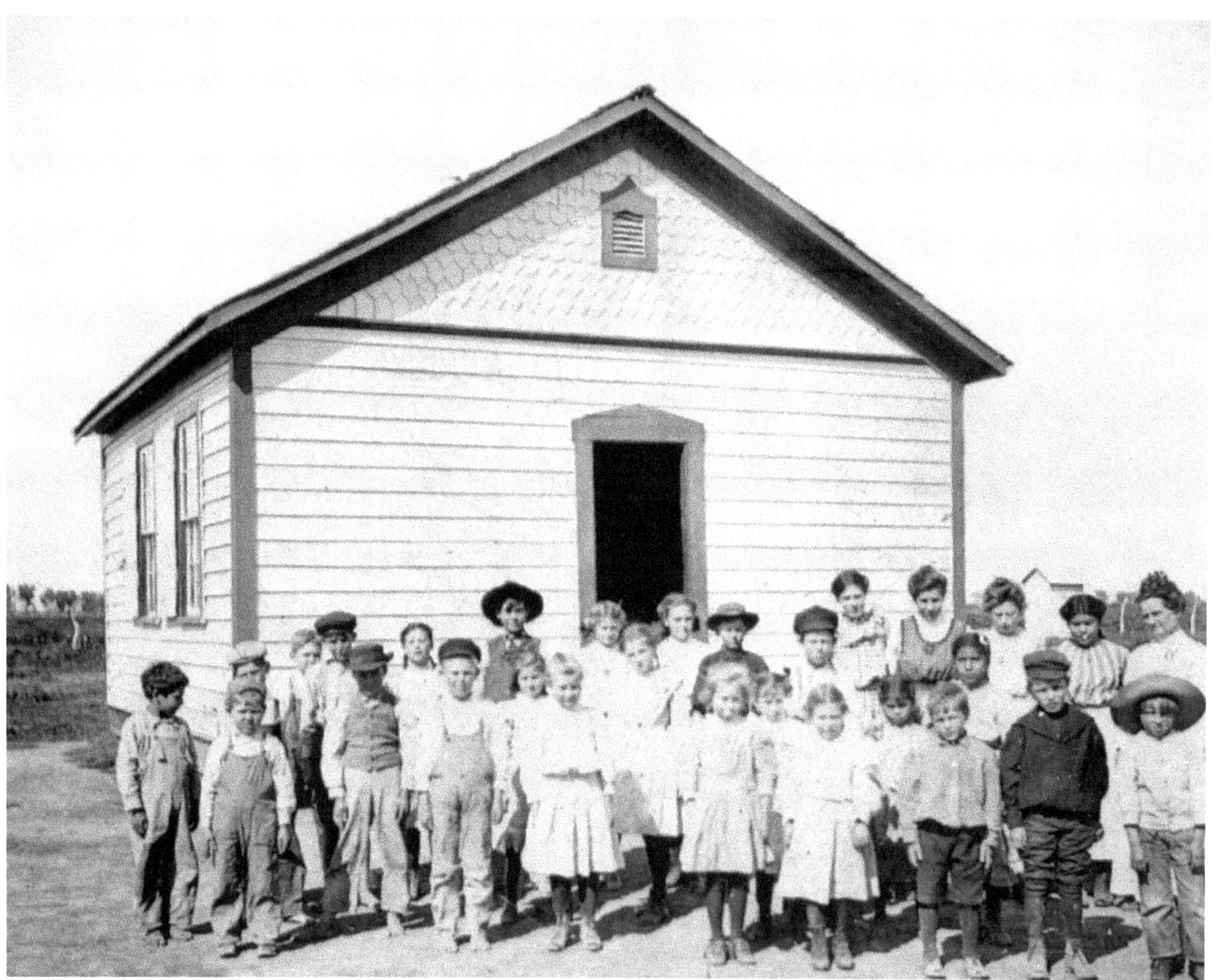

In 1900 Phoenix streets were unpaved. The hard-packed dirt streets were watered down by a horse-drawn water wagon in order to control the dust. The paving of Phoenix streets began in 1911 at Central Avenue and Jefferson Street in front of what was then the Commercial Hotel, later renamed the Hotel Luhrs.

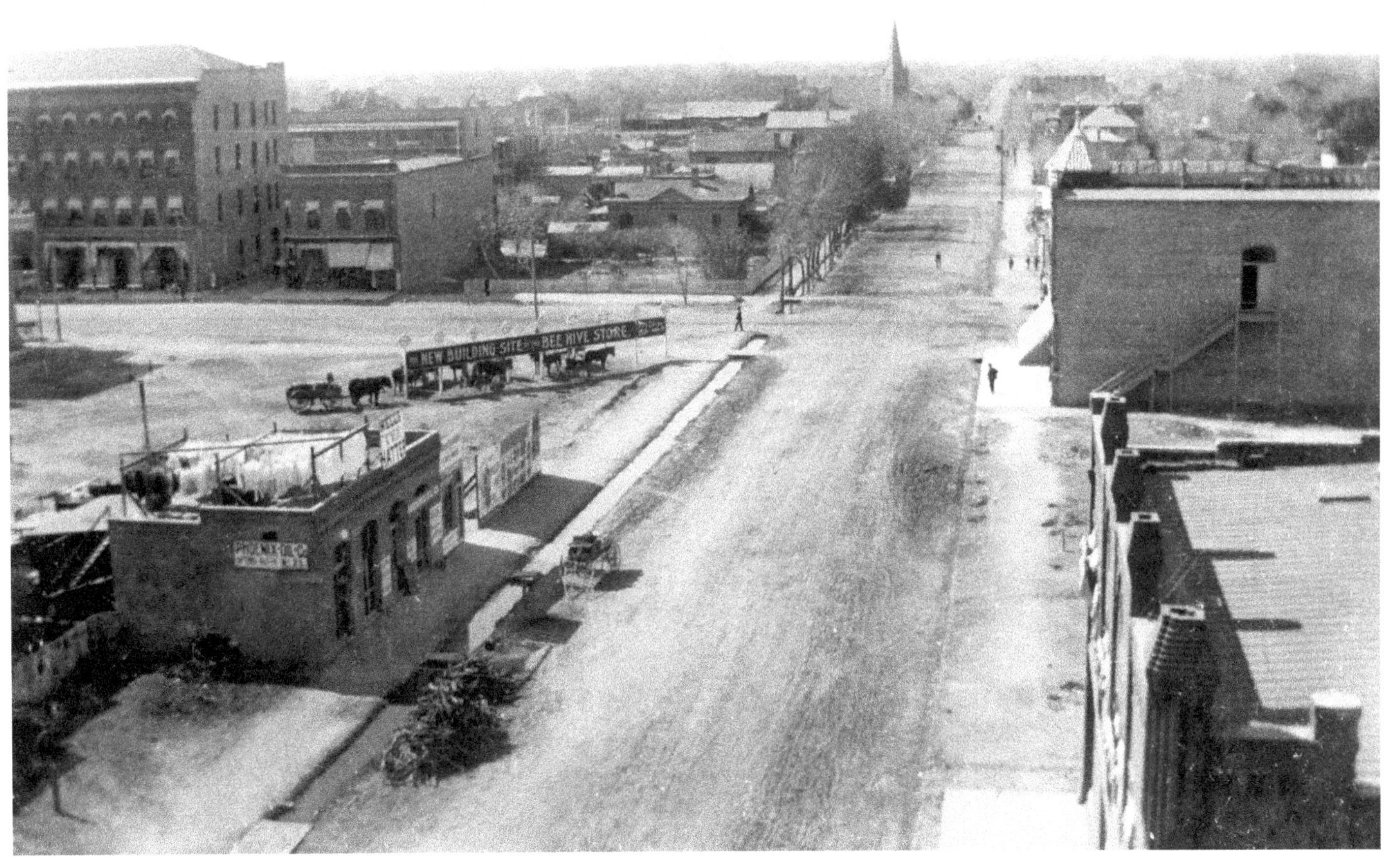

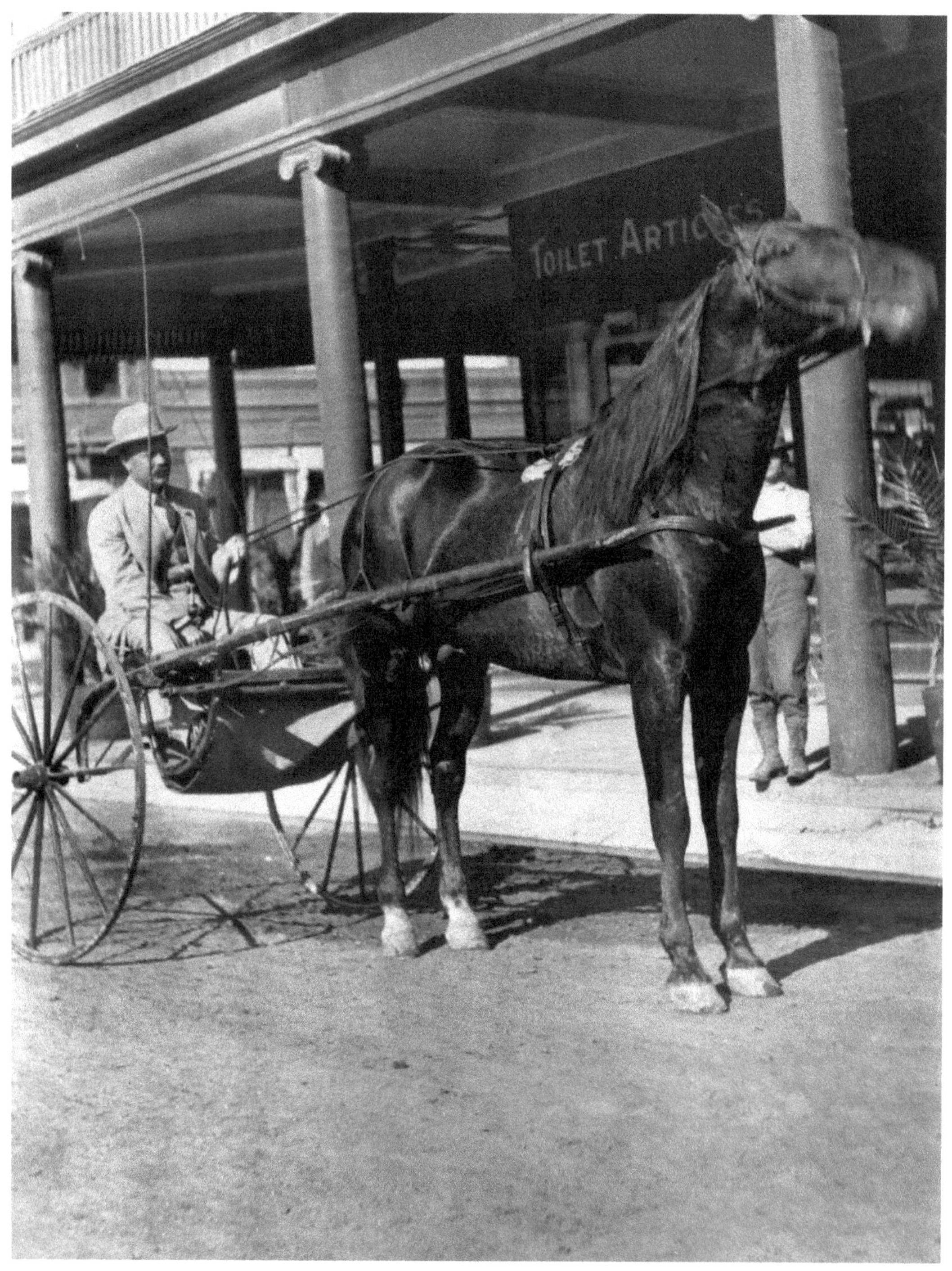

Shirley Christy, a Phoenix surveyor, territorial deputy treasurer, State Fair commissioner, and founder of the Arizona School of Music, enjoys a buggy ride down a Phoenix street around 1900.

The future of Phoenix looked very bright in 1900 when the State Capitol was completed. The Arizona Rough Riders had triumphantly returned from the Spanish-American War, Phoenix had its first library and first Grand Opera House, and more than 5,000 residents lived within the city limits.

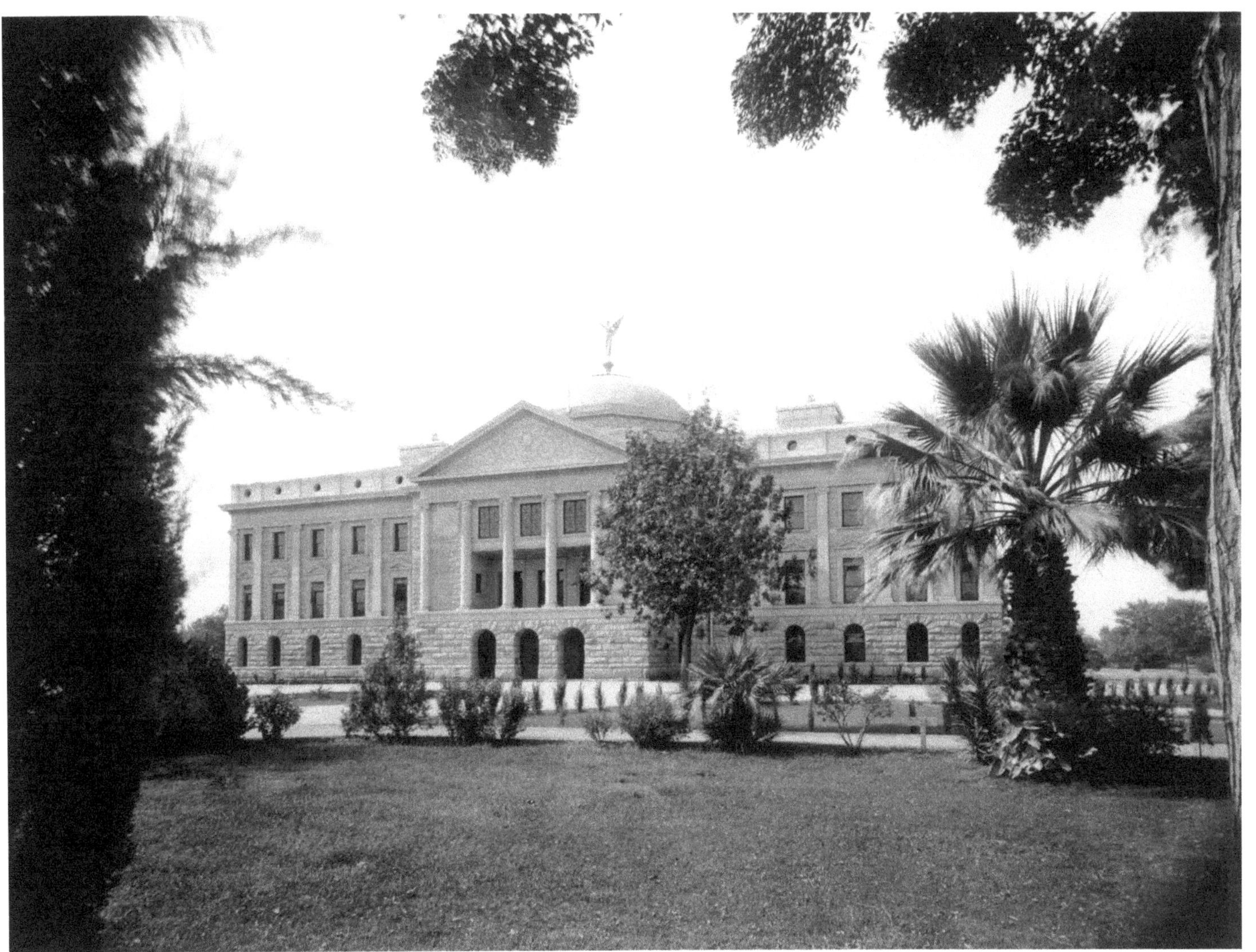

Pictured here is the home of John "Yours Truly" Smith on East Adams Street. He first came to the Phoenix area in 1866. The following spring, he built a hay camp near the future site of Phoenix to provide hay for the horses and mules at Fort McDowell. He went on to co-found the Arizona Canal Company, own the Phoenix Steam Mill, serve as postmaster, and later become a territorial representative.

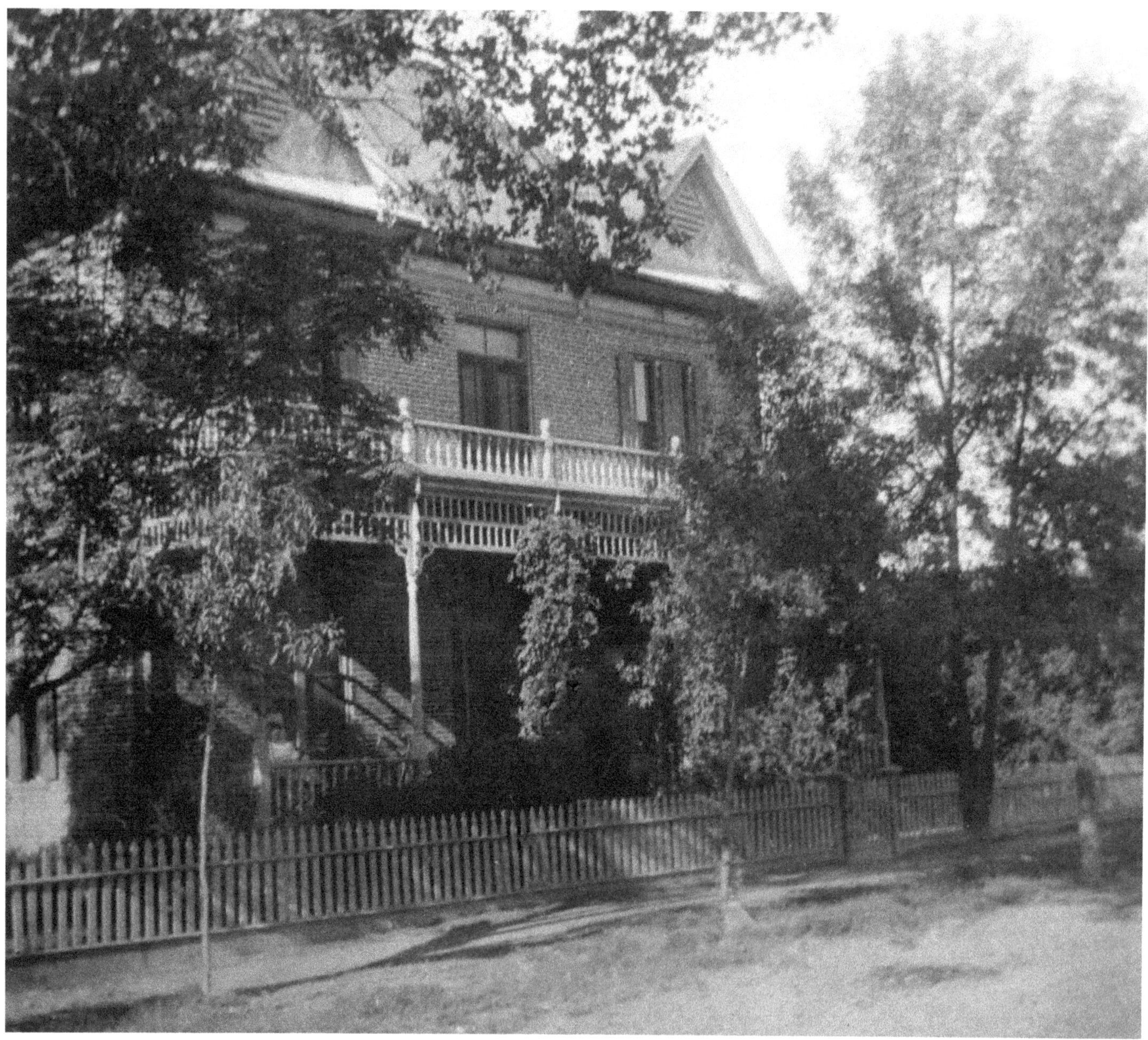

Captain James Harvey McClintock was wounded in the 1898 attack on the City of Santiago de Cuba during the Spanish-American War, and two years later he married Dorothy G. Bacon, a graduate of Stanford University. In 1902 McClintock was appointed Postmaster of Phoenix.

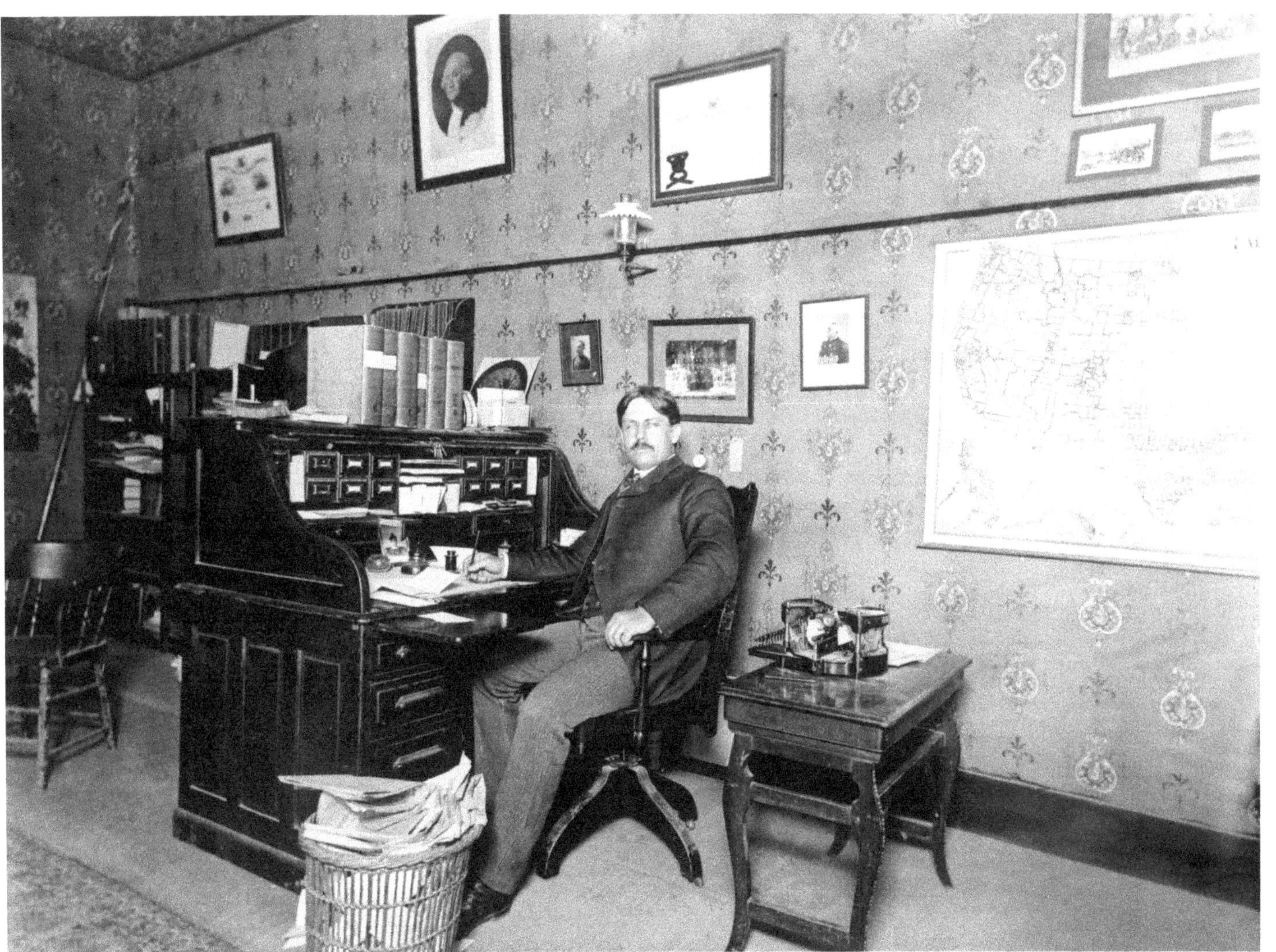

Early farmers in the Salt River Valley found that the fertile soil could sustain all kinds of fruit trees, including fig, quince, plum, orange, walnut, and peach. Farmers also planted barley, corn, alfalfa, oats, wheat, grapes, pecans, peanuts, and tobacco.

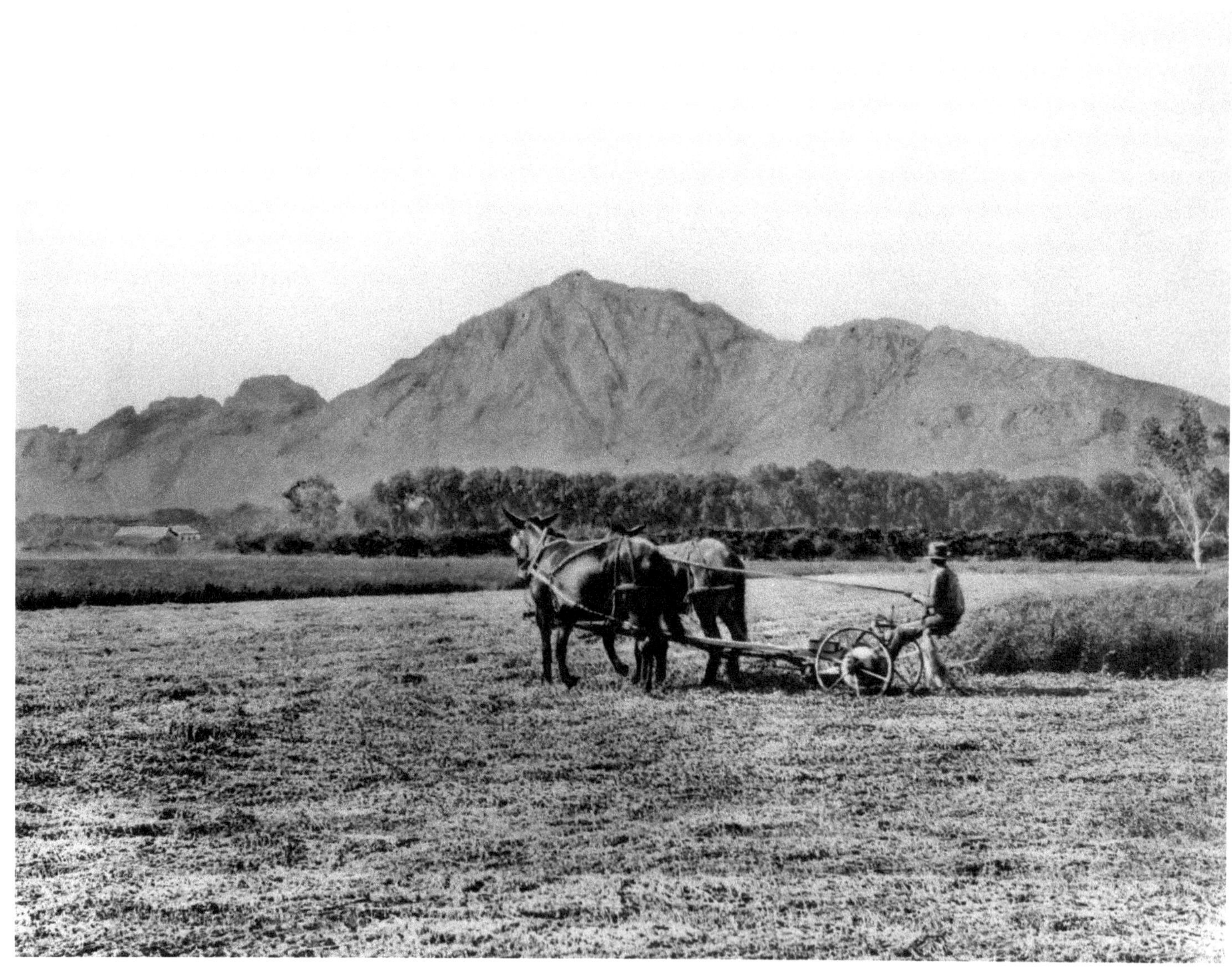

The Maricopa County Courthouse was built in 1884 on Washington Street between First and Second avenues. It was torn down in 1928 to make room for a new courthouse and city hall.

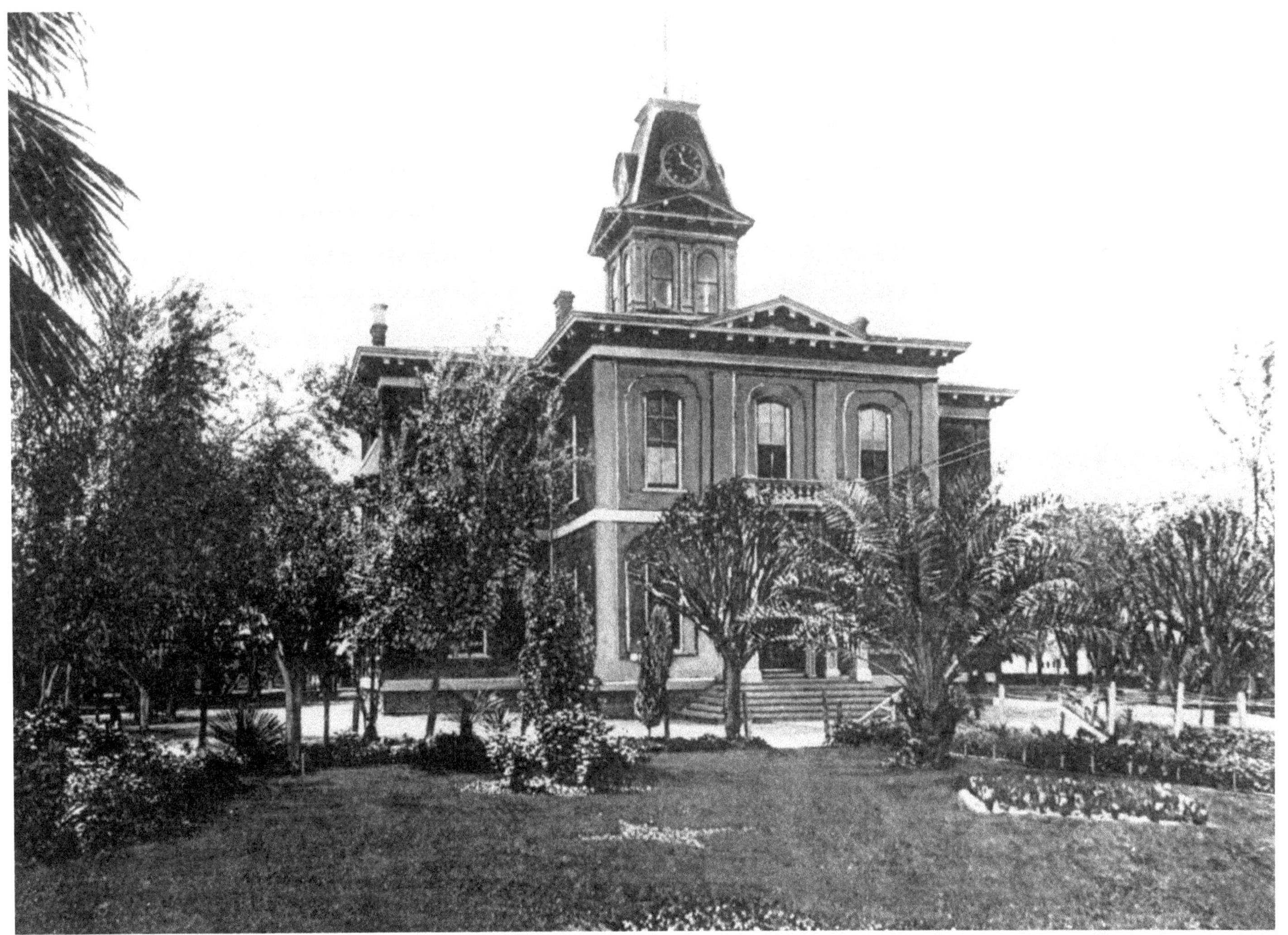

The all-volunteer Phoenix Fire Engine Company #1 was organized in 1881, but after two devastating fires that destroyed almost all of the business section in 1885 and 1886, the Phoenix city council authorized the formation of the Phoenix Fire Department, with Frank M. Czarnowsky, an immigrant from Poland, appointed as chief. Motorized fire equipment did not replace horse-drawn equipment until 1914.

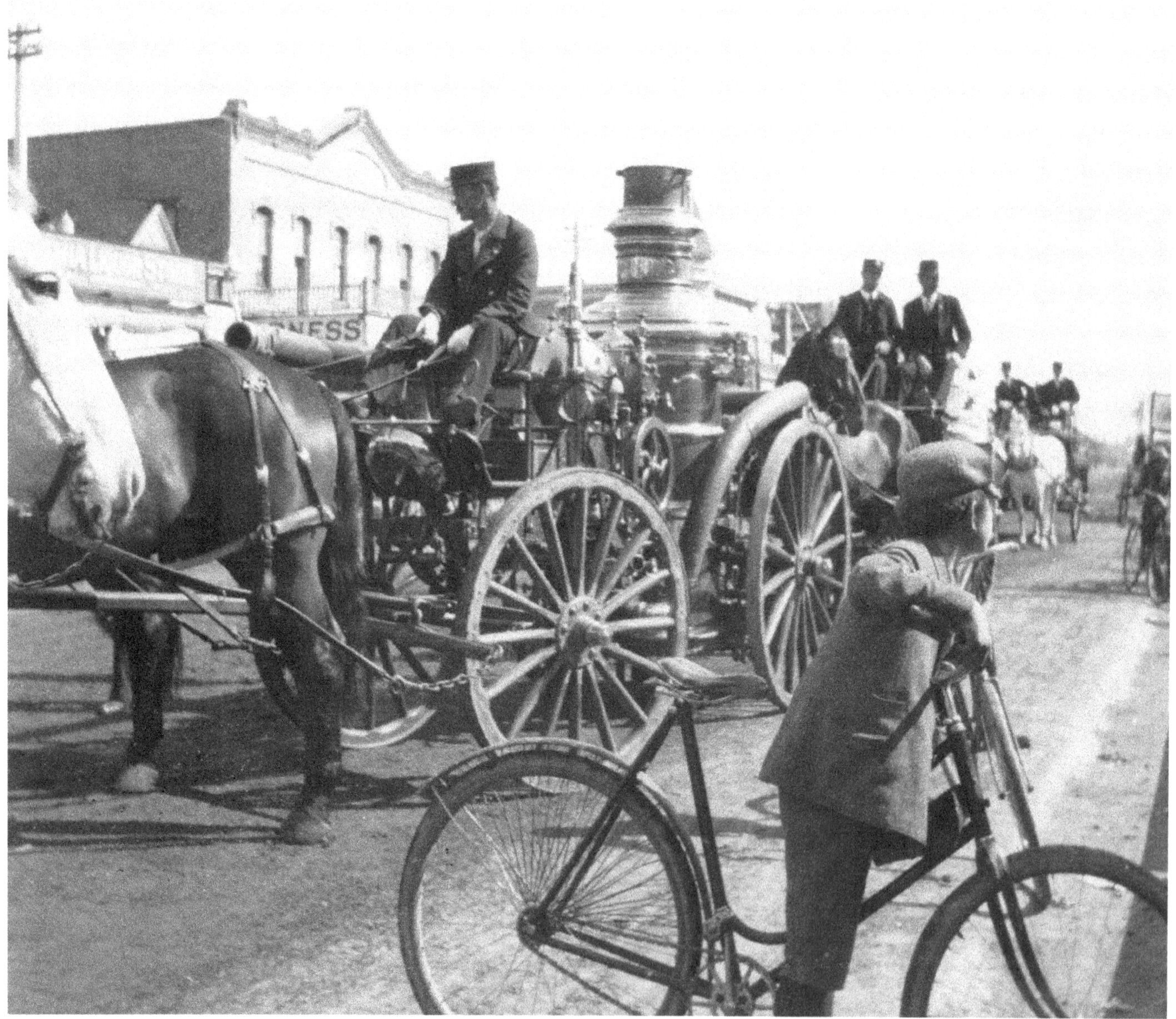

Shown here are 2nd Avenue and Washington Street around 1900, with trolley tracks running down the middle of the road.

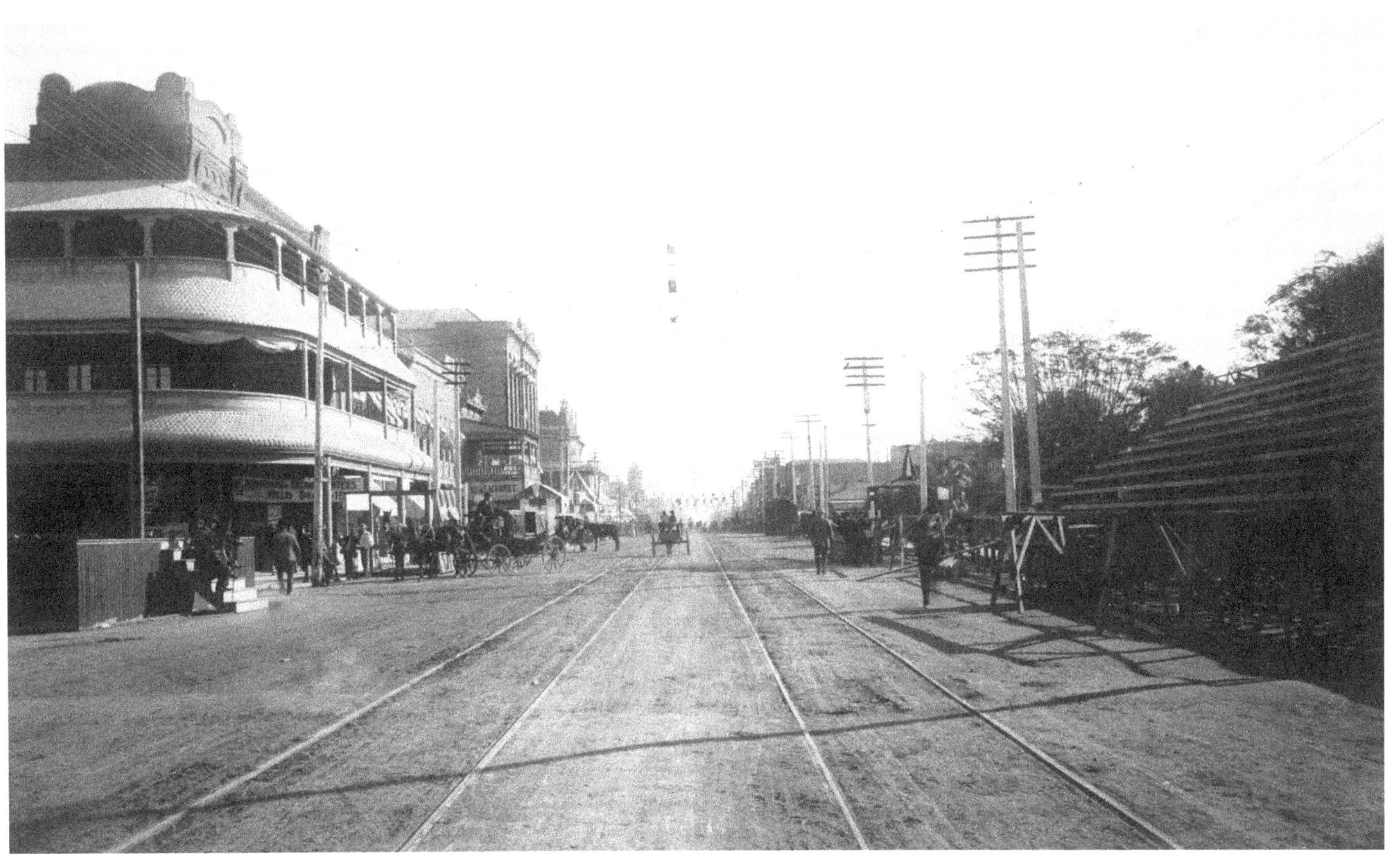

Arizona became a favored destination for those suffering from tuberculosis, and several tuberculosis hospitals were established in the Phoenix area, particularly in Sunnyslope. The disease was more popularly called "consumption" because it seemed to consume the individual, who suffered from dramatic weight loss, fever, and a bloody cough. The infected poor were sent to sanatoria that were quite modest. Some were little more than tents.

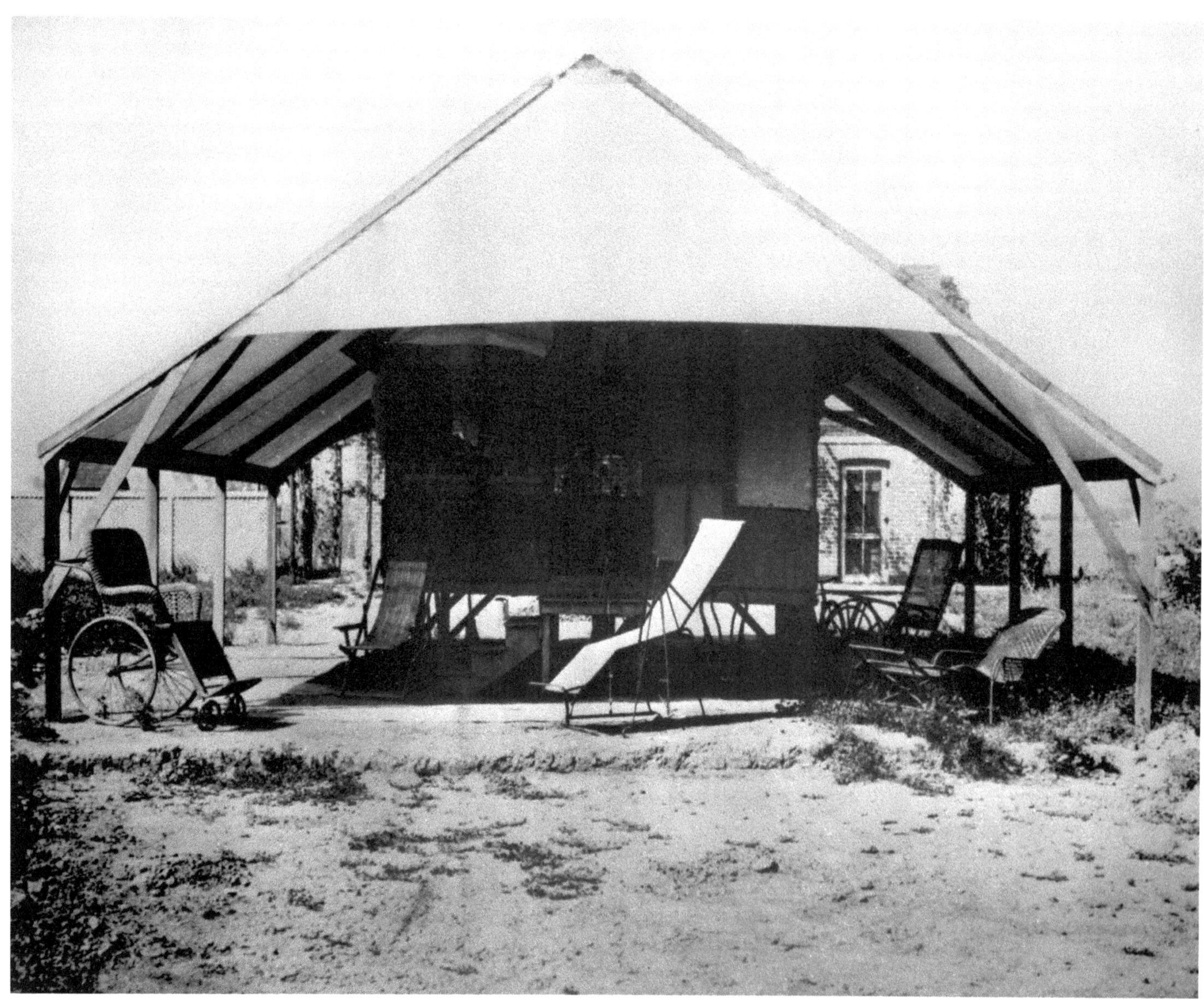

The Phoenix Indian School operated a tuberculosis sanatorium a mile from campus to train American Indian young women how to become care providers.

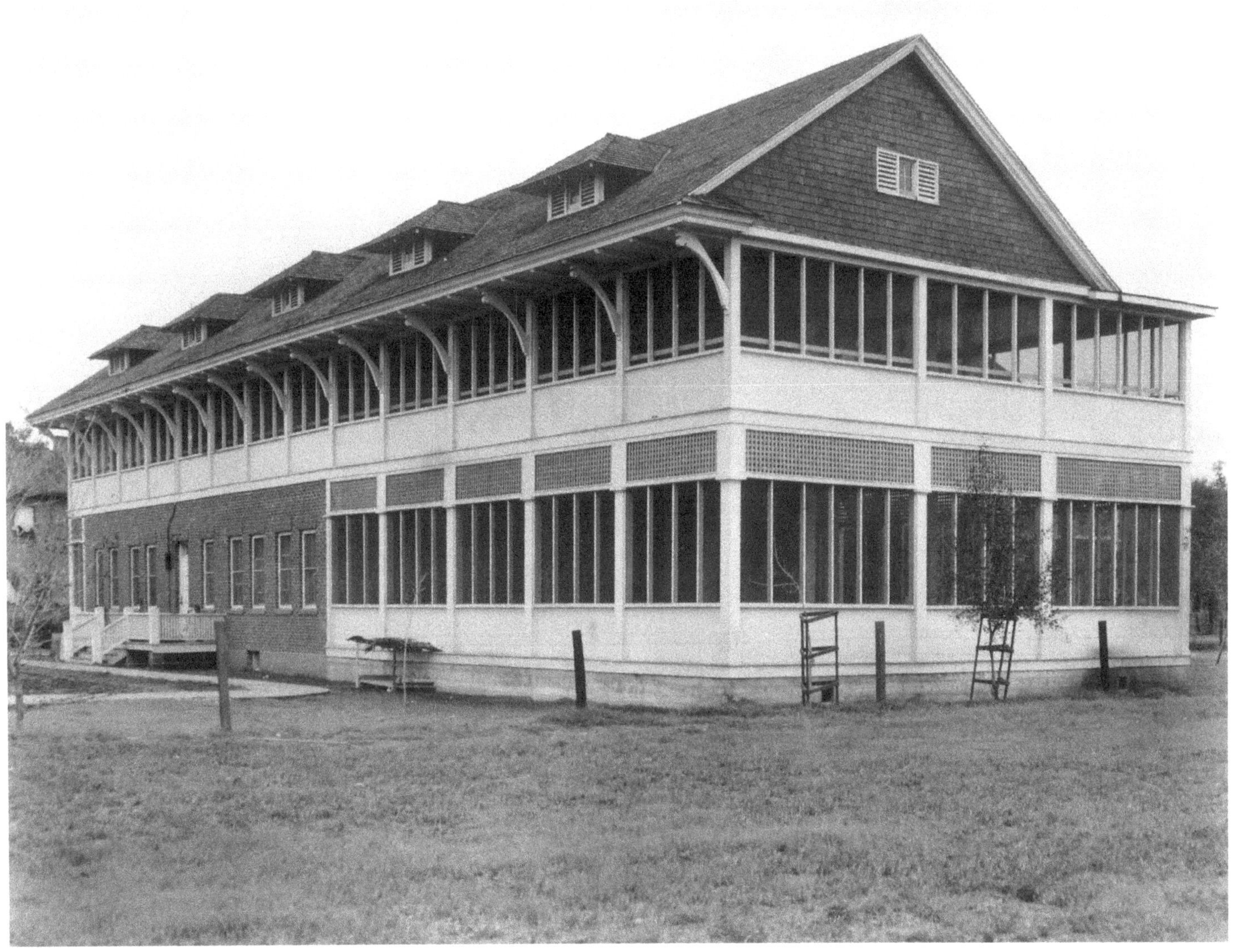

The wealthy suffering from consumption enjoyed more accommodating surroundings. In the 1880s doctors discovered that tuberculosis is contagious, and the National Tuberculosis Association—later the American Lung Association—led campaigns to promote covering the mouth and nose when sneezing and refraining from public spitting. Sadly, even under the best conditions, about half of those who came to Phoenix died within a few years.

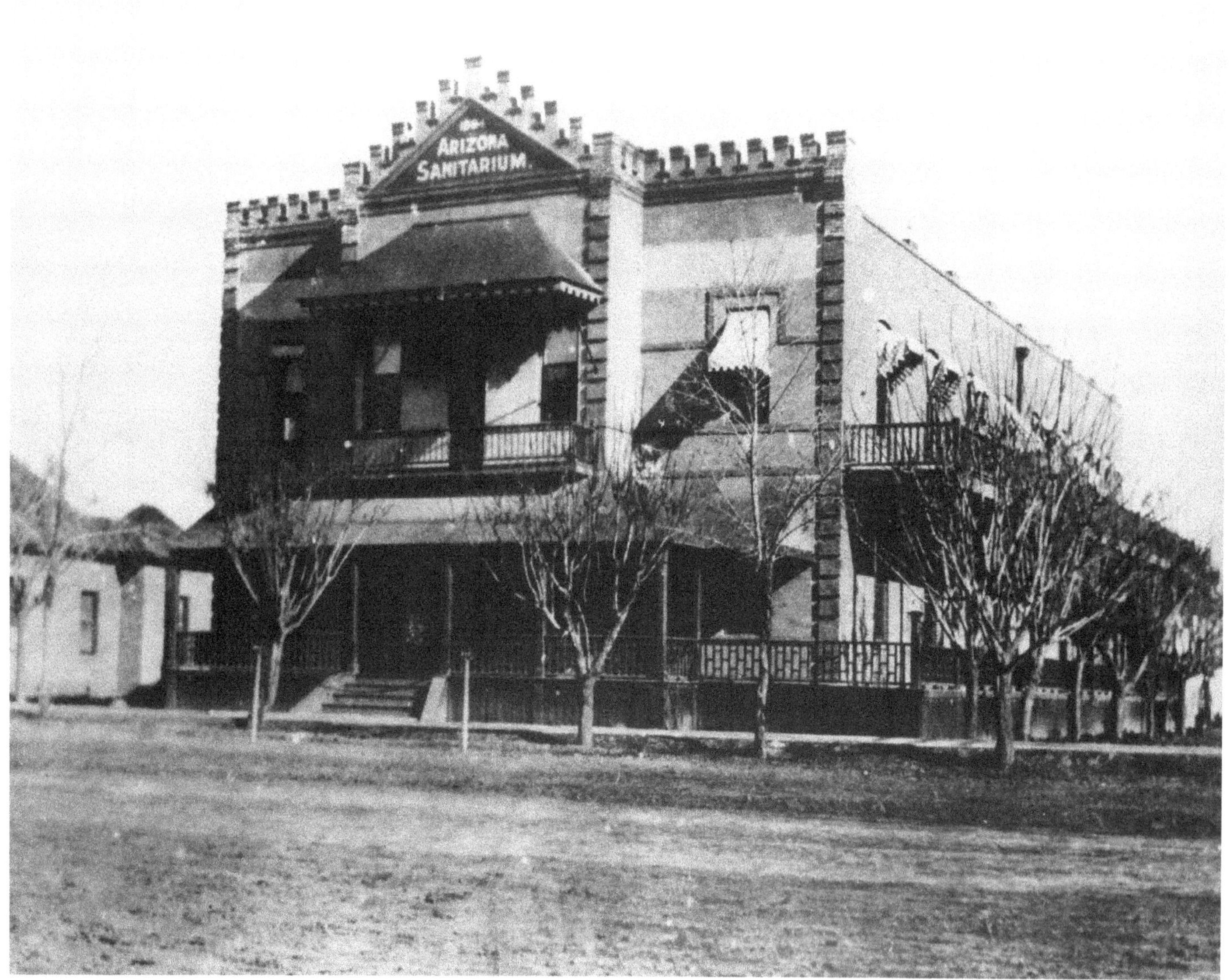

Members of the all-volunteer Phoenix Fire Engine Company #1 line up during a 1900 parade. Horse-drawn steam engines were freeing firefighters from having to pull their wagons by hand, decreasing the time needed to respond to emergency, and steam-powered pumps were increasing the range of water hoses. Motorized equipment did not replace horse-drawn until 1914.

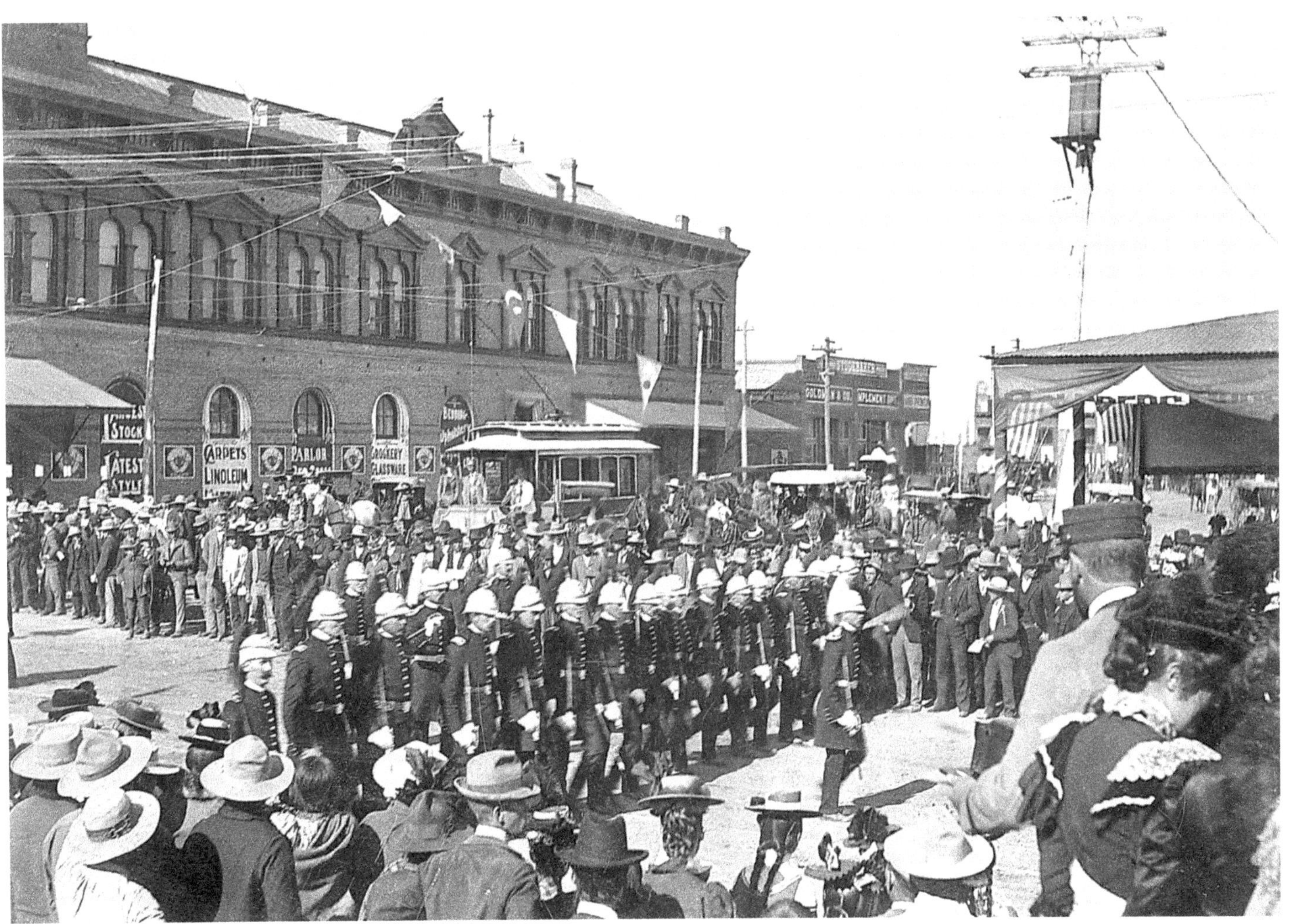

The Phoenix Bottling Works at 615 East Washington, owned by M. E. Morin and R. P. Bicknell, manufactured all kinds of carbonated beverages for Phoenix.

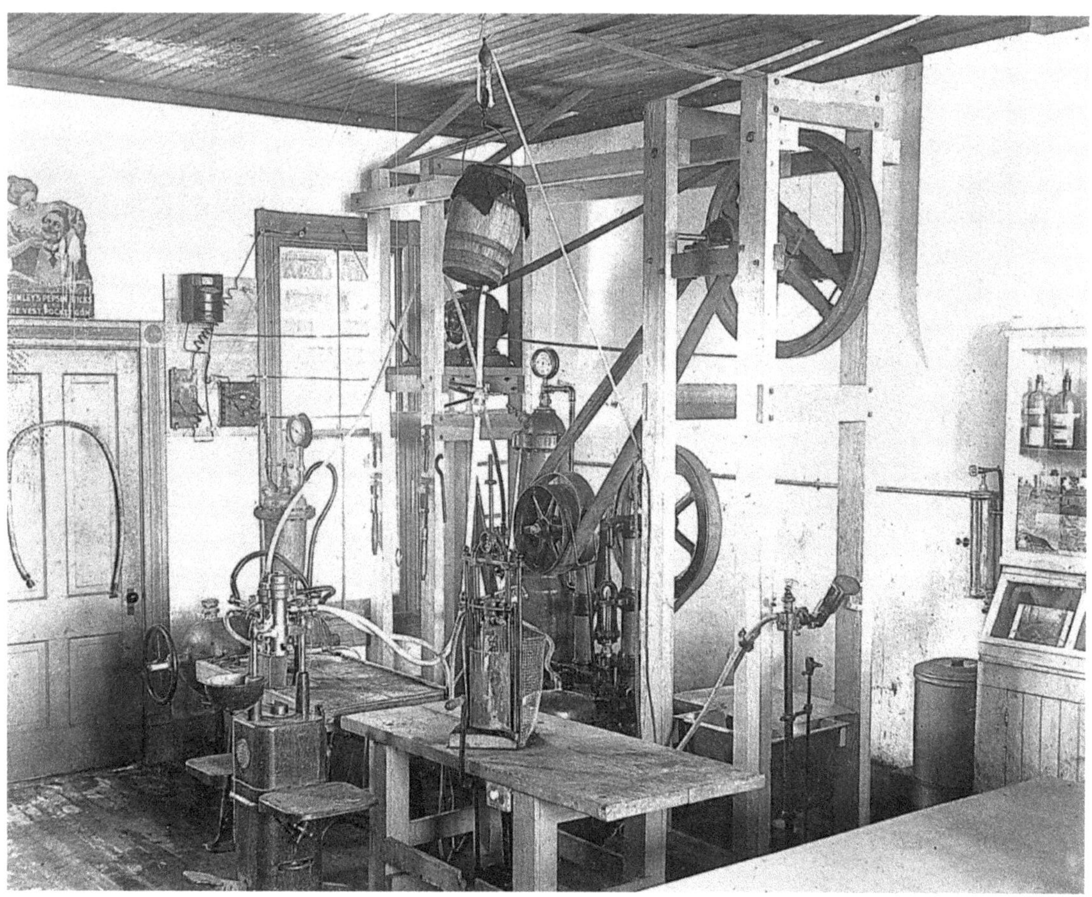

Riding a horse was a commonly used means of transportation in Phoenix in 1901.

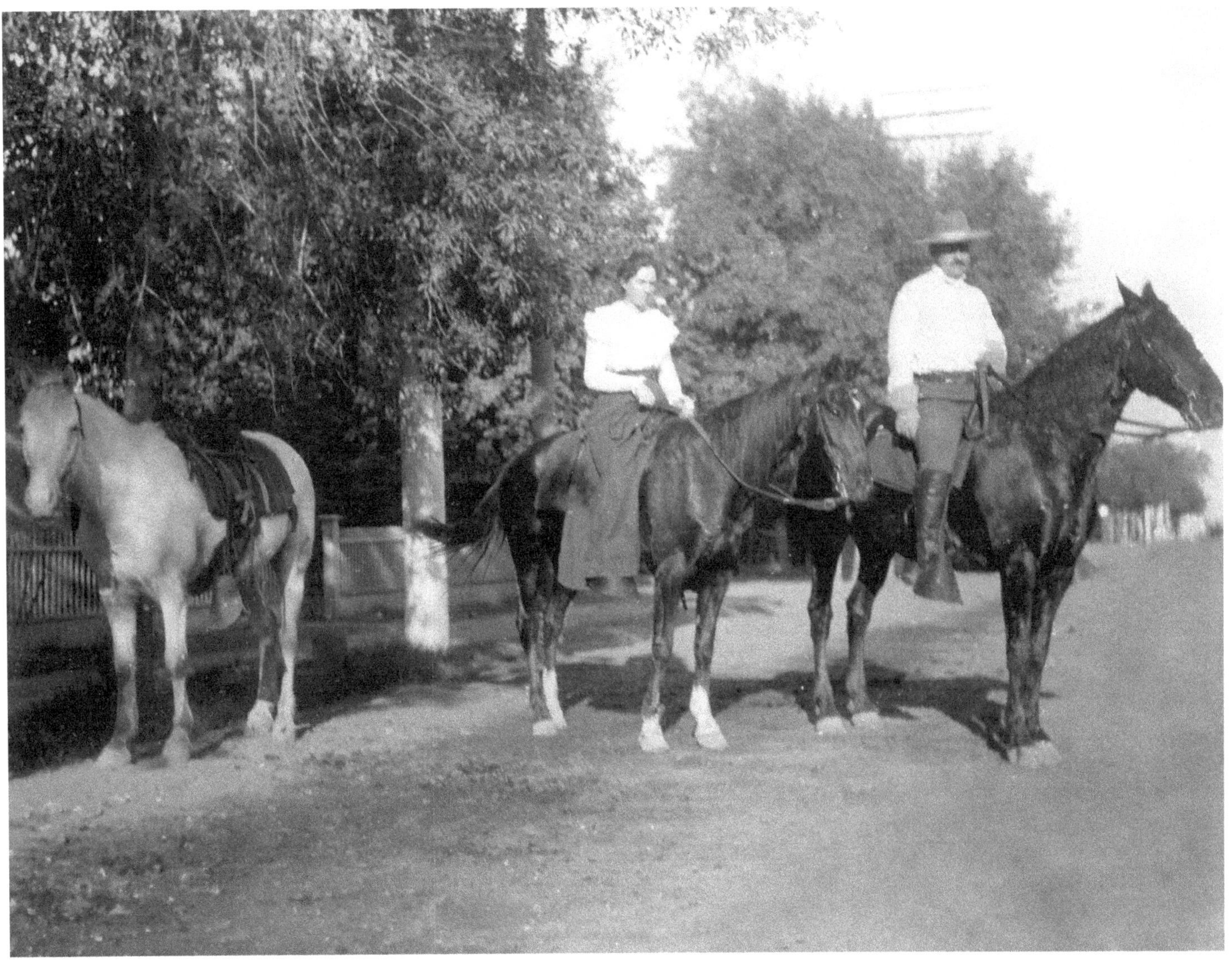

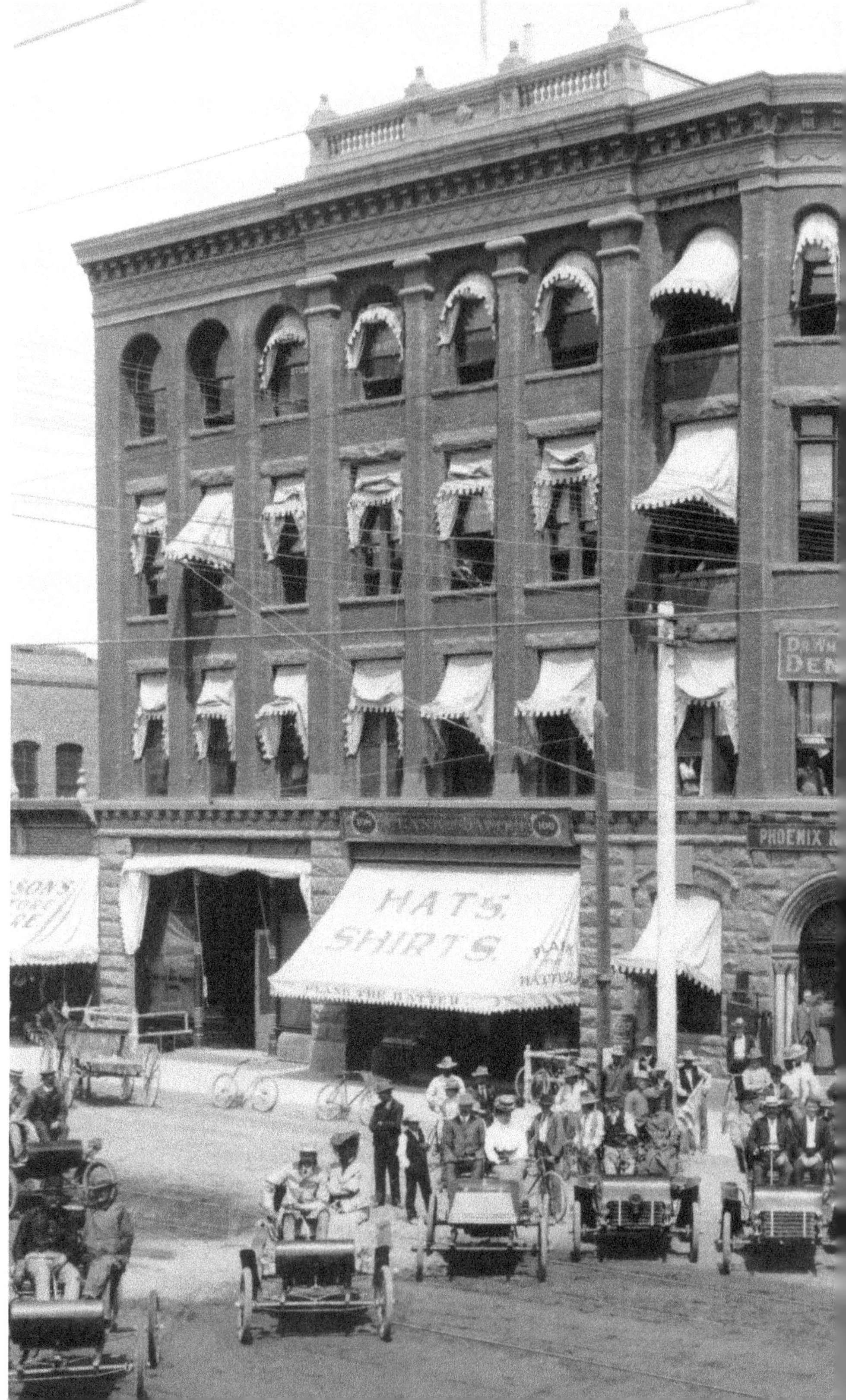
HATS
SHIRTS
PHOENIX

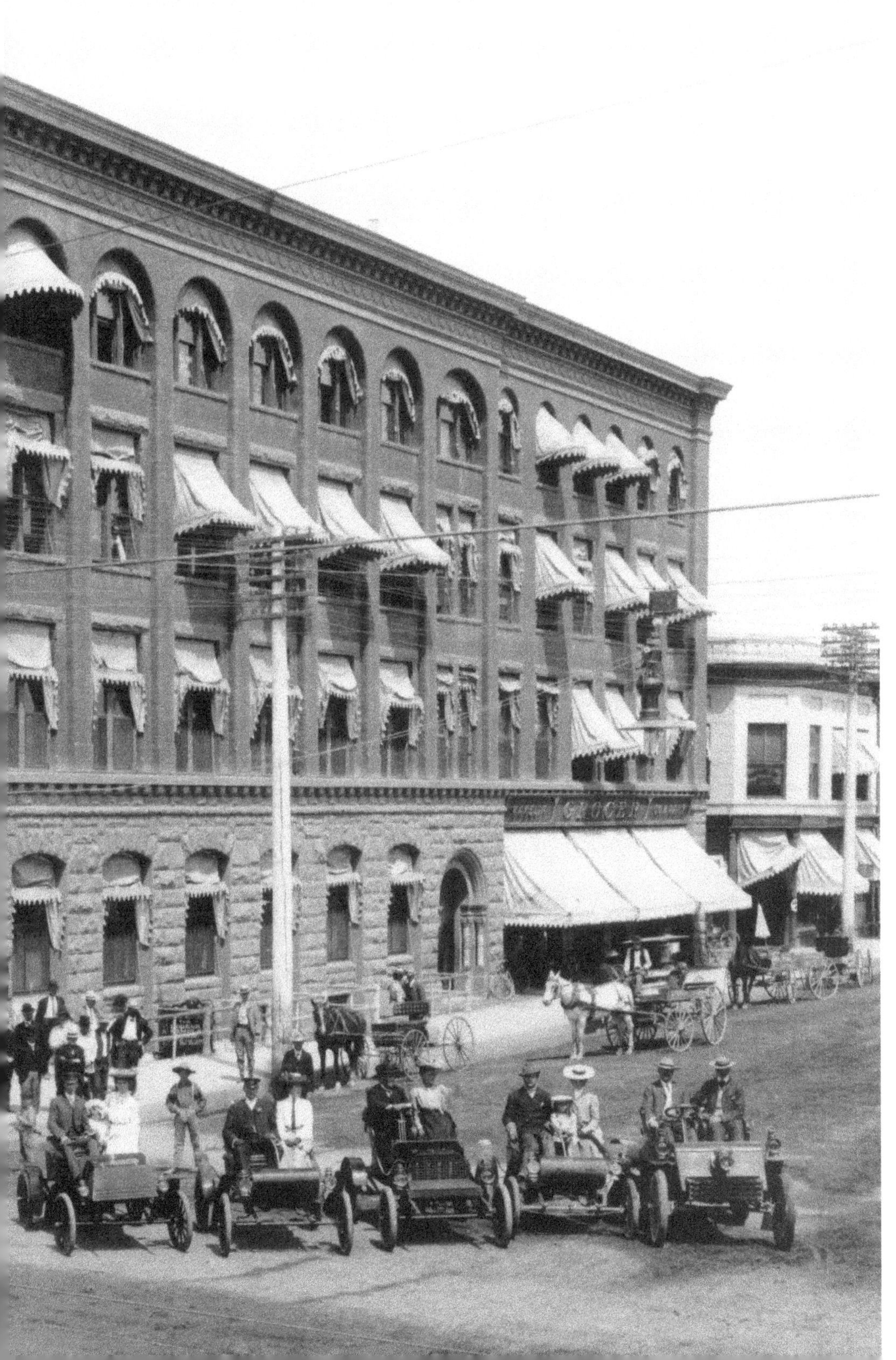

The first automobile arrived in Phoenix in 1900, and by 1904 Phoenix drivers were organizing road trips together. These drivers gather in front of the Phoenix National Bank.

German immigrant Edward Eisele baked all of the bread and pastries himself at the Phoenix Bakery and delivered them on foot, door to door. As the city grew, so did his need for better transportation. At first he learned how to balance his goods on a bicycle, but then he purchased the first horse-drawn bakery wagon in Arizona. In 1894, the Phoenix Bakery added seven more wagons to their fleet.

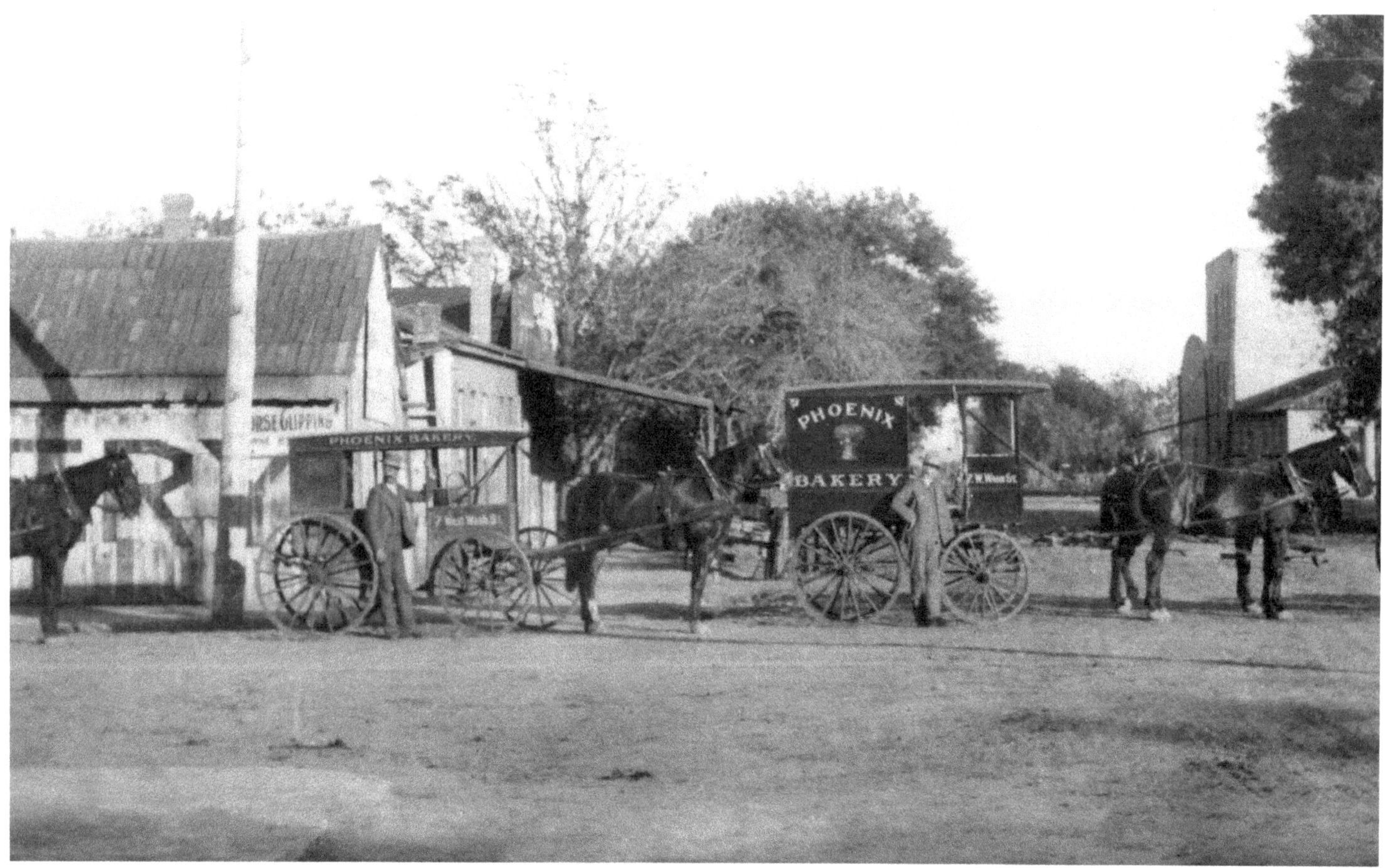

Floods repeatedly devastated the Salt River Valley in the late nineteenth and early twentieth centuries, and territorial representatives joined efforts by other Western states to lobby Congress for assistance in constructing reservoirs. The Newlands Act of 1902 authorized the building of a dam along the Salt River about 80 miles northeast of Phoenix, which began in 1905 and was dedicated by former president Theodore Roosevelt in 1911.

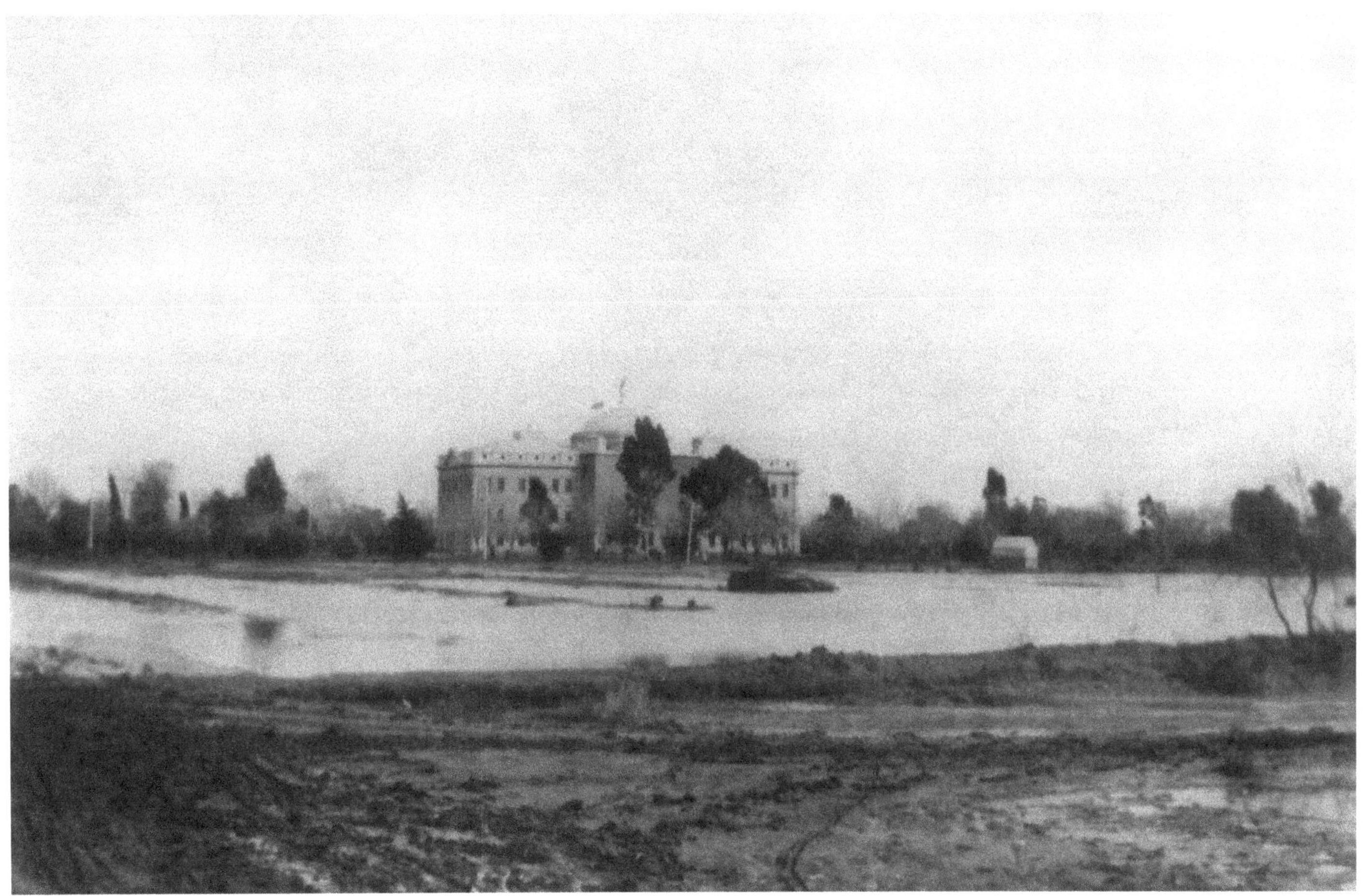

In 1843 the Sisters of Mercy first arrived in the United States from Ireland, dedicated to ministering to the sick and poor. The Sisters came to Phoenix in 1892 to open a parish school, and then expanded their mission to establish a sanatorium for poor tuberculosis patients. In 1895 they rented a six-bedroom brick cottage at Fourth and Polk streets and founded St. Joseph's Sanitarium, which grew into St. Joseph's Hospital, pictured here in 1905.

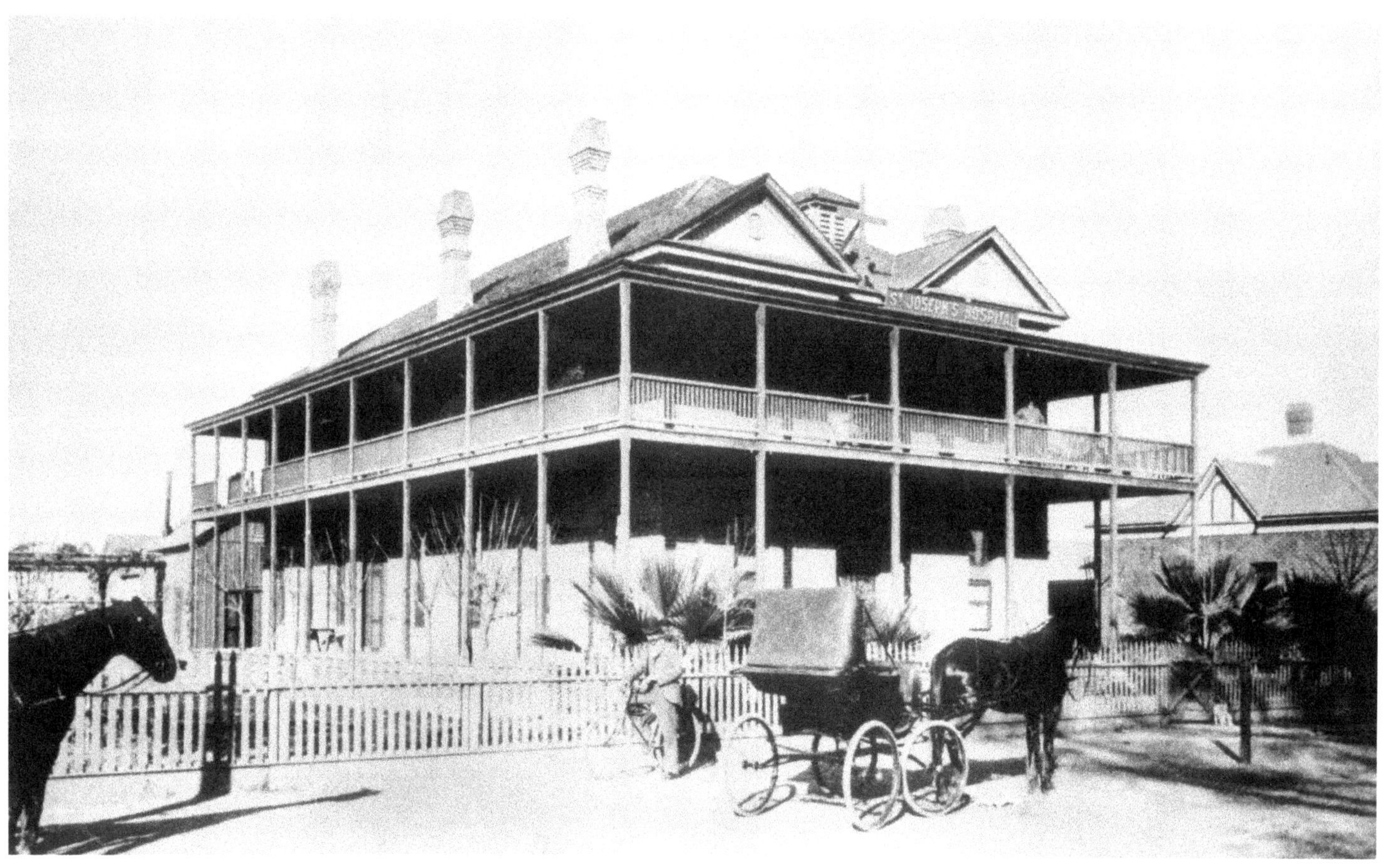

The Verde River flooded in 1905, causing moderate damage to Phoenix along the lower Gila River. Citizens gather at the State Capitol to witness what was called the "Cave Creek Flood."

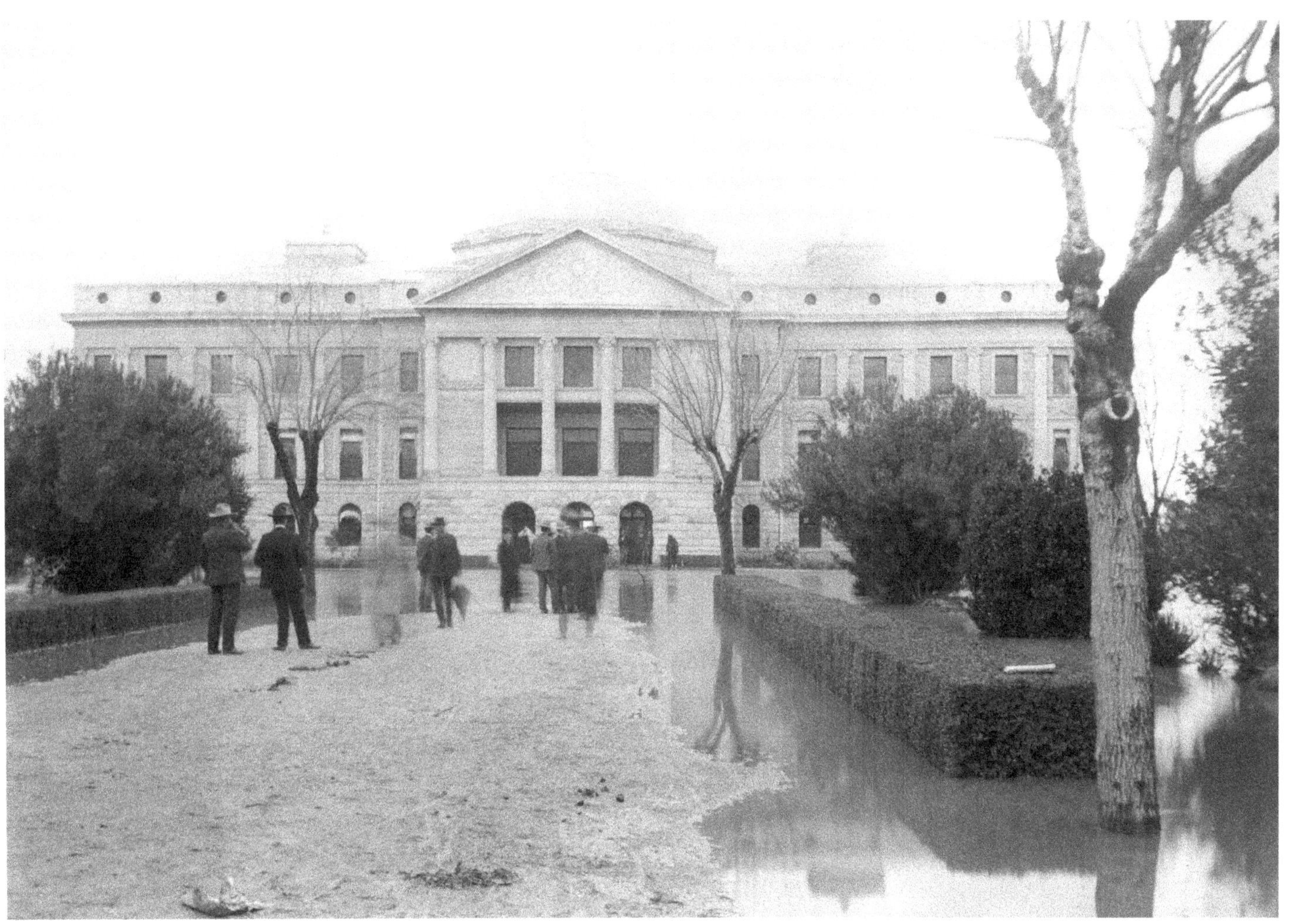

Phoenician Lew Collins takes aim in the desert with his two hunting dogs, probably at desert quail, in 1905.

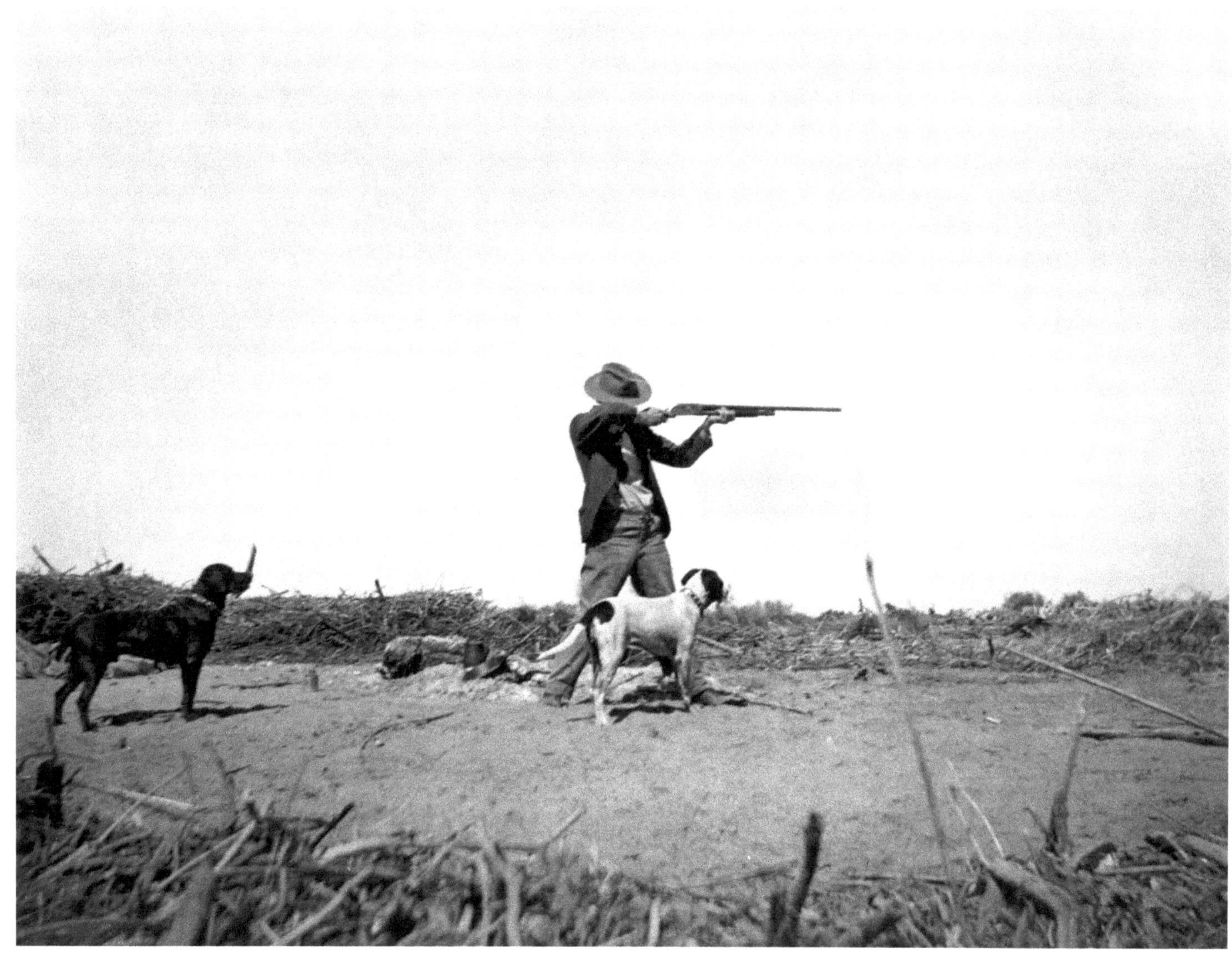

Territorial legislator George Wylie Paul Hunt, kneeling, picnics in the desert near Phoenix in 1905 with Doctor R. N. Looney, Paul Patrick, Wallie Washington, and another woman (unidentified). Sun umbrellas provided relief from direct sunlight.

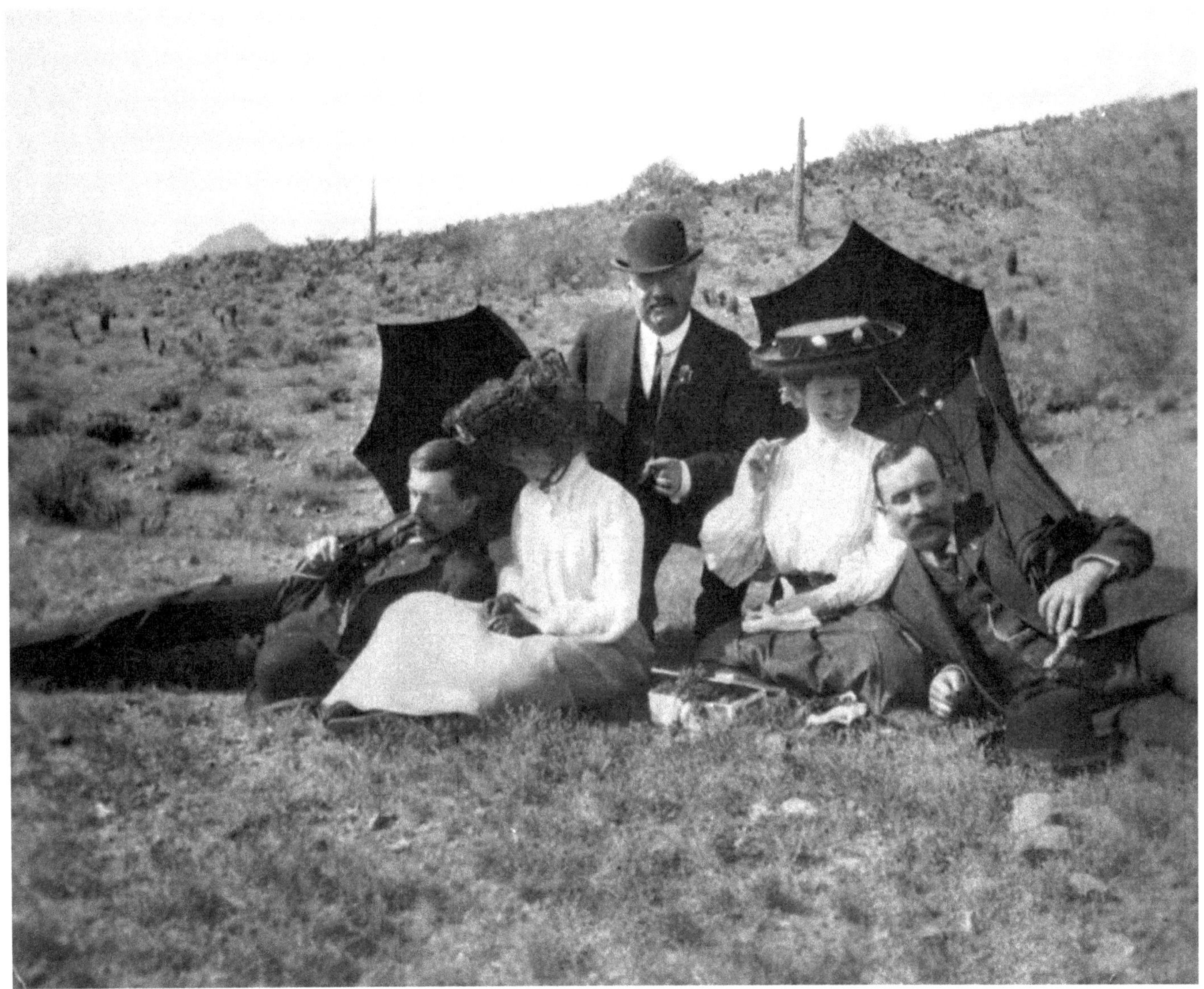

With the "closing" of the West in 1890, the federal government embraced a plan to assimilate American Indian children through compulsory education. The United States Industrial Indian School at Phoenix, later known as the Phoenix Indian School, was founded in 1891 as a coeducational institution for American Indian children. This 1907 image shows the main administrative building of the school.

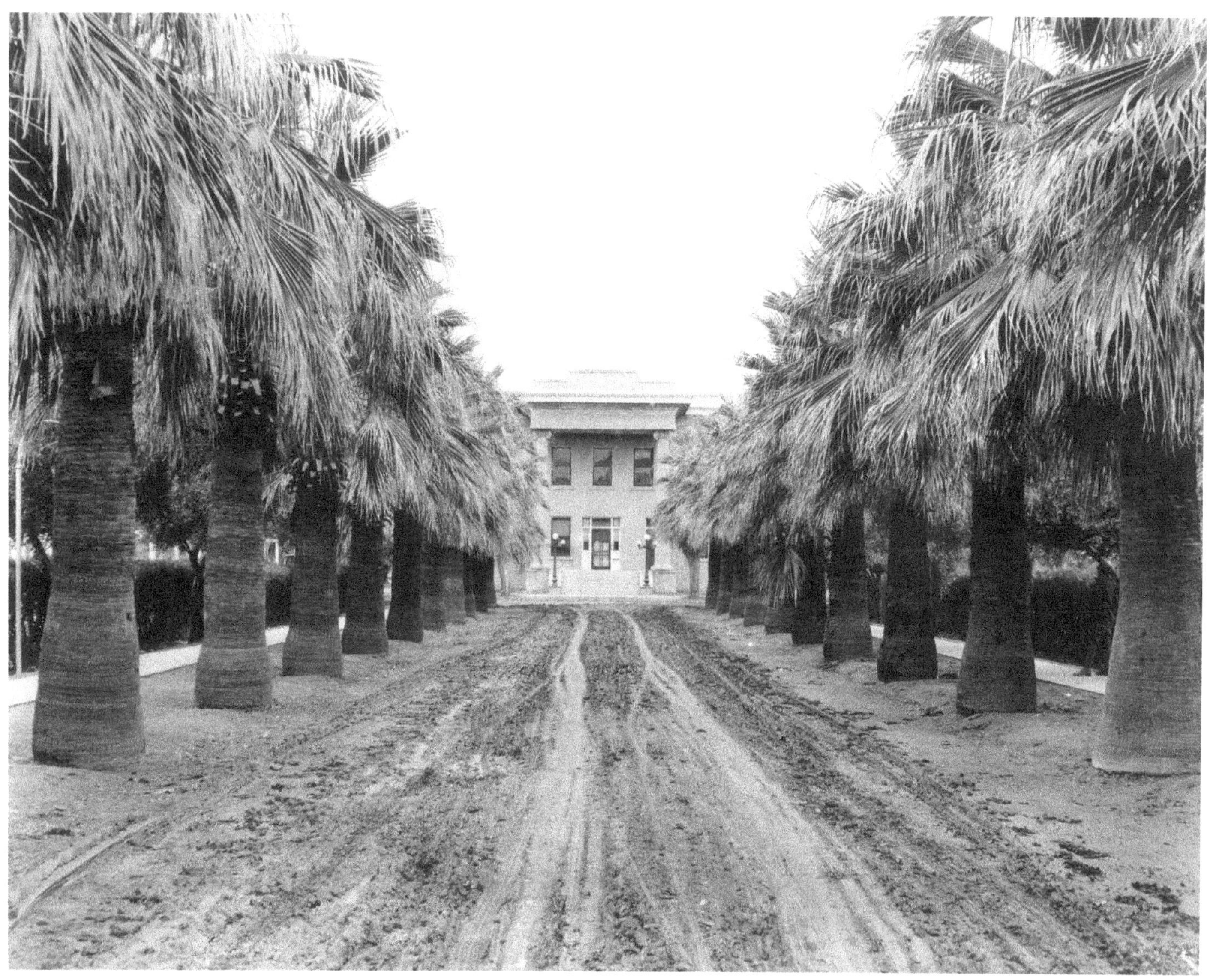

The curriculum at the Phoenix Indian School was designed to invest children with American values, customs, and religion, and train them in productive American trades such as wagon-making, shoemaking, blacksmithing, and carpentry. Children pictured here in 1907 are learning about dairy production.

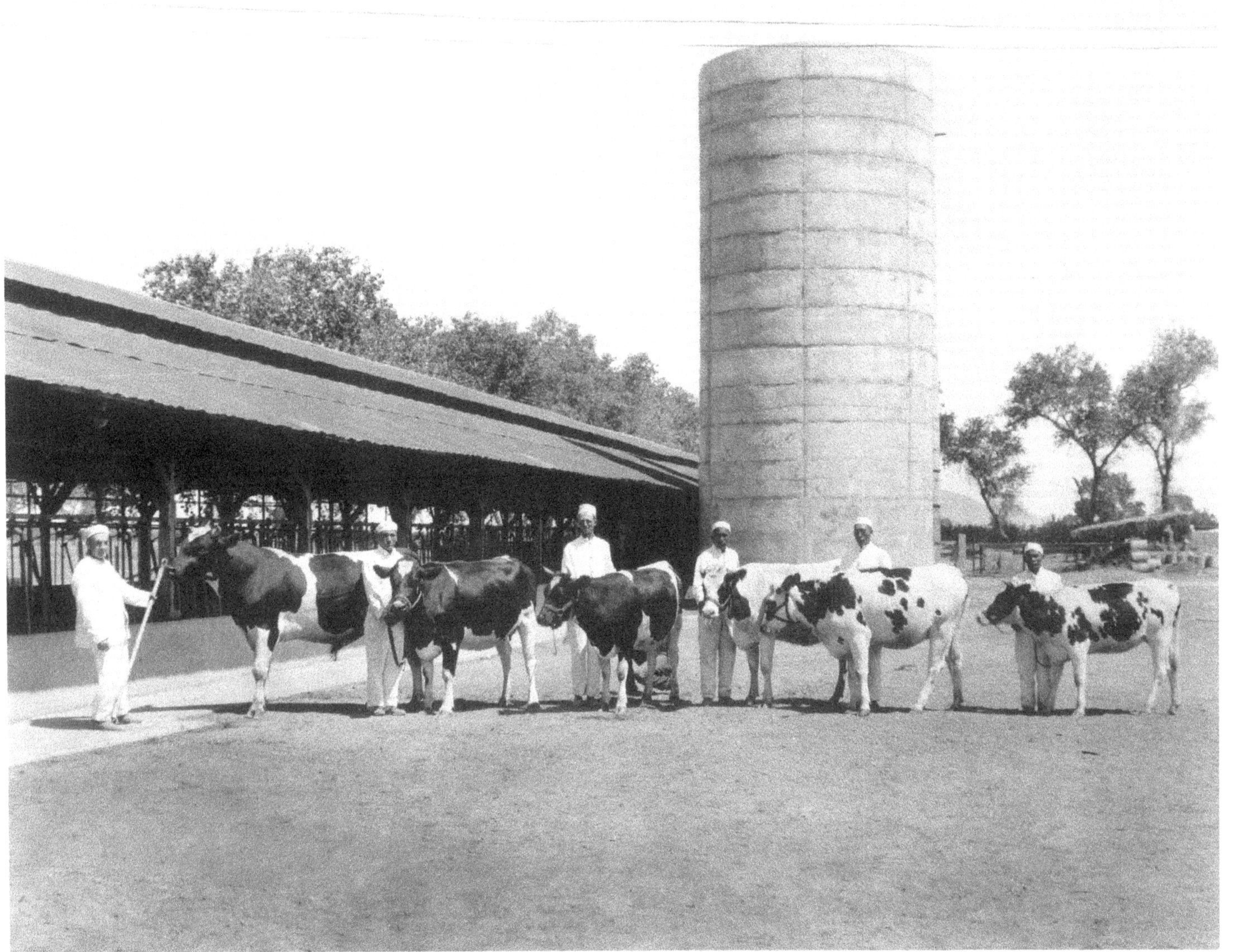

The 1909 Territorial Fair was probably the first time most Phoenicians had seen an airplane. The airplane pictured here flew into town only six years after the Wright Brothers successfully flew at Kitty Hawk, North Carolina.

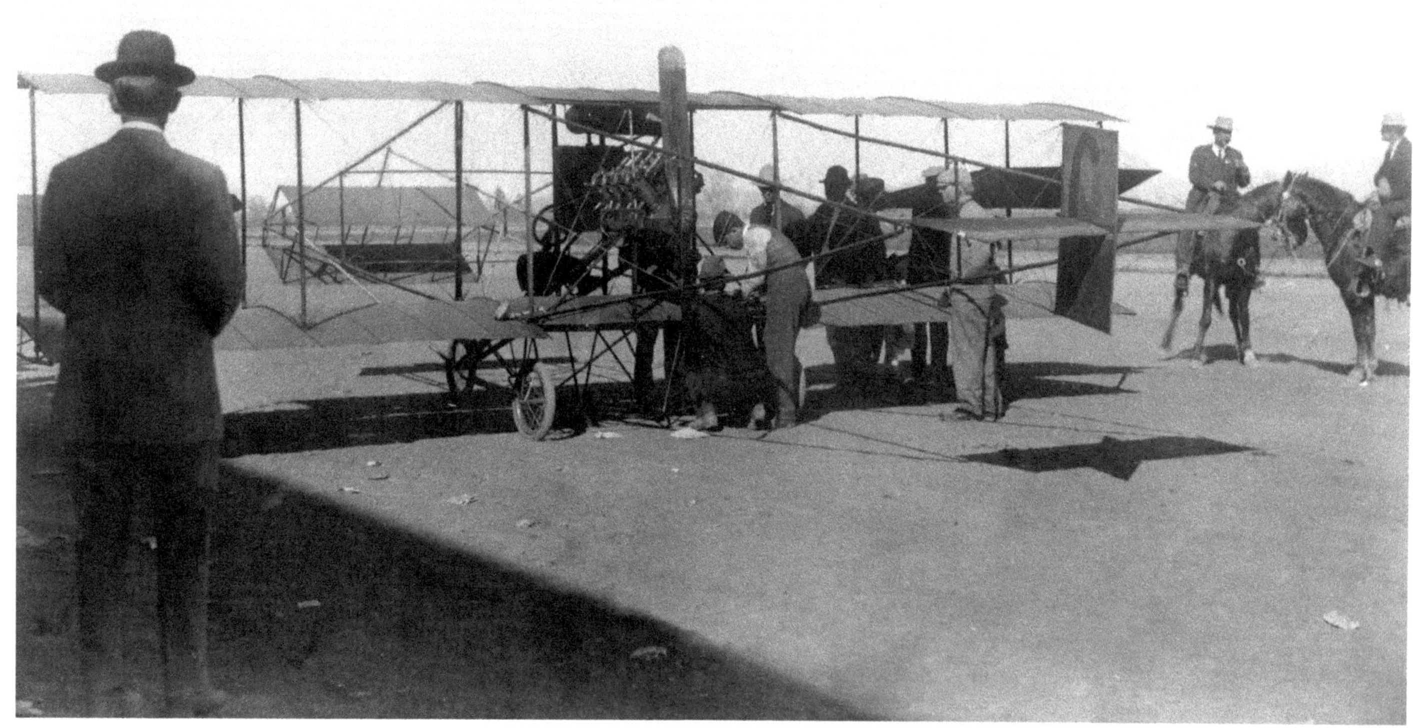

Horse racing was a favored activity at the Arizona Territorial Fair. A harness race is in progress here.

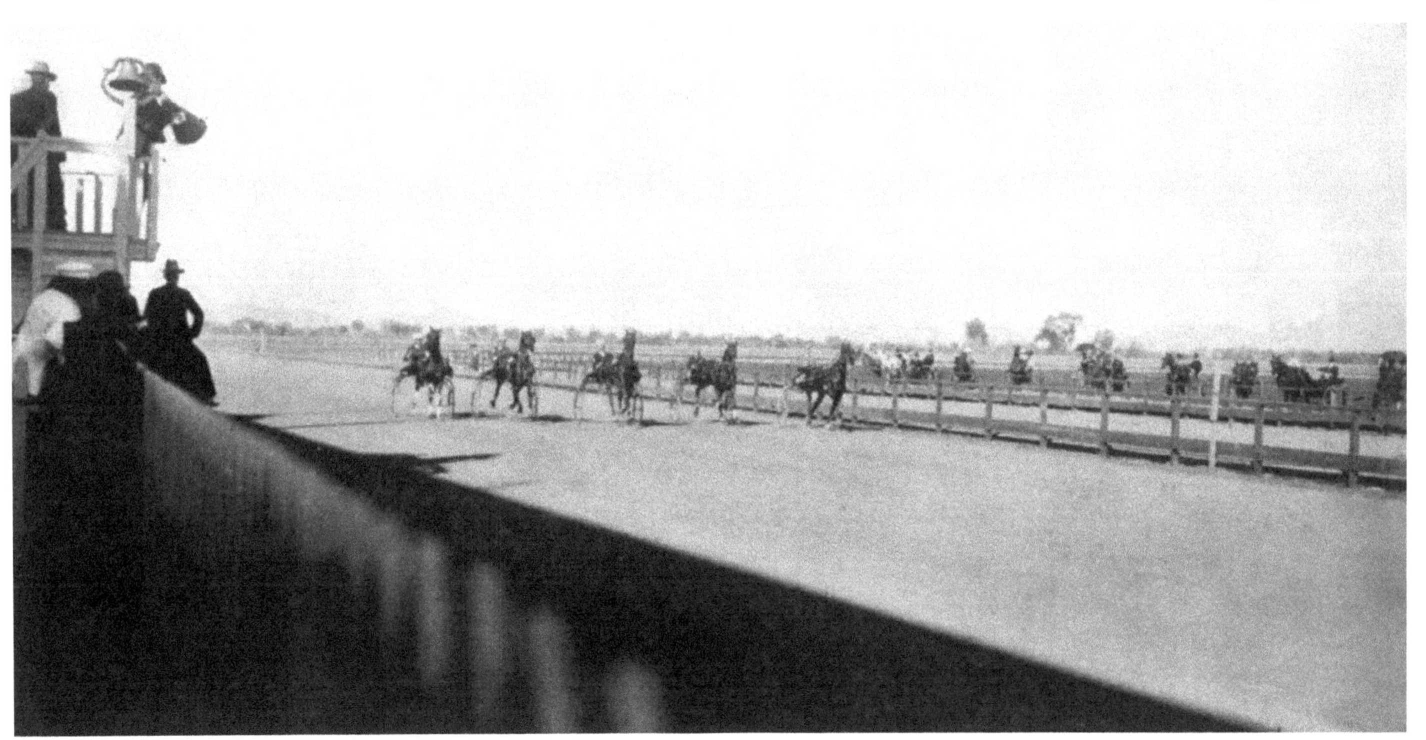

By 1910 women's fashions had become tailored to align more closely to the female form. These Arizona women are attending an event at the State Capitol.

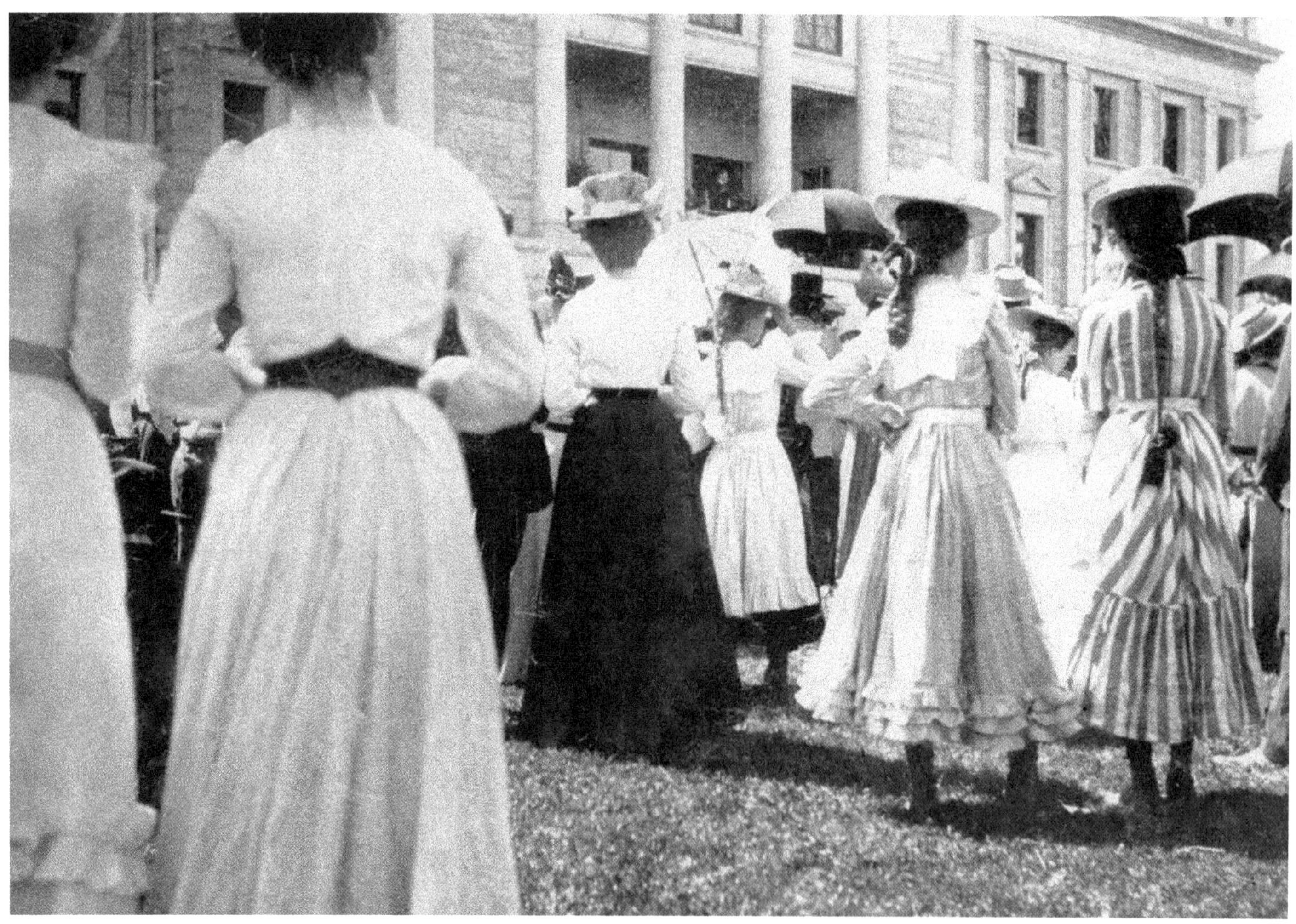

President-elect William Howard Taft rides through Phoenix in 1909 in a parade in his honor.

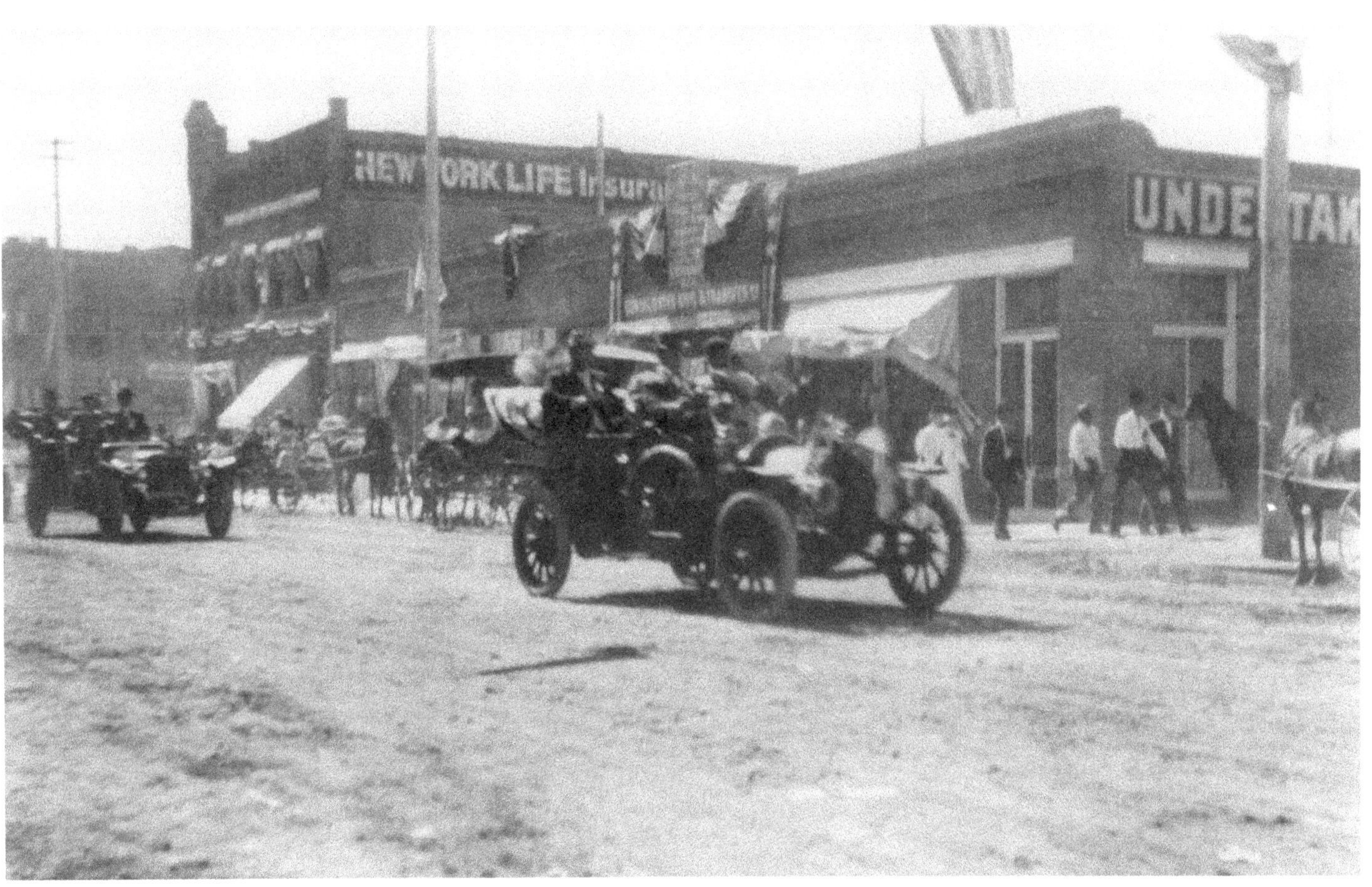

James McClintock, on the left, was postmaster of Phoenix from 1902 to 1914, but became better known as an expert on Arizona history as the state's first official historian and archivist.

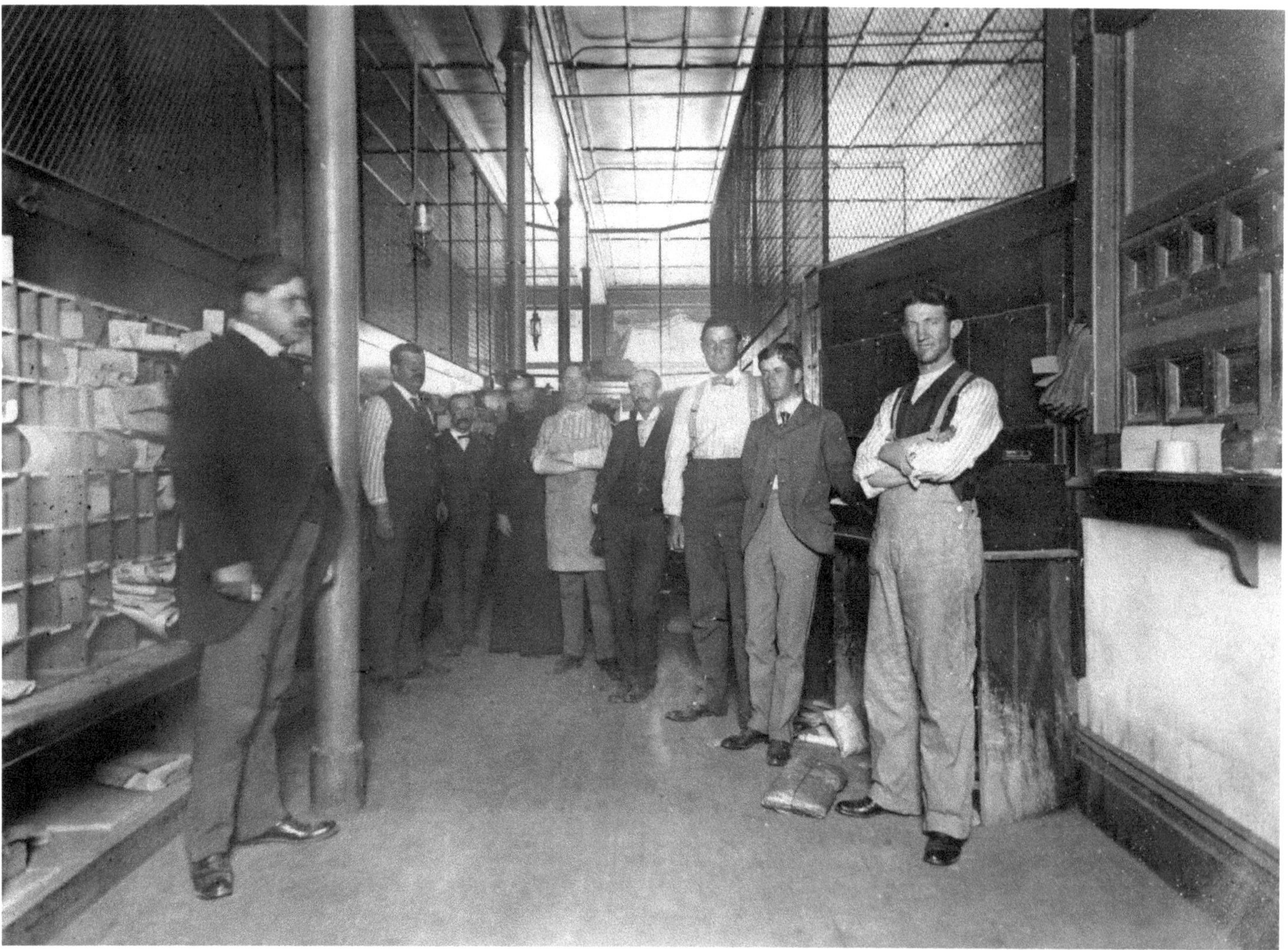

Despite the valiant efforts of downtown residents, the Adams Hotel, built of wood, burned down in 1910, sending plumes of smoke and flame hundreds of feet into the air. The following year the hotel was rebuilt with brick and renamed the Hotel Adams, pictured here.

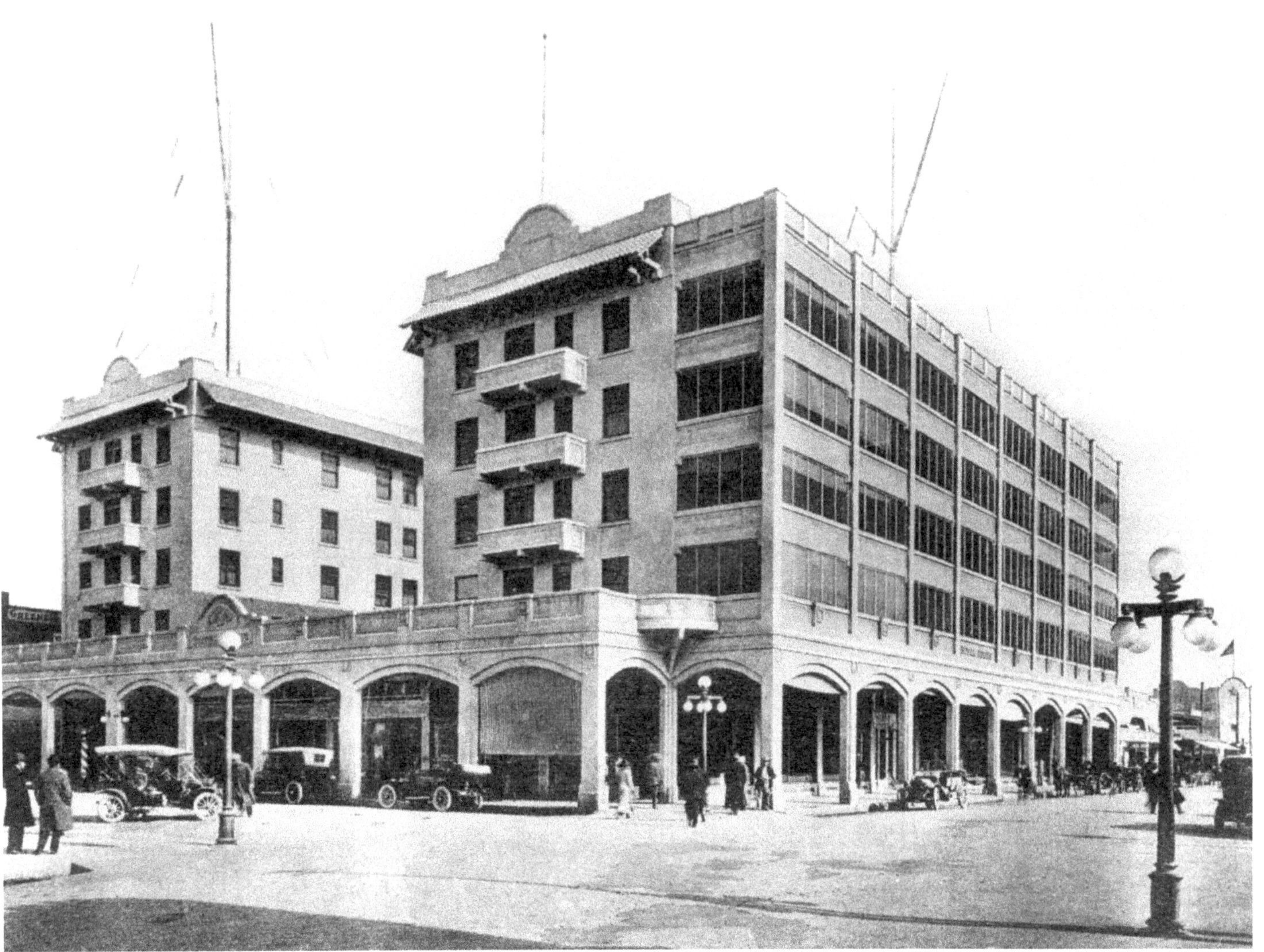

Washington Street, around 1910, with a drugstore in the foreground. Before 1920, drugs such as heroin, morphine, and other derivatives of opium were sold legally. Reputable drug companies of the late nineteenth century sold over-the-counter drug kits that contained glass-barreled hypodermic needles and vials of opiates. Laudanum—opium mixed with alcohol—was also a popular elixir that was administered freely to children and adults to treat a variety of ills.

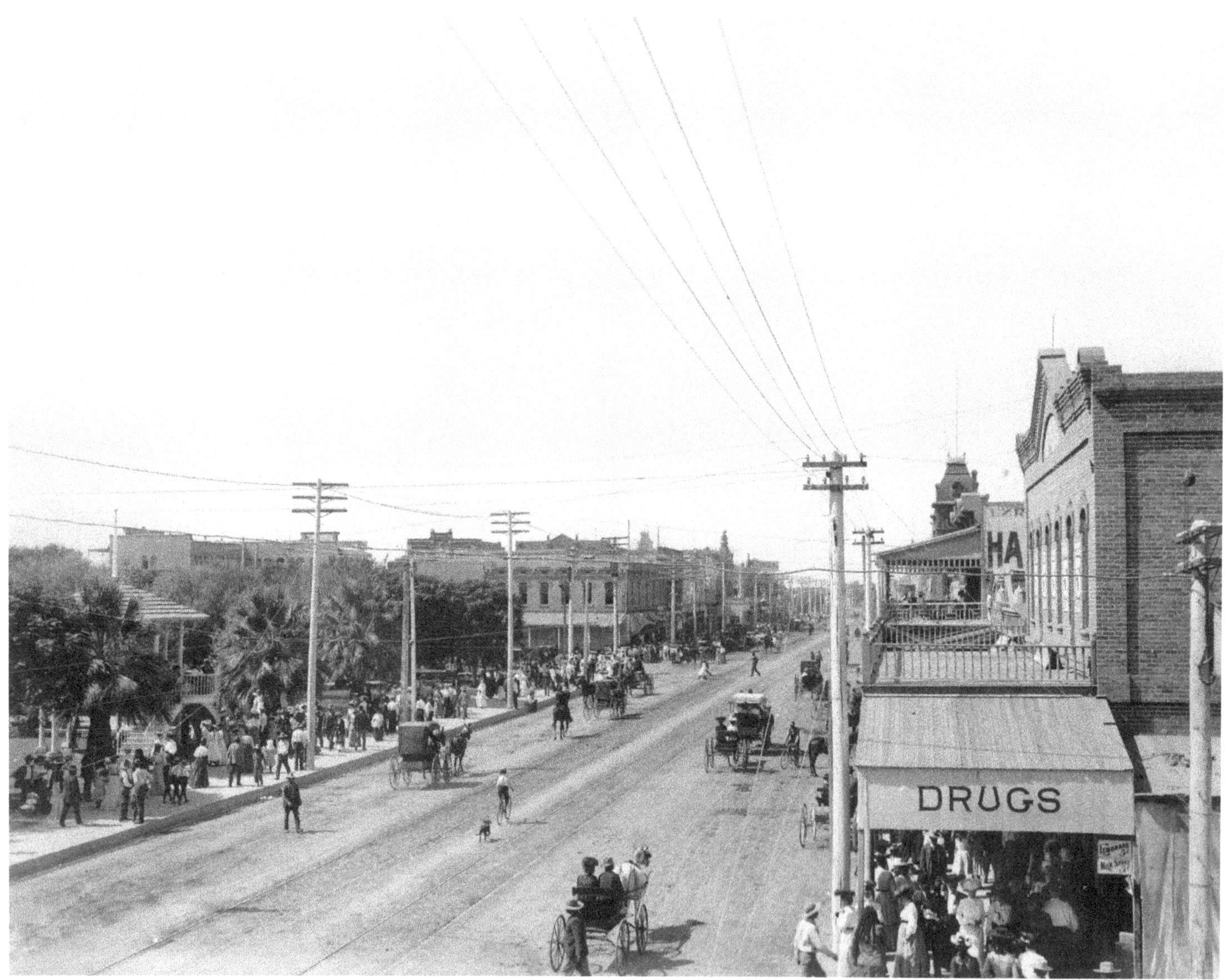

Andrew Carnegie, Scottish-born American steel tycoon turned philanthropist, donated money to build more than 2,500 public libraries around the world. Dorothy Bacon McClintock, wife of James McClintock, was instrumental in getting a Carnegie grant to build the Phoenix Public Library, which was located on Eleventh Avenue and Washington Street and dedicated February 14, 1908. Today the building is home to the Arizona Hall of Fame Museum.

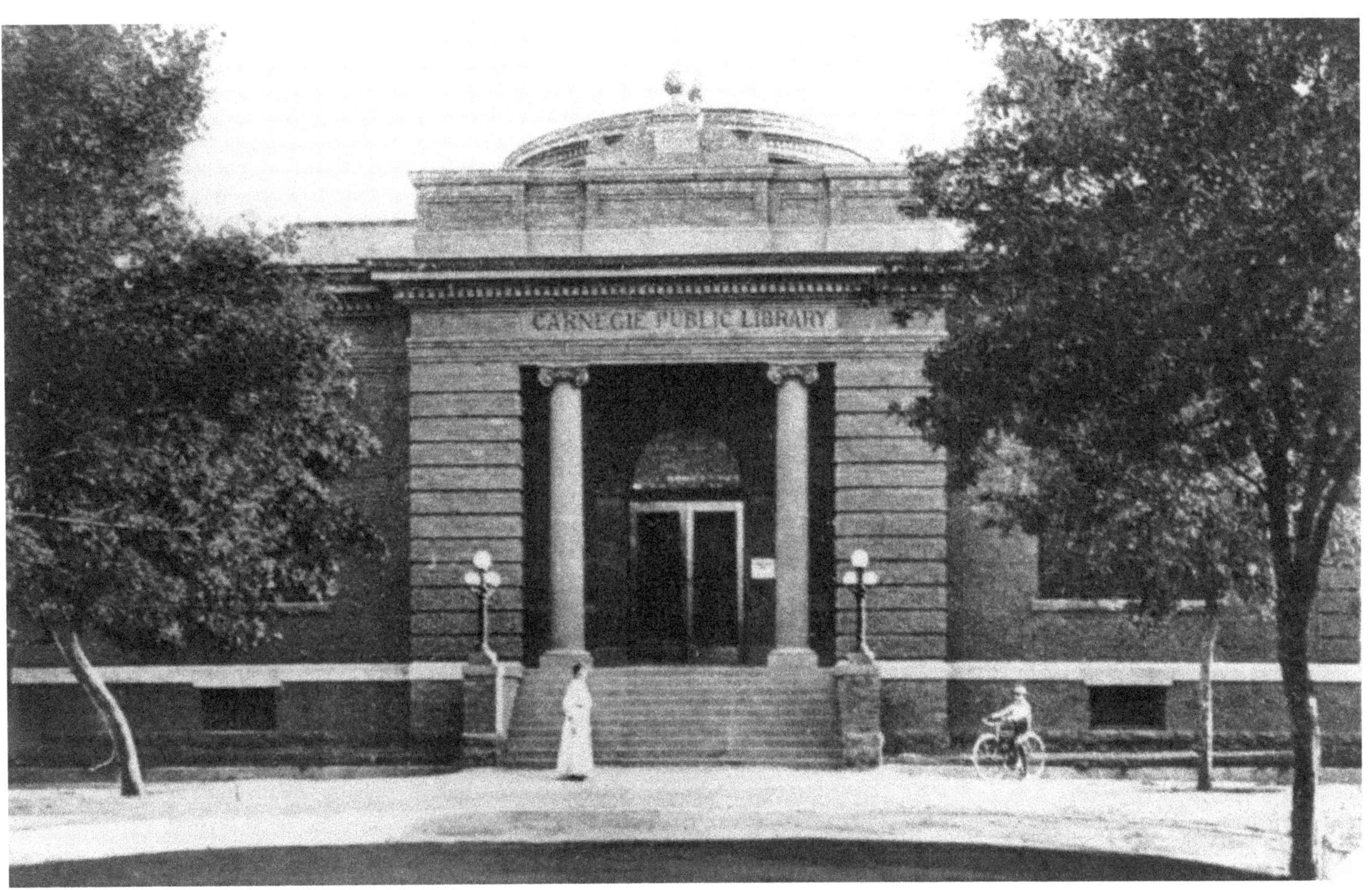

Phoenicians were an inventive lot, willing to try almost anything. One enterprising soul drives a team of dogs attached to a small wagon in front of the State Capitol in 1912 as passersby watch in awe. The idea might have caught on were it not for the advent of automobiles.

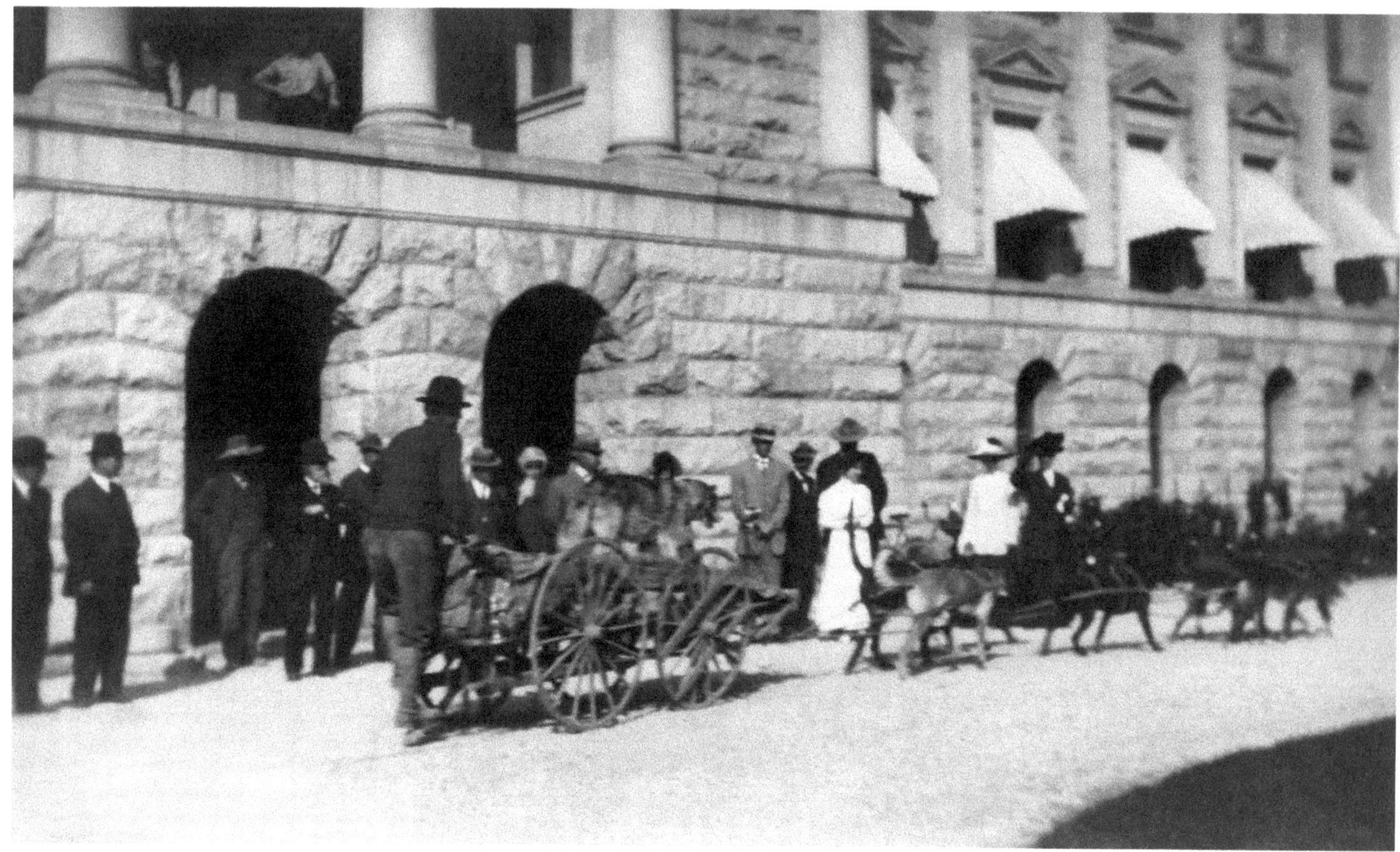

The Westward Ho Hotel, completed in 1927, was the city's premier luxury hotel and the tallest building in Arizona until 1960. This photograph shows the glory of the Westward Ho Dining Room, built to look like a Spanish palace.

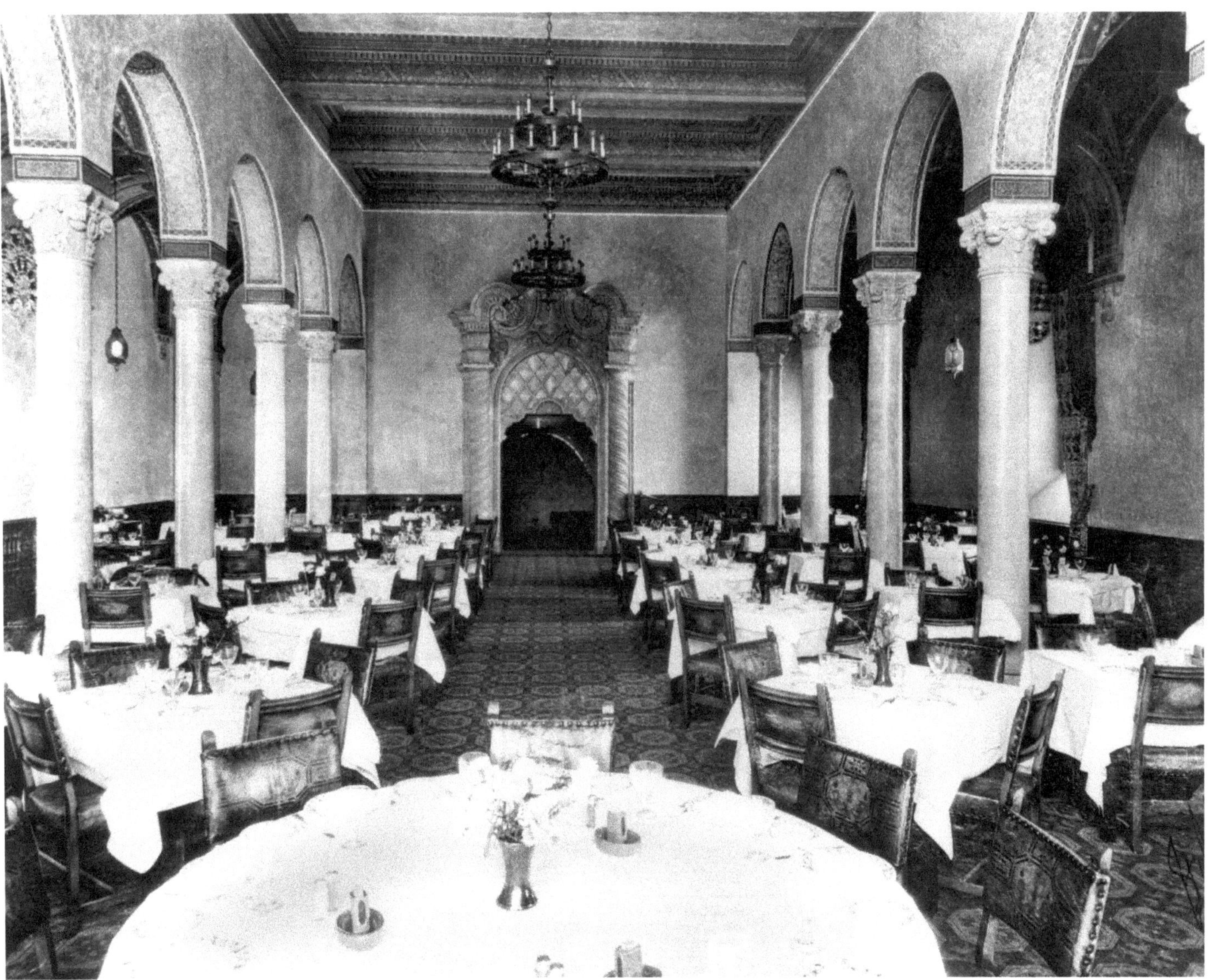

Governor-elect George Hunt poses in front of the State Capitol with delivery boys for the *Saturday Evening Post* in 1912.

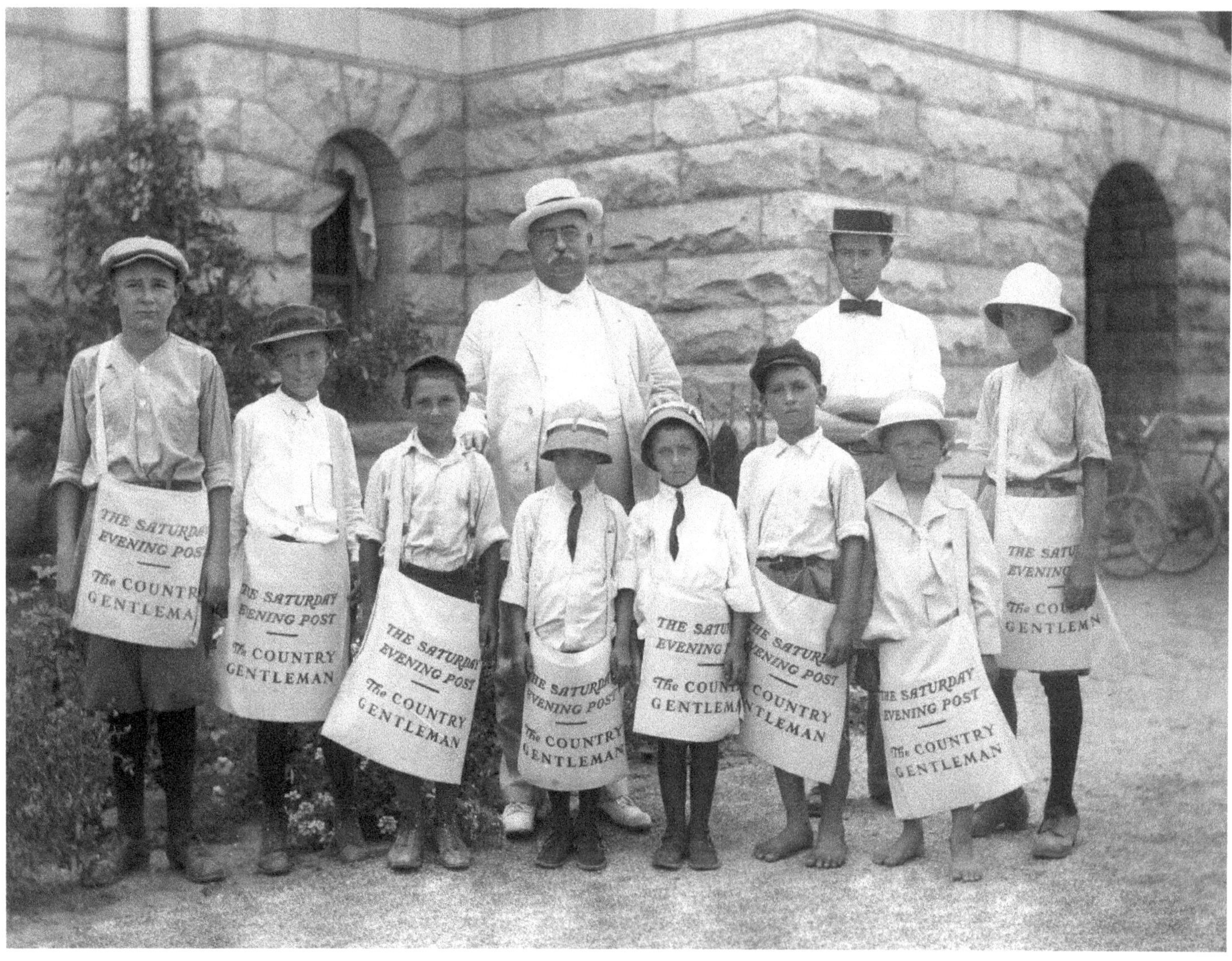

Arizonans gather at the State Capitol for the inauguration of George Hunt as the state's first governor in 1912.

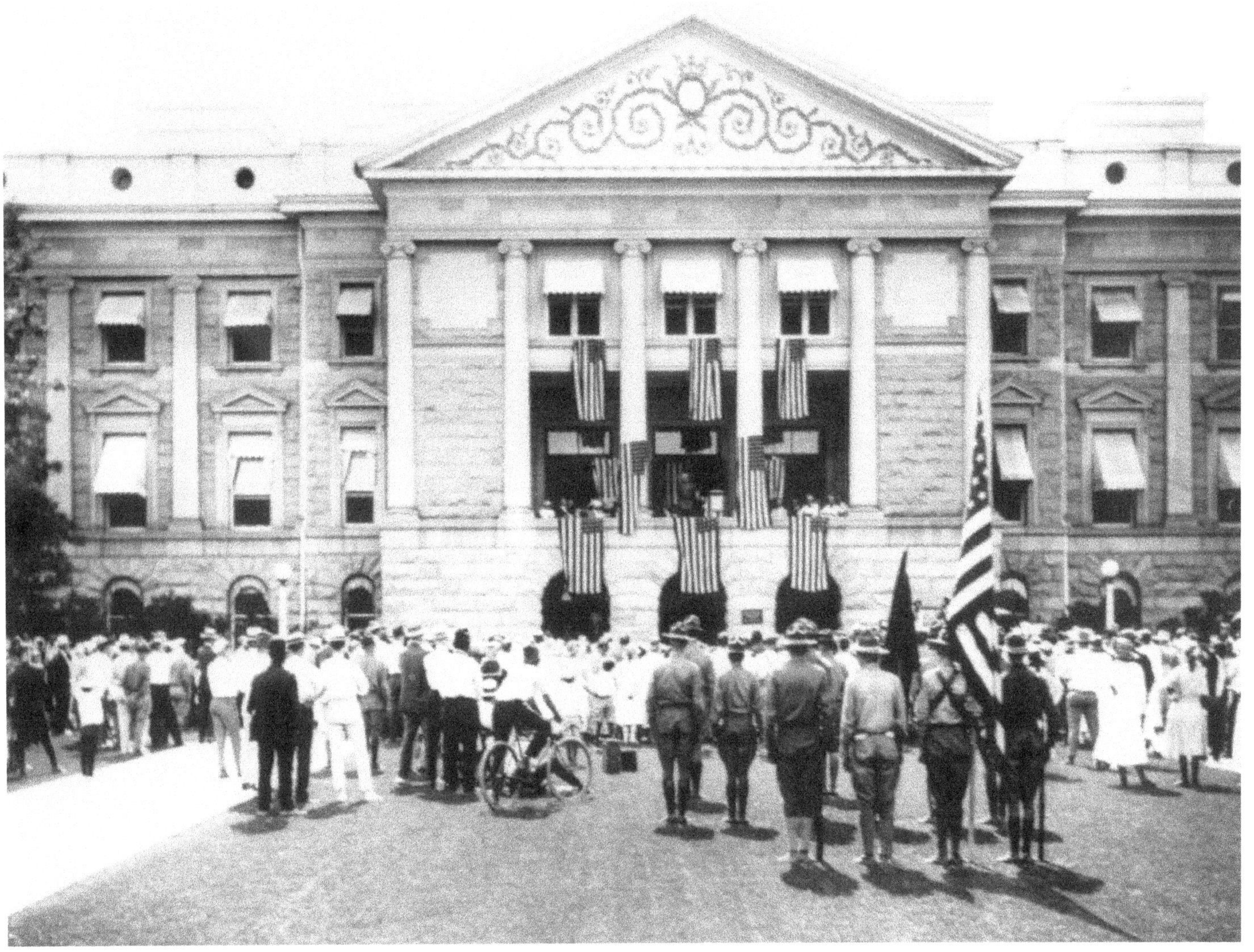

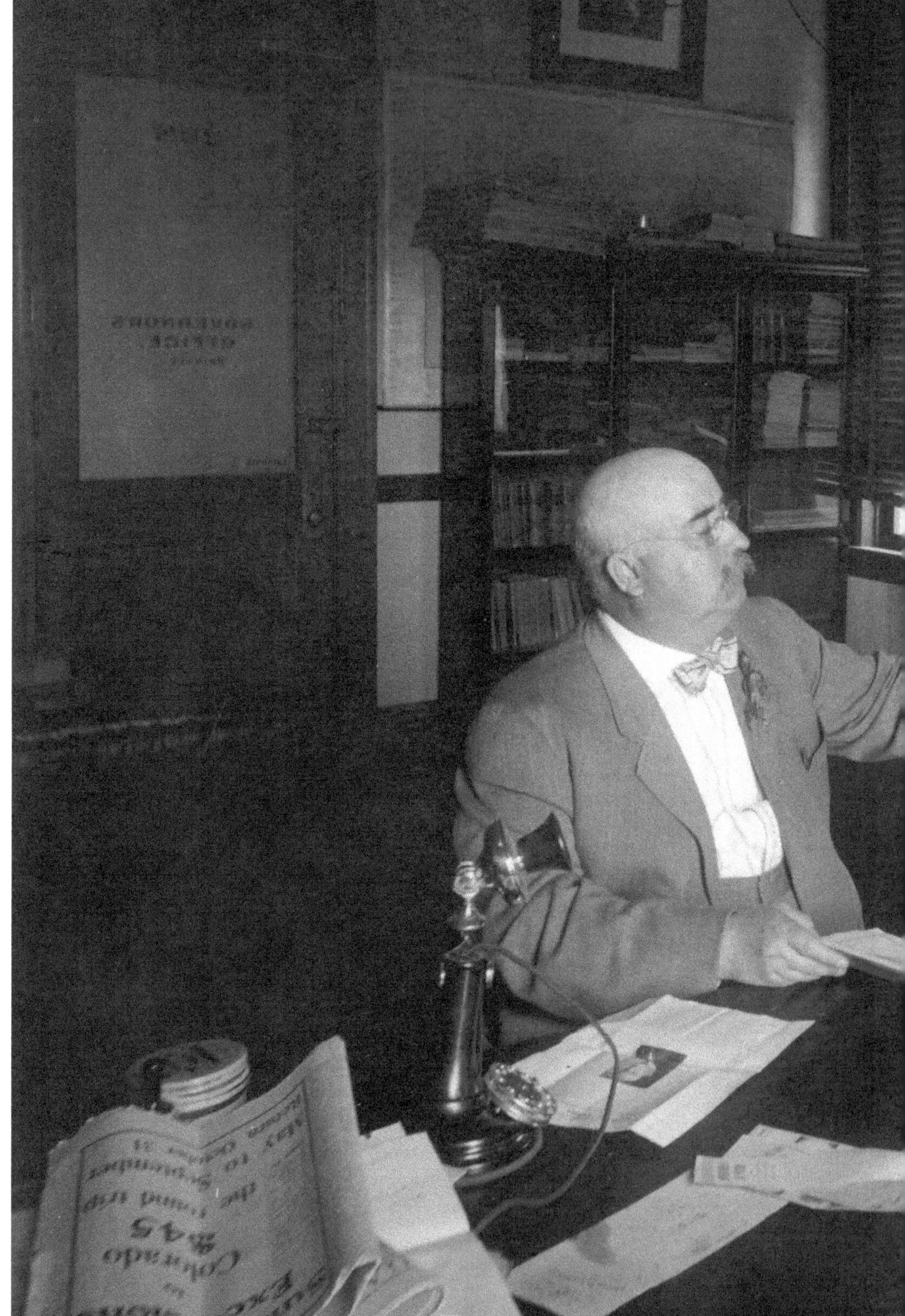

Arizona's first governor George W. P. Hunt was born in Missouri in 1859 and left home at the age of nineteen. For three years he worked and traveled until he settled in Globe, Arizona. Within a few years he was elected to the Arizona Territorial Legislature and would serve from 1892–1900, and again from 1904–1910. He was president of Arizona's Constitutional Convention and became the state's first governor in 1912.

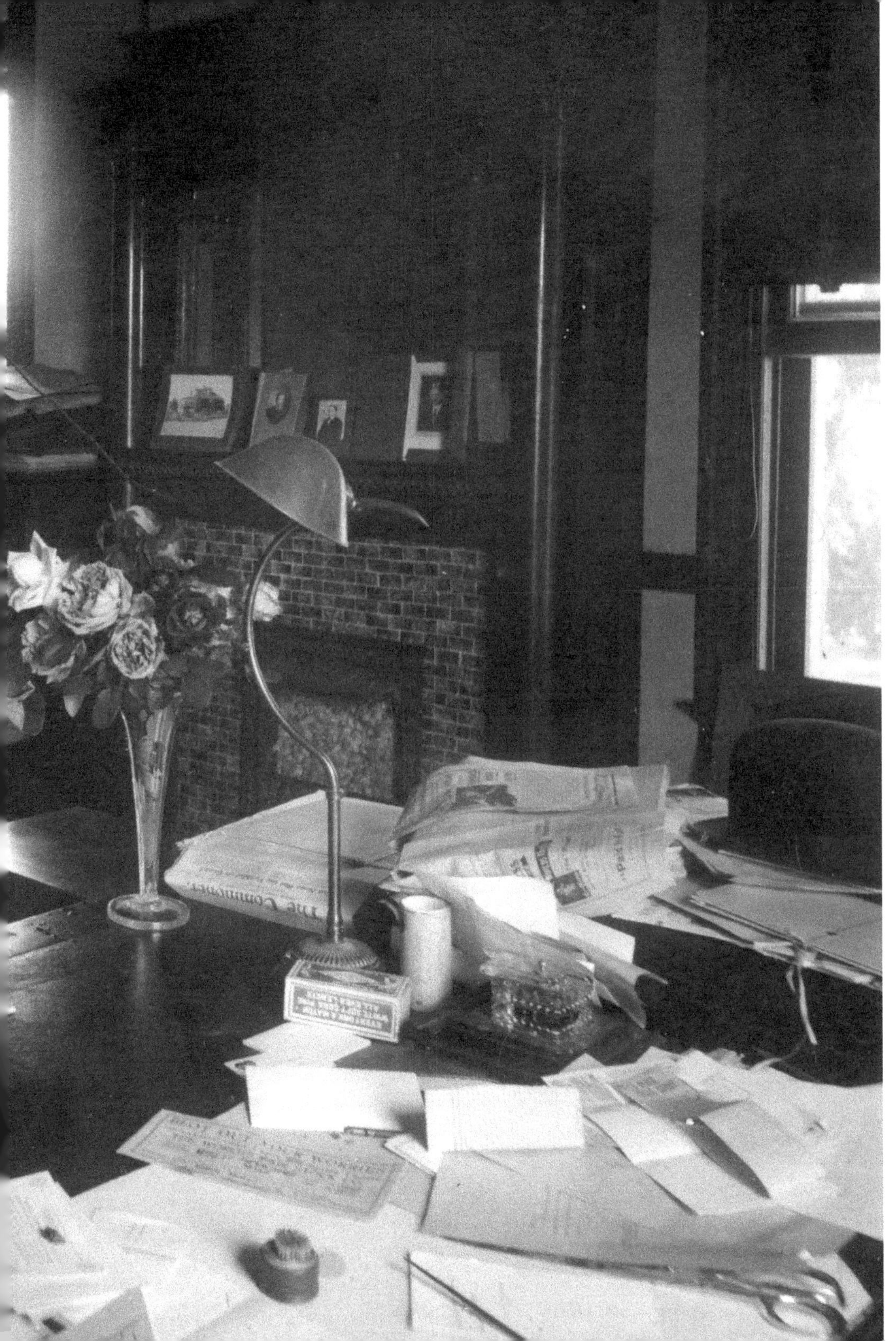

Automobile racing is almost as old as the invention itself. The first automobile race in the United States took place in Chicago in 1895 over a 54-mile course, involving four gas-fueled cars and two electric cars. Spectators pictured here have gathered in 1912 at the Phoenix State Fairgrounds to watch a dusty race.

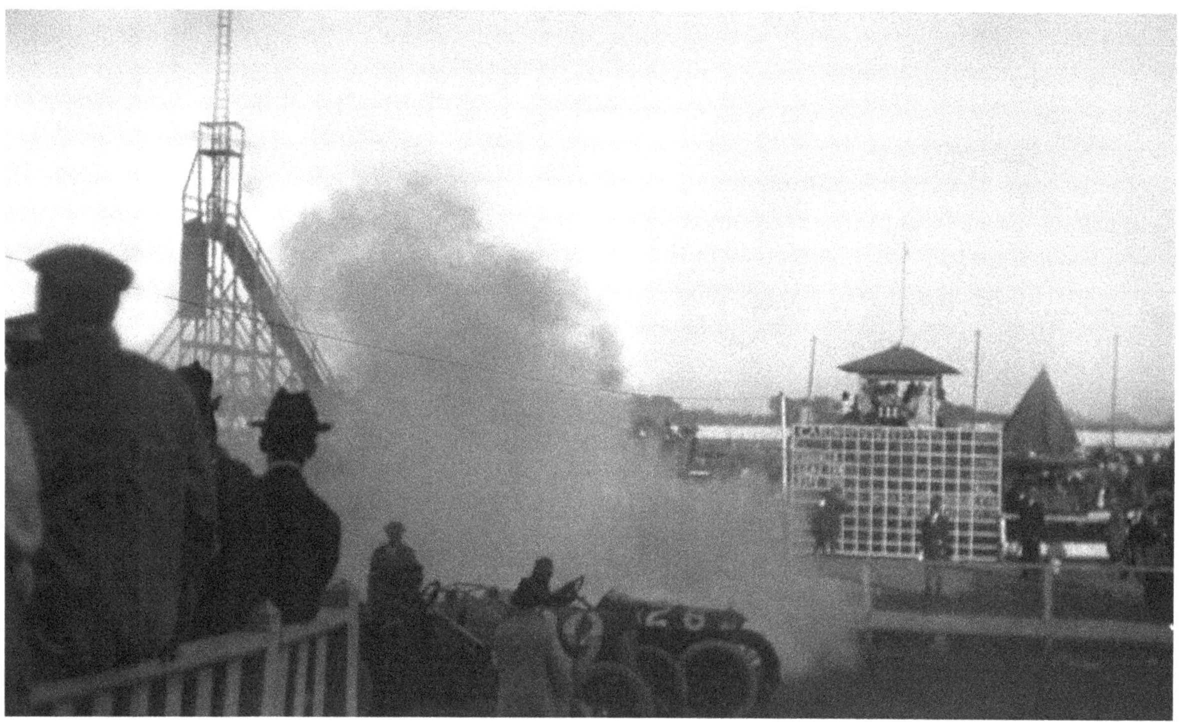

Arizona legislators pause to commemorate the first meeting of the Arizona State Legislature in 1912.

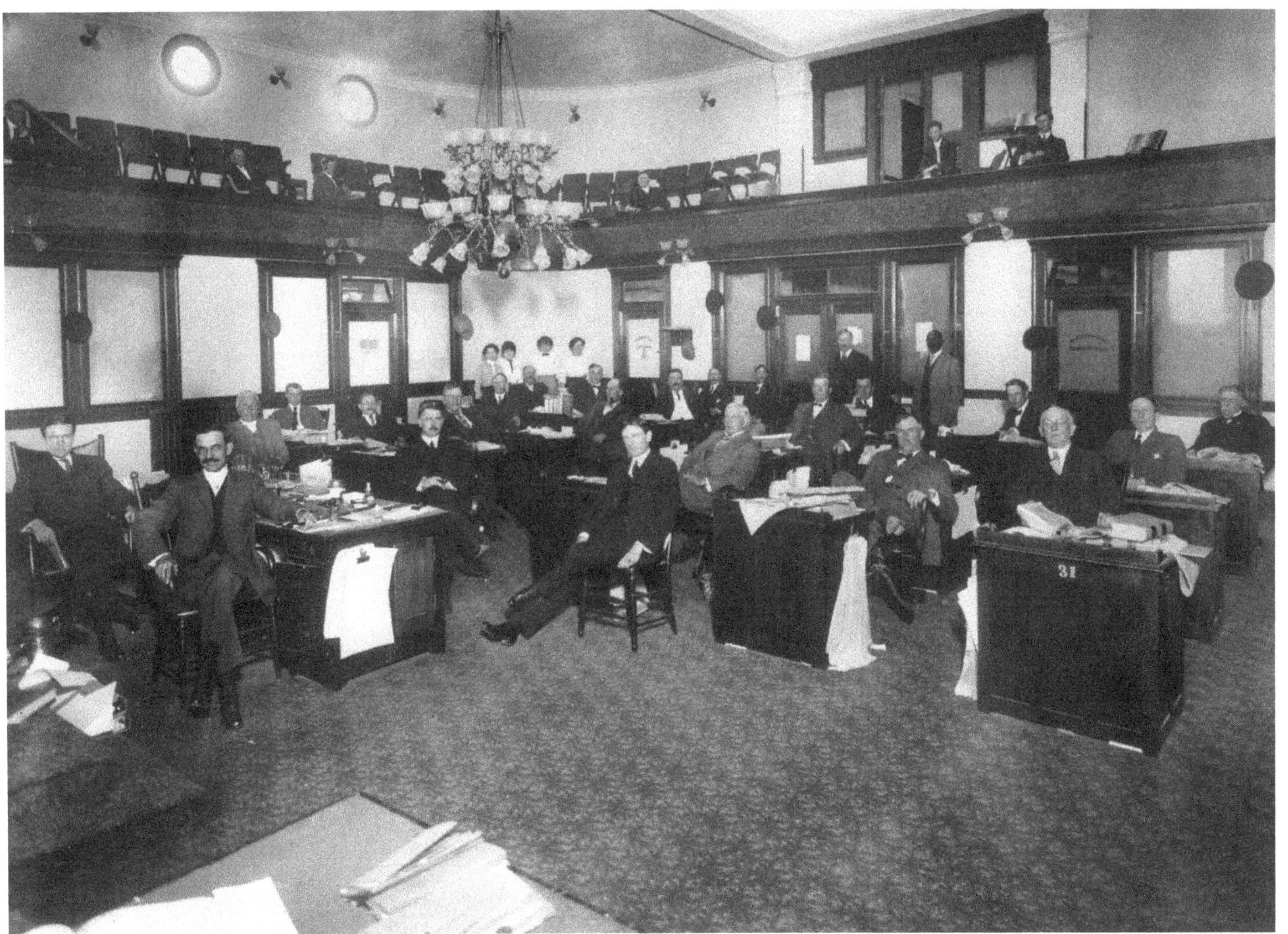

Families gather outside Phoenix Union High School for 1915 graduation.

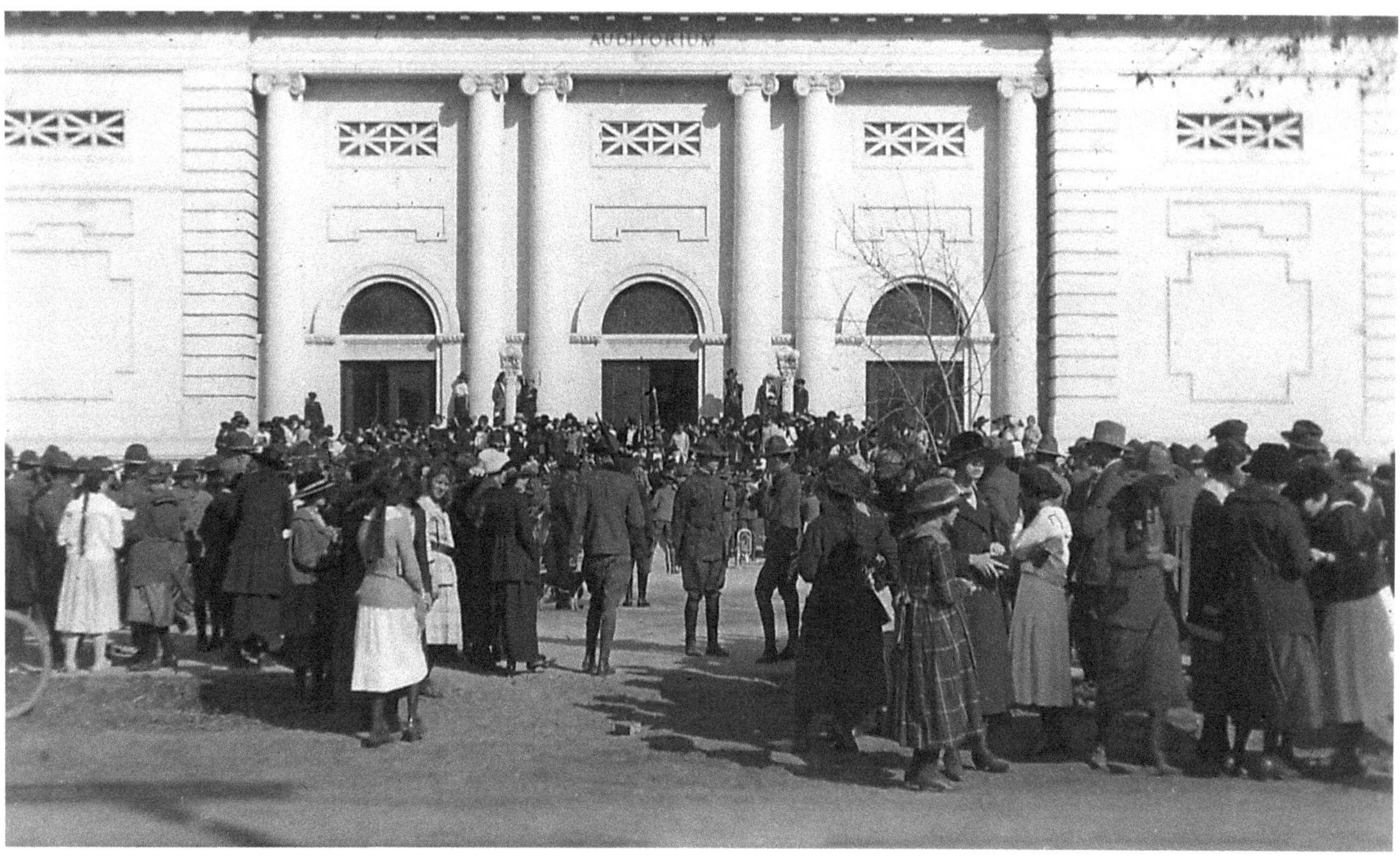

Roosevelt Dam was the first large-scale irrigation project of the Federal Reclamation Act of 1902 and helped increase the amount of land that could be farmed. Constructed between 1905 and 1911, it was the world's tallest masonry dam. It forms Roosevelt Lake as part of the effort to control flooding caused by the Salt River and to store water for irrigation.

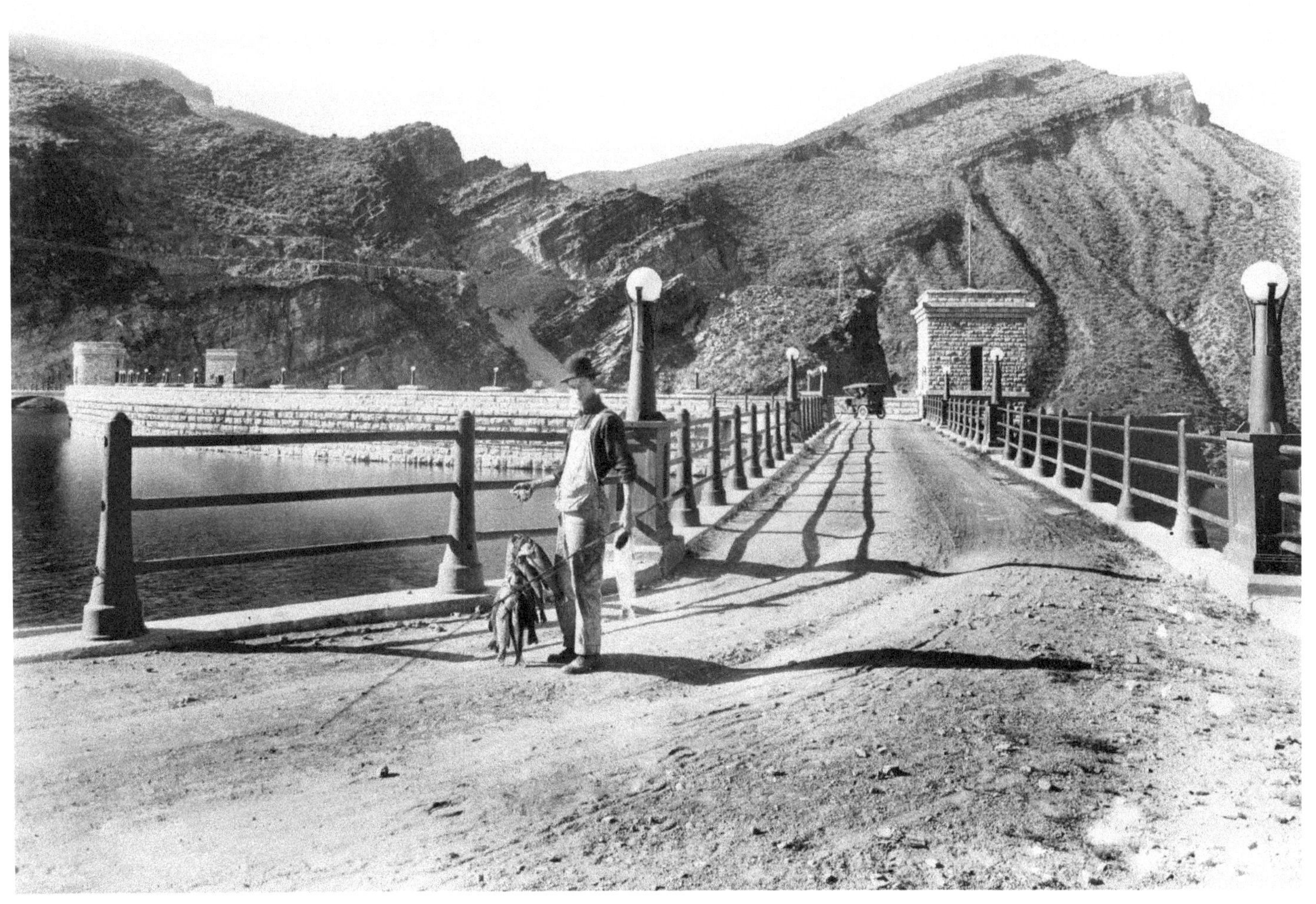

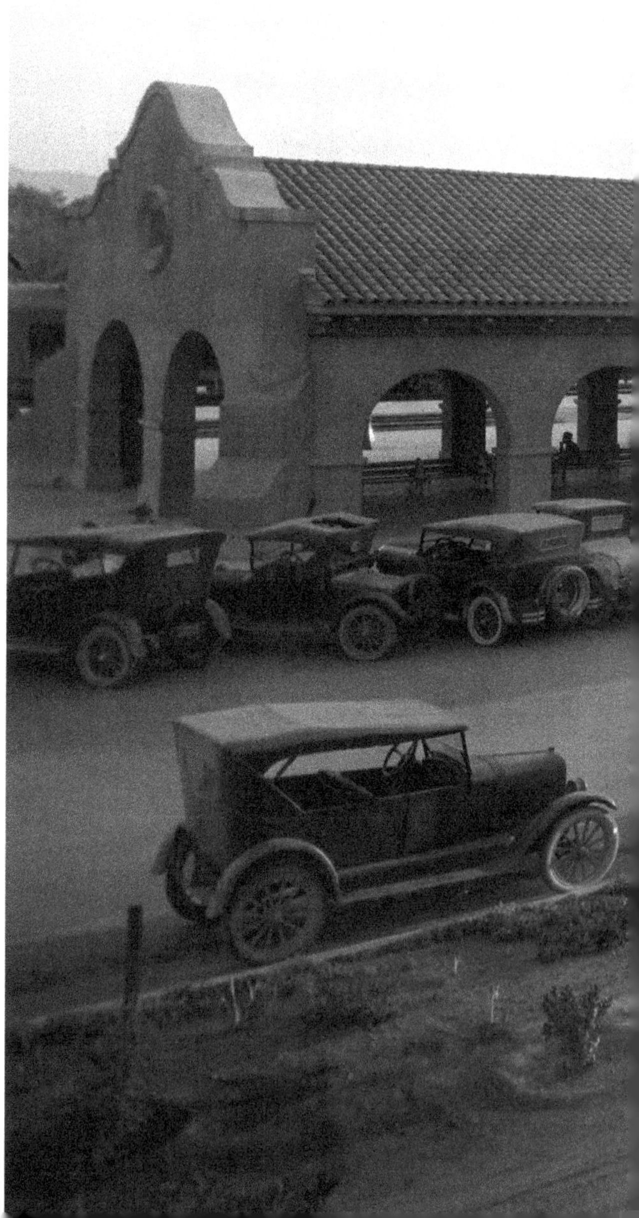

The Union Pacific Railroad began with an act of Congress in 1862. The line started in Omaha, Nebraska, and ran westward through southern Wyoming and northern Utah, connecting with the Central Pacific Railroad line in Promontory Summit, Utah, in 1869 to create the first transcontinental railroad in North America. The Union Pacific acquired several smaller lines and in 1901 took control of Southern Pacific Railroad, which operated the line into Phoenix. In view here is Union Station.

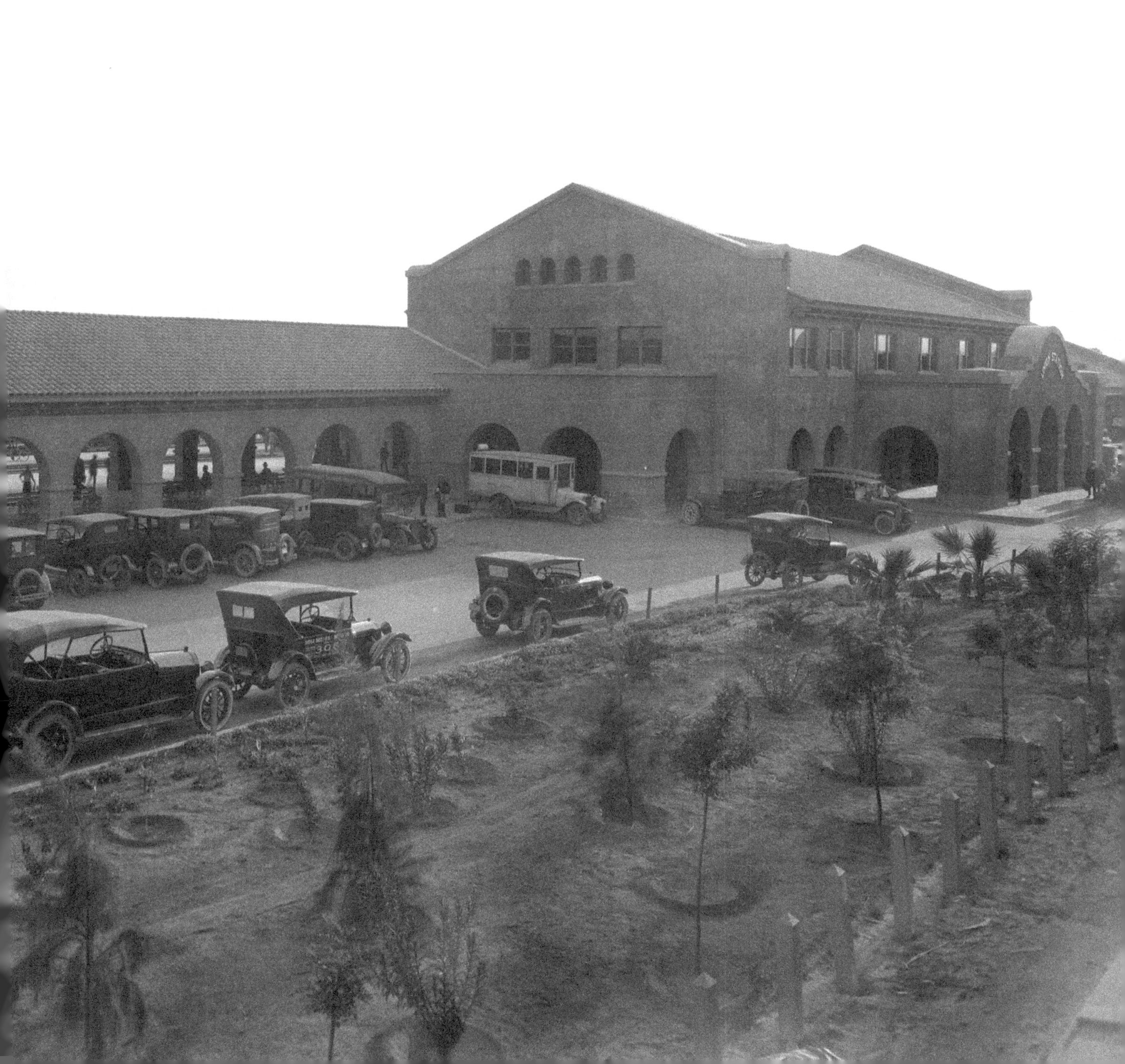

Airplane technology rapidly advanced following the Wright Brothers' successful flight in 1903. Airplanes were first used for peacetime activities like cotton dusting. General "Black Jack" Pershing was the first to employ airplanes for military purposes in 1916 when he led the unsuccessful attempt to capture Pancho Villa, and thereafter airplanes quickly became a crucial instrument of war. The biplane pictured here at the 1918 State Fair in Phoenix may have been used for recruiting purposes.

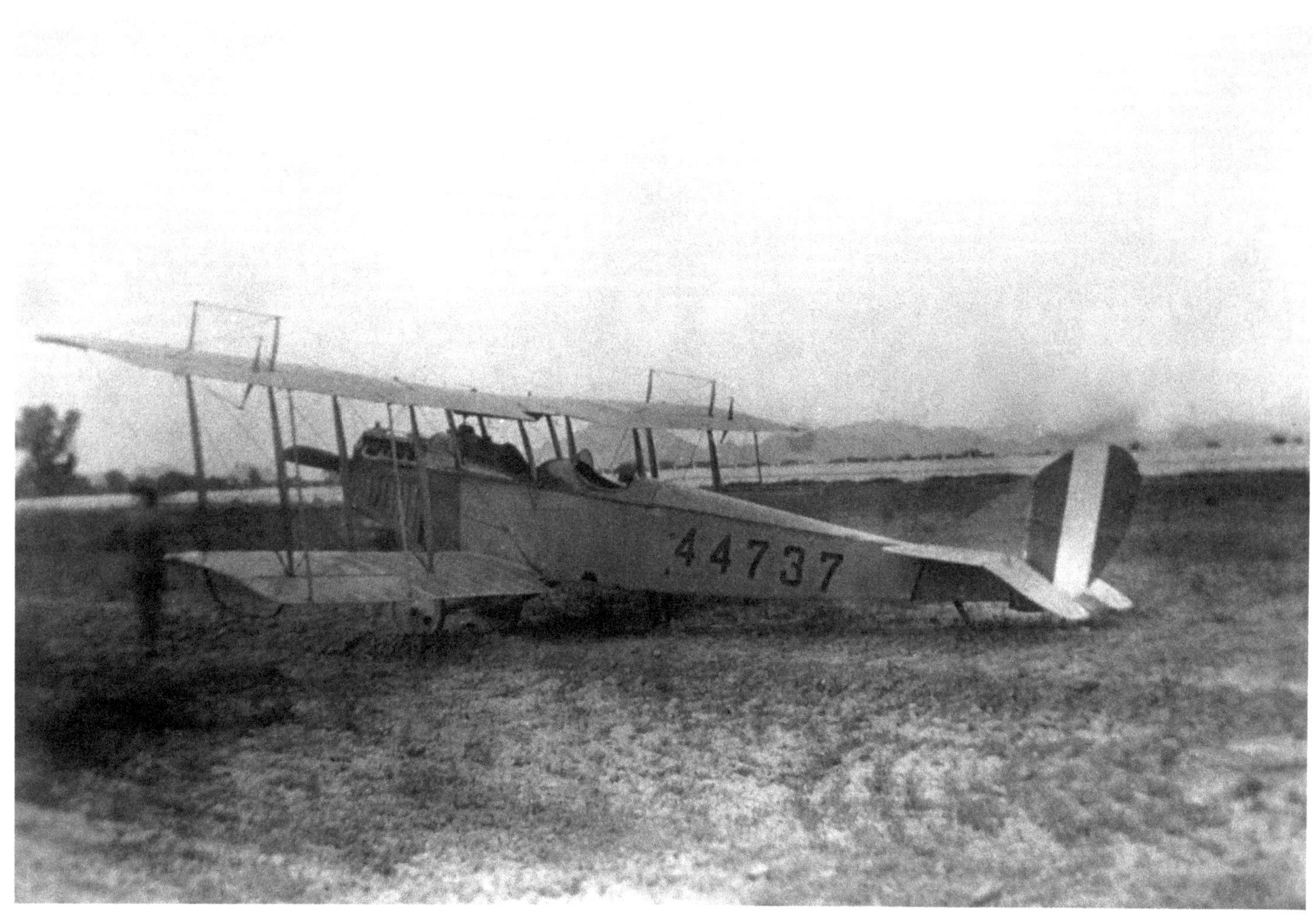

Hot-air balloons were used in China as early as the third century A.D. as unmanned military signals. Studies suggest that the Inca could have used manned air balloons in the sixth century A.D. to create the geoglyphs on Peru's Nazca plain. The first documented manned flight lifted off in France, in 1783, carrying paper manufacturers Josef and Etienne Montgolfier, who had begun experimenting after observing ash rising in fires. Shown here, Phoenix fairgoers enjoy a hot-air balloon ride in 1918.

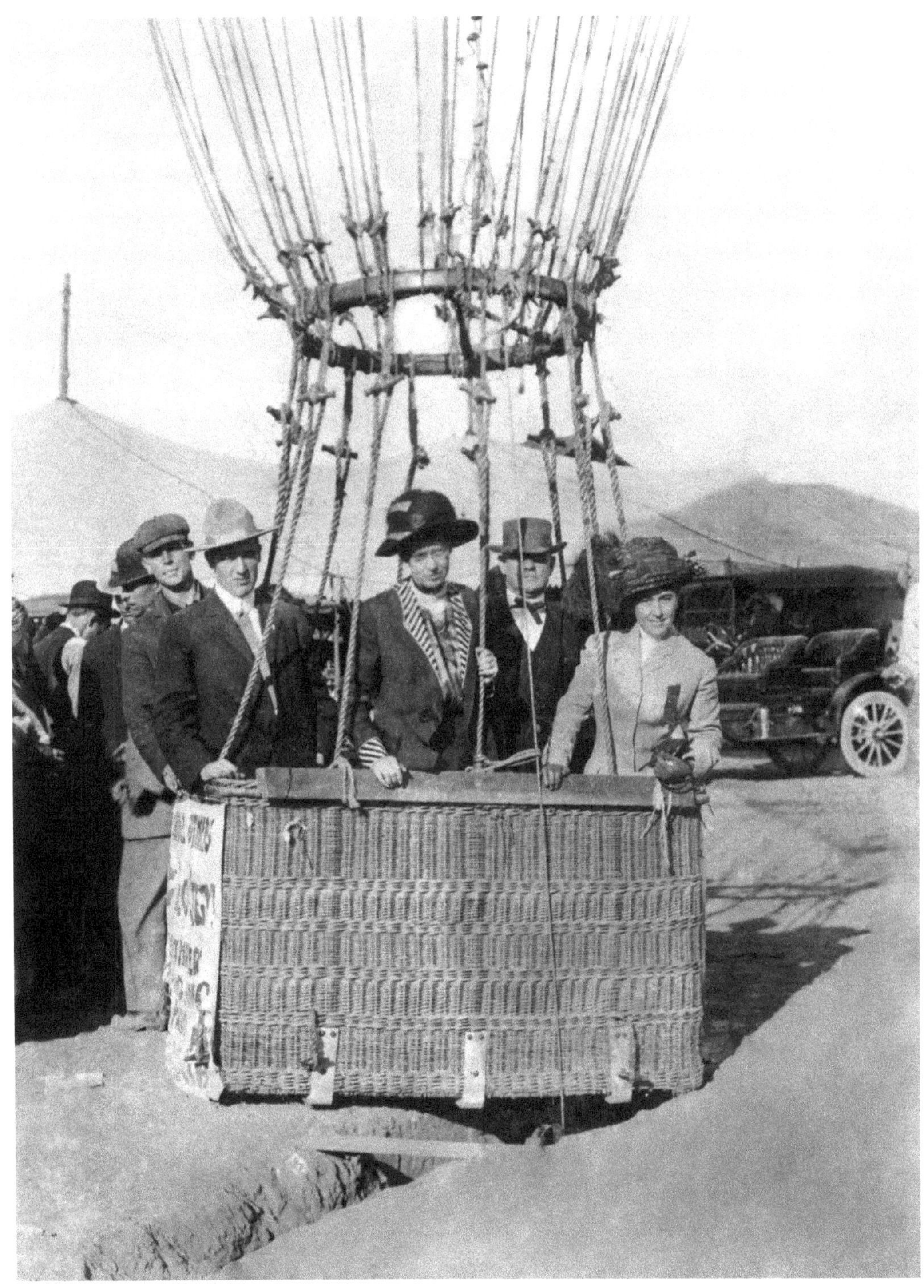

Automobiles remained out of reach for most Americans until Henry Ford began mass producing the Model T. The growing popularity of automobiles required better streets, and Central Avenue was the first paved street in Phoenix, beginning at Jefferson Street and running north. In those early days, it was not uncommon for frightened horses to run away down Phoenix streets causing excitement and sometimes damage.

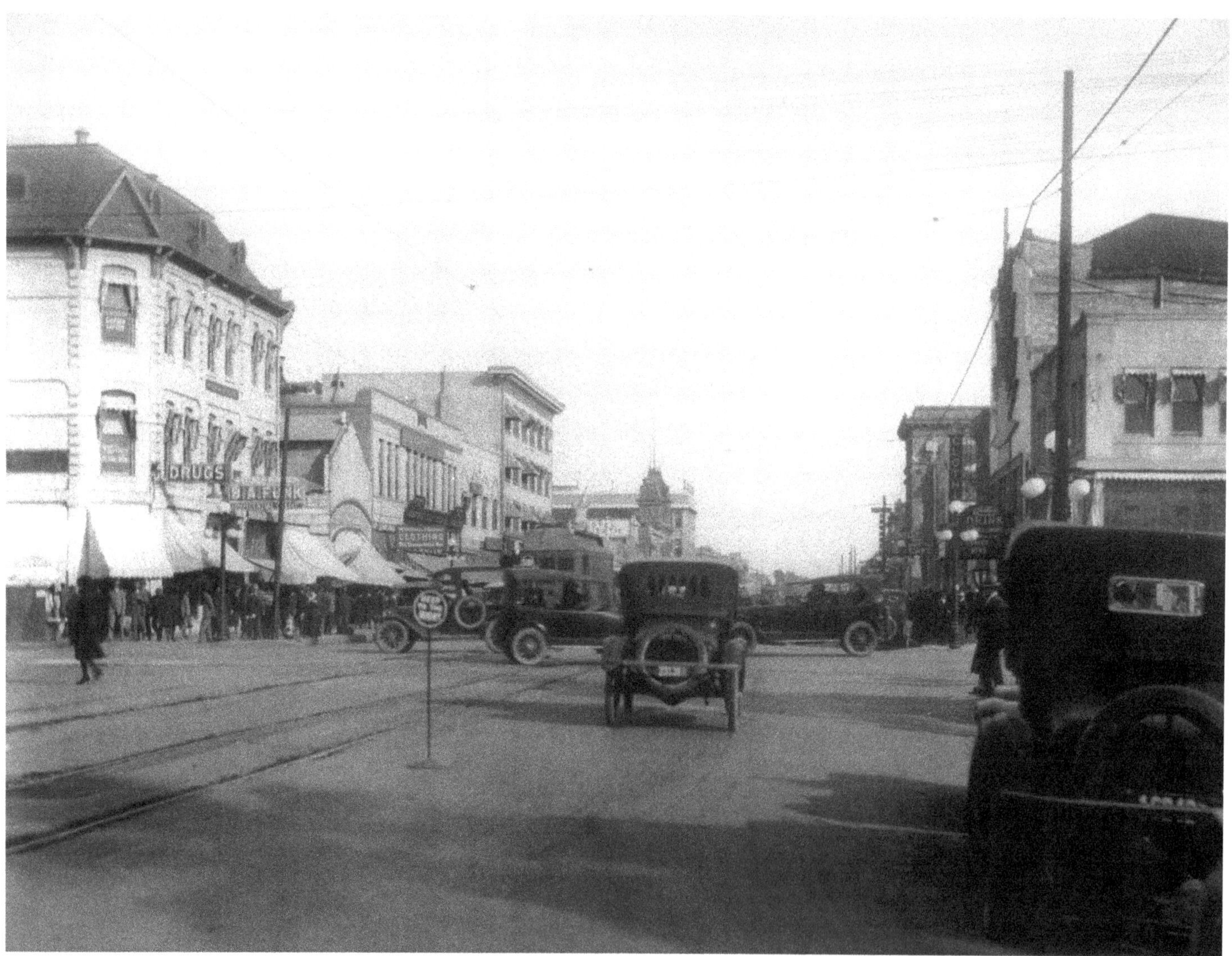

Phoenicians enthusiastically gather around the newest automobile to roll into town.

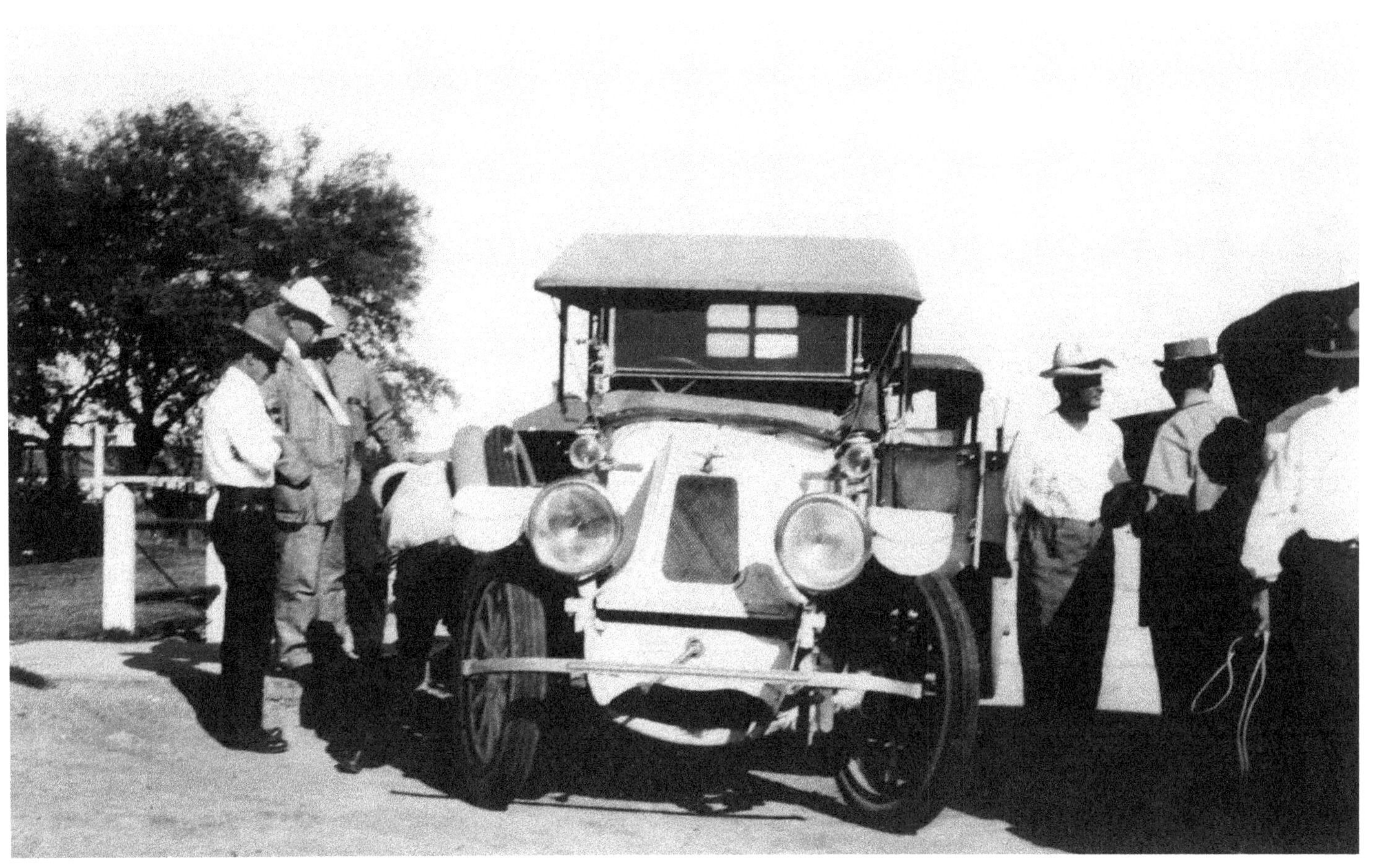

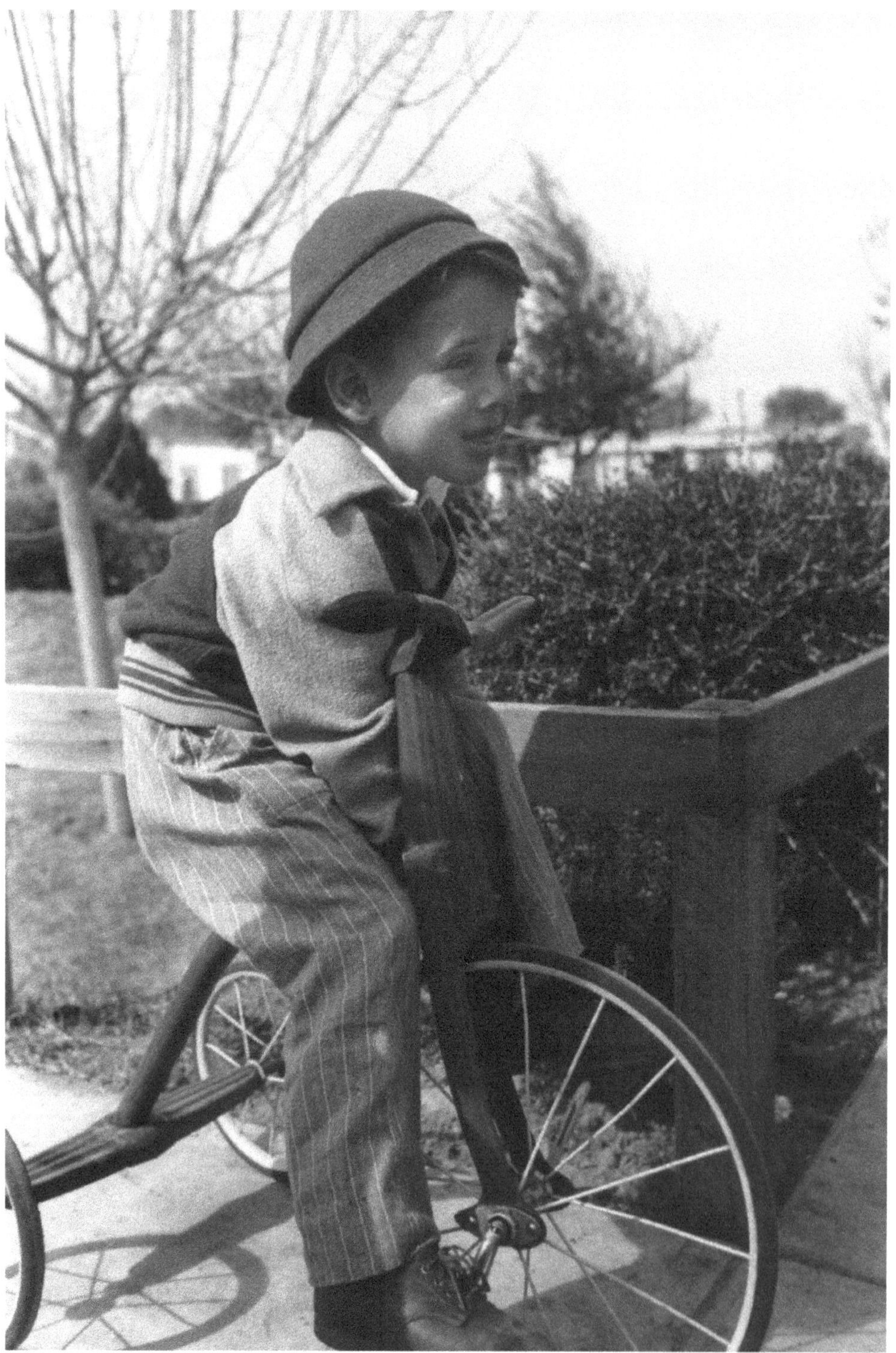

This little boy enjoys a tricycle at the Phoenix Camelback Farms. The farms were an effort by the Farm Security Administration during the Great Depression to combat rural poverty and improve the lifestyle of sharecroppers, tenants, and farmers. The FSA purchased marginal lands owned by poor farmers and resettled them in group farms on land more suitable for efficient farming, teaching them to use modern techniques under the tutelage of experts.

The Modernizing City

(1920–1939)

By 1920, Phoenix was no longer a town, but a city of almost 30,000, with more than 1,000 buildings constructed in 1920 alone. The seven-stories-tall Heard Building was the city's first high-rise. Phoenix Union High had a student enrollment of 2,000 and Phoenix Junior College opened that year. Recognizing that an era was quickly passing, the city held its first Pioneer Reunion in 1921. Phoenix's first radio station began broadcasting in the 1920s and by the end of the decade, regular flights from Los Angeles had begun arriving at Sky Harbor Airport. In 1929, the Heard Museum opened, dedicated to preserving American Indian life and culture.

The 1920s were characterized by the jazz age, the postwar rebellion against Victorian values of the previous generation, which altered social attitudes and behavior. The growing affordability of the automobile changed how Americans viewed leisure time, social propriety, and sex. Religious fervor resurged in reaction to changing social values and the growing influence of science and secularism in schools.

Winston Hackett, Phoenix's first black physician, opened Booker T. Washington Memorial Hospital to provide care for unserved Phoenician minorities, and Phoenix's first black high school, Carver High, began admitting students.

The massive collapse of the national economy, signaled by the stock market crash of 1929, spread throughout the world. Prices and profits fell as demand declined from international markets, decreasing personal incomes and tax revenues. Construction, mining, and farming, all vital to the Phoenix economy, stagnated. The Great Depression was on.

Thousands of Dust Bowl refugees passed through Phoenix on their way to California, and many stayed. With an average of 25 percent of the national work force unemployed, President Franklin Roosevelt championed federal activism on an unprecedented scale. Public utilities projects, parks, roads, and farms throughout Phoenix benefited handsomely from federal programs designed to put people back to work.

The worldwide depression influenced the rise of aggressive militaristic government—fascism—in Europe and Asia, and soon Phoenix would again be altered by war.

The original Maricopa County Courthouse was built in 1884 and torn down in 1928 to make room for the combined Courthouse and Phoenix City Hall, pictured here on West Washington Street between First and Second avenues.

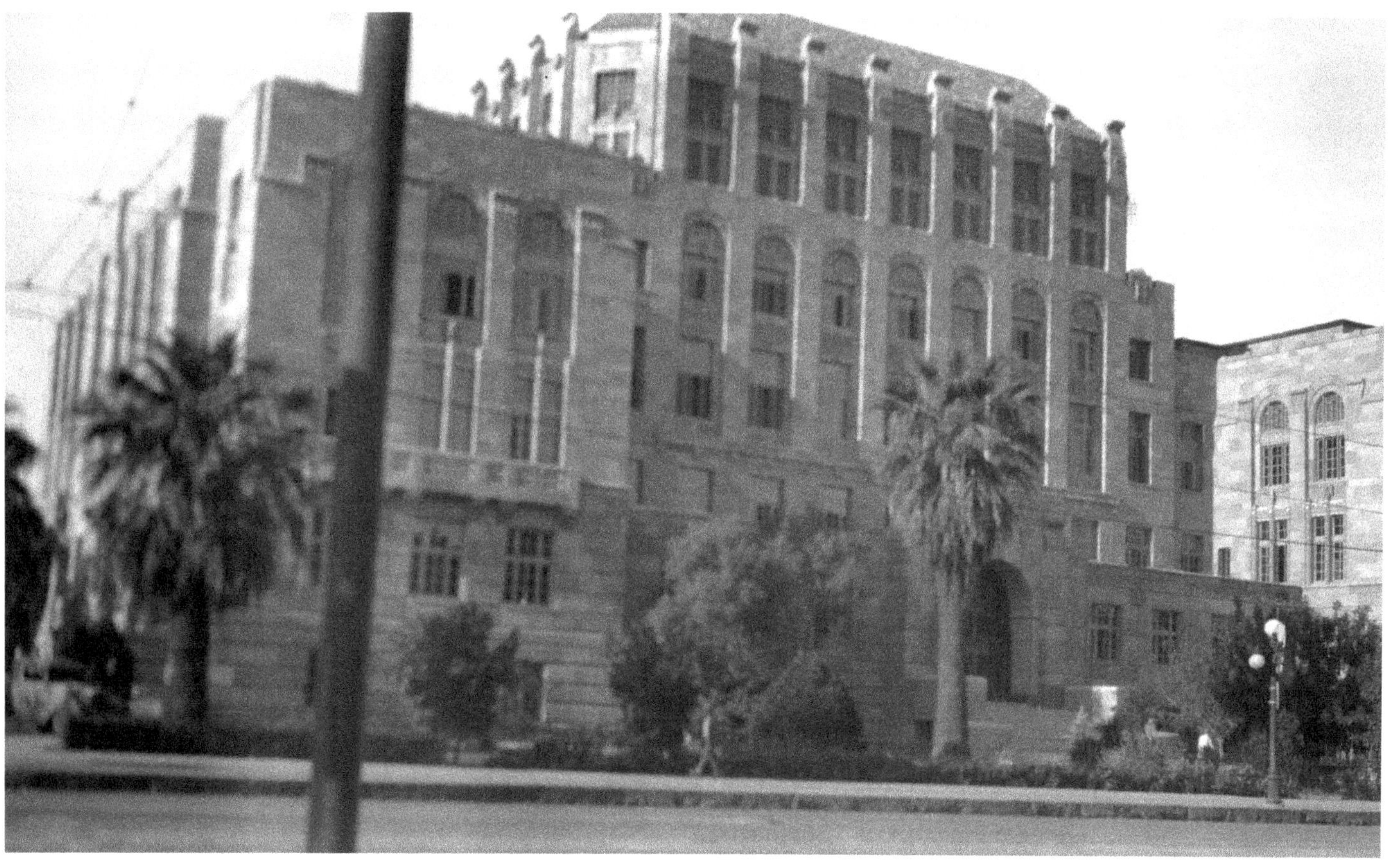

Railroads spurred the growth of many industries in Arizona, particularly the cattle industry. This 1920s photograph shows the Tovrea Stockyards, owned by Edward Ambrose Tovrea. In the 1880s, Tovrea had left Sparta, Illinois, and worked as a butcher in Bisbee. He eventually moved to Phoenix and founded the Arizona Packing Company in 1920. By 1928 the Tovrea Stockyards was the largest packing plant west of Fort Worth. The stockyard and slaughterhouse fostered the cattle, hog, and sheep industries in the area and made Tovrea a fortune.

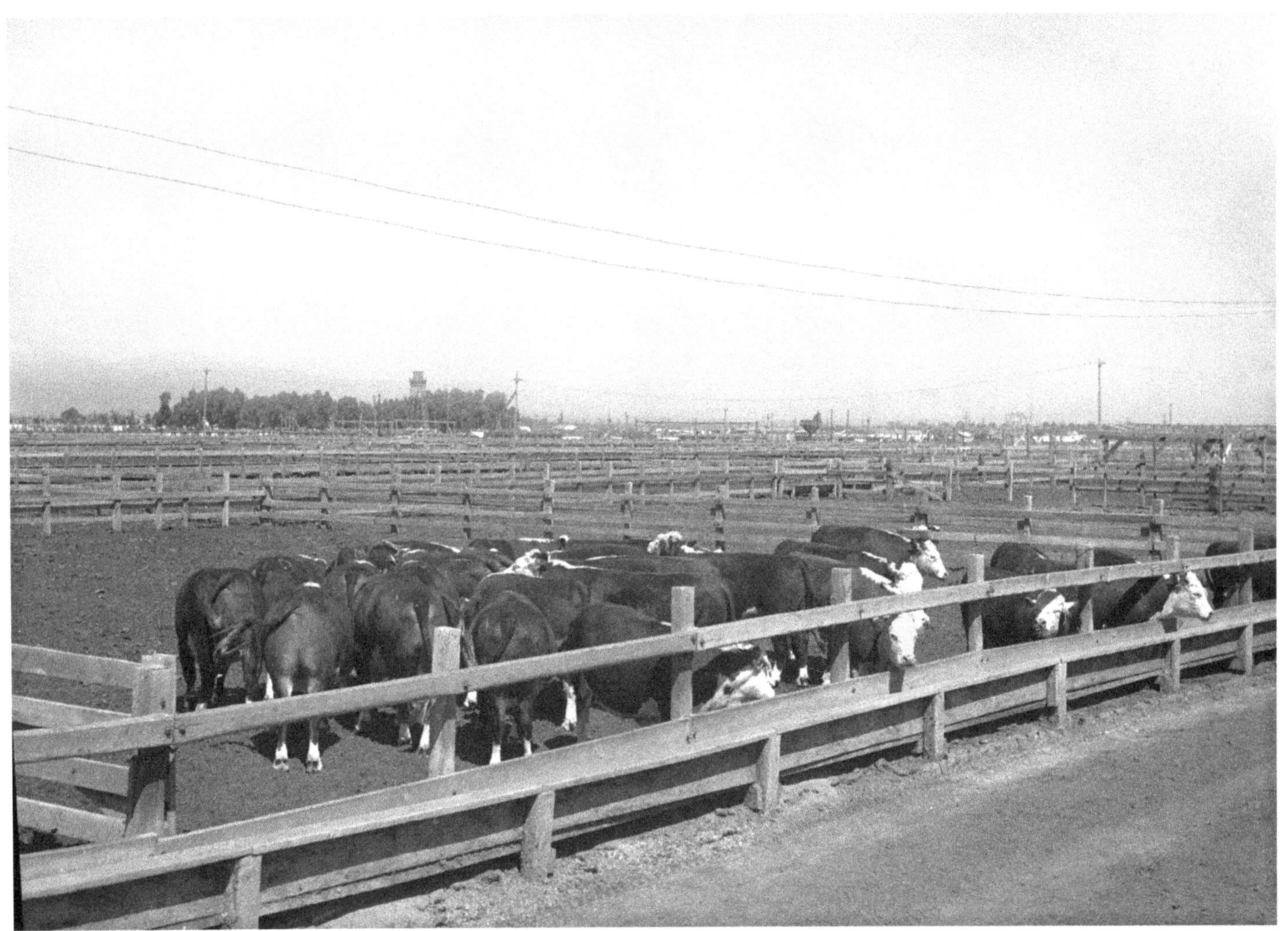

In 1920, drugstores such as the one pictured here were more regulated than they had been in earlier years—Congress passed the Dangerous Drug Act that year, which made purchases of addictive drugs illegal. By that time, however, there were an estimated 200,000 heroin addicts in the nation and untold numbers of opium and morphine addicts.

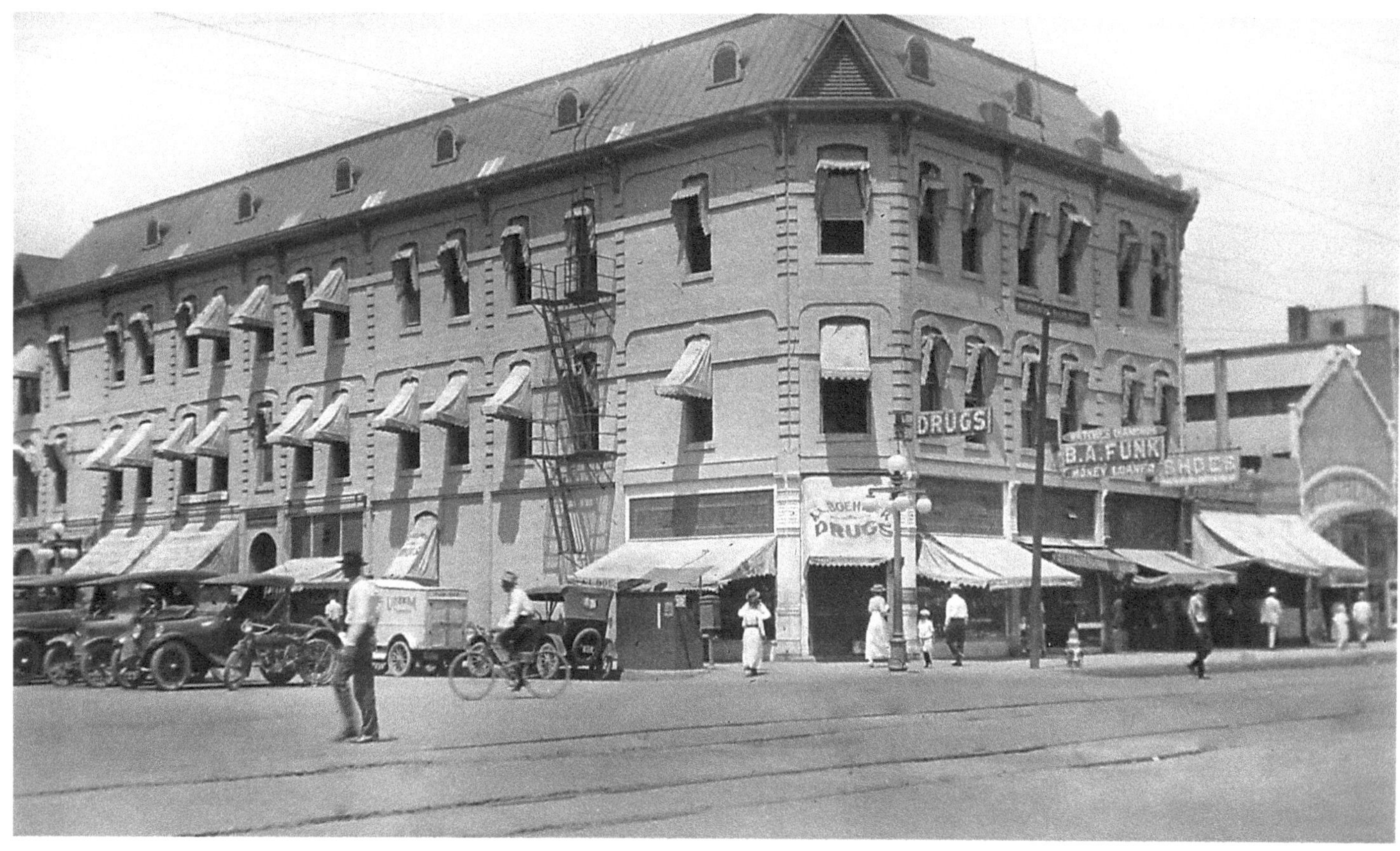

The Ford Hotel coffee shop on West Washington and Second Avenue was a popular gathering place. When coffee was first imported to the United States, colonists much preferred imported tea, but they acquired a taste for it when British forces blockaded American ports during the War of 1812. Coffee was in high demand by the time the Civil War broke out, and coffeehouses increasingly replaced the pub as the social center of communities.

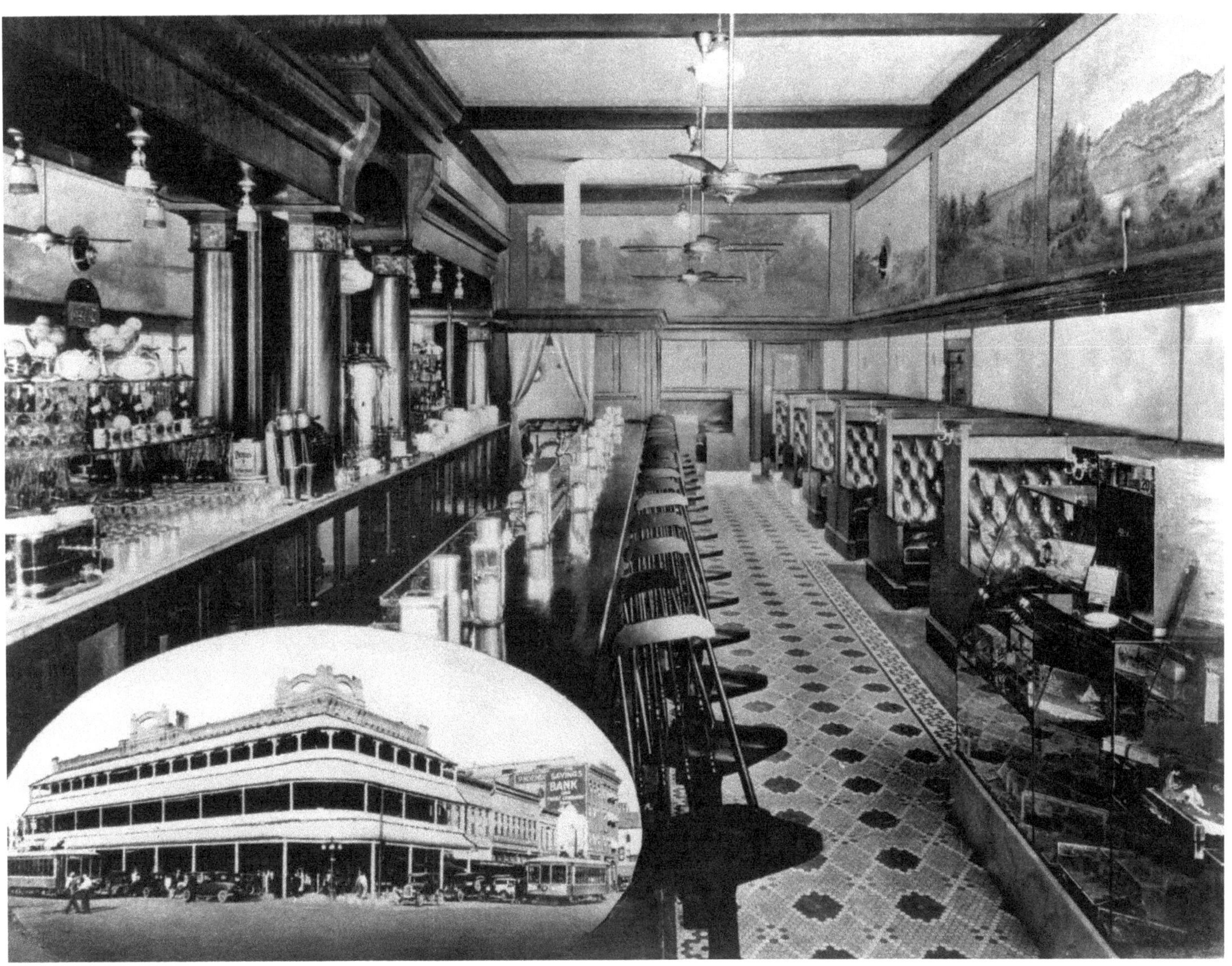

Following Spread: Horses, liveries, and feed stables were still a common part of life in Phoenix during the 1920s. Automobiles were expensive and horses were still needed on farms and ranches.

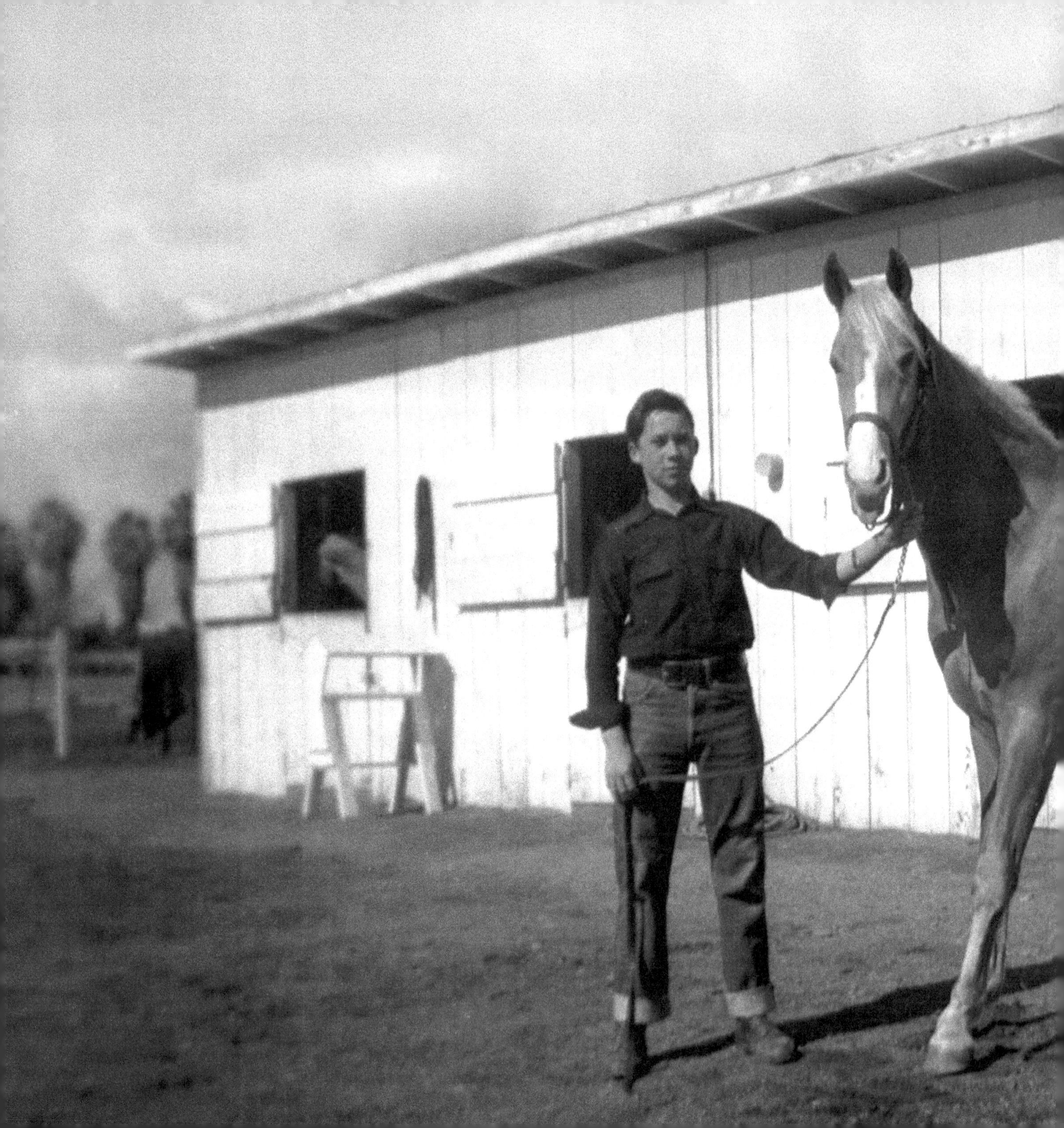

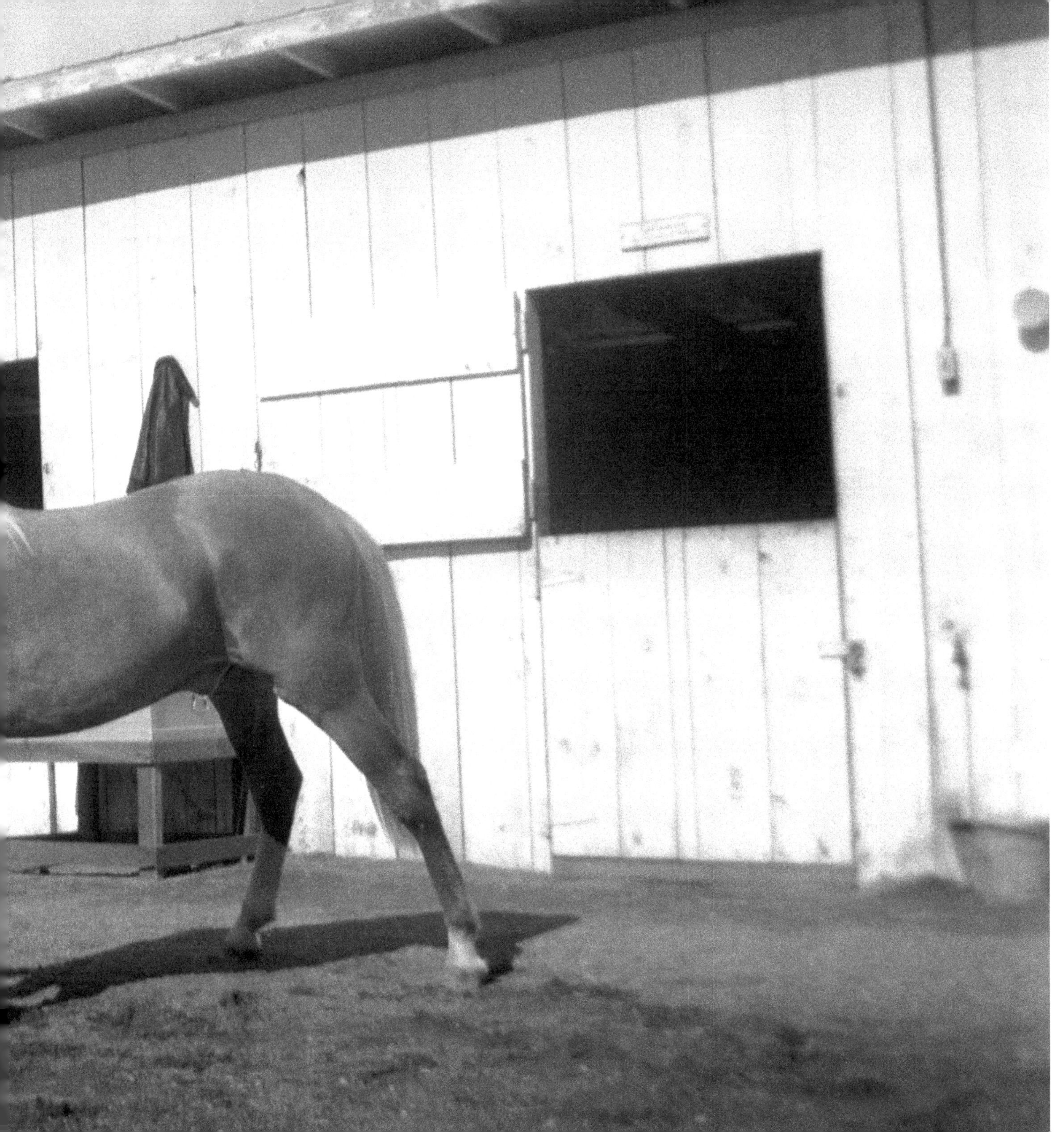

Home swimming pools did not become popular until after World War II. Most Phoenicians swam in swimming holes or public swimming pools. The Riverside Park was a favored destination to escape the summer heat.

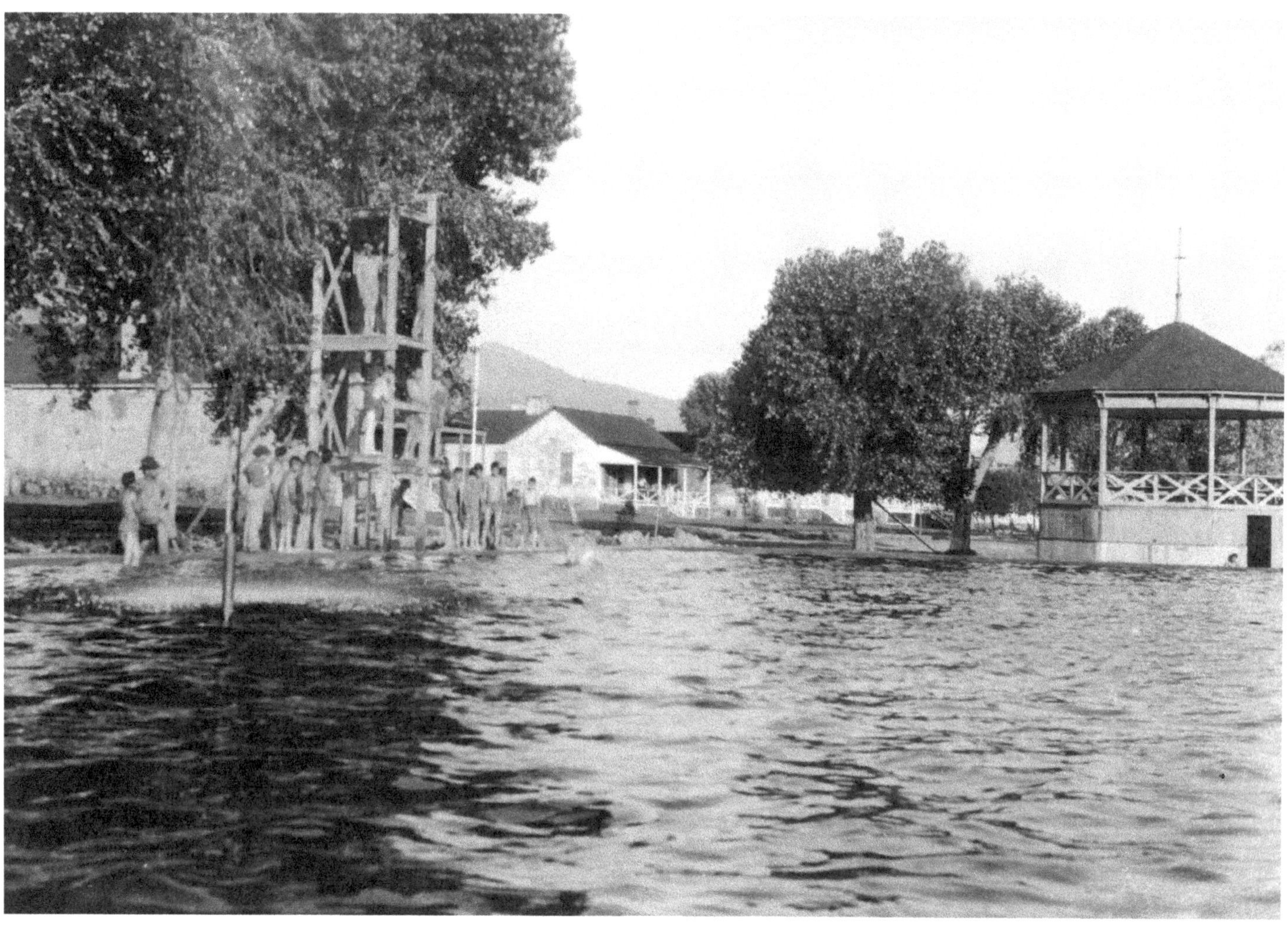

The writers and staff of the *Arizona Republic* pause for a moment in 1920 for a photograph. The newspaper began in 1890 as the political voice for Territorial Governor Lewis Wolfley, Attorney General Clark Churchill, and other Arizona officials.

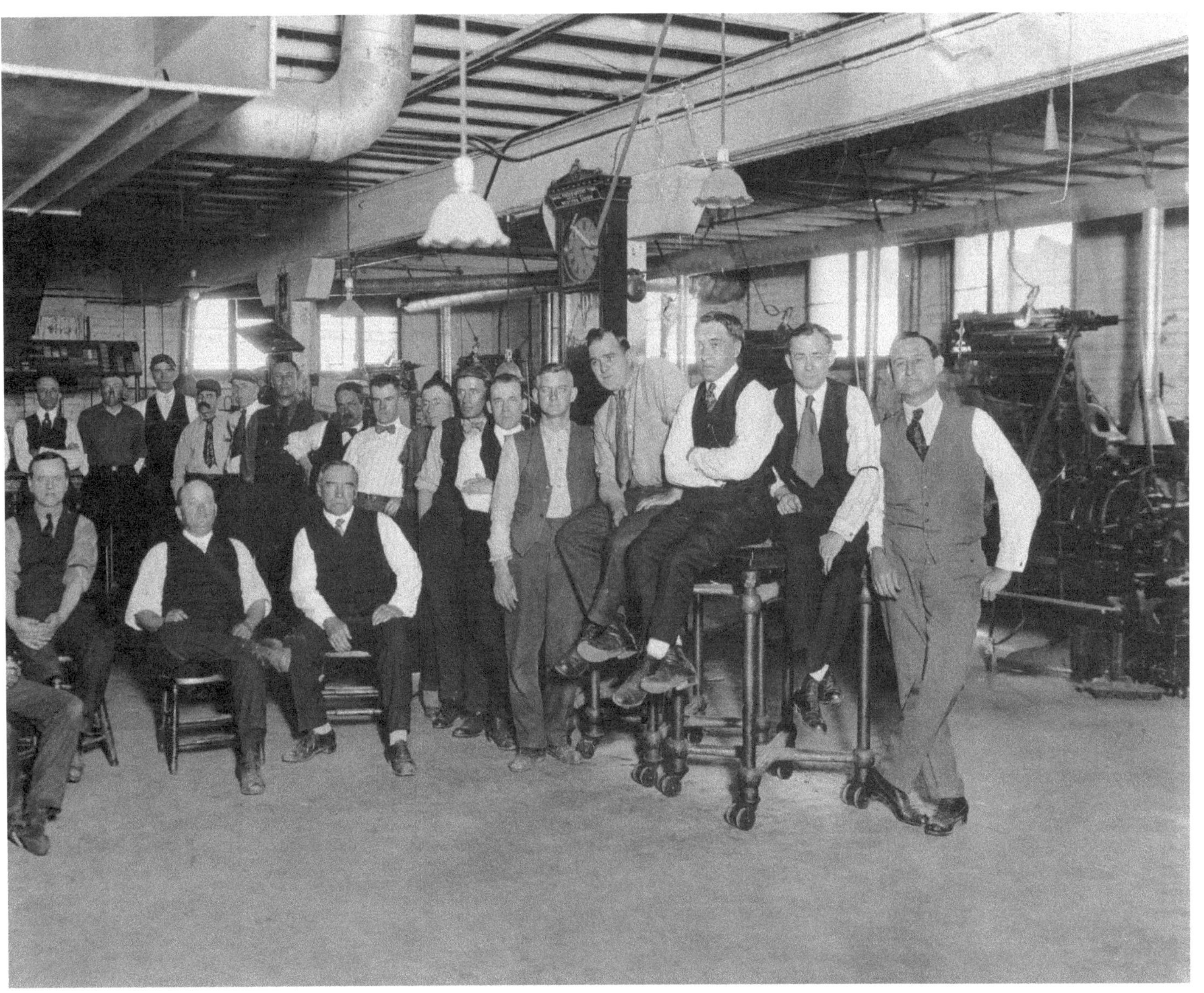

Cars park outside the Phoenix Post Office in 1920, shaded by majestic palm trees.

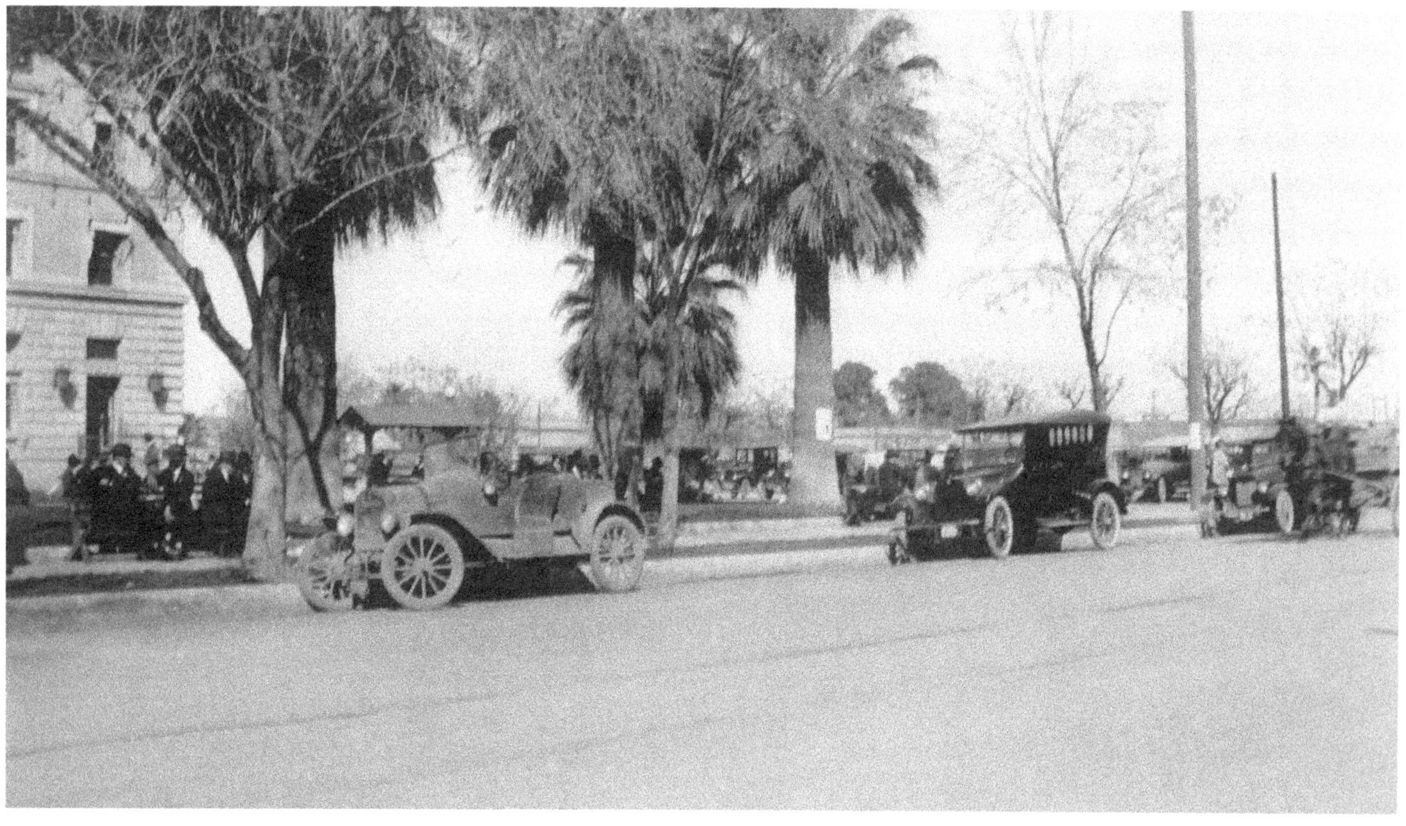

Phoenicians enjoy a summertime swim at the Riverside Park pool, around 1920.

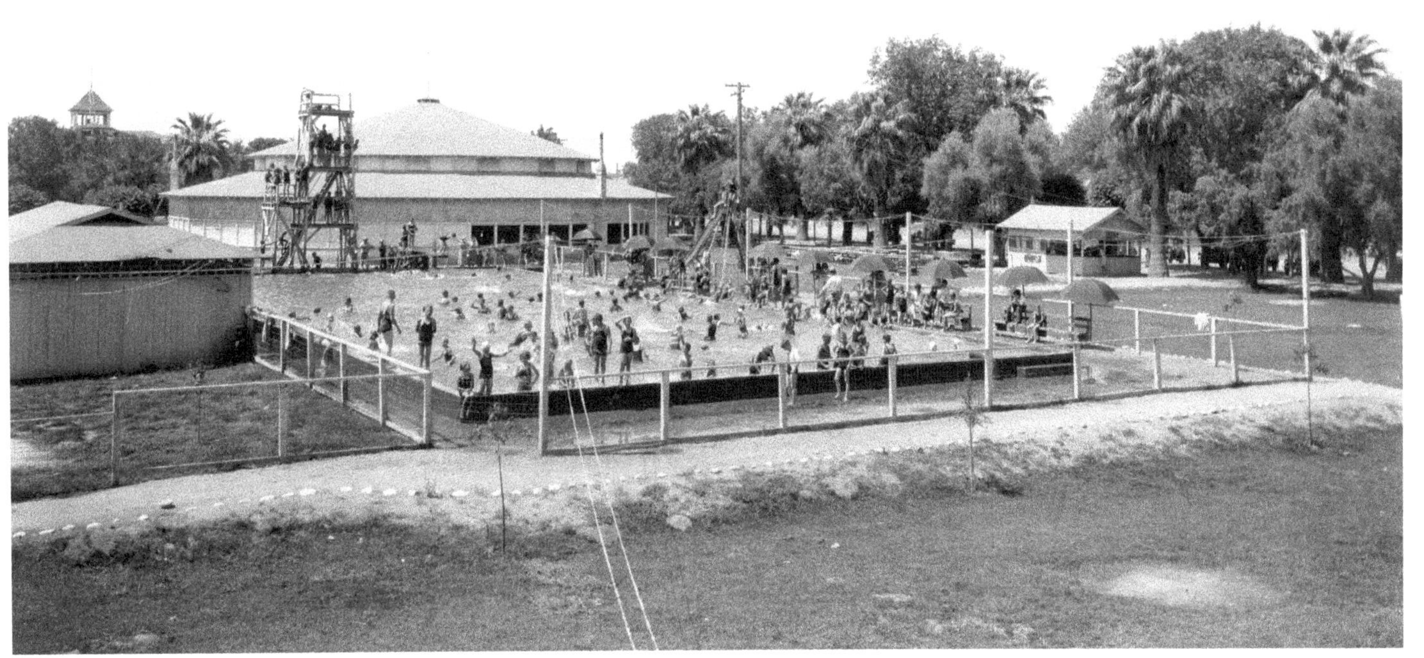

Many professions that are now mostly staffed by women were handled by men in the early twentieth century, when it was expected that most women would stay at home. Three female employees of the Arizona Title Company were ahead of their time. They are standing in the Maricopa County Courthouse Park with the Phoenix business district visible behind them.

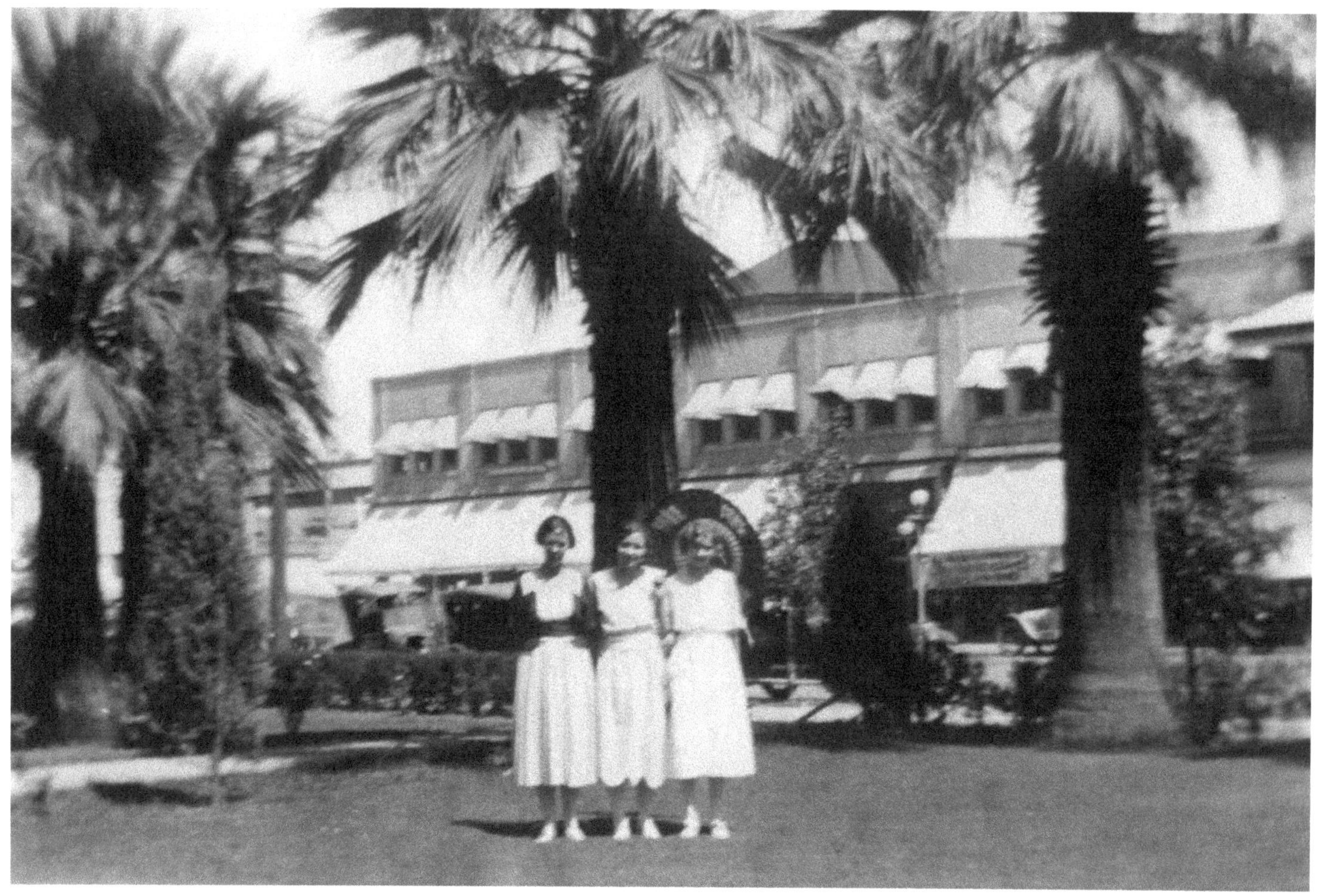

Phoenix had a series of post office facilities until 1913, when the U.S. Treasury Department built the Phoenix Post Office and Courthouse, pictured here in 1920.

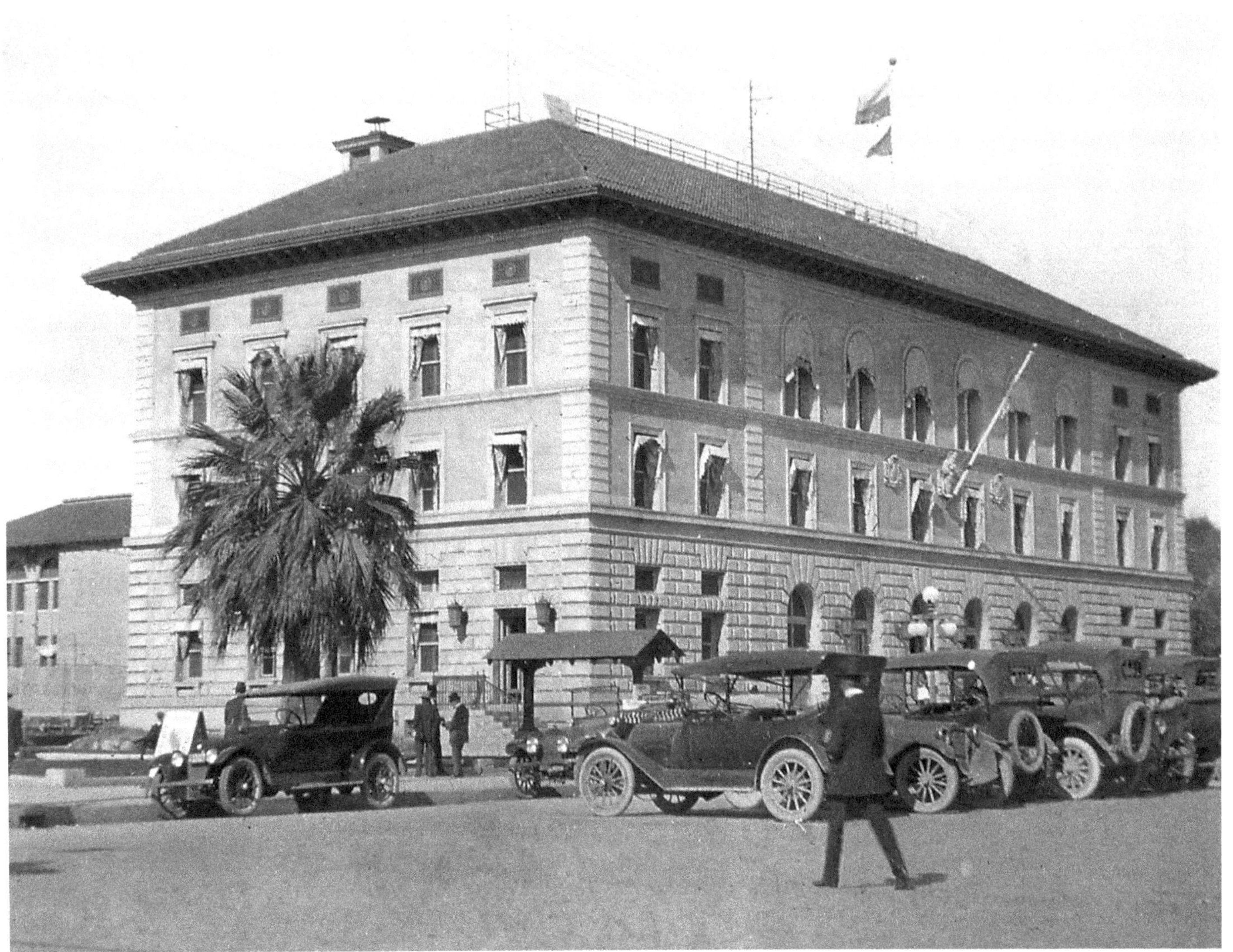

As automobiles emerged as the preferred mode of transportation in the 1920s, the Arizona Highway Department widened its role beyond maintaining the roadways. Many states created magazines to appeal to motorists—engineers in the Arizona Highway Department, pictured here, began publishing *Arizona Highways* in 1925 with travel stories and scenic black-and-white photographs.

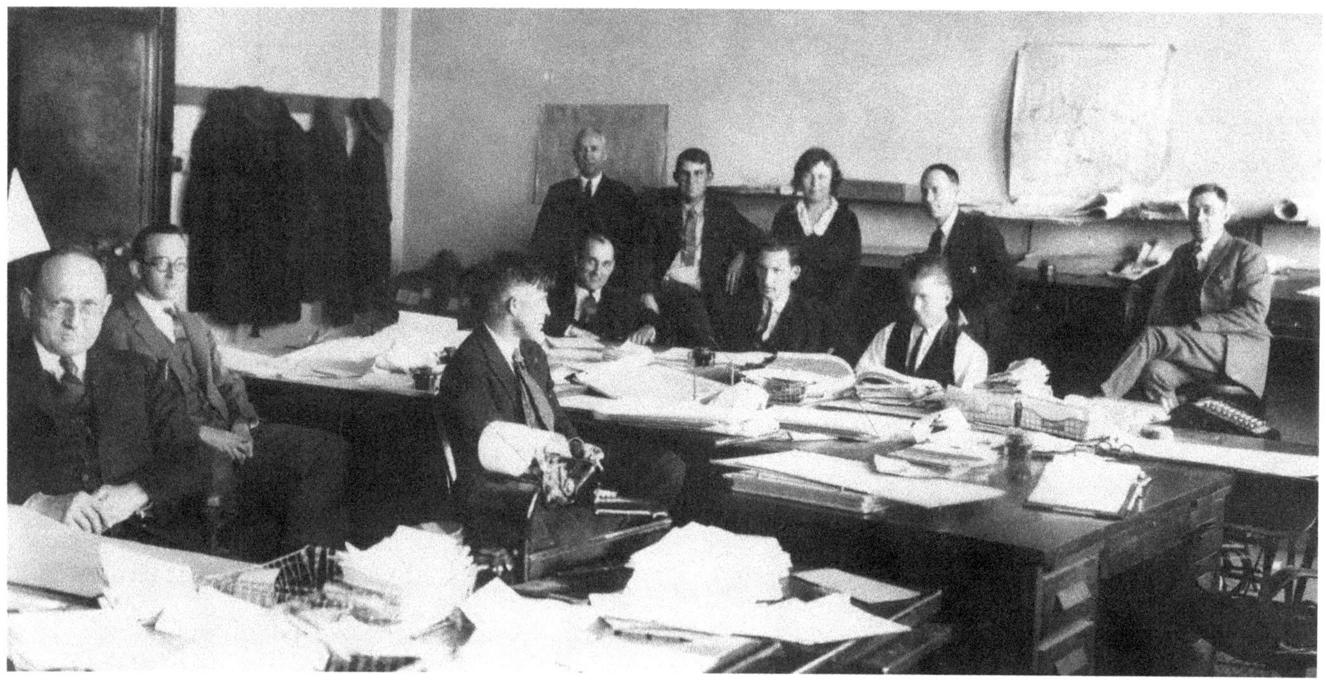

Two young women enjoy a pleasant afternoon at the Riverside Park in Phoenix, around 1922.

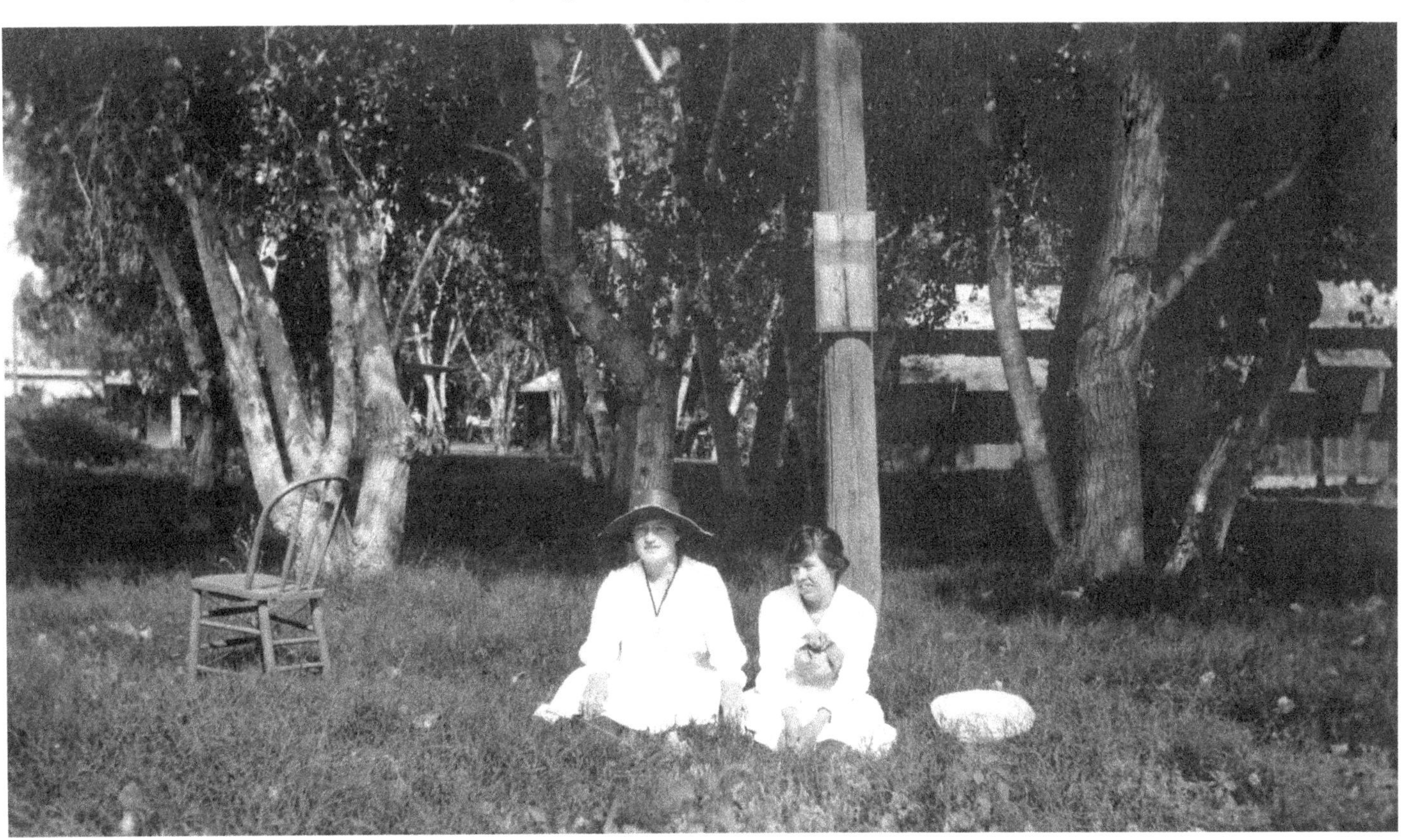

Governor Hunt poses with his driver Harry Shea in front of the pyramid-shaped cairn built for Charles Debrille Poston, the Father of Arizona, near Florence. Poston organized the first mining company in Arizona when it was part of the Territory of New Mexico, and he is credited with giving Arizona its name in 1863 when he obtained President Lincoln's signature to create the territory. He was also Arizona's first elected delegate to Congress.

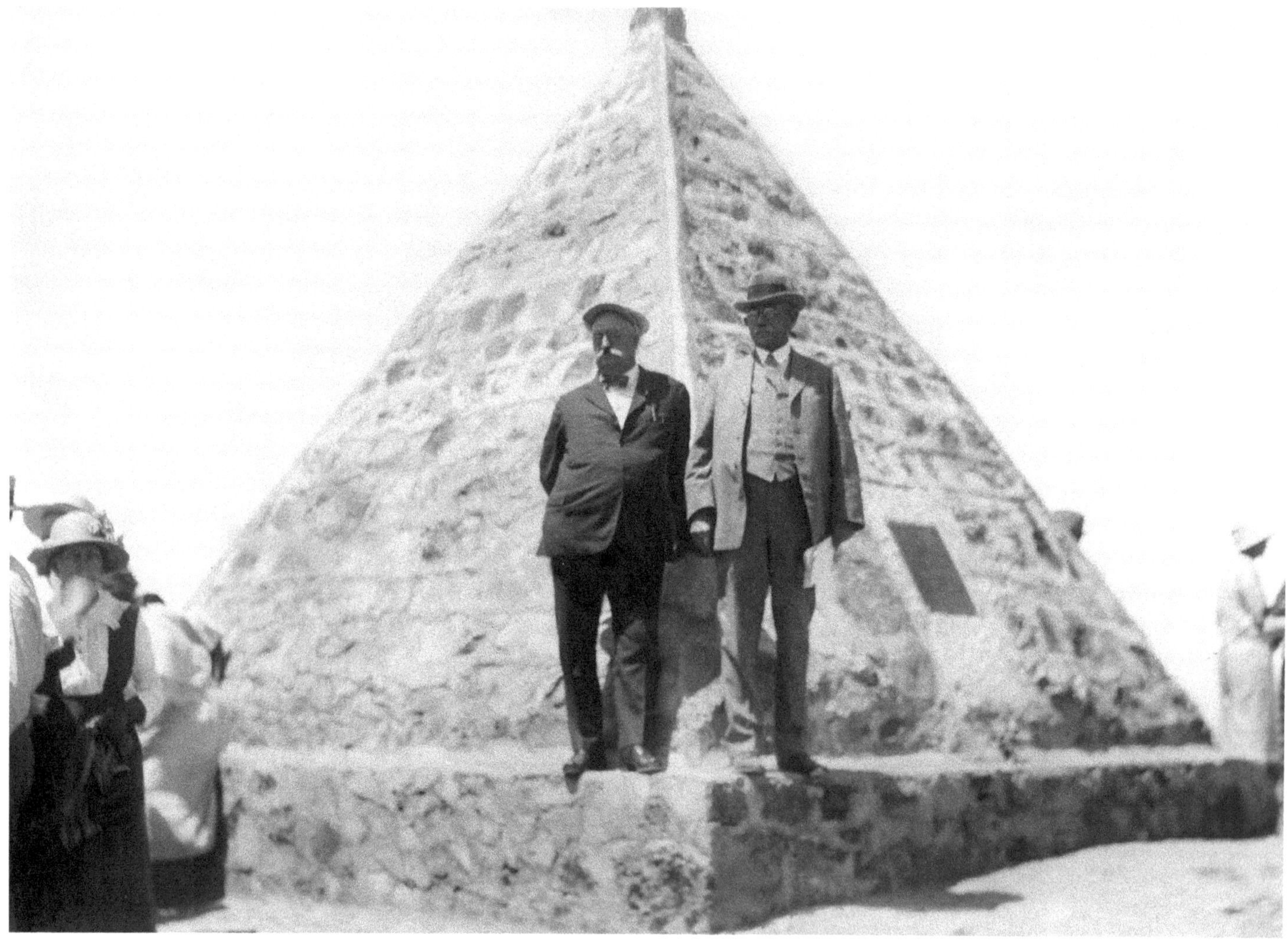

Governor Hunt poses with pilots of a military airplane that landed in Phoenix in 1925.

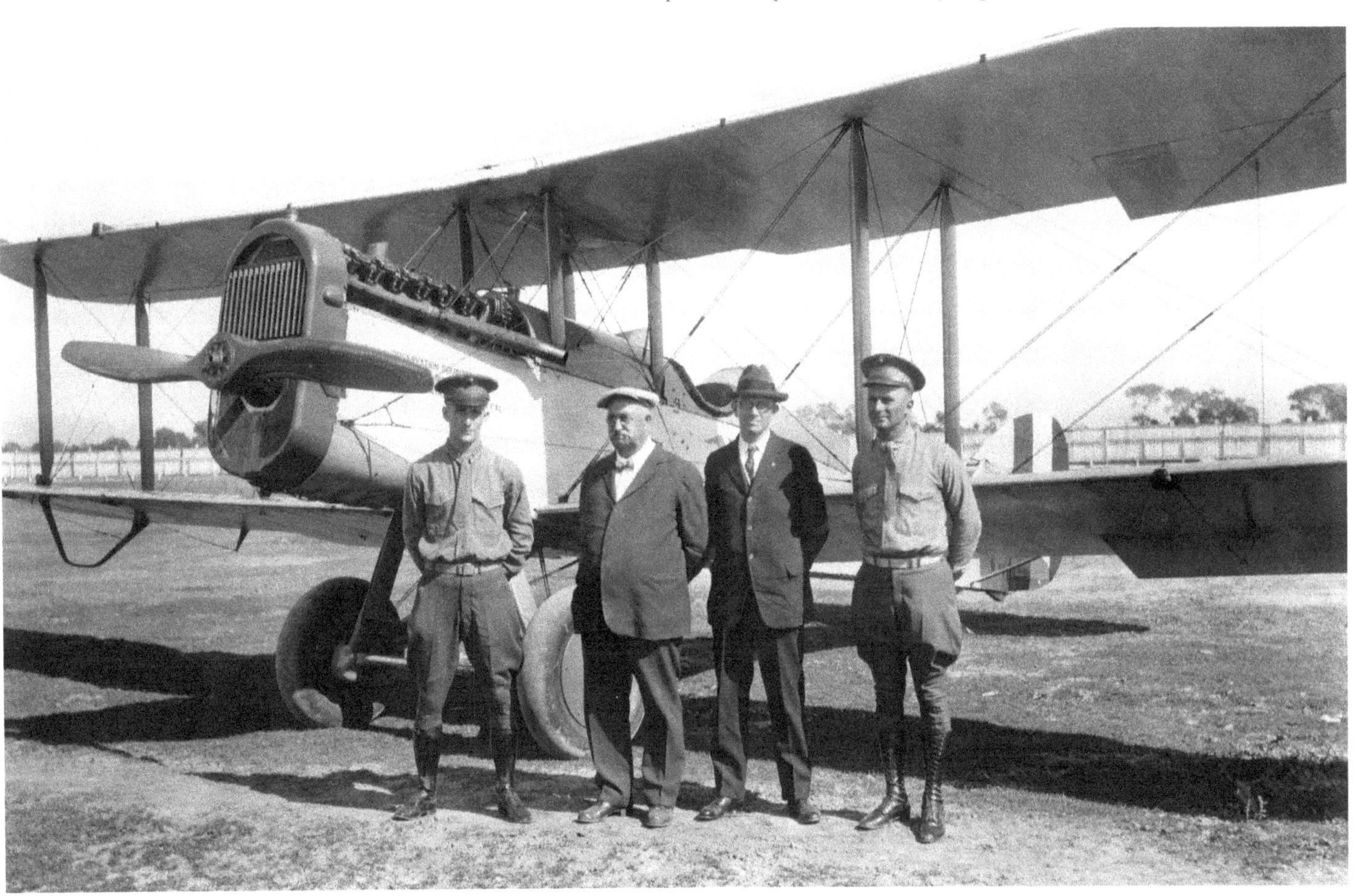

Governor Hunt poses with his driver Harry Shea and a traveling party of young women on their way to Roosevelt Dam in the Tonto National Forest, east of Phoenix. Automobiles made such day trips possible, along scenic roads and at relatively minimal cost.

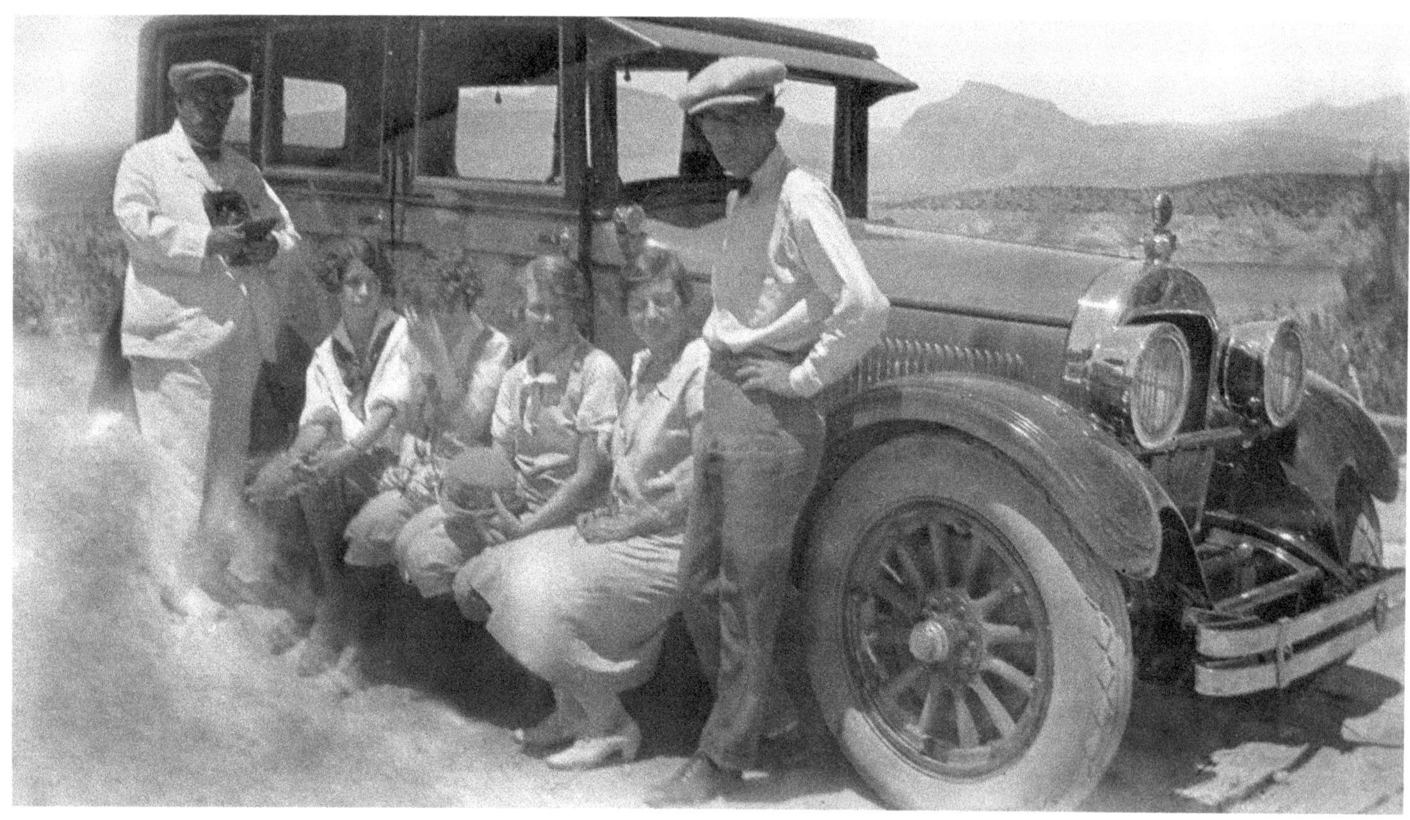

The DH.4A, pictured here in 1925, was designed by famed British aviation pioneer Sir Geoffrey de Havilland and built by American manufacturers for service in World War I. It was considered to be a versatile daylight bomber, well armed and equipped with a powerful twelve-cylinder engine. After the war the DH-4 was modified for carrying airmail.

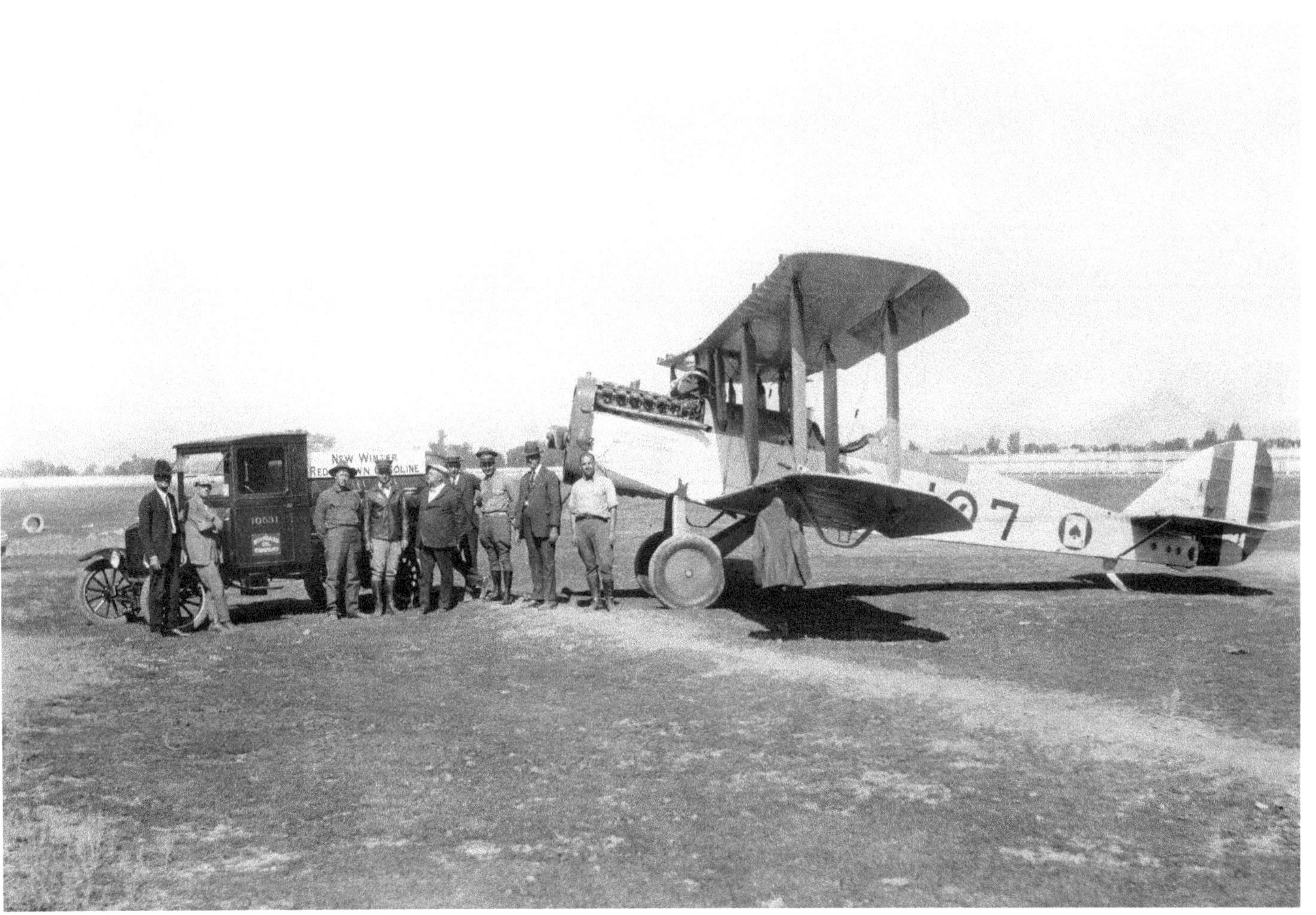

Governor Hunt signs the Women's Minimum Wage Law at the Arizona State Capitol in Phoenix in 1923.

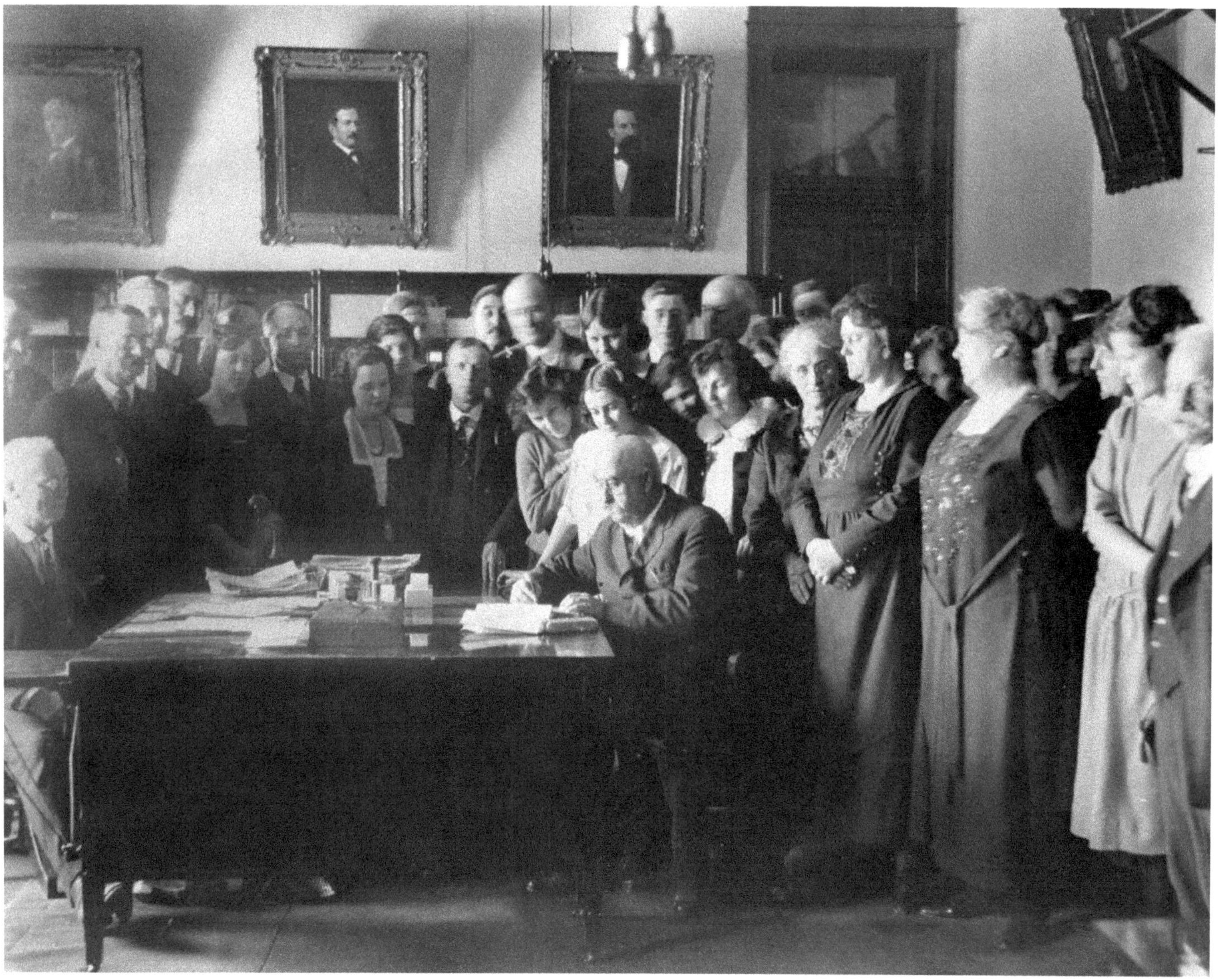

Governor Hunt playfully poses with a lawn mower at the Arizona State Capitol, although it is doubtful that he actually mowed the lawn. The first lawn mower was invented by an English engineer in 1827 as an alternative to the scythe for cutting lawns on sports grounds and in gardens. The rising popularity of lawn sports after World War I, such as tennis, croquet, football, and rugby, spurred lawn mower sales.

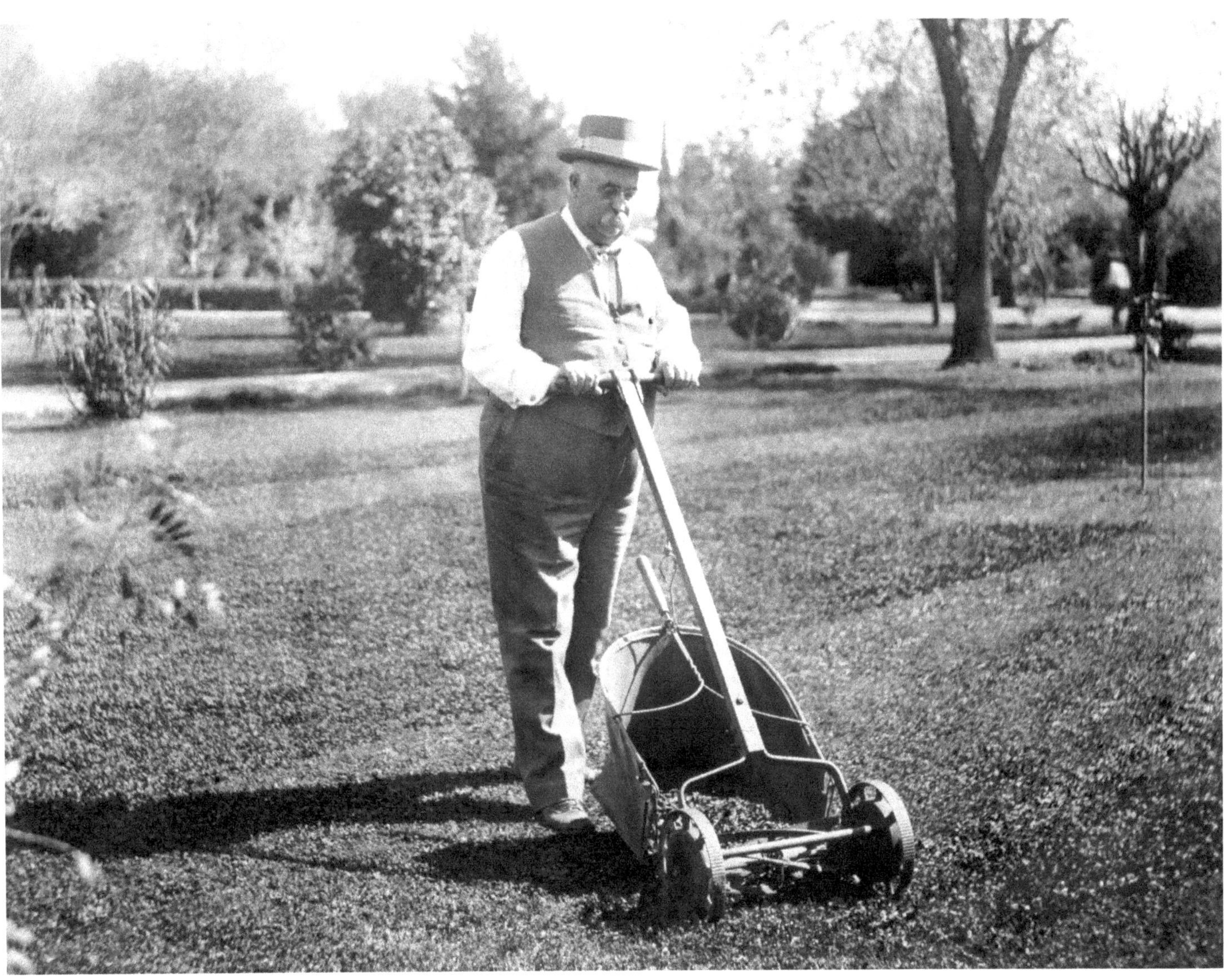

Phoenicians enjoy an afternoon picnic at South Mountain Park. Originally called Phoenix Mountain Park, South Mountain Park was created in 1924 when President Coolidge sold 13,000 acres to the City of Phoenix for $17,000.

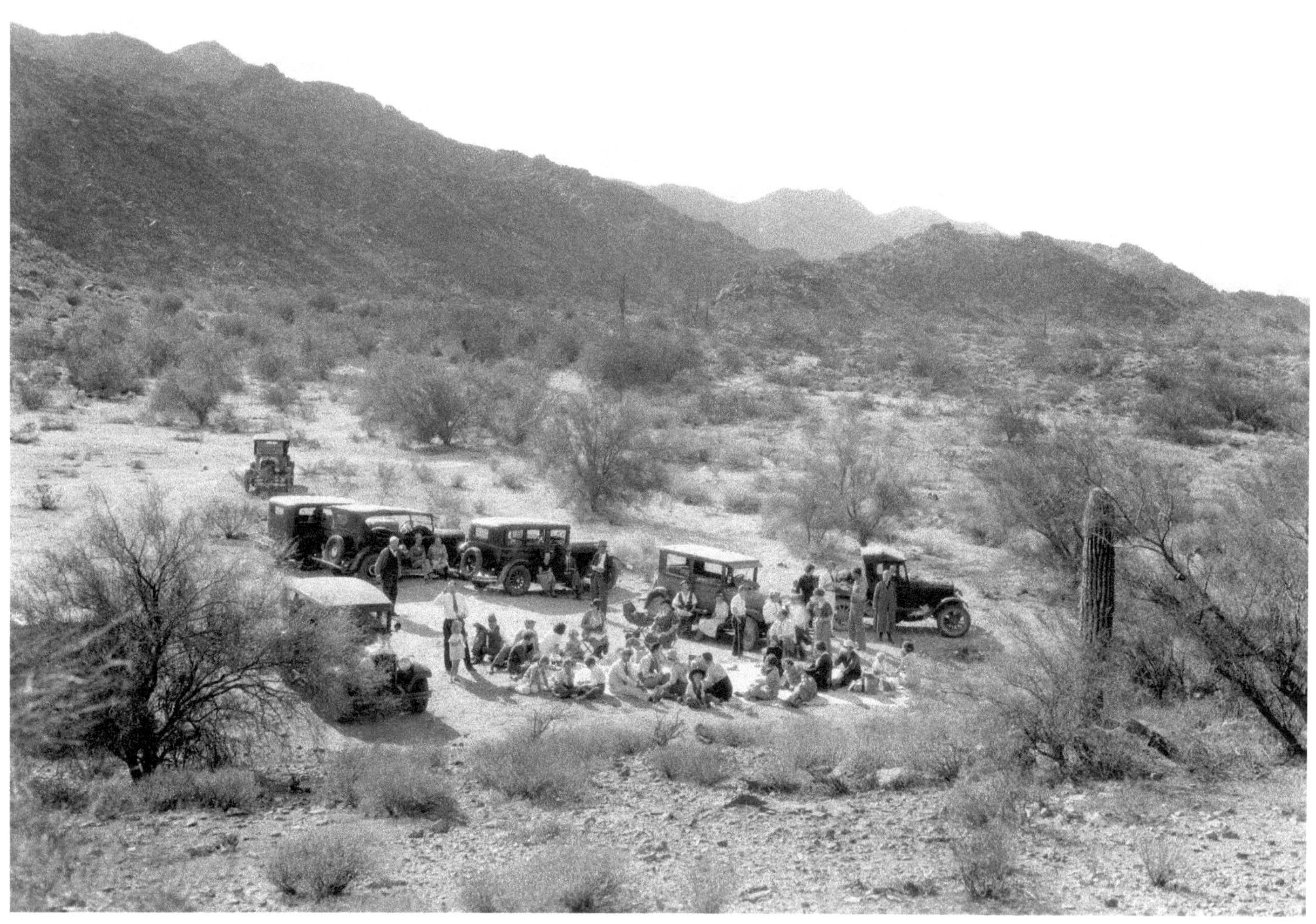

Pietistic denominations were convinced that prohibition would cure society of a host of ills and spearheaded the "dry" movement in the United States from as early as the 1840s. Arizona passed a prohibition law in 1914, and many Americans, in an anti-German mood after World War I (leading beer distributors like Schlitz, Pabst, Anheuser-Busch, and Coors were all founded by German Americans) supported an amendment to the Constitution prohibiting the manufacturing, sale, or transportation of alcohol.

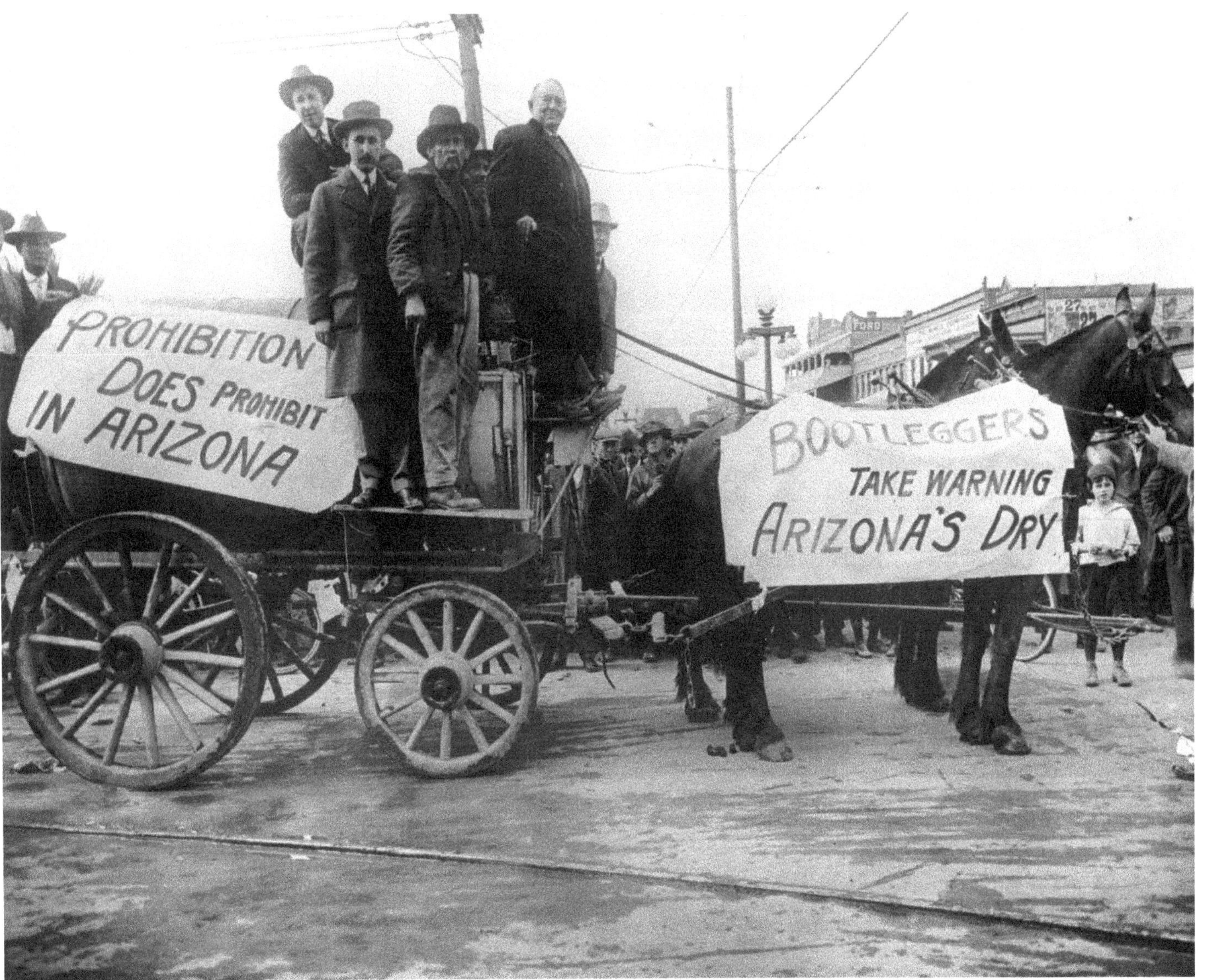

Superintendent of Highways Lee Coffelt poses with Governor Hunt in front of a Ford Model A.

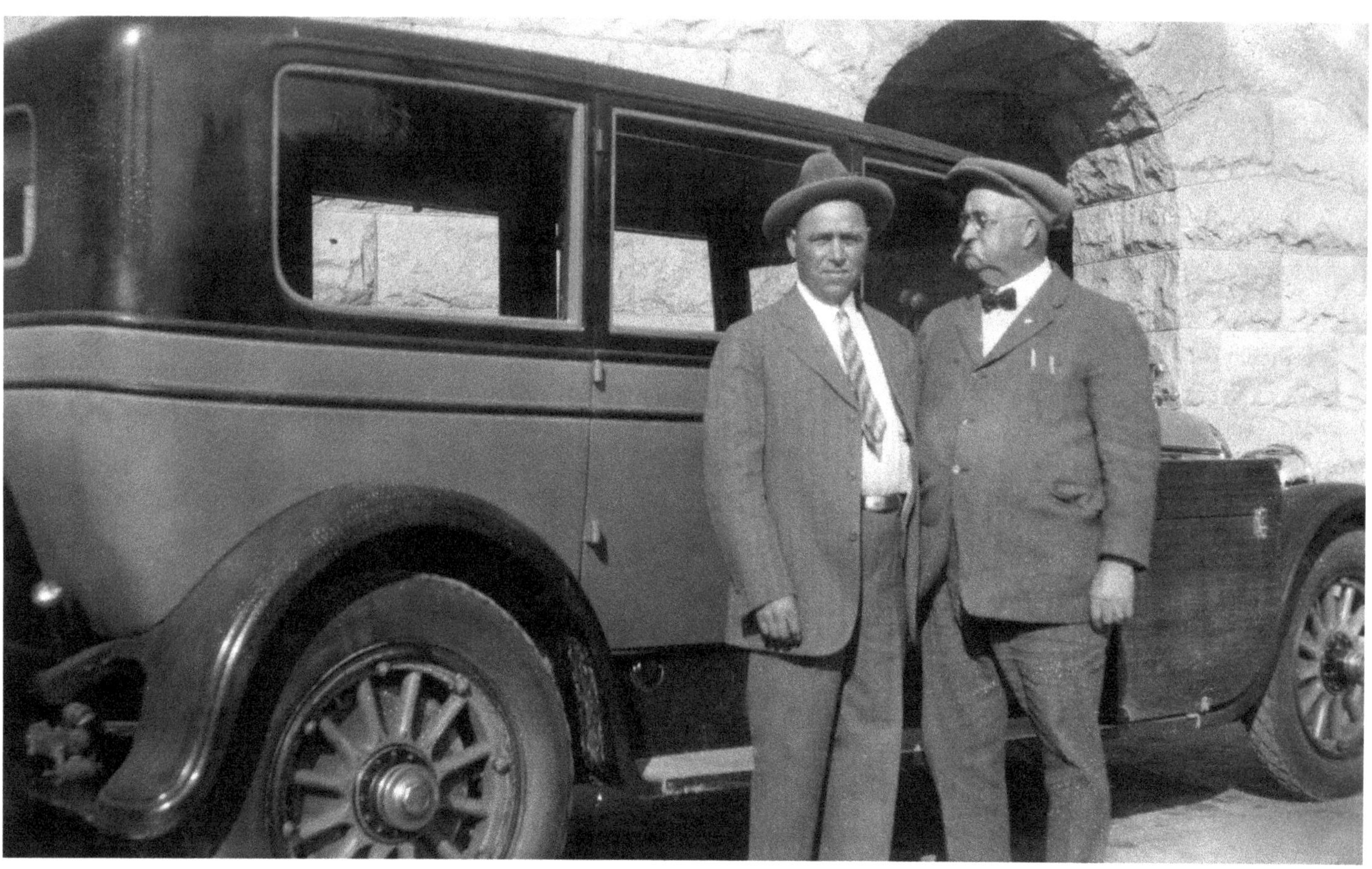

Fair goers enjoy a hot-air balloon ride, with a little advertising, at the 1925 Arizona State Fair.

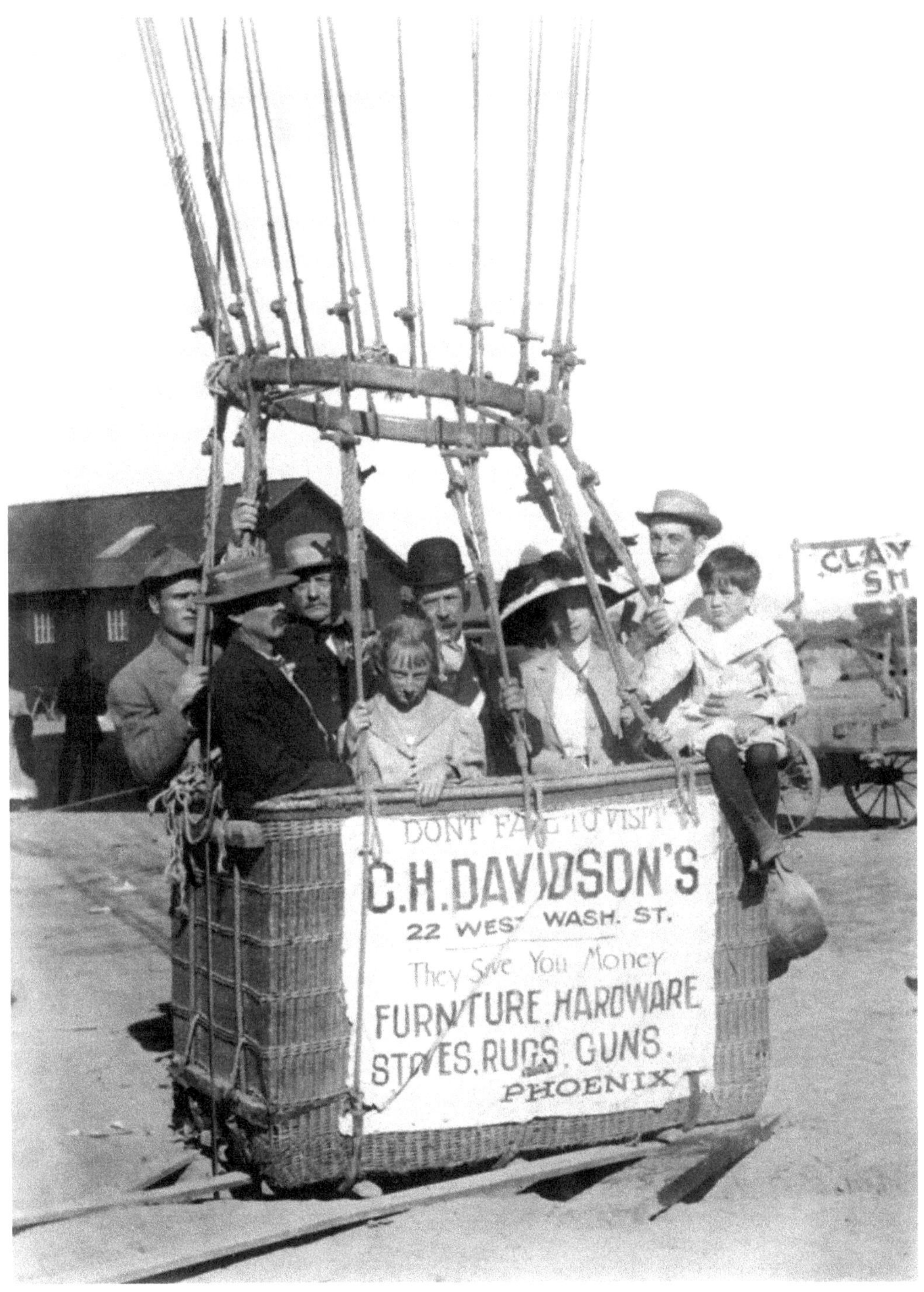

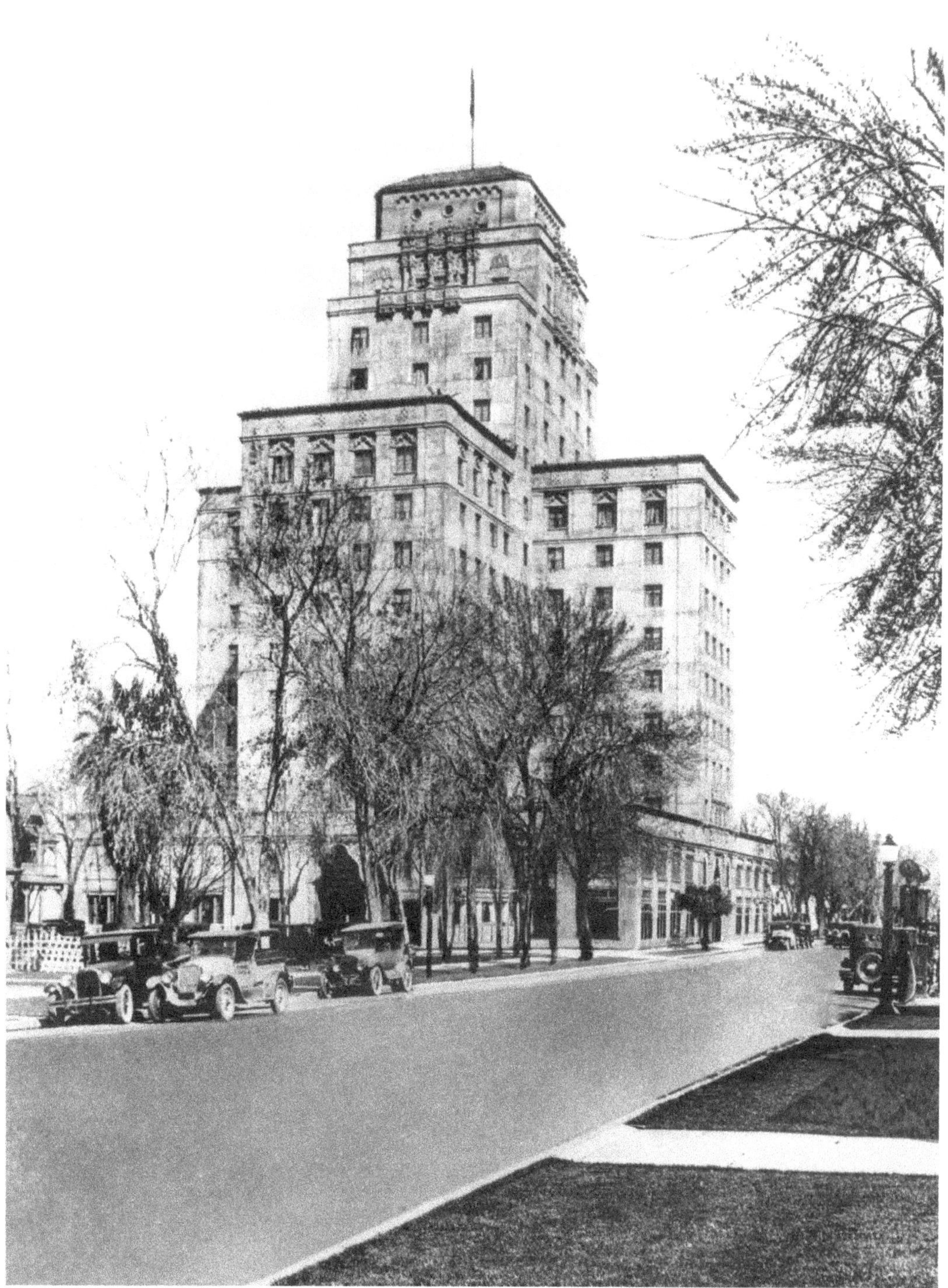

Phoenix businessman Guy Bennett envisioned a luxury hotel for elite visitors. He demolished his home to make way for the Roosevelt Hotel, but he ran into financial difficulties and sold the uncompleted hotel in 1928 to George L. Johnson. Inspired by Charles Kingsley's Western novels, Johnson renamed it the Westward Ho.

Frank Moy, Ralph Rollins, and J. W. Stoad observe Governor Hunt signing the invitation to President Calvin Coolidge to attend the dedication of Coolidge Dam in 1928.

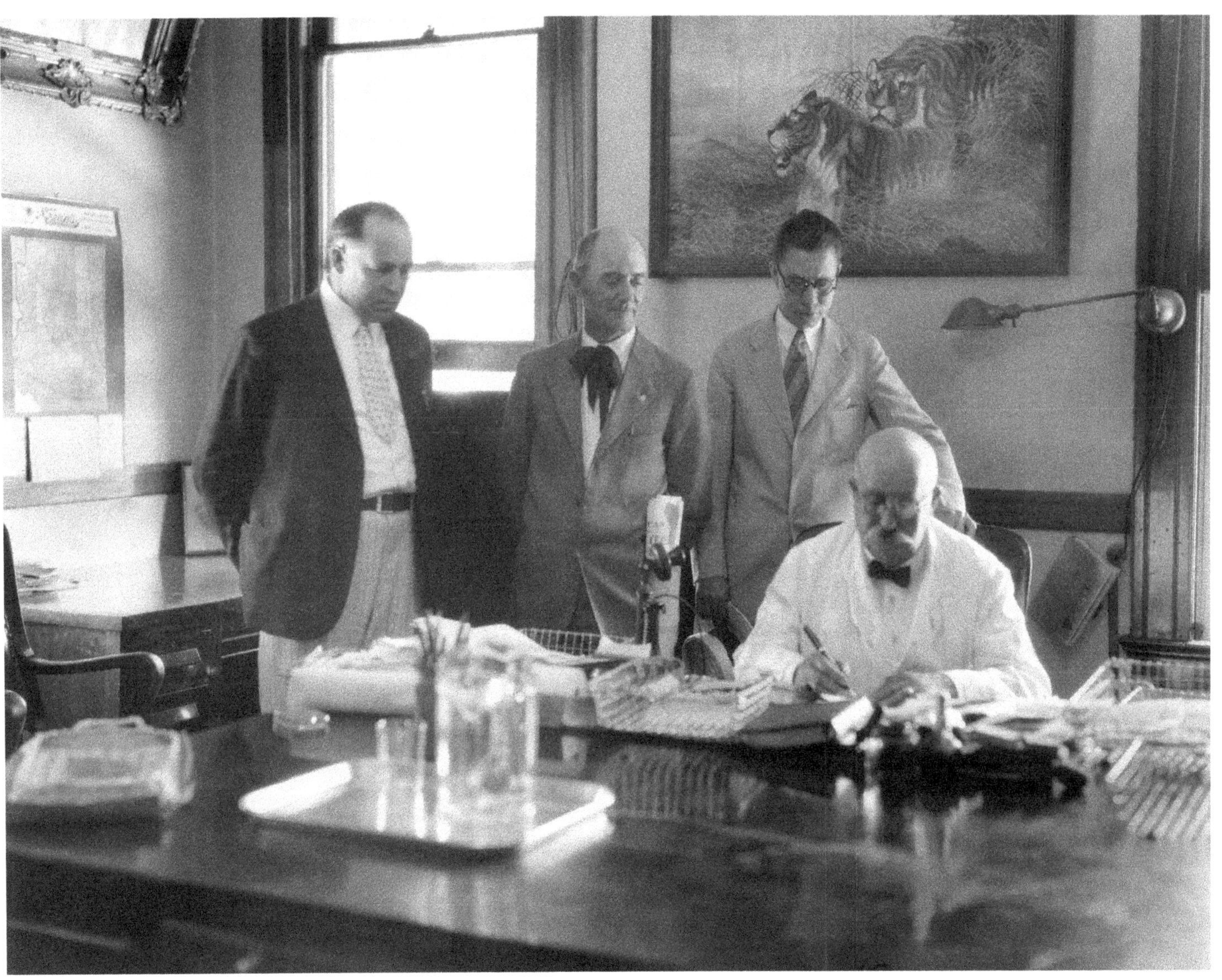

By the time this 1930 photograph was taken of a Phoenix citrus grove, with Camelback Mountain in the background, citrus was a well-established part of the economy. The industry in Phoenix began during the growing season of 1870 when early settlers imported orange trees from Southern California that were first planted by Spanish missionaries.

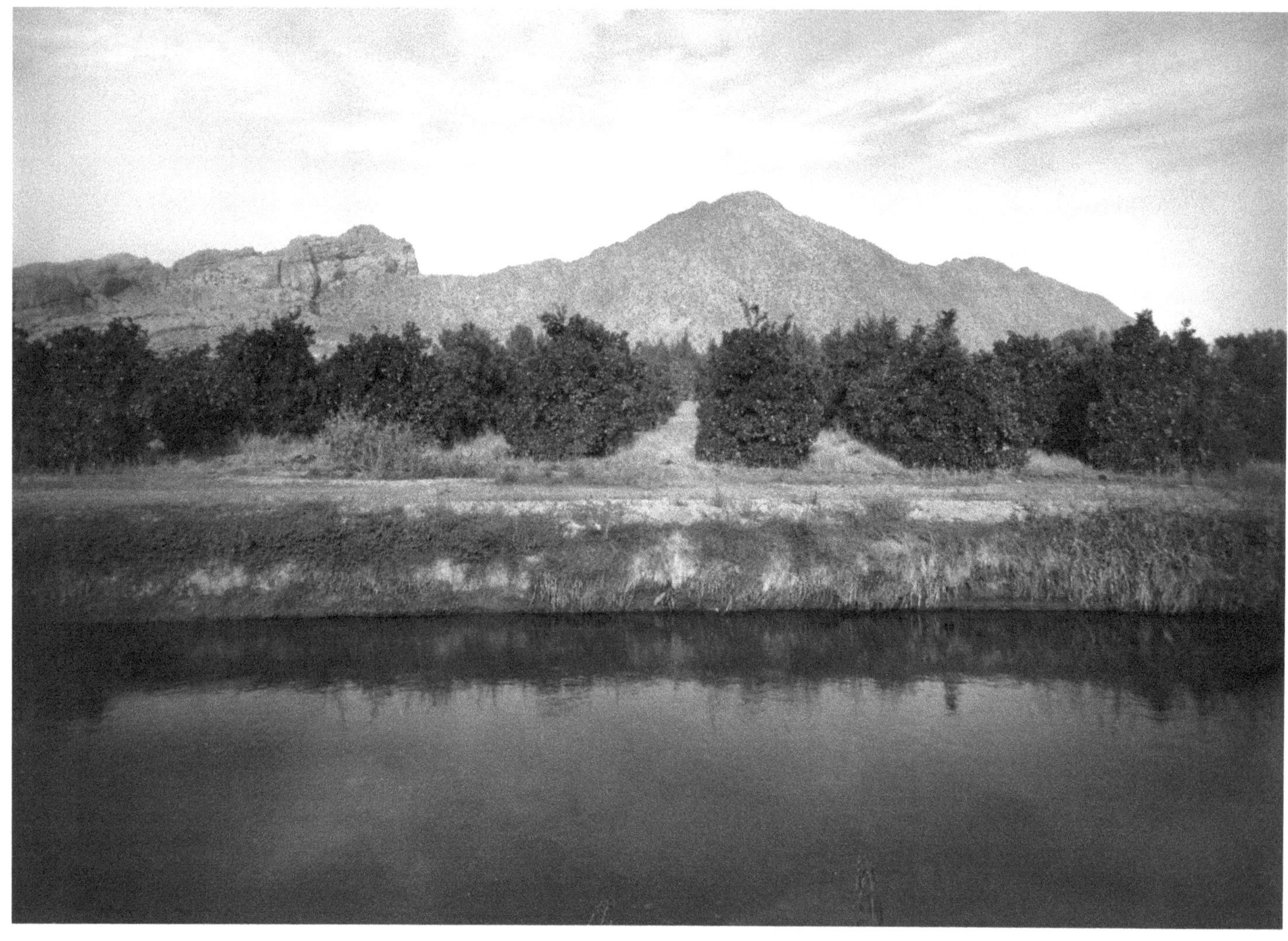

Arizona Rough Riders celebrate their 33rd anniversary in Phoenix. Originally 1,000 men volunteered for the Arizona Rough Riders, but only 210 were allowed to join Teddy Roosevelt in Cuba.

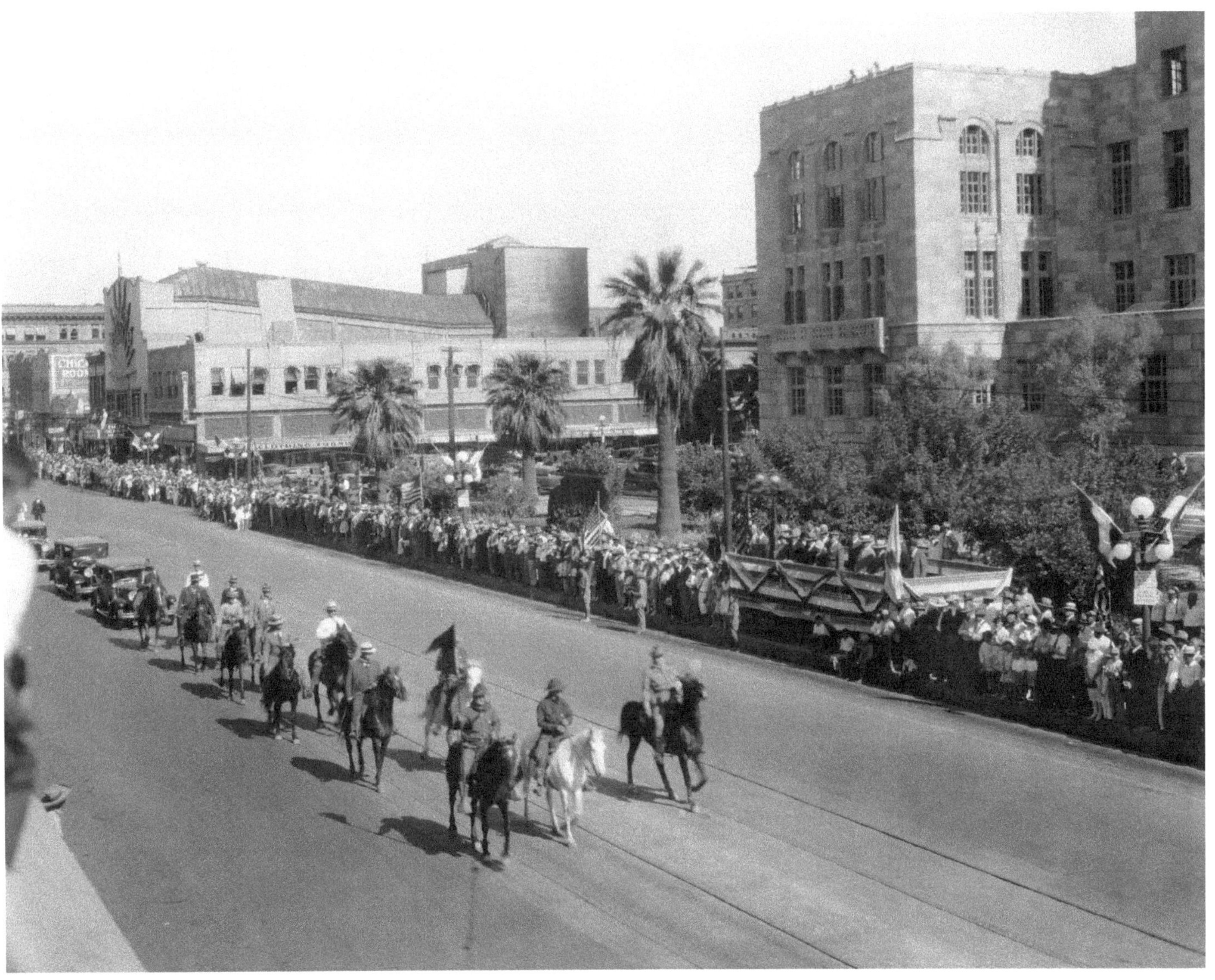

By the time this 1930s photograph was taken of First Avenue, near Van Buren Street, Phoenix had a population close to 50,000, its own radio station, a new Union Station for the Southern Pacific and Santa Fe railroads, and regular flights to Los Angeles from the new Sky Harbor Airport.

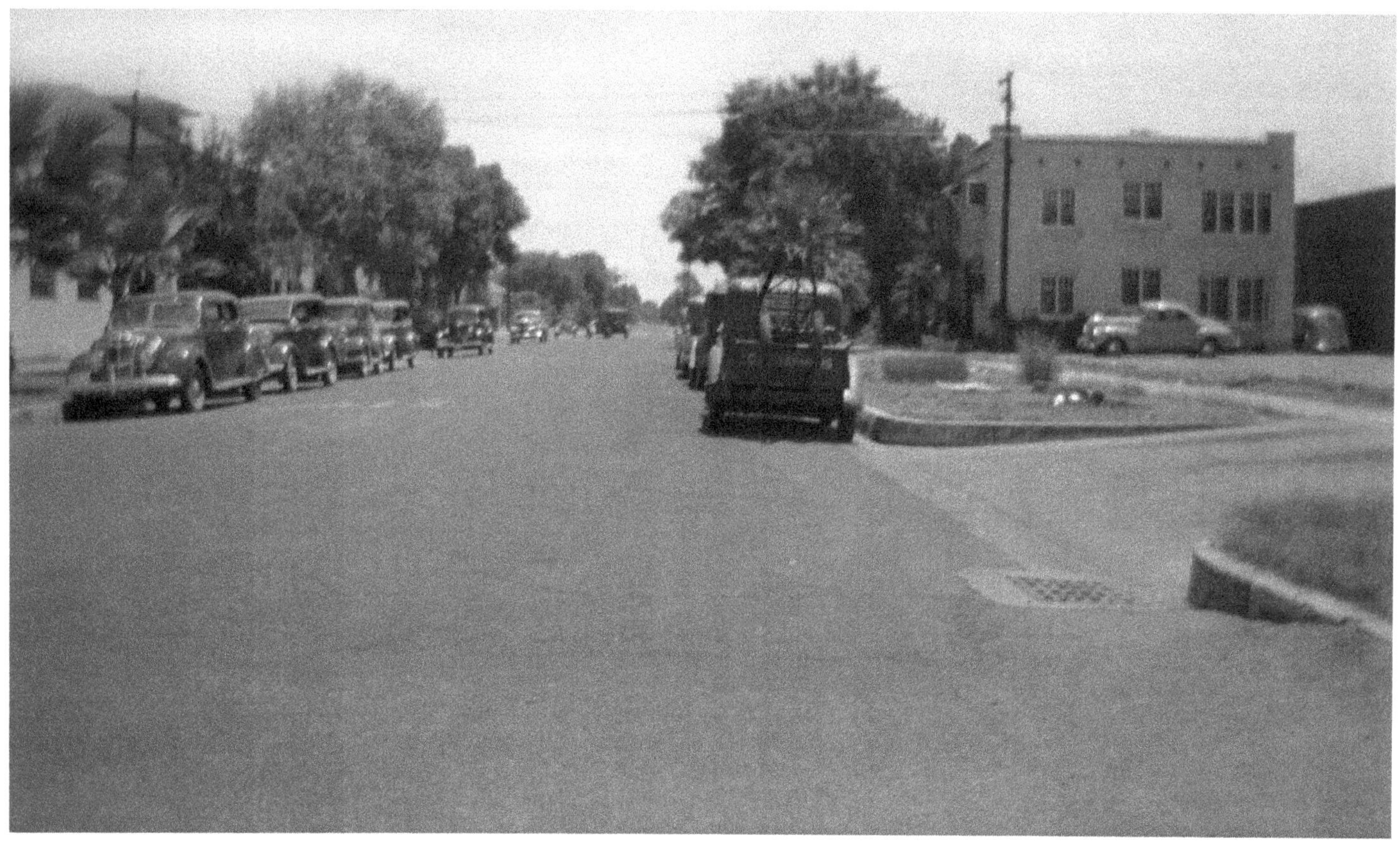

For many years, Phoenicians used canals for swimming, and in this particular case, to water ski by a car driving along the canal bank. When this 1930s picture was taken the sport was still young, having been introduced in 1922 by Ralph Samuelson, who created his own pair of water skis, attached a cord to a boat driven by his brother, and reached a speed of 20 m.p.h. on Lake Pepin in Minnesota.

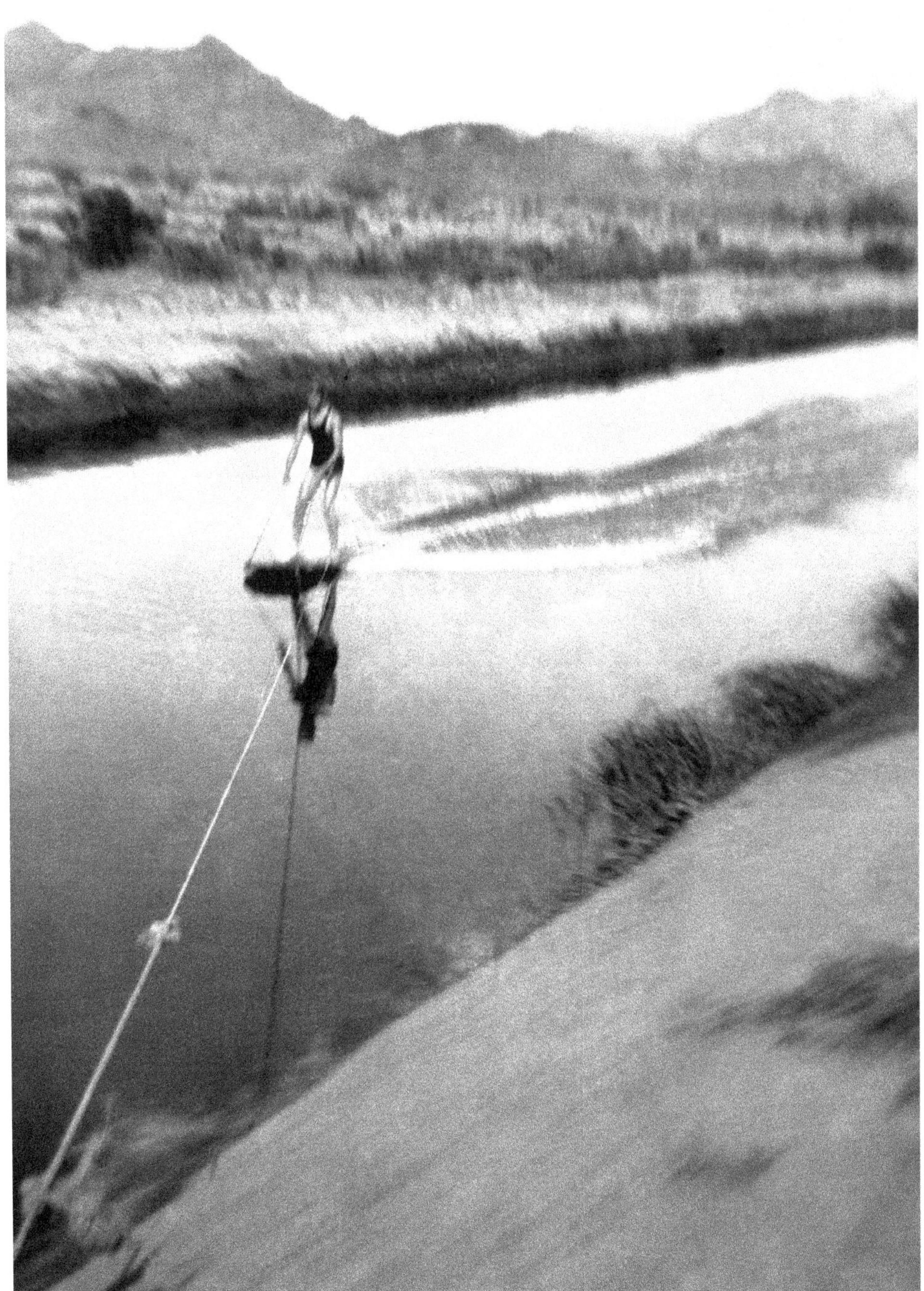

In 1935 President Roosevelt unveiled the largest and most comprehensive New Deal agency. The Works Progress Administration (WPA) employed millions of unemployed to work on construction projects, build roads, and operate arts, drama, media, and literacy projects. WPA photographers documented the social and cultural life of Americans, including these students on the playground at Madison School. Founded in 1890, Madison School was originally located in a citrus grove on 12th Street and Missouri.

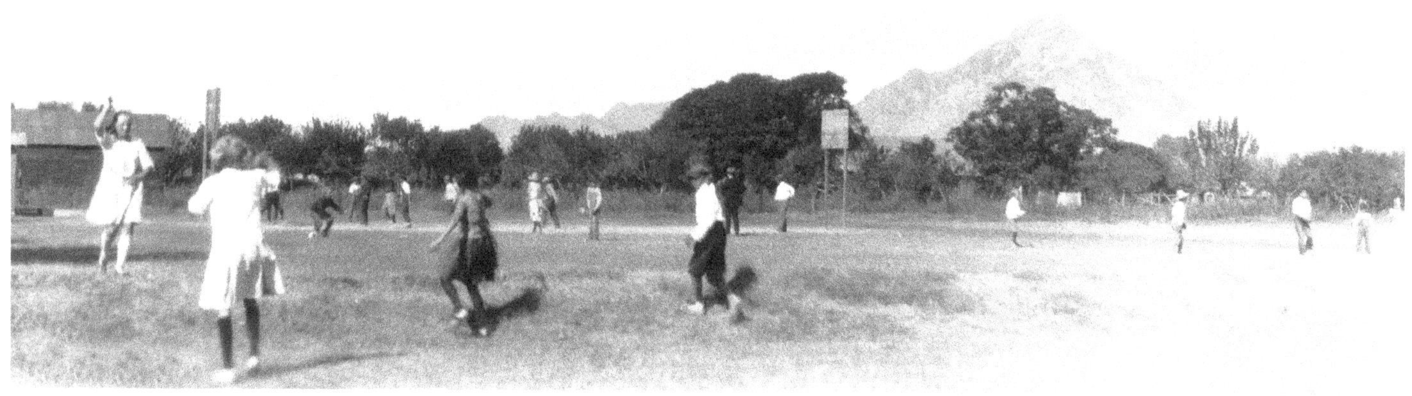

A series of violent winds during the early 1930s stripped massive amounts of topsoil from the Great Plains states, blowing dust as far away as Boston, New York City, and Washington, D.C. With their land barren and homes seized in foreclosure, hundreds of thousands of Midwestern farm families were forced to leave what would be called the "Dust Bowl." Pictured here is one such family making their way out West in search of employment.

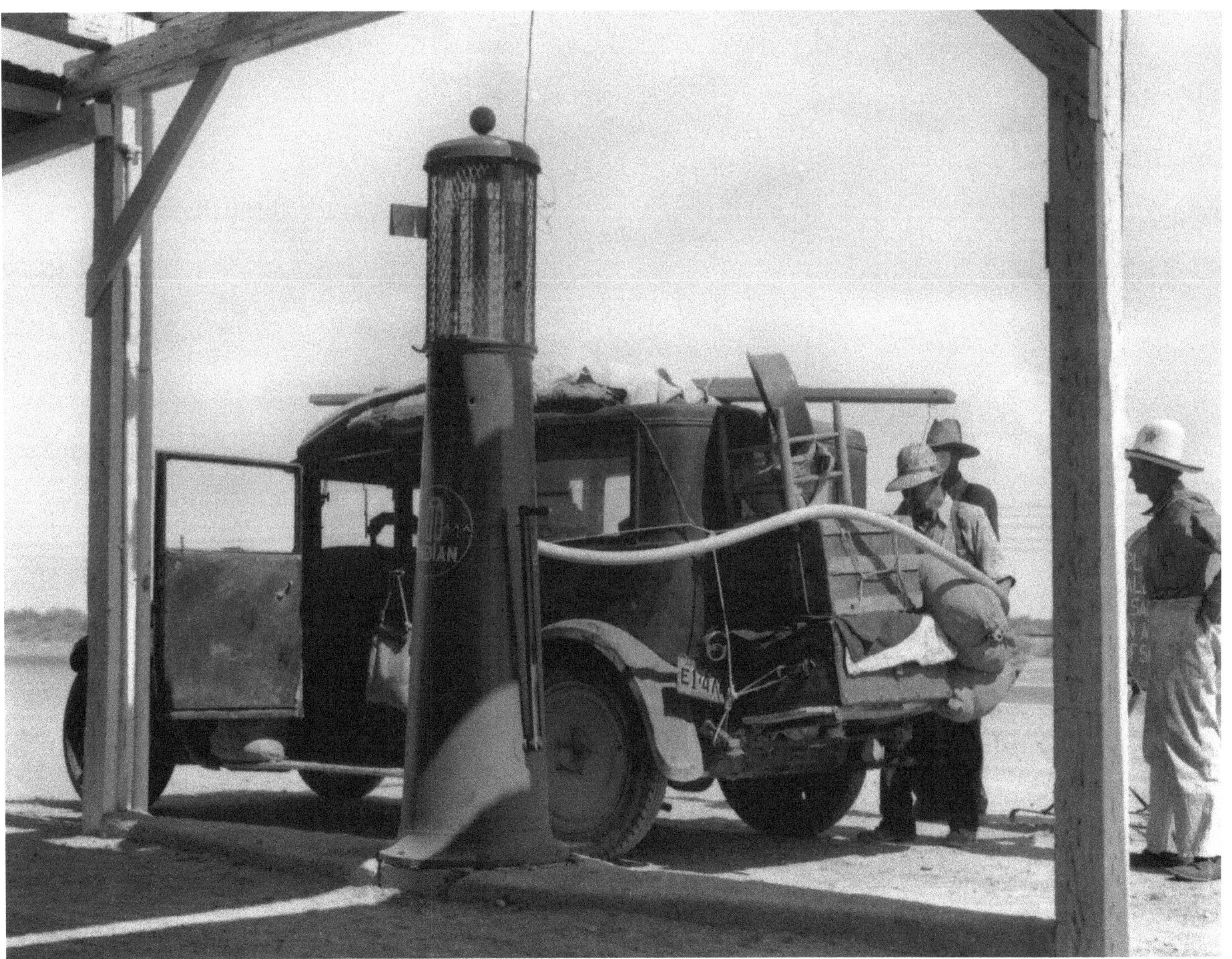

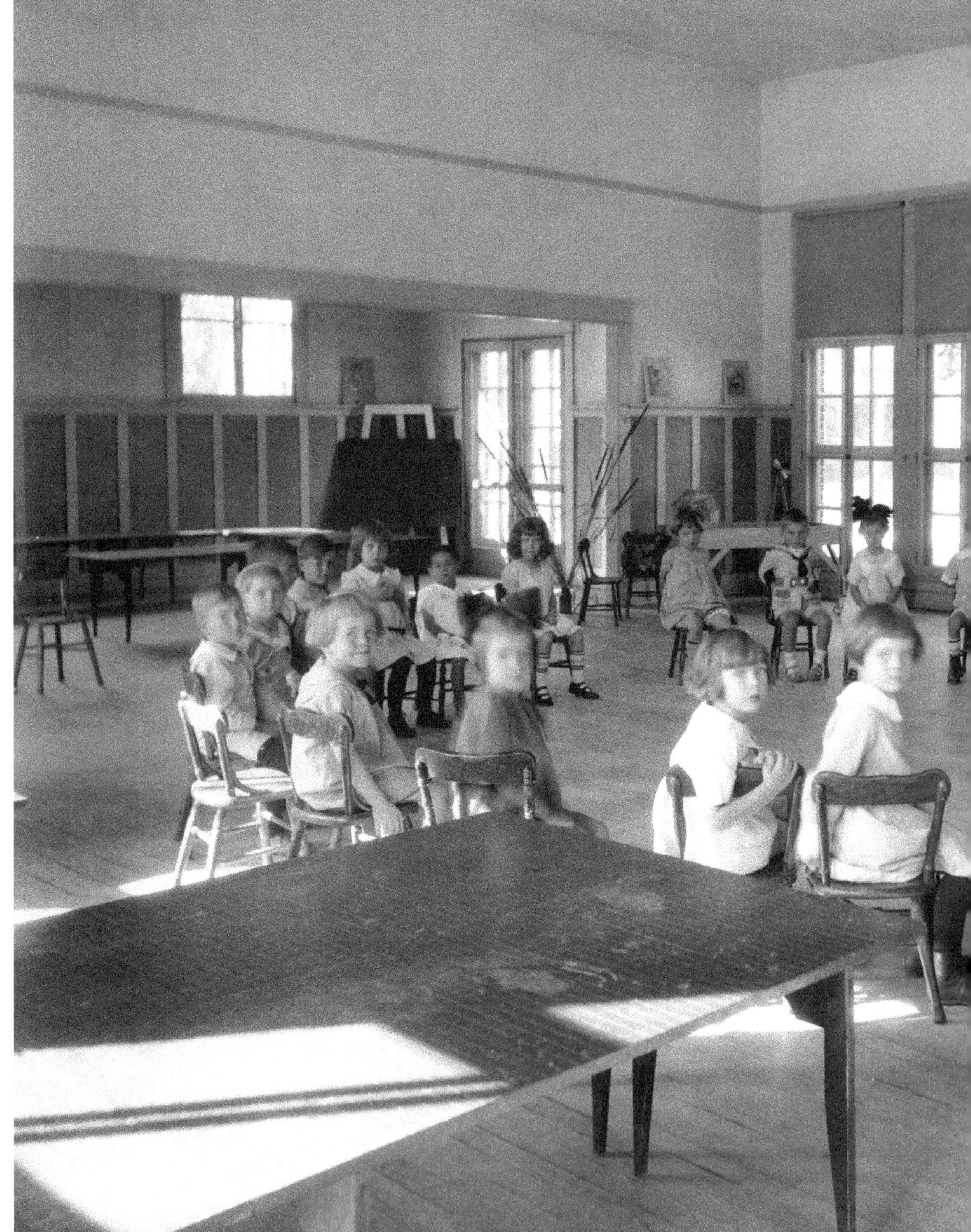

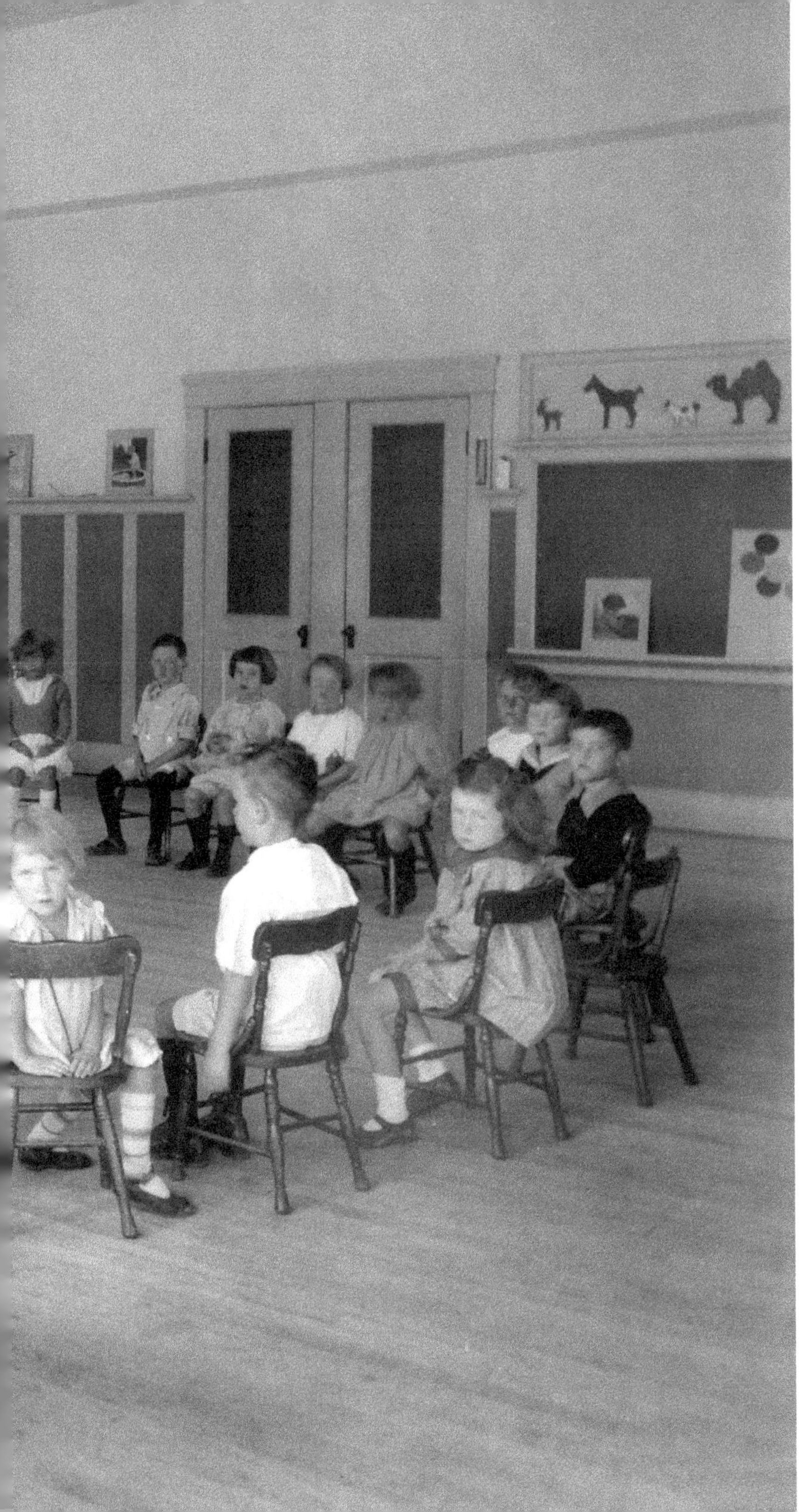

In 1840 Friedrich Wilhelm August Froebel of Germany opened the first kindergarten in commemoration of the four-hundredth anniversary of Gutenberg's invention of movable type. In the United States, the first kindergarten was established in Wisconsin by German immigrants in 1856. The first English-language kindergarten in America started three years later in Boston. It wasn't until 1873 that kindergarten became part of public education. Pictured here is a 1930s kindergarten class at Phoenix's McKinley School.

The first chartered flight from Sky Harbor Airport took place in November 1928, when Scenic Airways flew passengers to the opening of the Rocky Point Fishing Club. Pilots who used Sky Harbor, which started as a cotton field, nicknamed it "the Farm" because they often had to buzz the field before landing in order to clear the runway of grazing cows. Governor Hunt stands before an airmail service airplane here in 1931.

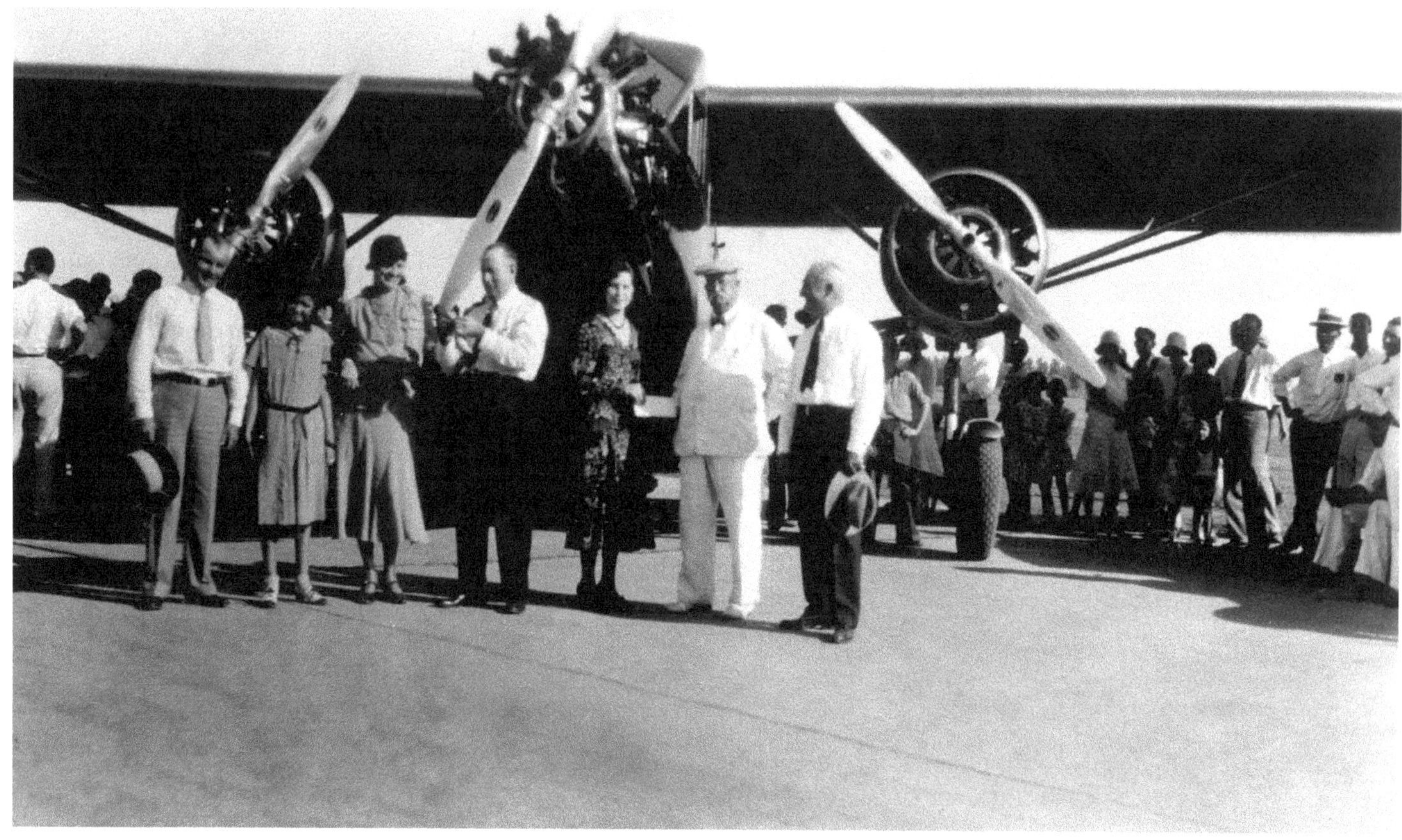

A 1930s view of the Phoenix cityscape, probably from the Westward Ho Hotel, which was the tallest building in Phoenix at the time.

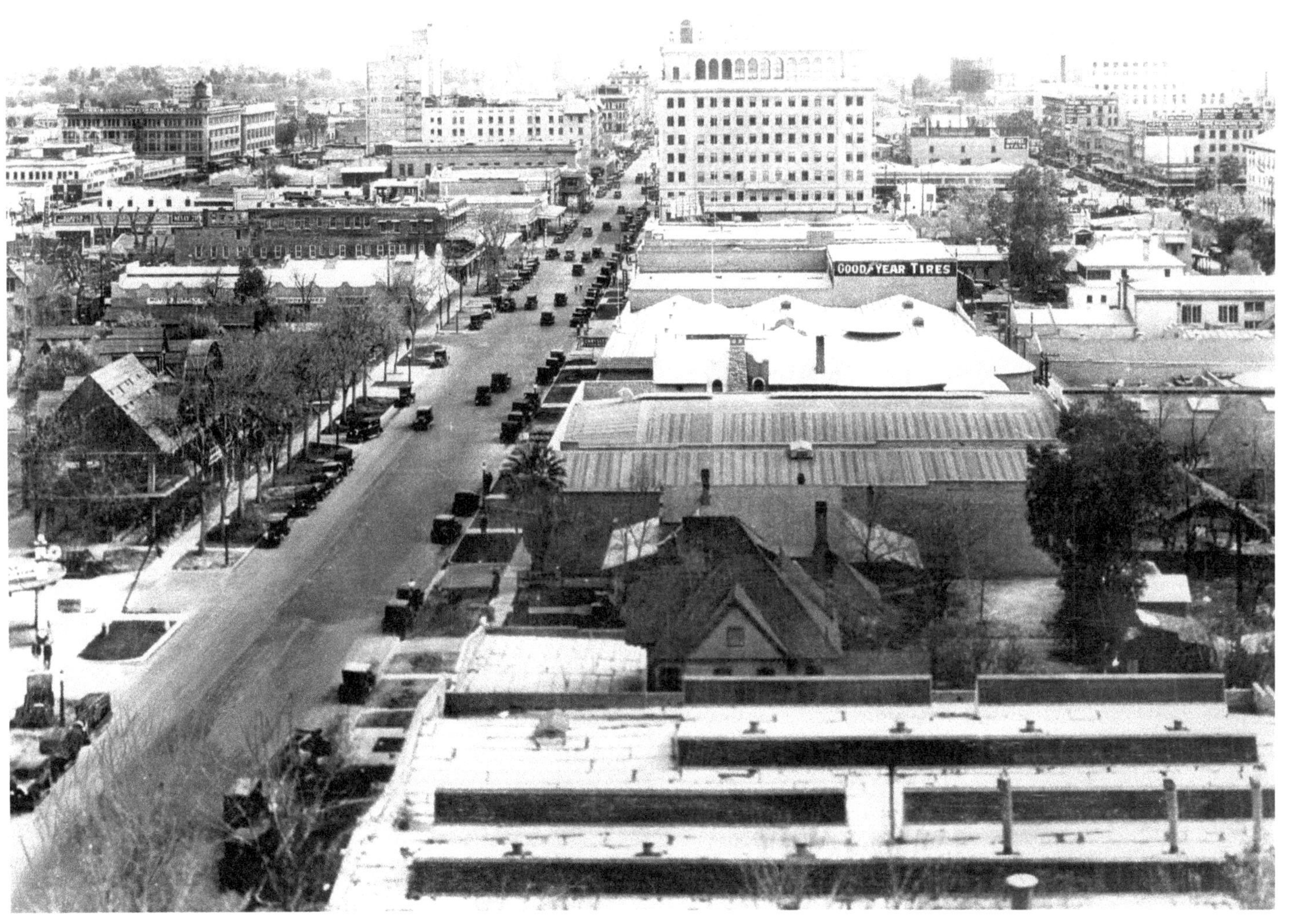

Mary Green and her two children were the first African Americans to arrive in Phoenix. As agricultural production grew in the Phoenix region, farming associations such as the Cotton Growers or Farm Bureau recruited African Americans to the area. In time, African Americans became the second-largest minority in Phoenix after Mexican Americans. Although race relations were not as strident in Phoenix as in other parts of the country, Phoenix was a segregated city.

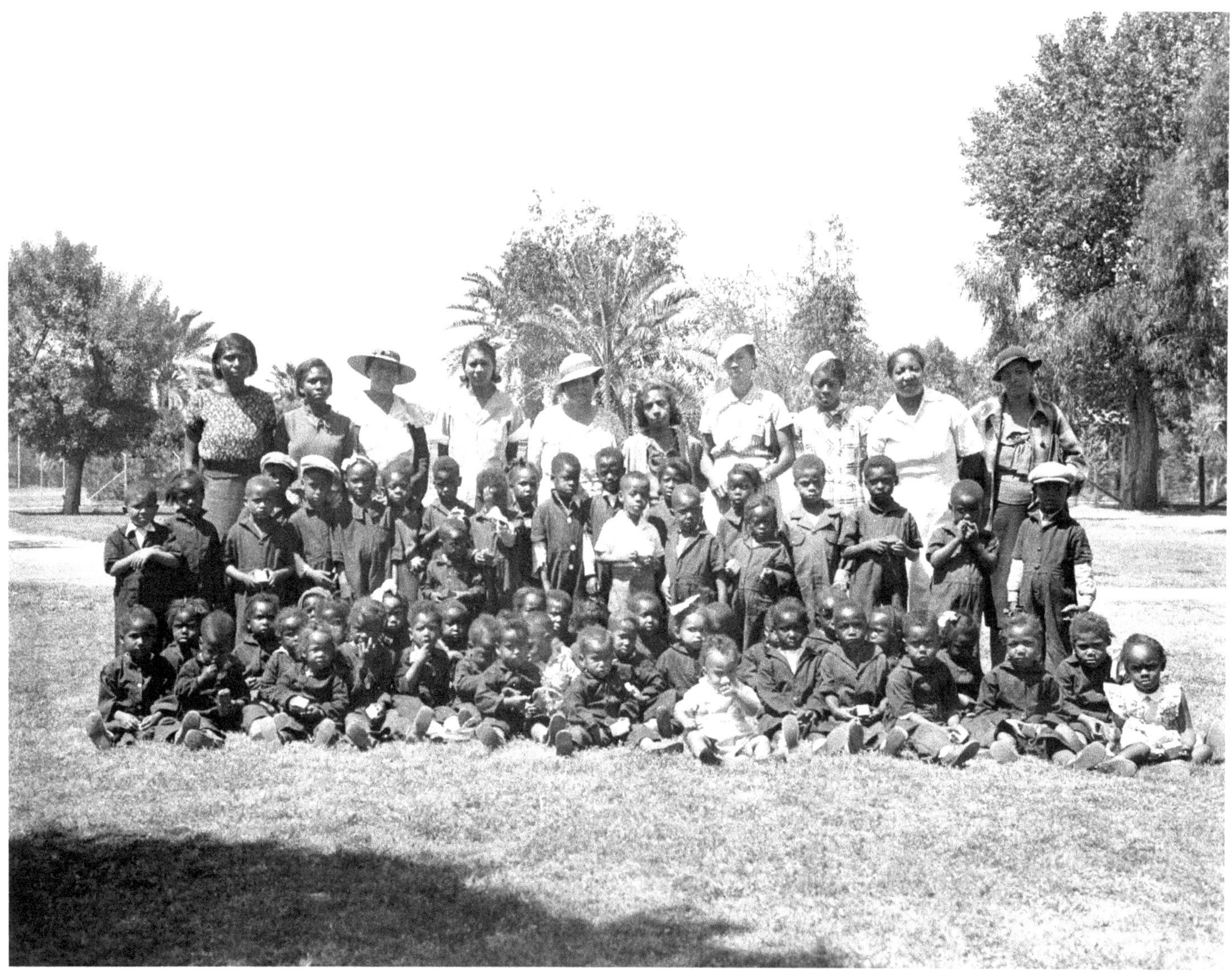

Swimming in the canals for recreation was a favorite pastime for Arizonans. Pictured here are three men wearing the latest fashion in swimming suits.

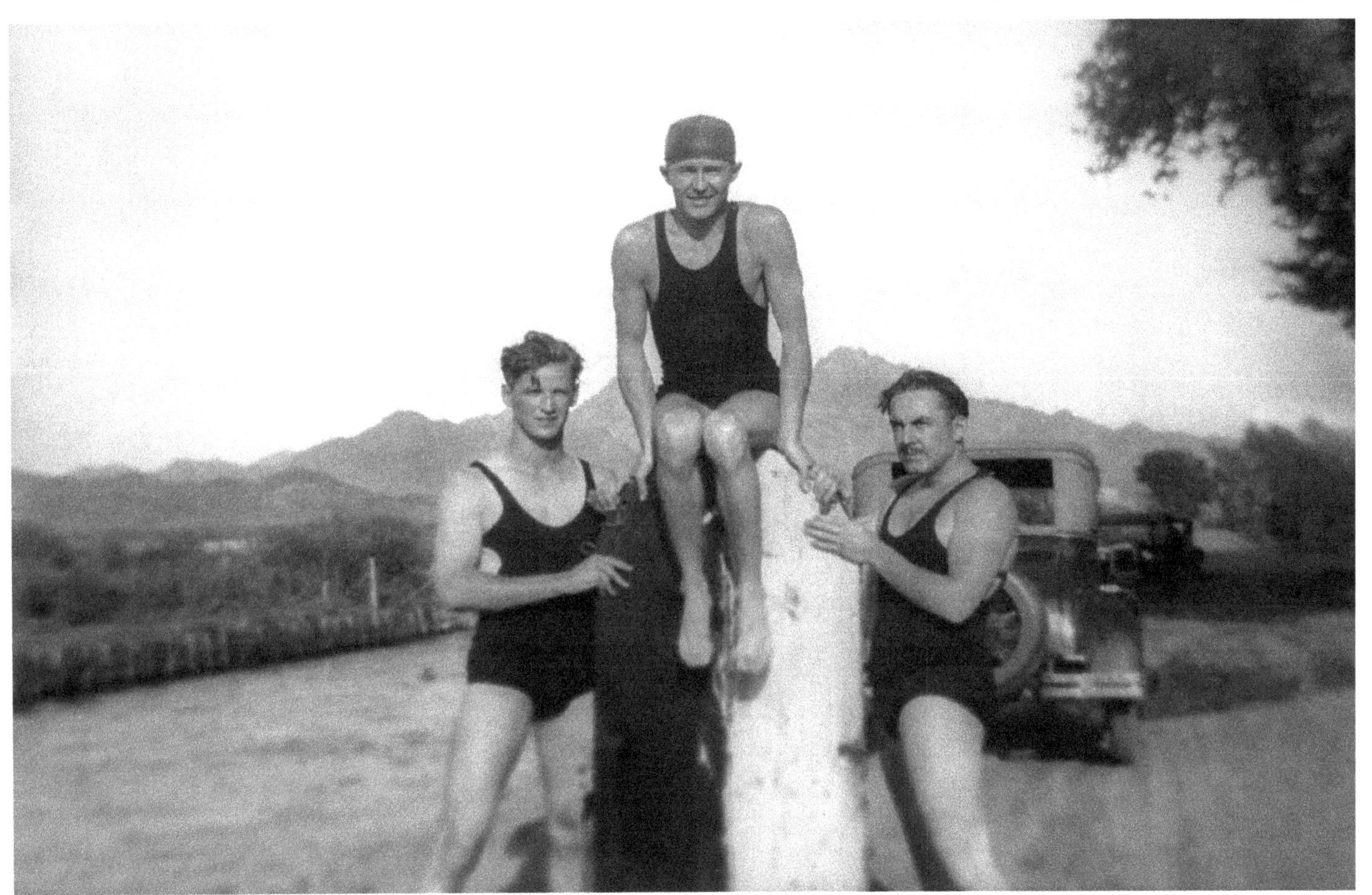

Children playing on the playground at Trinity Cathedral in 1934 were part of a program sponsored by the WPA.

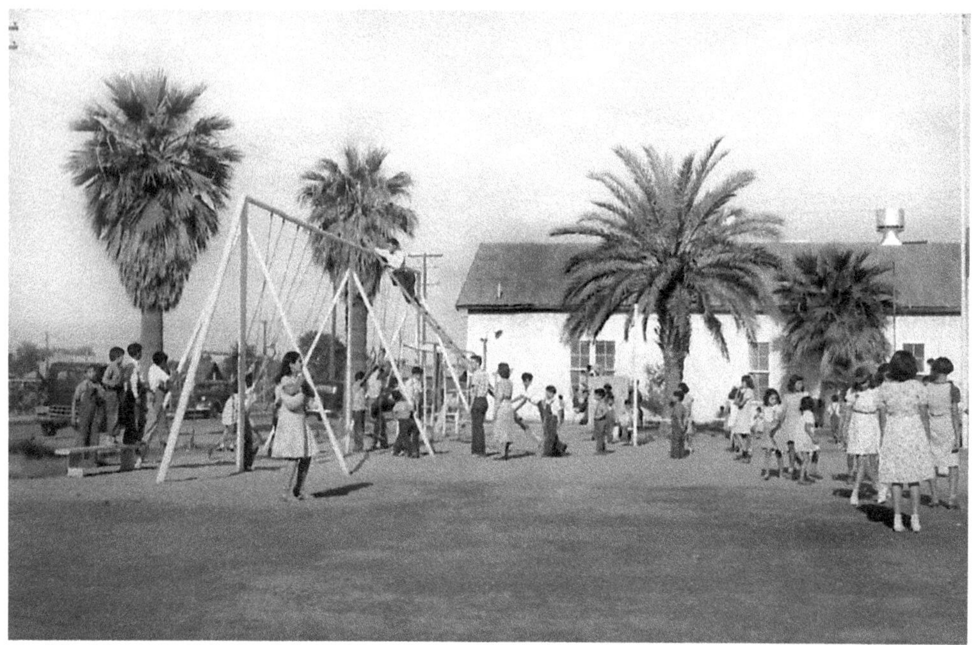

The development of new fabrics made possible more comfortable and practical swim wear than had been enjoyed by earlier generations. In 1907, not so long before this 1930s photograph was taken, Australian swimmer Annette Kellerman was arrested for indecent exposure while touring in the United States because her swimsuit exposed her arms, legs, and neck. In 1916, she became the first film star to pose fully nude, in the film *A Daughter of the Gods.*

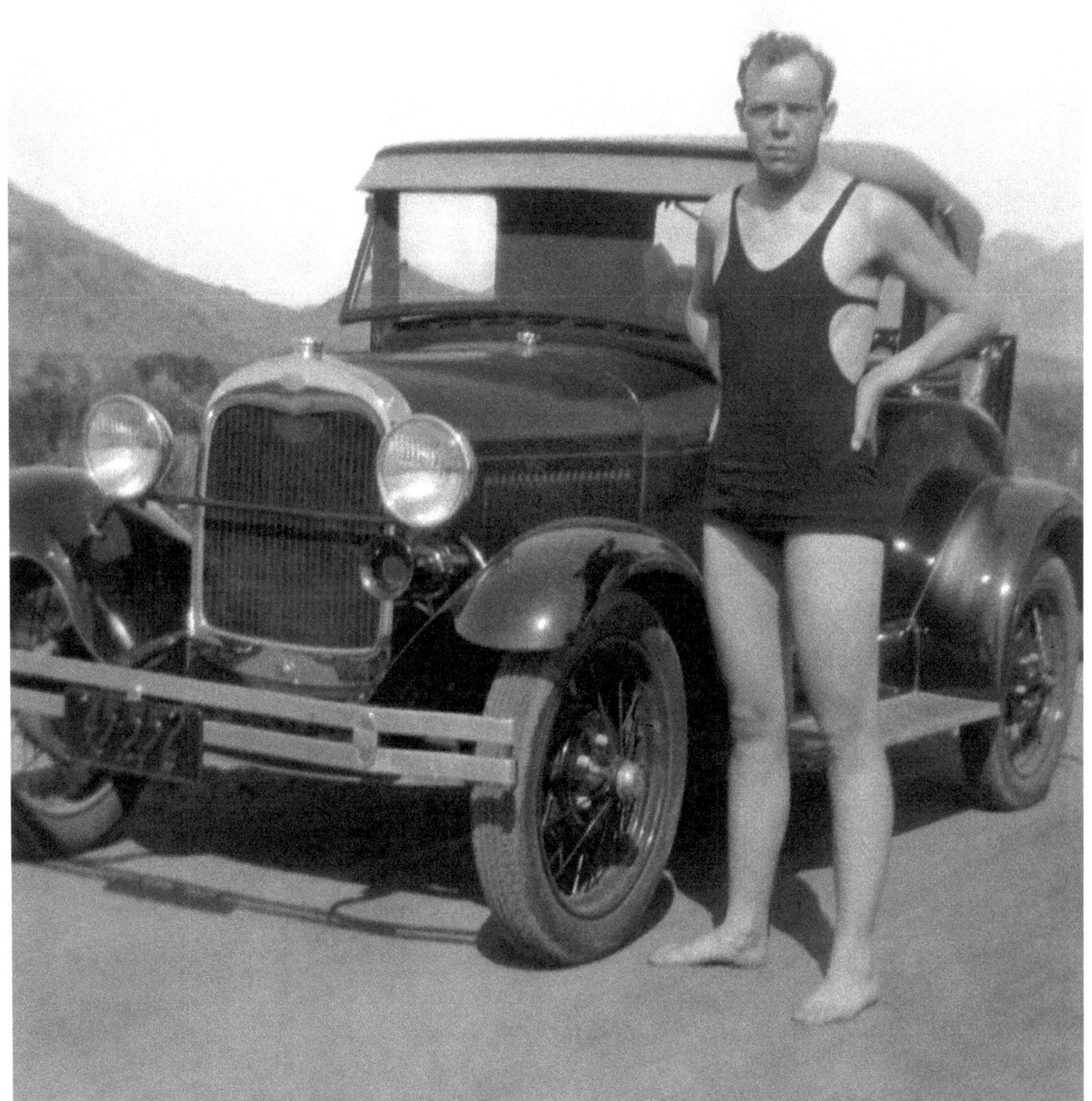

As Phoenix spread outward from the city center, many roads remained unpaved. Here a Civil Works Administration road construction crew is preparing Henshaw Road and 24th Street for paving.

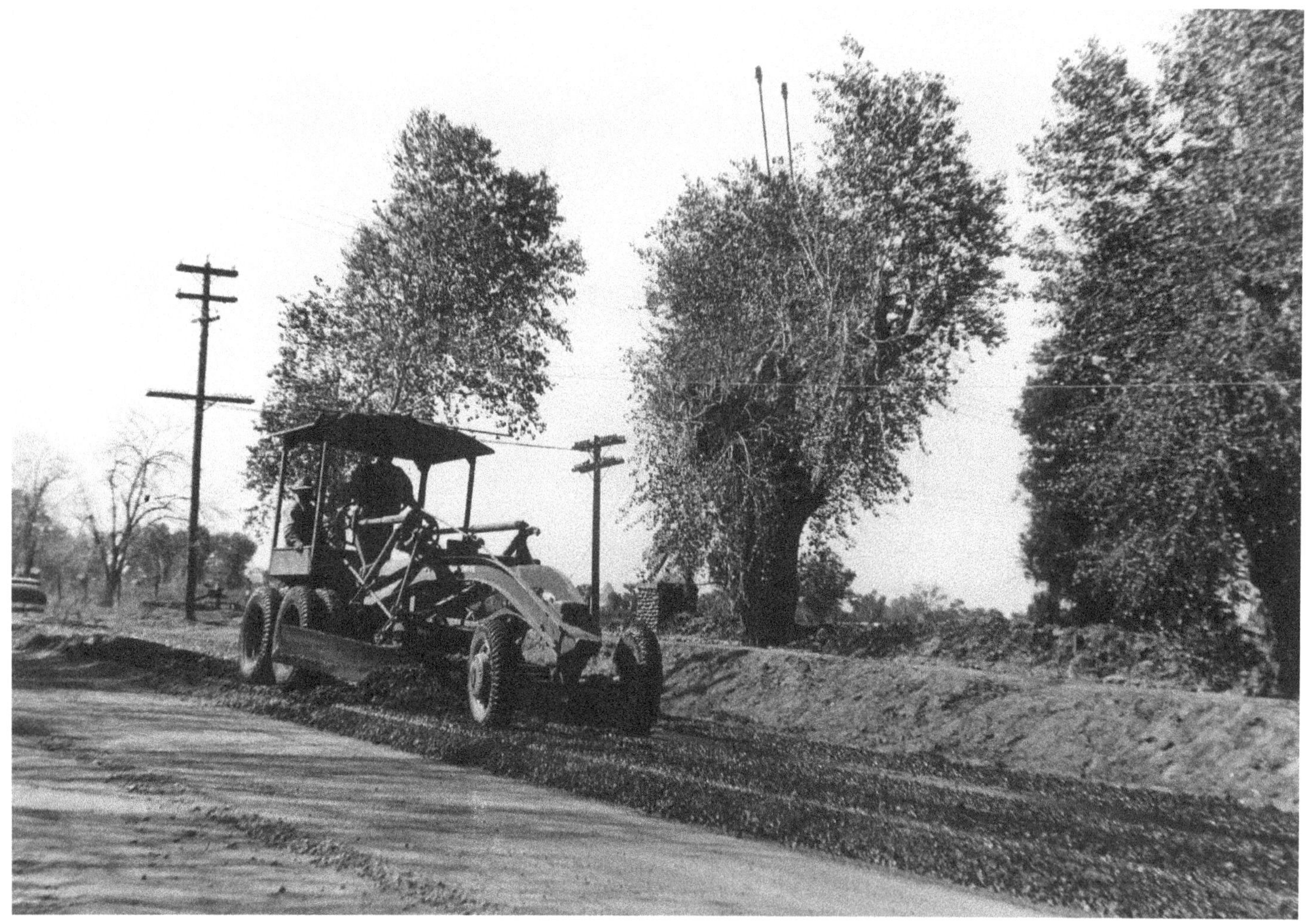

President Franklin D. Roosevelt unveiled the Civil Works Administration (CWA) in 1933 to create temporary jobs for millions of the unemployed. The CWA focused mainly on construction—improving or constructing buildings, bridges, and roadways. This 1934 photograph shows CWA workers paving 19th Avenue in Phoenix.

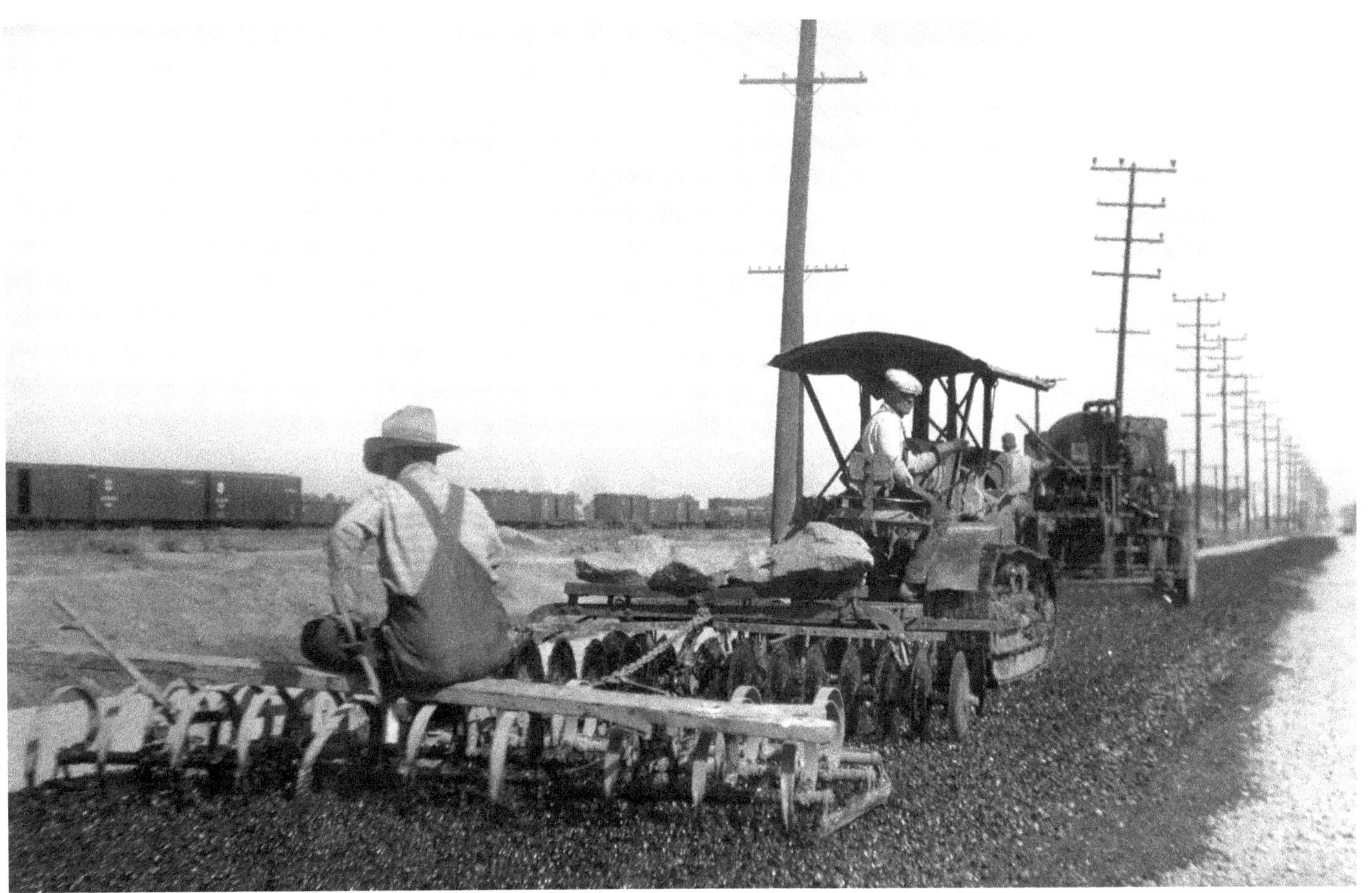

The Boy Scouts of America was one of the leading youth organizations that arose during the Progressive Movement in the early twentieth century. With rural families migrating to urban areas, many social activists became concerned that young men were failing to learn the values of self-sufficiency and patriotism. This Phoenix amphitheater was built for the Boy Scouts by the Civil Works Administration.

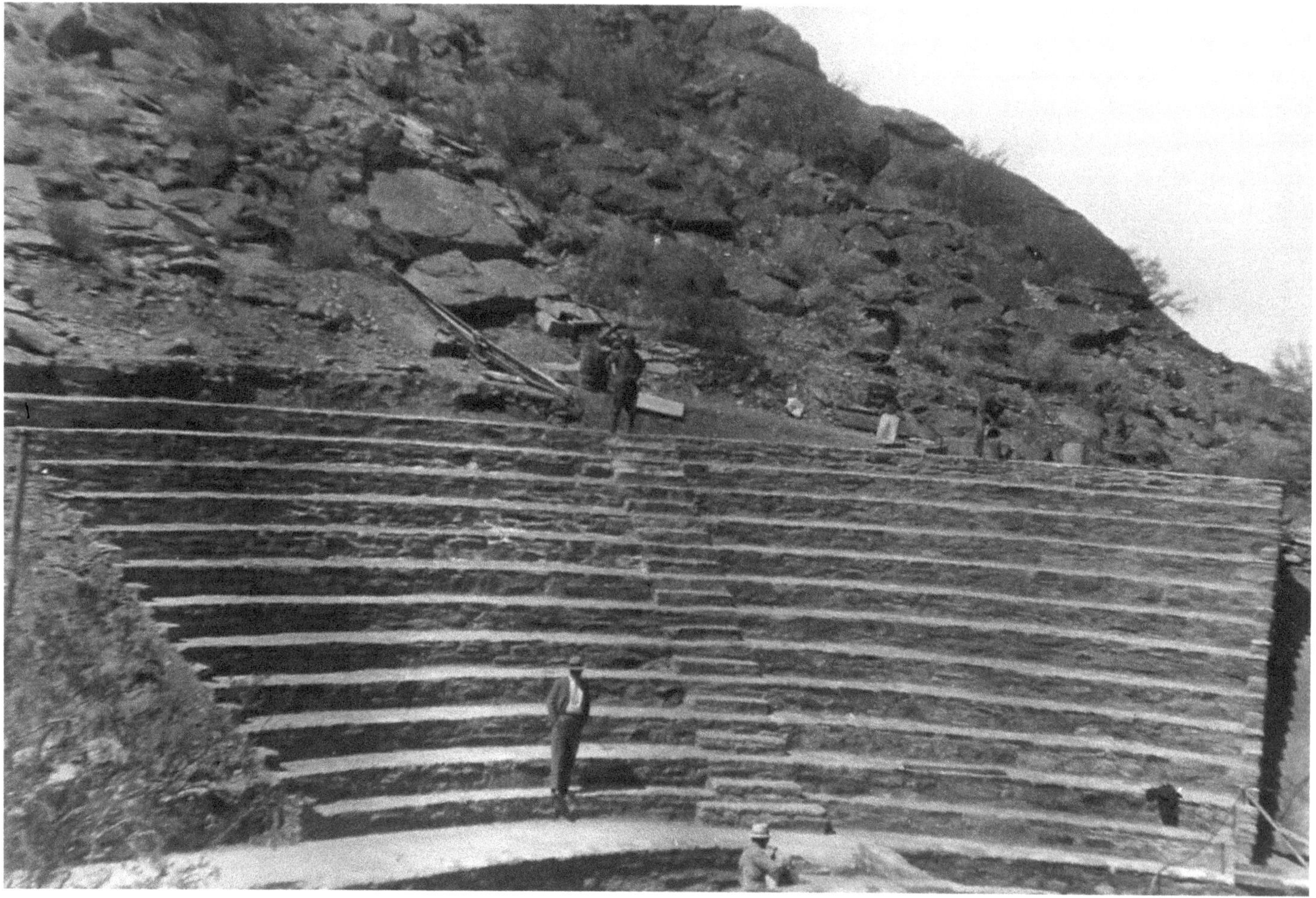

The WPA also offered job training for the underemployed. The young women pictured here are being trained in food preparation.

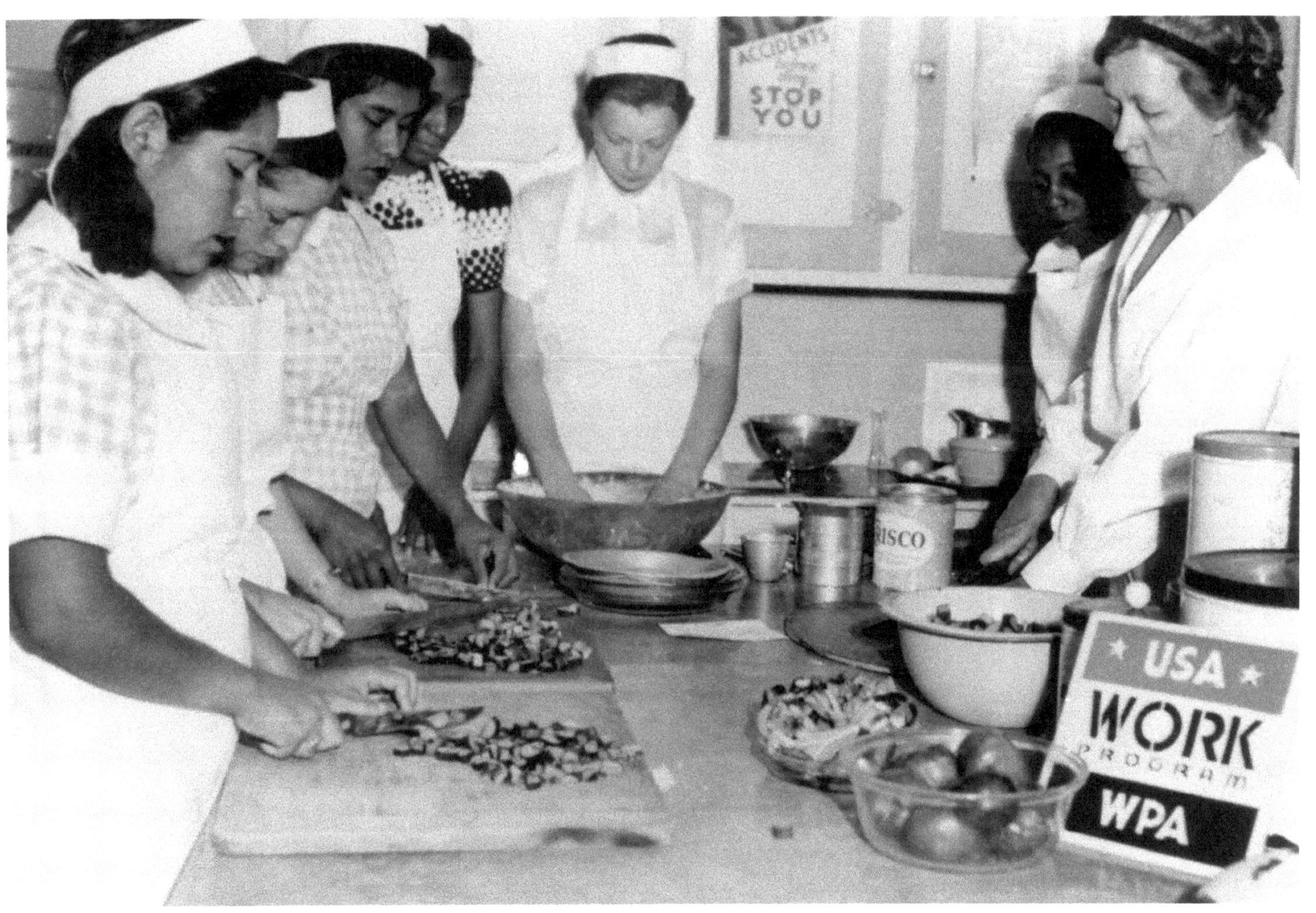

Phoenix meat cutters are working on an Emergency Relief Administration project in 1934.

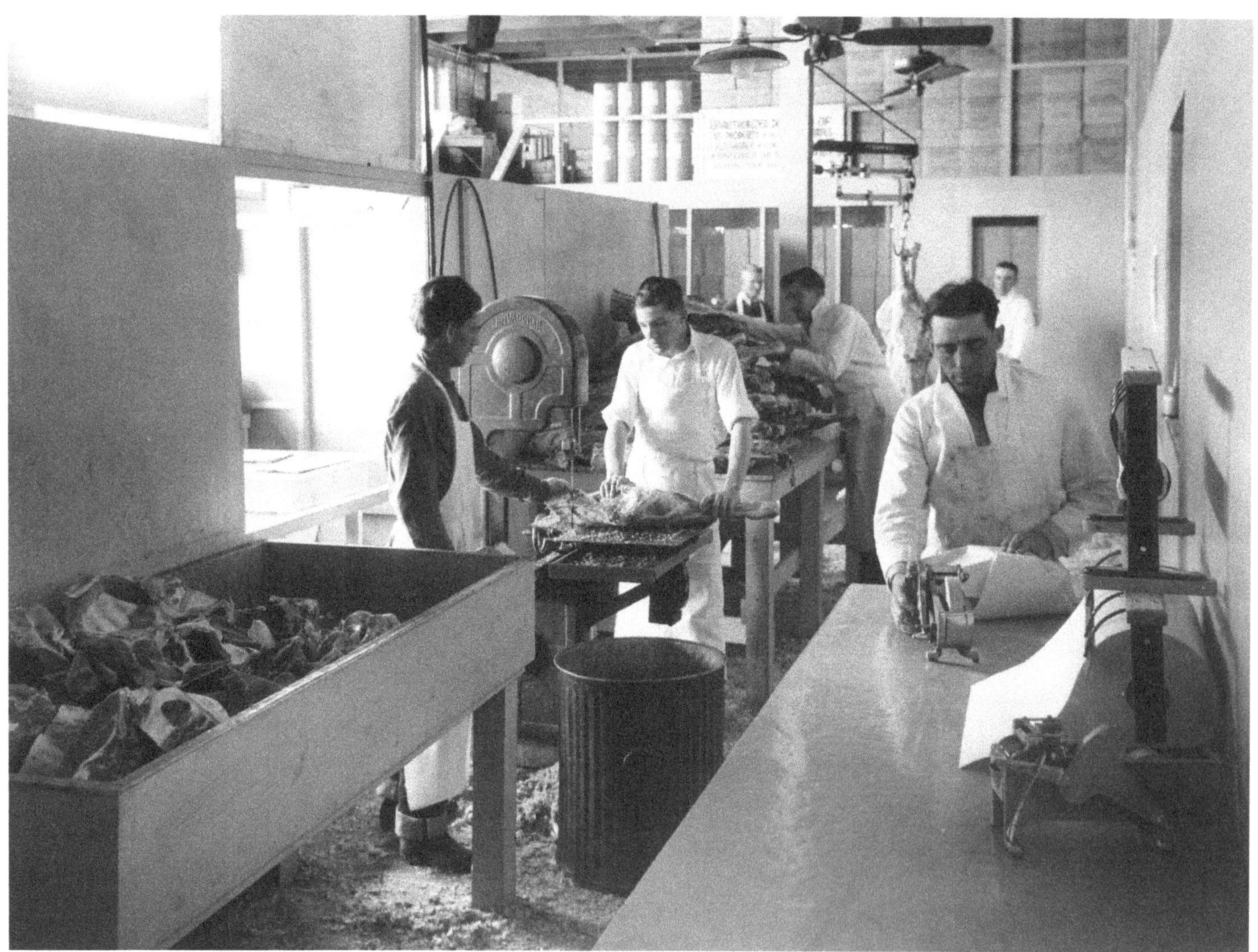

Much of South Mountain Park's infrastructure was constructed by the Civilian Conservation Corps in the early 1930s. South Mountain Park is the largest city park in the United States, the second largest urban park in North America, and among the largest municipal parks in the world. These Civil Works Administration employees gather to enjoy a picnic at the park in 1934.

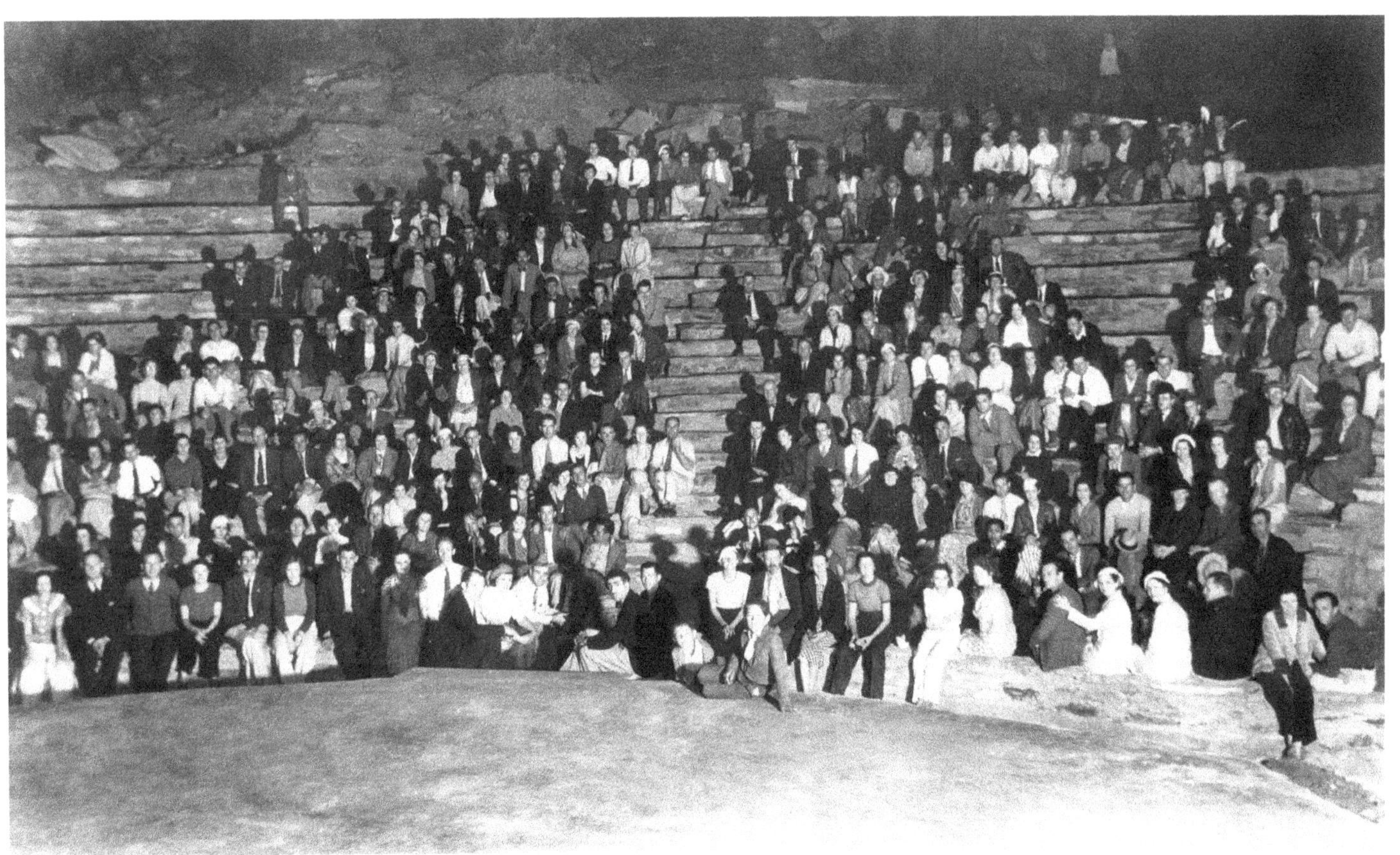

Artists and dramatists employed by the Works Progress Administration produced plays and pageants in part to entertain but also to educate. This 1934 Thanksgiving play was presented by the WPA in Phoenix, complete with faux Indians in anachronistic costume.

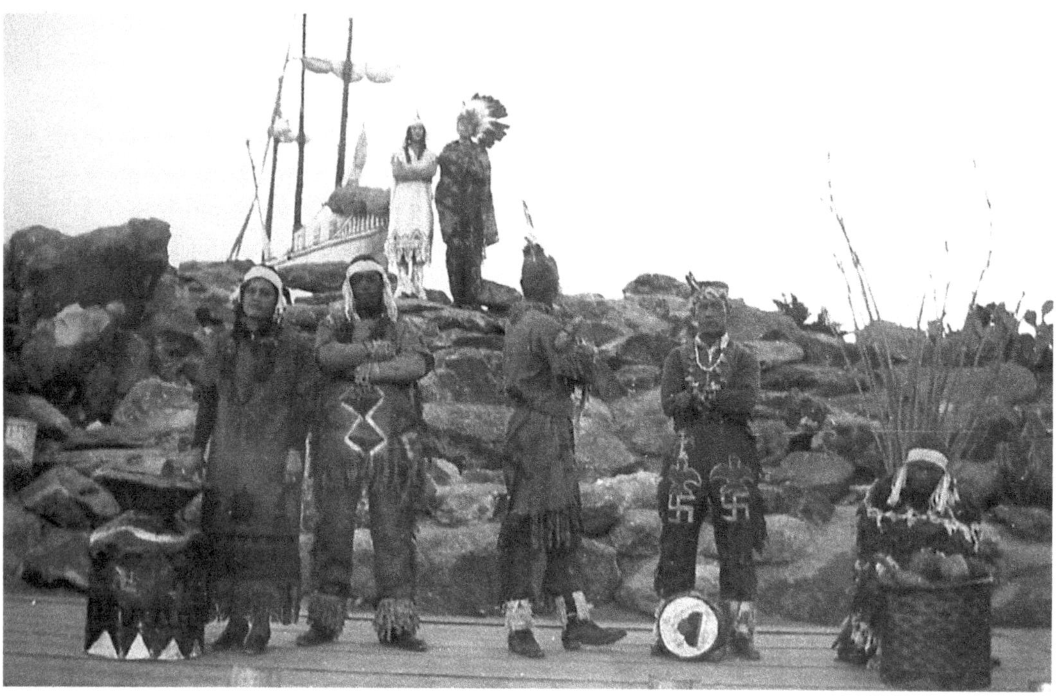

Children gather around a handicraft table sponsored by the Phoenix Optimist Club in cooperation with the WPA. The veranda providing shade to the children was a common feature of older Phoenix homes and buildings.

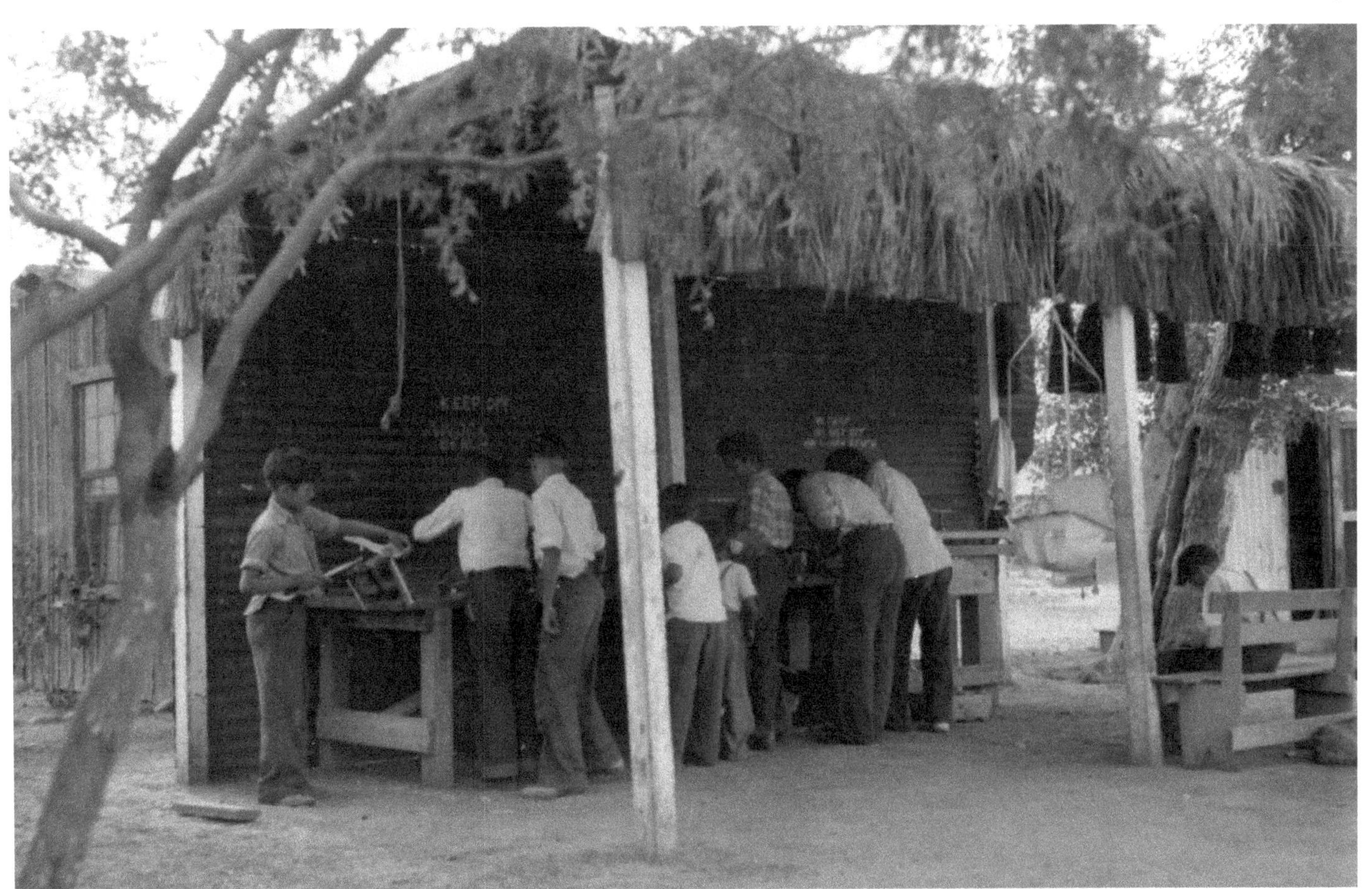

The Civil Works Administration employed laborers in all kinds of work. Pictured here are CWA clerks in 1934.

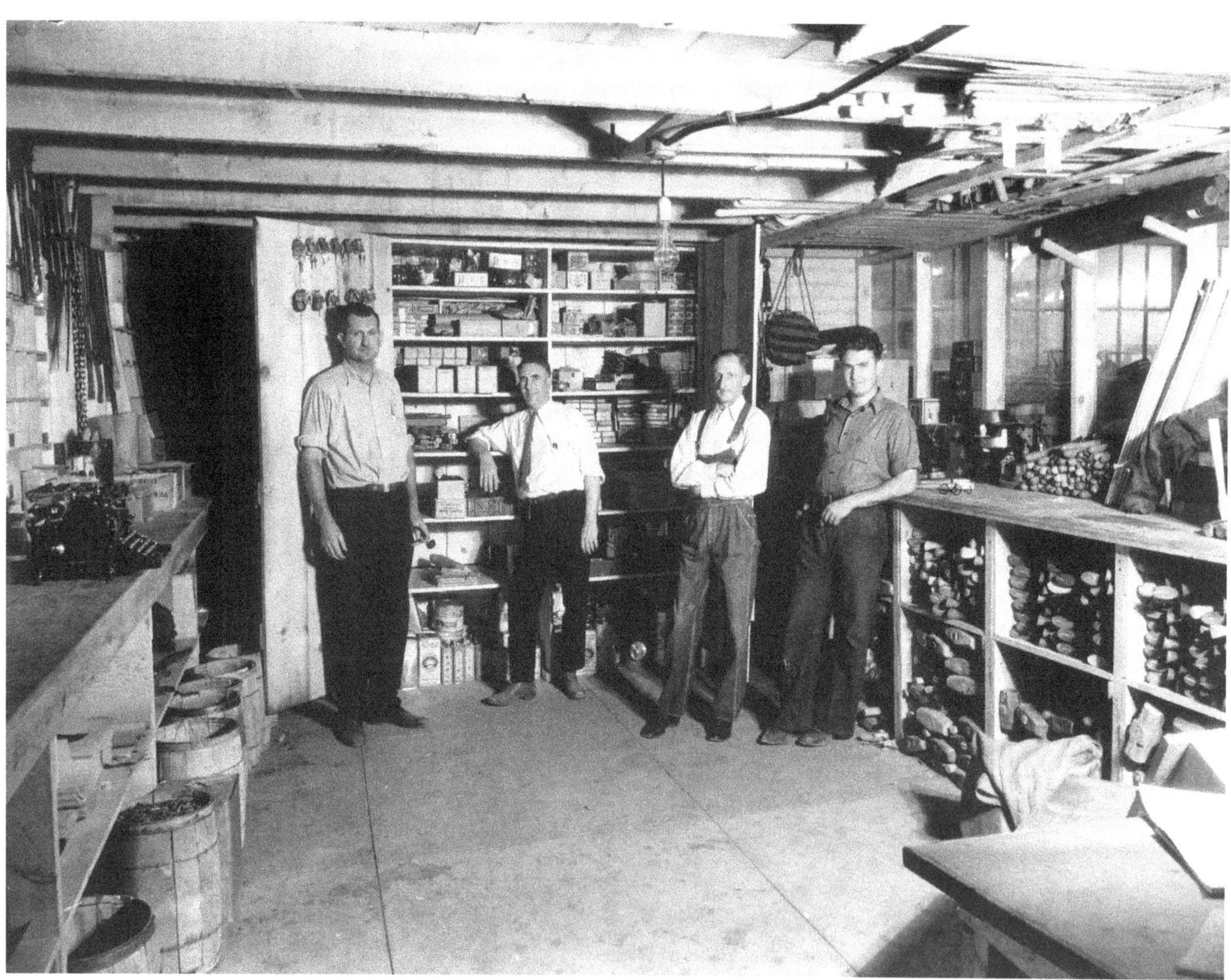

CWA crews apply cement with a high-pressure gun as part of a 1934 road construction project in Phoenix.

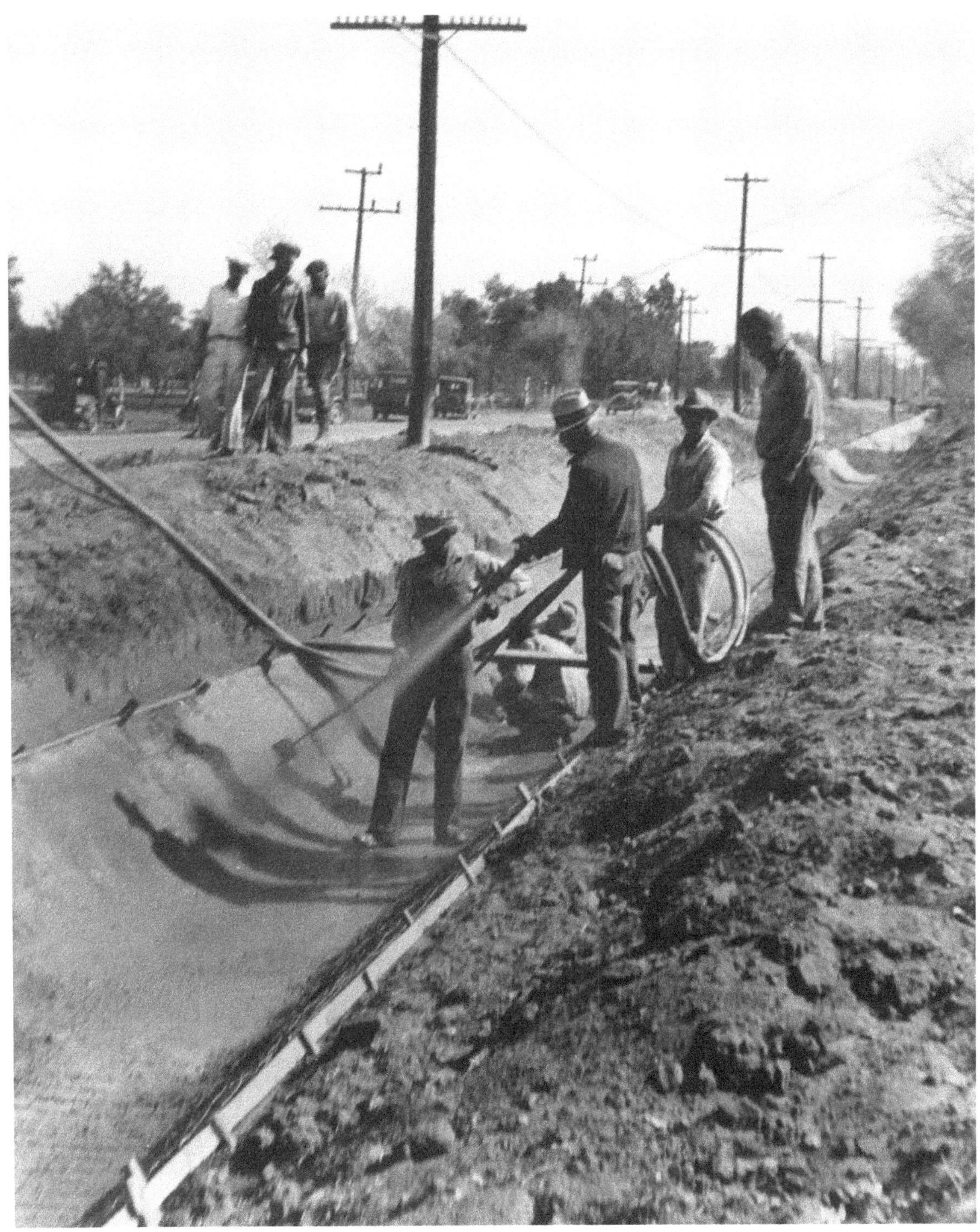

The Civil Works Administration built "transient camps" for out-of-state workers employed on projects. These camps, built out of prefabricated housing sections, included dormitories, showers, an infirmary, a bakery, an outdoor stage, and recreational fields for sports. Pictured here are residents playing baseball at an Emergency Relief Administration Transient Camp in Phoenix.

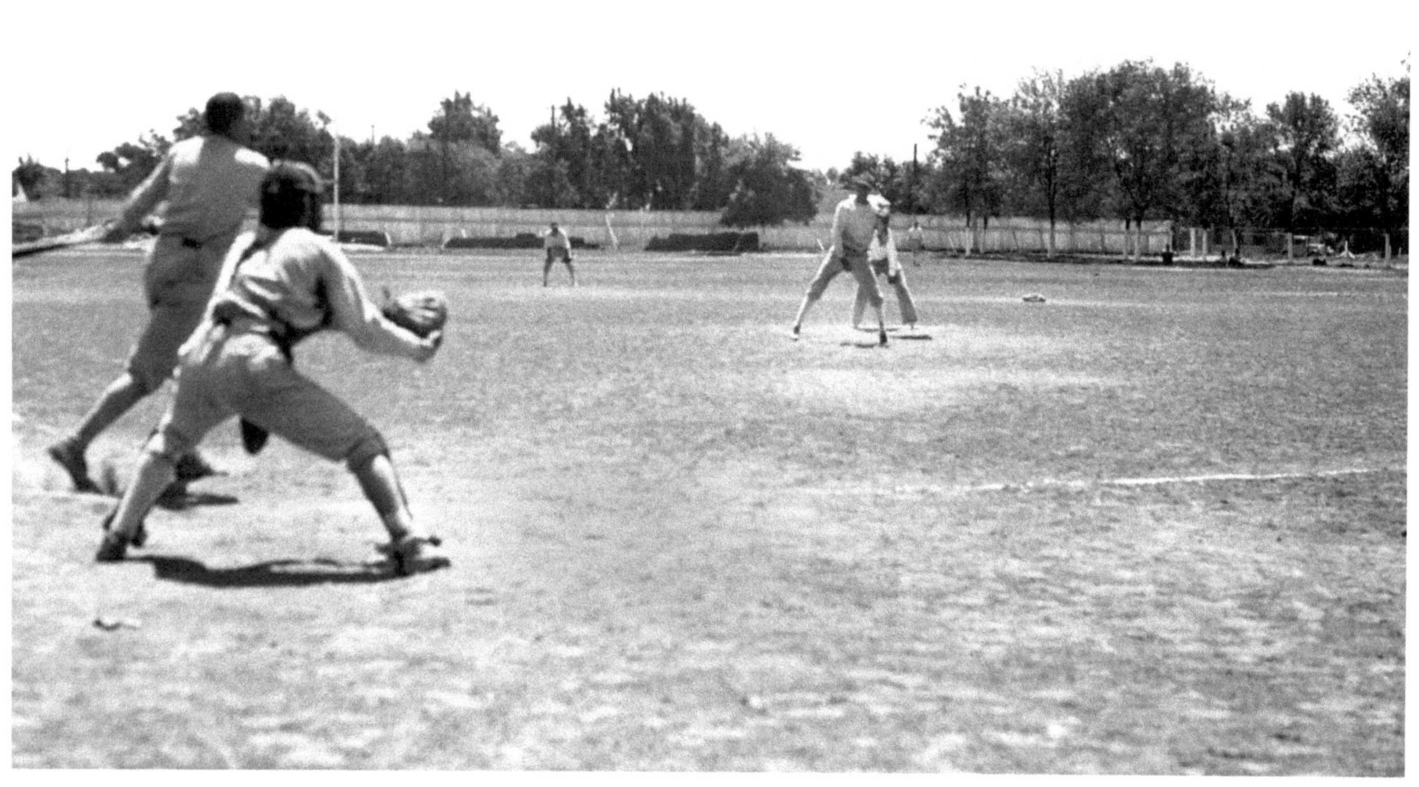

Part of modernization for many Phoenicians meant having a green lawn, made possible largely by the invention of sprinklers. The appreciation of desert landscaping would come only decades later when the demand for water began to challenge supply and water conservation became an important part of life in the desert.

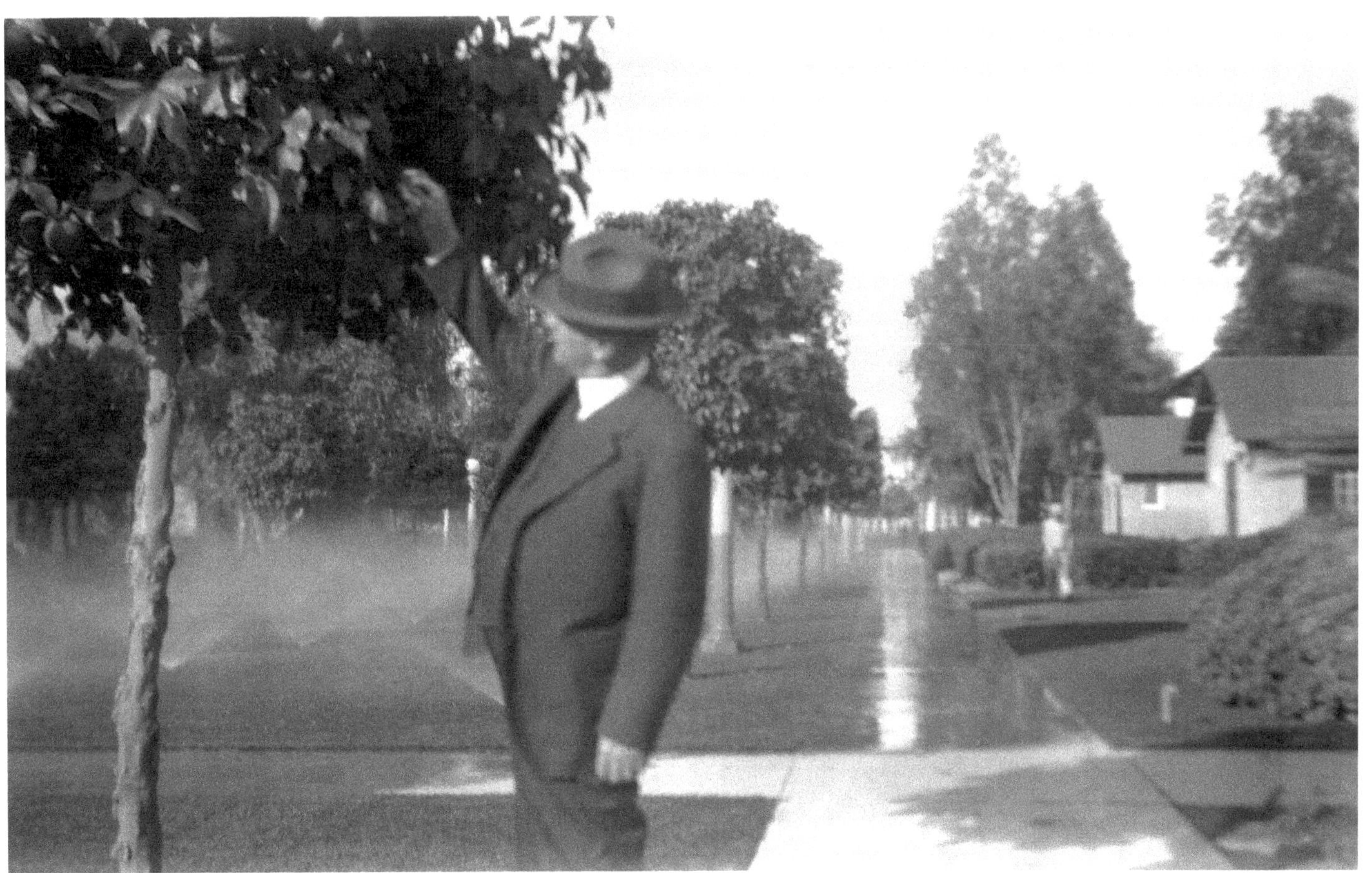

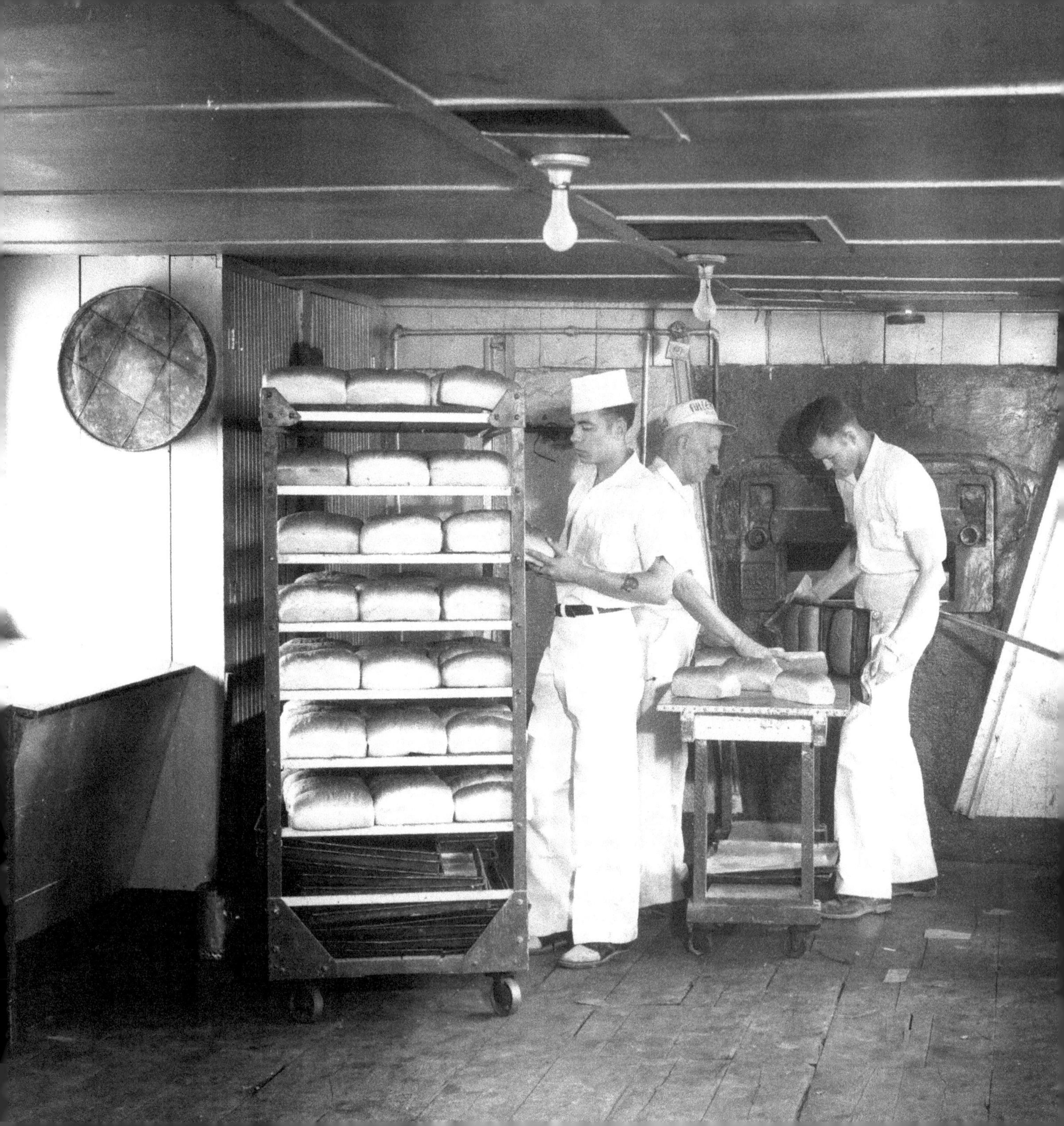

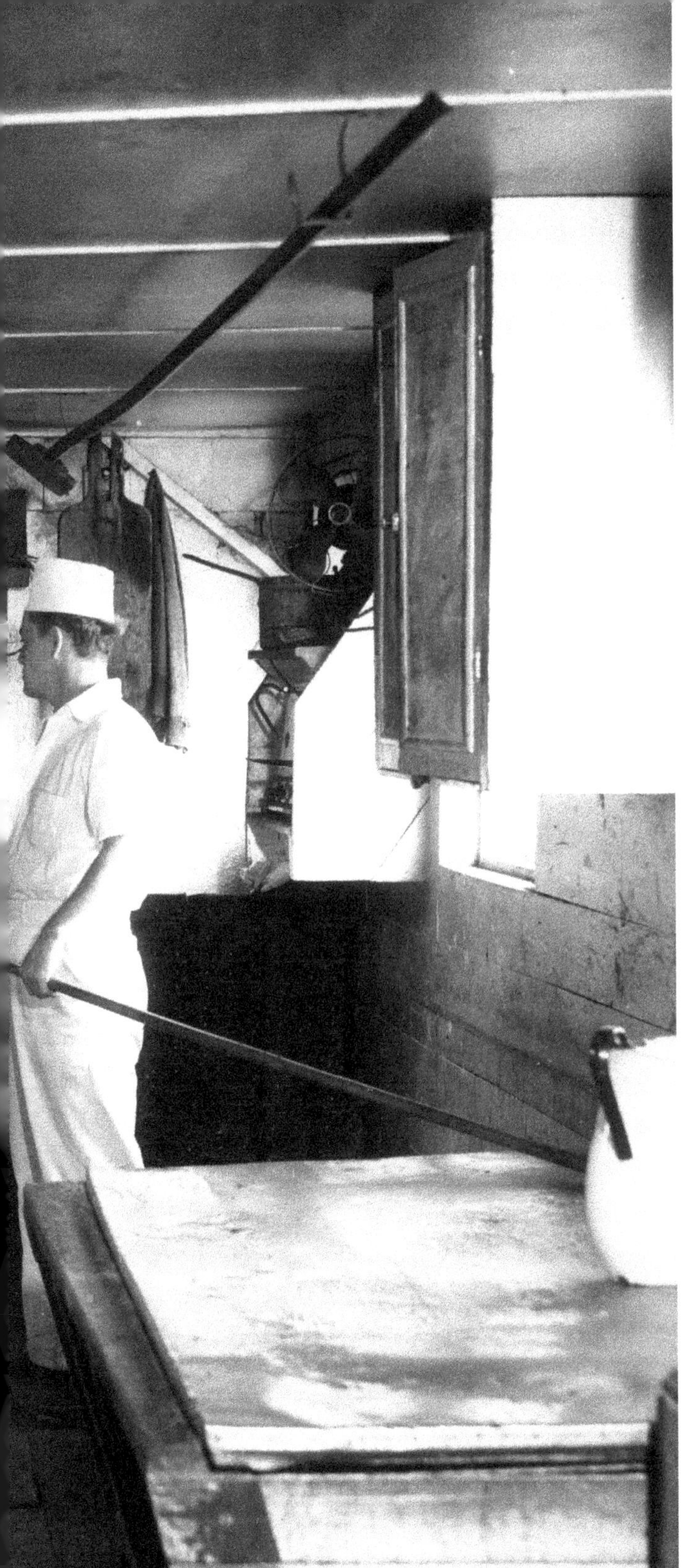

Emergency Relief Administration workers in 1935 bake bread at a transient camp.

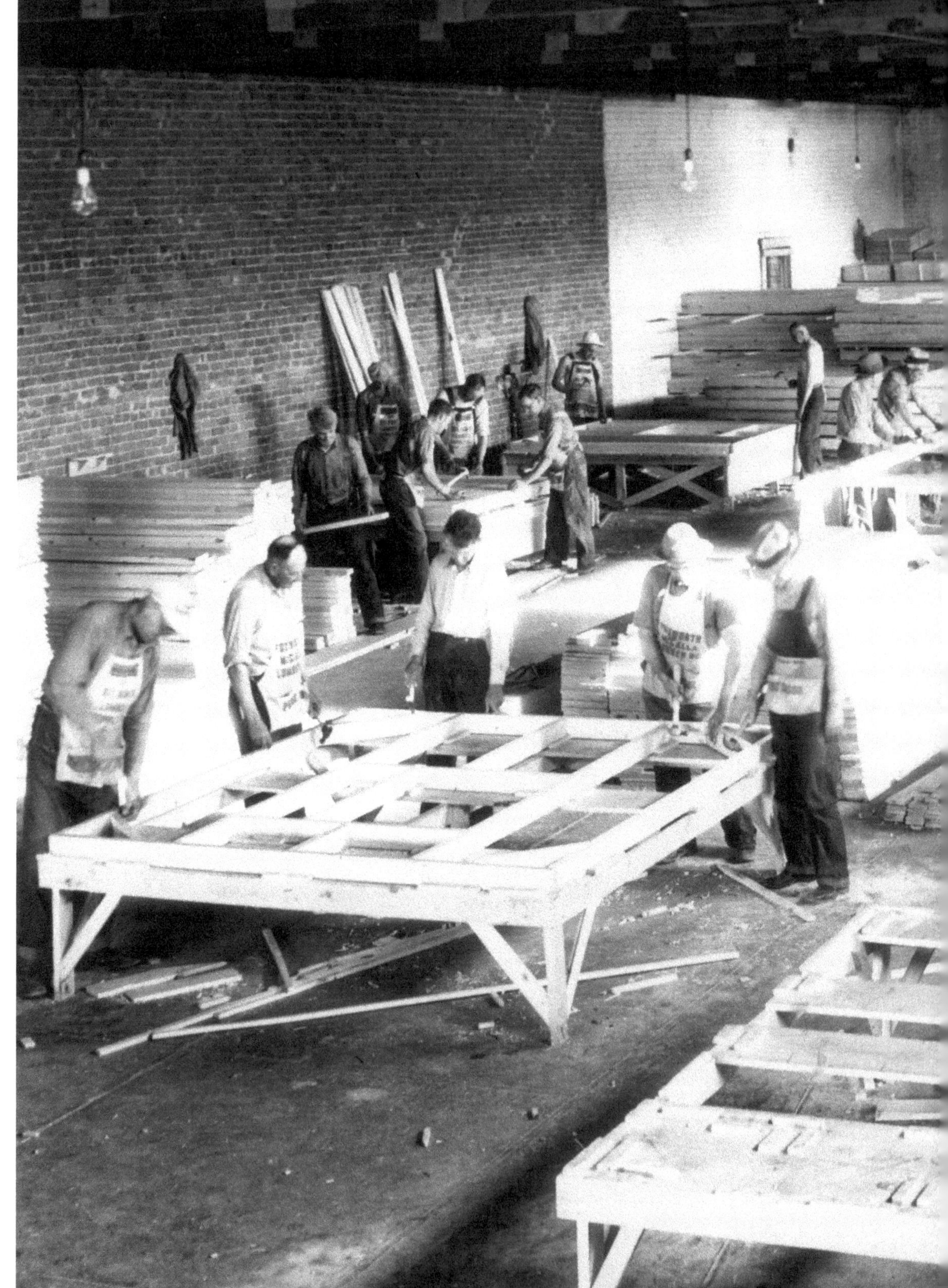

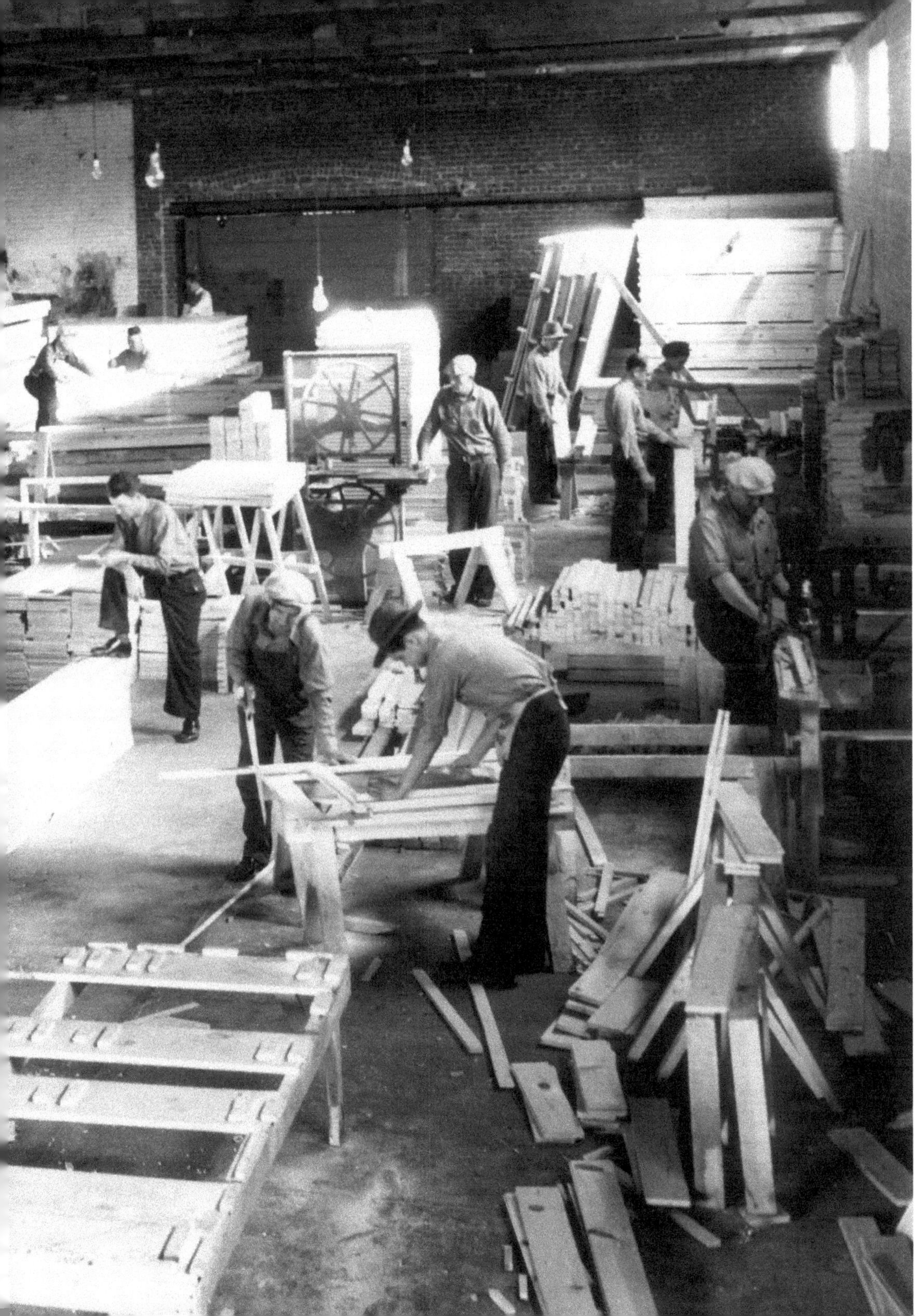

Shown here are Emergency Relief Administration workers in Phoenix building prefabricated housing units for transient camps.

Older American cities once used wood stave pipes for their sewers, but after the 1850s cities generally used vitrified clay, cement mortar, or brick for sewer lines. The Arizona Highway Department is installing concrete pipes here in 1935.

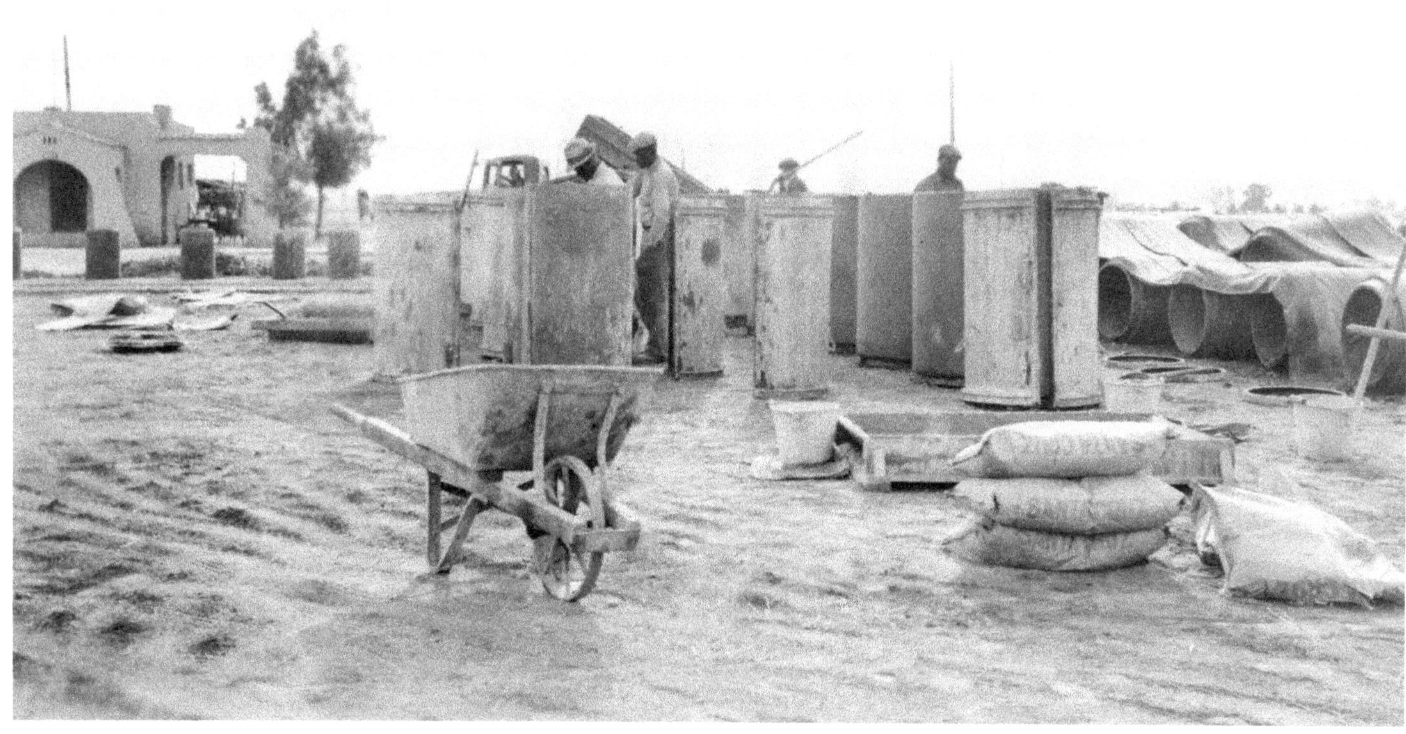

The working area of the Civil Works Administration office in Phoenix.

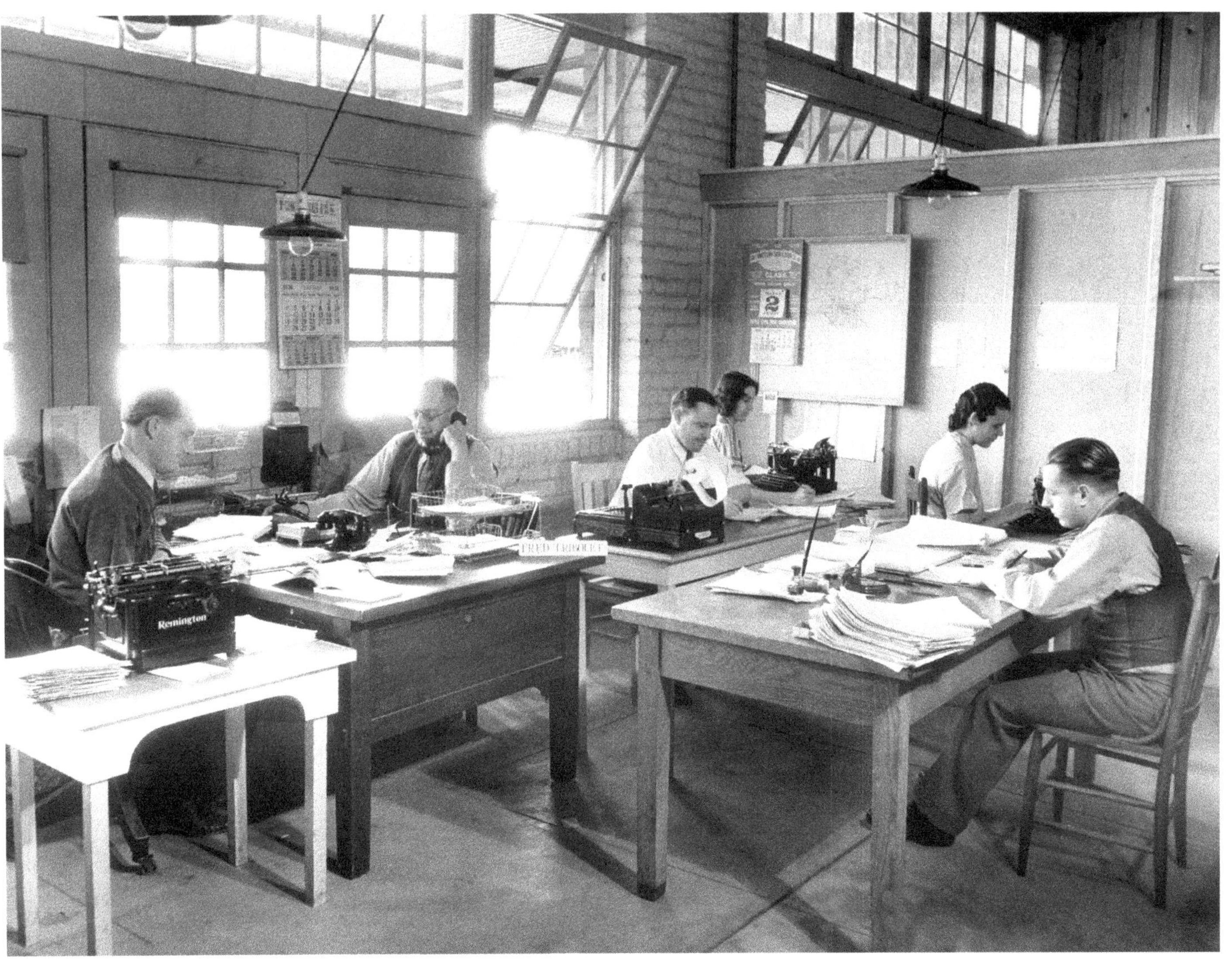

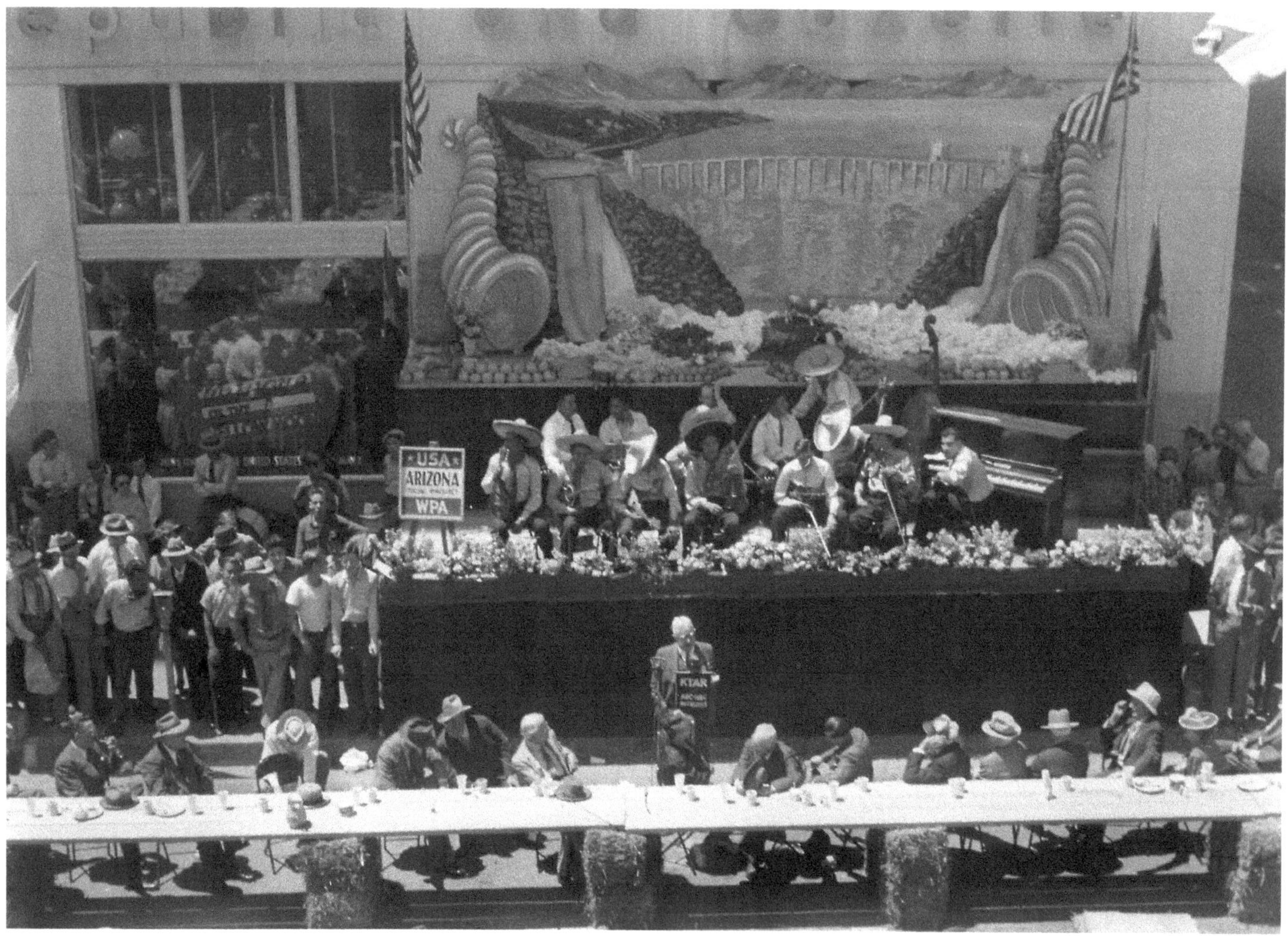

Mariachis play as citizens gather in 1936 in front of the *Arizona Republic–Phoenix Gazette* offices. A cornucopia exhibit is shown in front of a replica of Hoover Dam with a Works Progress Administration sign. Construction of the dam began in 1931 and generators began transmitting electricity from the Colorado River to Phoenix in 1936.

Emergency Relief Administration artists were employed to create friezes to adorn the Phoenix Fairgrounds. The artist pictured in this 1935 photograph is working in a stable with a horse as her model.

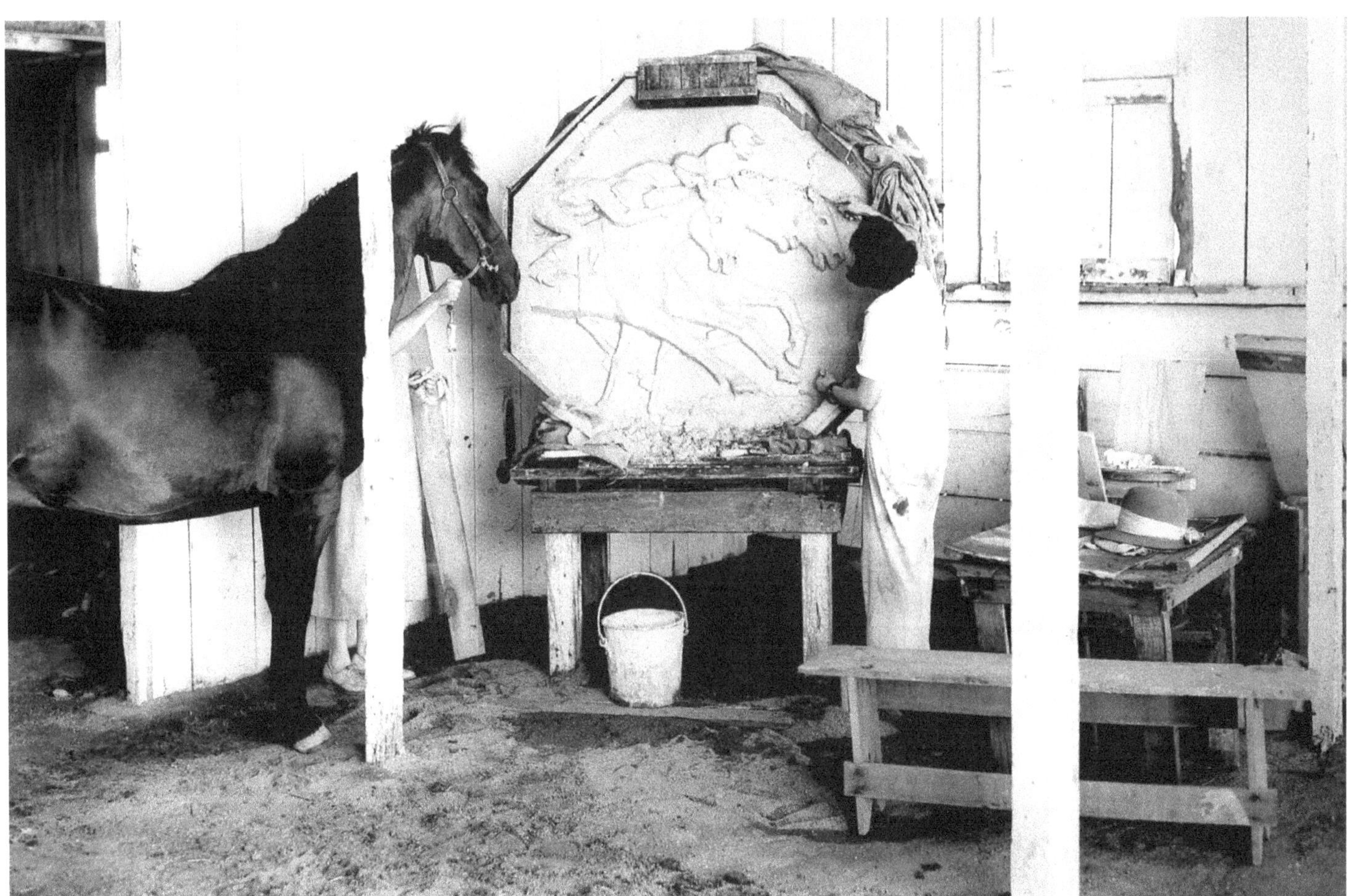

In 1869, the Swilling Canal Company built a canal east of Phoenix in an area that classically educated Darrell Duppa called "Tempe," after the Vale of Tempe in Greece. Charles Trumbull Hayden was the first white settler in Tempe and a Mexican by the name of Mendoza had established a ranch there. In 1936, WPA workers pave East Van Buren in Phoenix, which connected with Mill Avenue in Tempe, linking the two cities together.

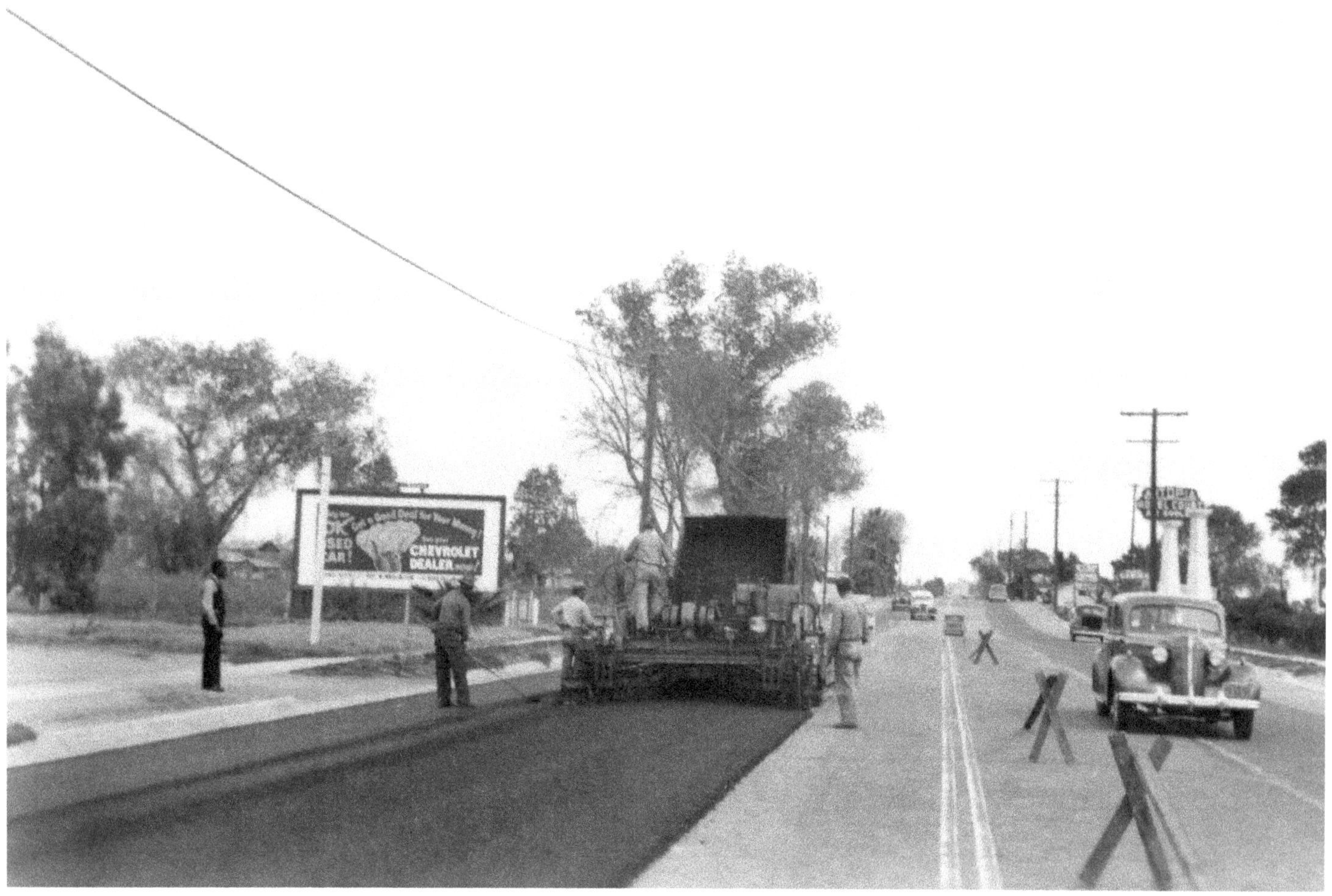

By 1935 downtown Phoenix looked like most modern business districts. Pictured here are stores and shops along Washington Street, including the O. C. Coffee Shop, First National Bank, Valley Lunch Shop, the Hoeppner Electric Company, Hotel Luhrs, and the Angeles Hotel. Note the porticos common to Phoenix shops, protecting customers from the desert sun.

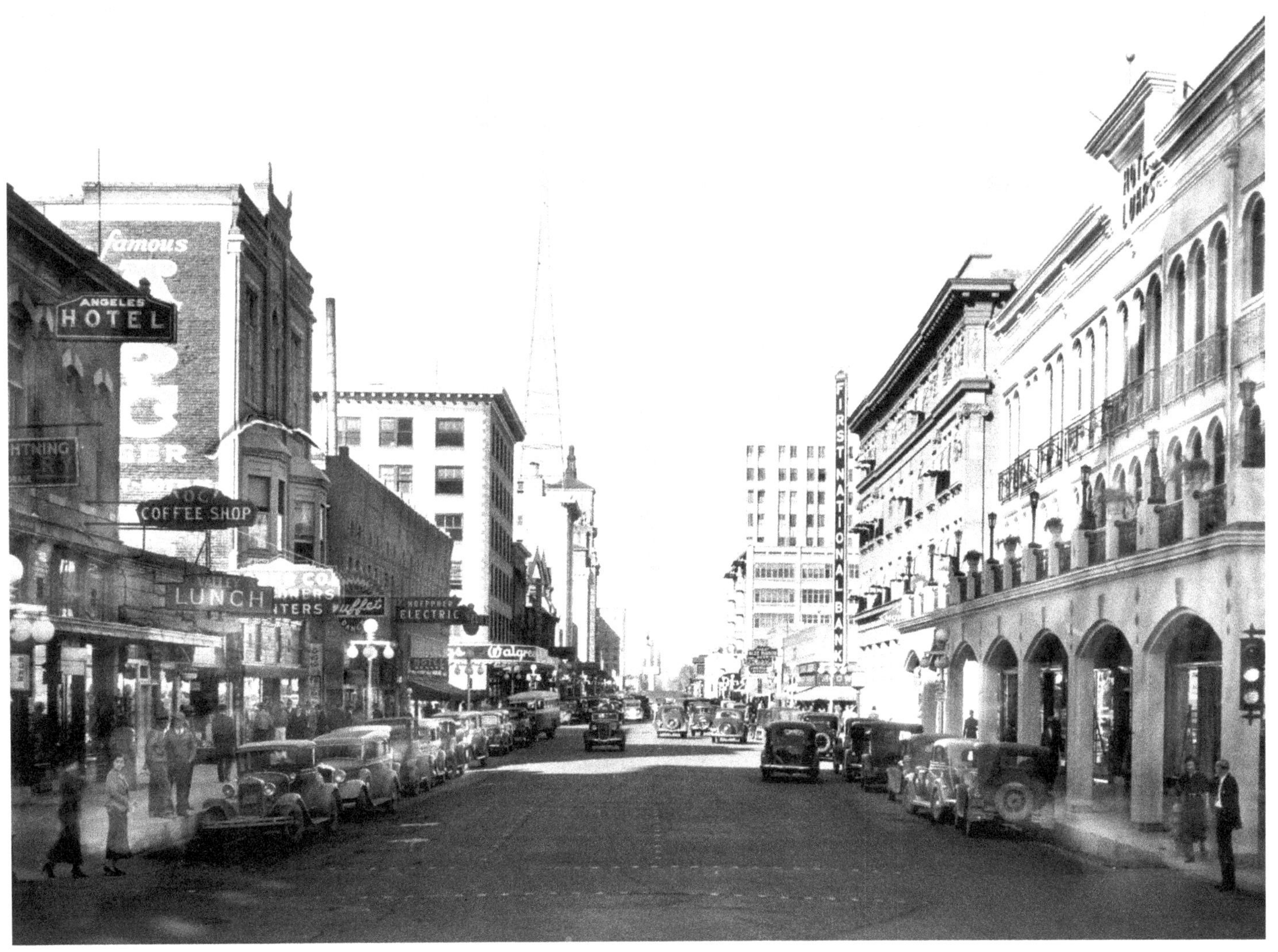

A view of the city's St. Vincent's Hospital.

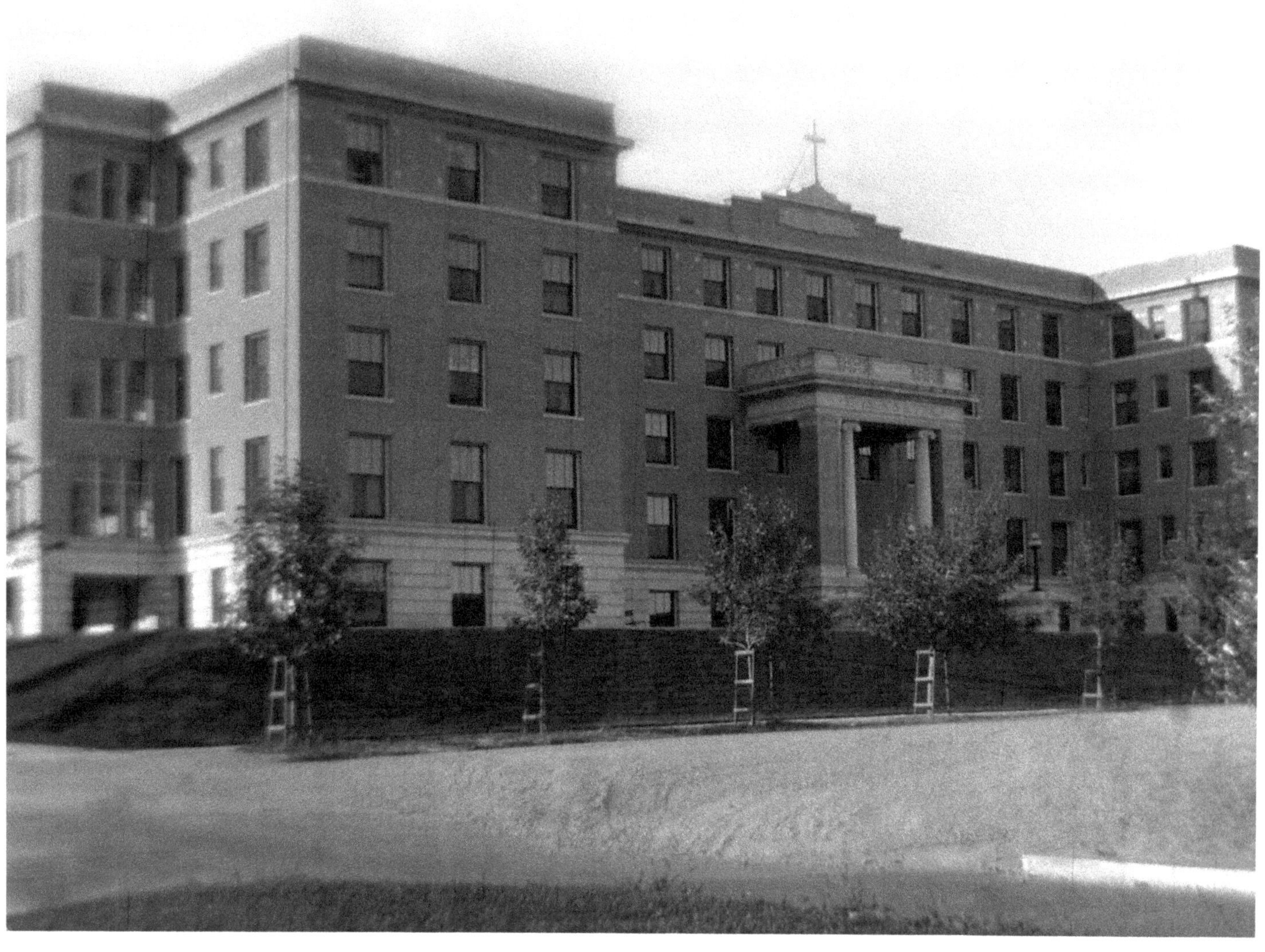

In 1877, a party of six men, three women, and ten children from Creston, Iowa, headed to Arizona and founded a settlement southwest of Phoenix that was to become the town of Buckeye. WPA road construction workers are pictured here in 1936, paving the road that connects Buckeye to Phoenix.

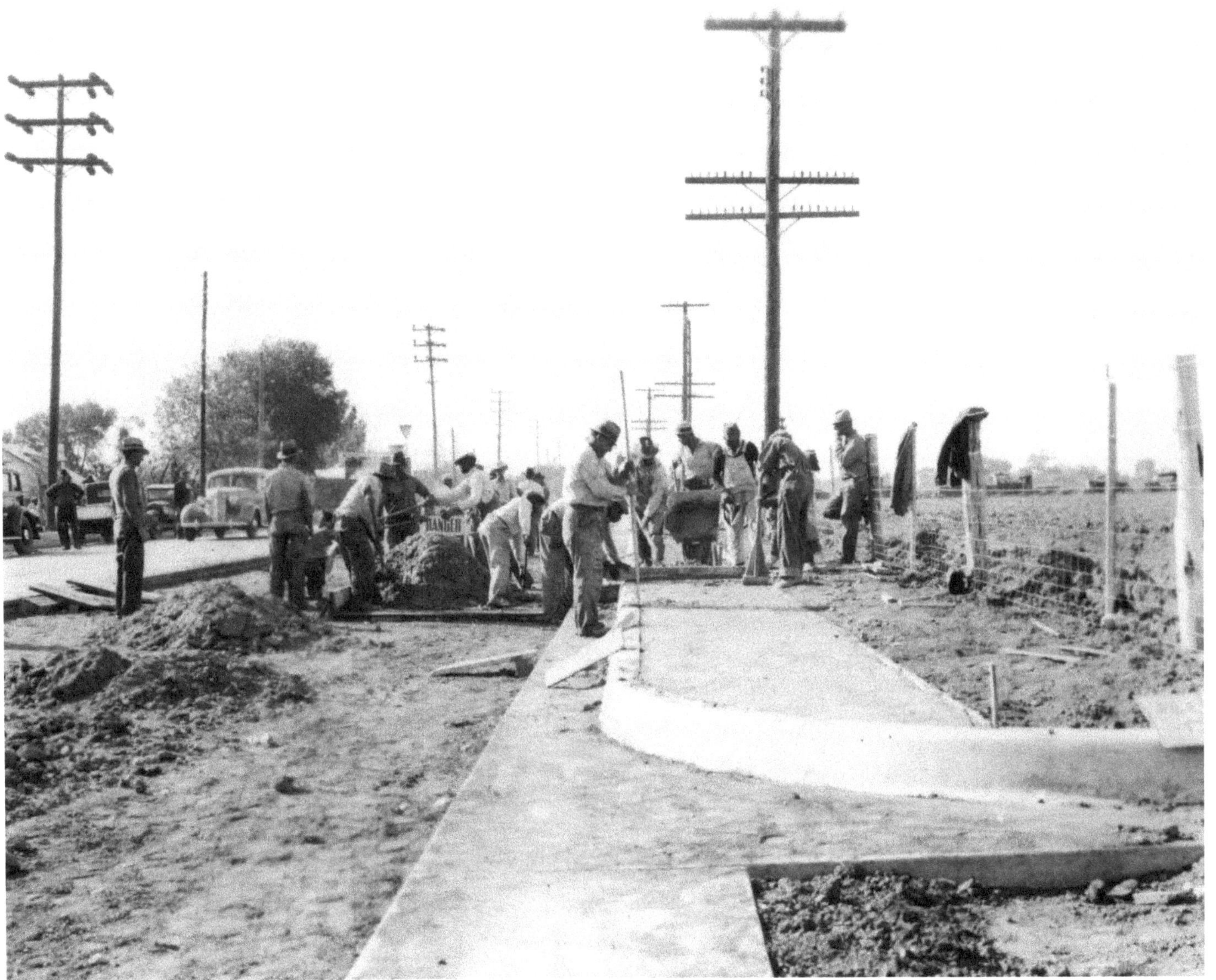

Twenty senators of the 1937 Arizona State Senate gather outside the Capitol in Phoenix for a group shot.

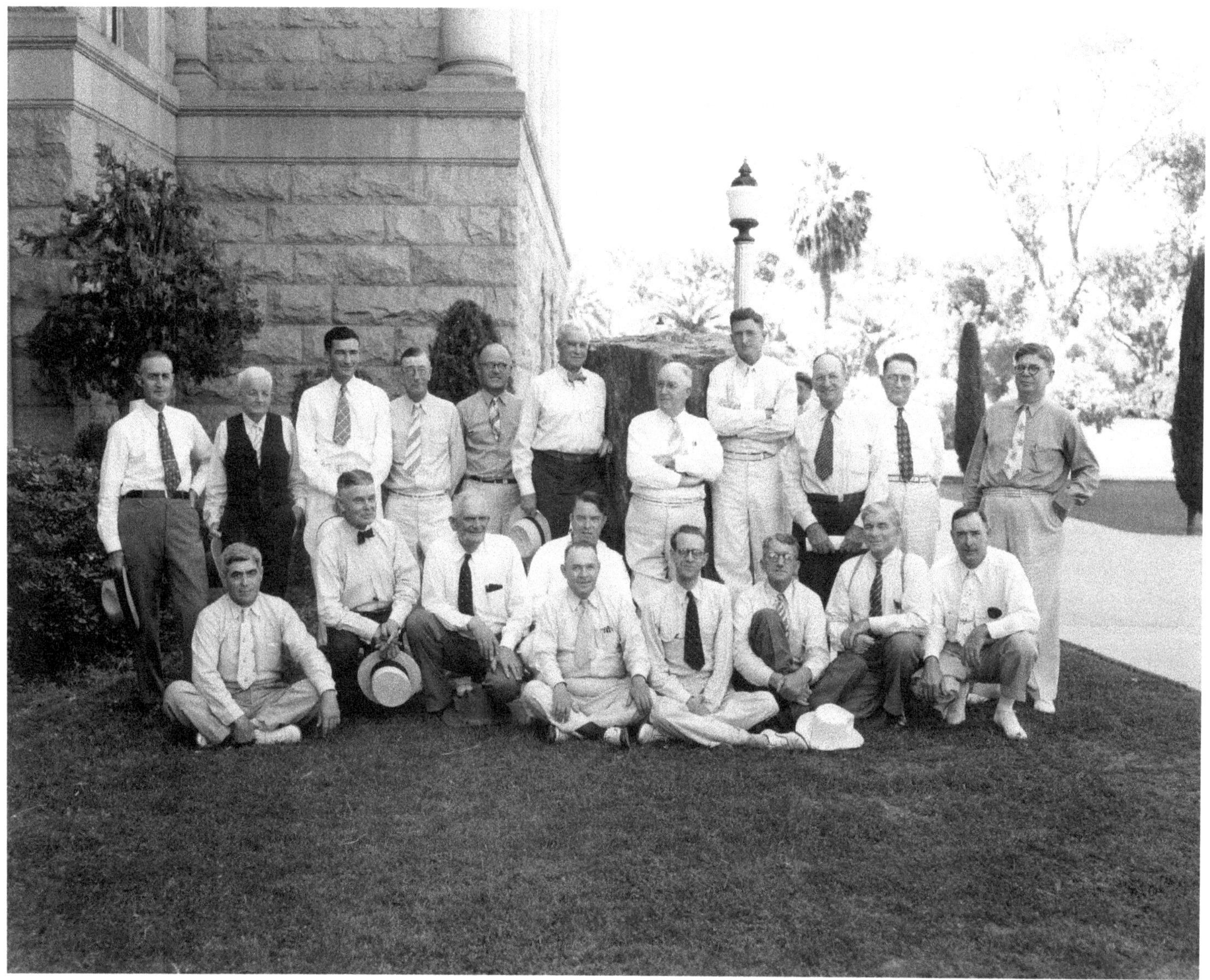

The Sprawling Metropolis (1940–1970s)

A little more than a decade after the Black Tuesday stock market crash, a second world war lifted Phoenix, and the rest of the nation, out of the Great Depression. Gone were the soup lines and the desperate procession of migrants passing through Phoenix in search of employment.

In 1940, the U.S. Army selected a site near Phoenix that was to become the largest fighter training base for an Army Air Corps. The city of Phoenix bought 1,440 acres of land in Litchfield Park and leased it to the government for $1 a year. Sky Harbor Airport served as temporary training grounds for pilots, overseen by Captain Barry Goldwater, who was director of ground training. Locally owned Del. E. Webb Construction began excavating for the first buildings of Luke Air Base, named after Phoenix native and World War I Medal of Honor recipient Frank Luke, Jr. Thousands of pilots passed through Phoenix to train at Luke, as well as at Higley Field (later named Williams Air Force Base) and Falcon Field in Mesa.

The war transformed Phoenix from an agricultural center to an industrial and product distribution center. Hoover Dam, which had been completed in 1935, brought energy to the rapidly growing city. Small business boomed as a result of the influx of military men and their families, who required goods and services.

After the war, many servicemen returned to Phoenix. The G.I. Bill provided access to college and the socioeconomic mobility that had been unavailable to them before the war. In the fall of 1945, 553 students were enrolled at Arizona State Teacher's College at Tempe (later renamed Arizona State University); the next semester enrollments jumped 110 percent to 1,163 students. Air-conditioned homes and businesses became standard in Phoenix as technological advances improved affordability. Large industries located plants and factories in Phoenix to capitalize on the growing and educated labor force and steady climate.

Much of Phoenix's growth during the postwar era spread outward from the downtown area in low-density suburbs. Land was cheaper outside the city, and developers could build inexpensive cement homes for the postwar population boom. Much of the historic district in downtown Phoenix was destroyed in the urban renewal projects of the 1960s and 1970s. Despite the city's changing landscape, Phoenix was slow to embrace integration, and rural parts of Phoenix, especially South Phoenix, remained predominantly a segregated enclave of African Americans and Americans of Mexican and Asian ethnicities.

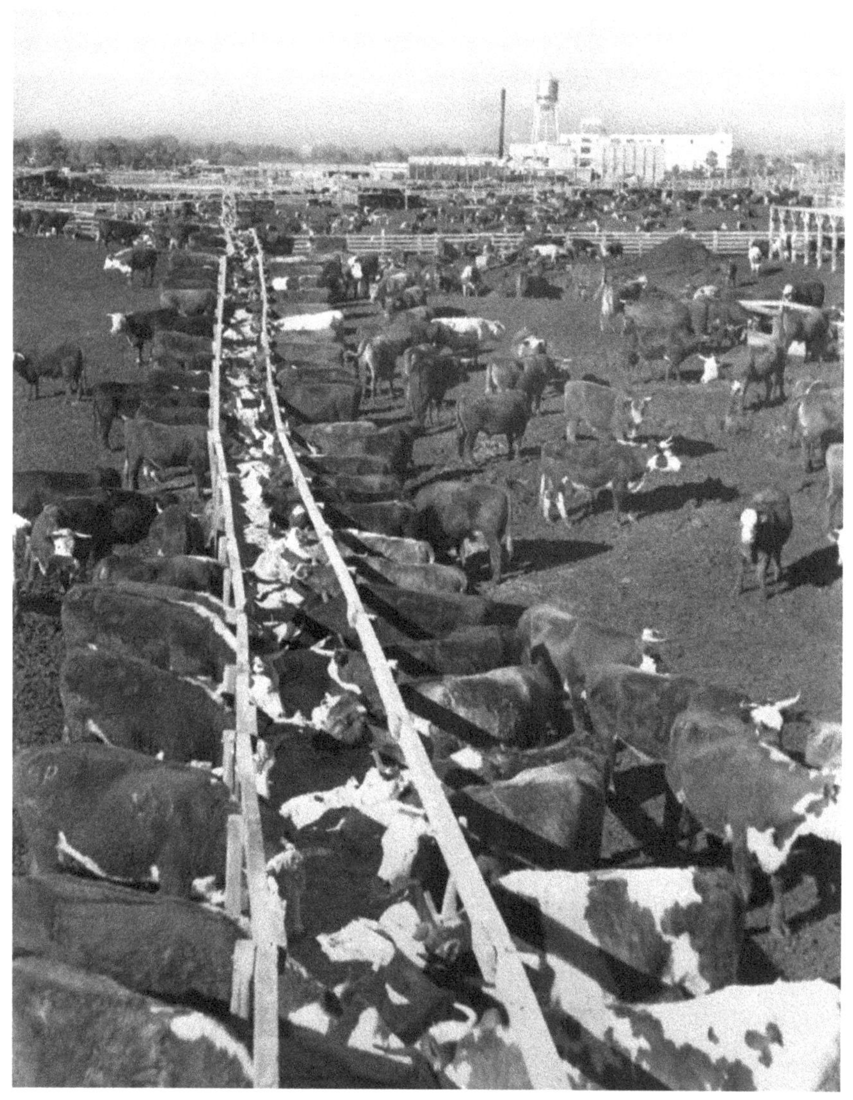

By the 1940s the Tovrea Land and Cattle Company in Phoenix was the world's largest feedlot, with nearly 40,000 head of cattle and 200 acres of cattle pens.

The street-lamp posts in front of the Westward Ho Grill Room, next to the luxurious Westward Ho Hotel on Central Avenue between Filmore and Pierce streets, were designed to resemble a saguaro cactus.

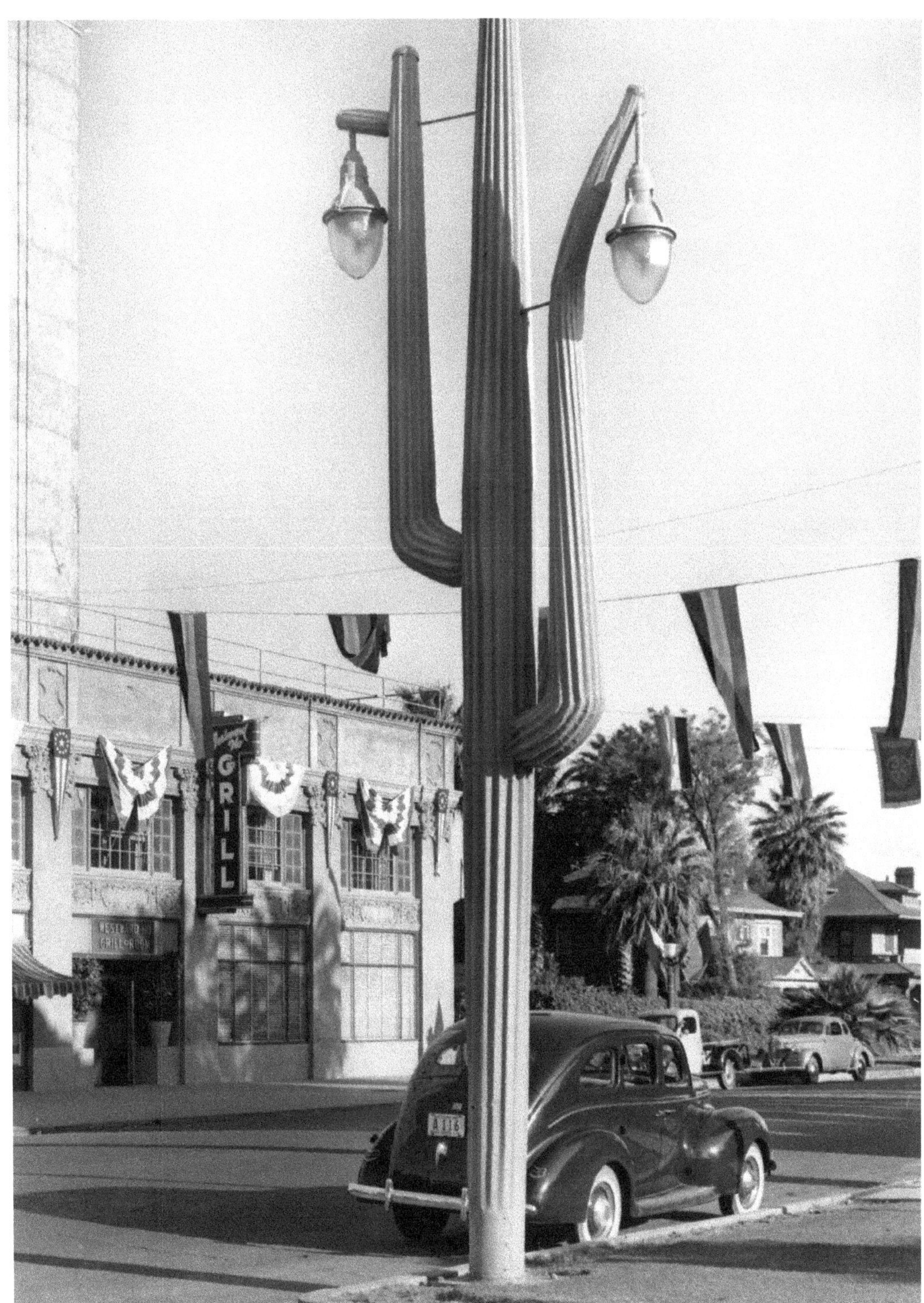

The card catalog at the Arizona State Library, pictured here in 1943, was the descendant of a tradition that began following the storming of the Bastille in 1789. Information about confiscated books and manuscripts was recorded on the backs of playing cards for the Bureau de Bibliographie. By the 1930s most modern libraries, such as the Arizona State Library, used typewriters to record information, although some librarians still preferred to use longhand.

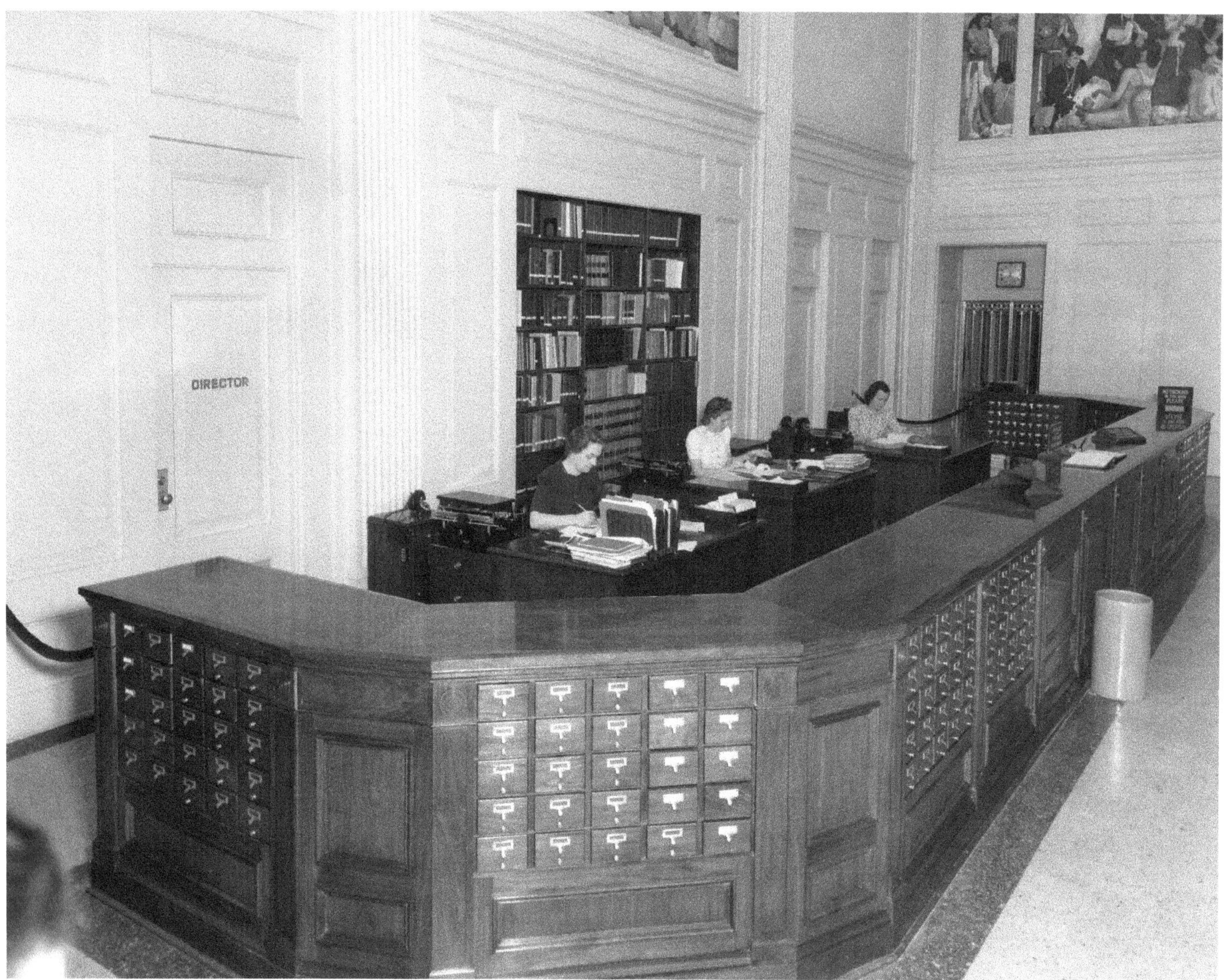

In 1878, German immigrant Georg Heinrich Nicholas Luhrs rode on horseback into the small settlement of Phoenix. The modest adobe shop where he set up business as a wheelwright grew into the Commercial Corral & Fashion Livery Stable, and then it became the Commercial Hotel, later renamed the Luhrs Hotel. The Luhrs Tower pictured here was built in 1929. At 14 stories tall, it was the tallest building in Arizona at the time.

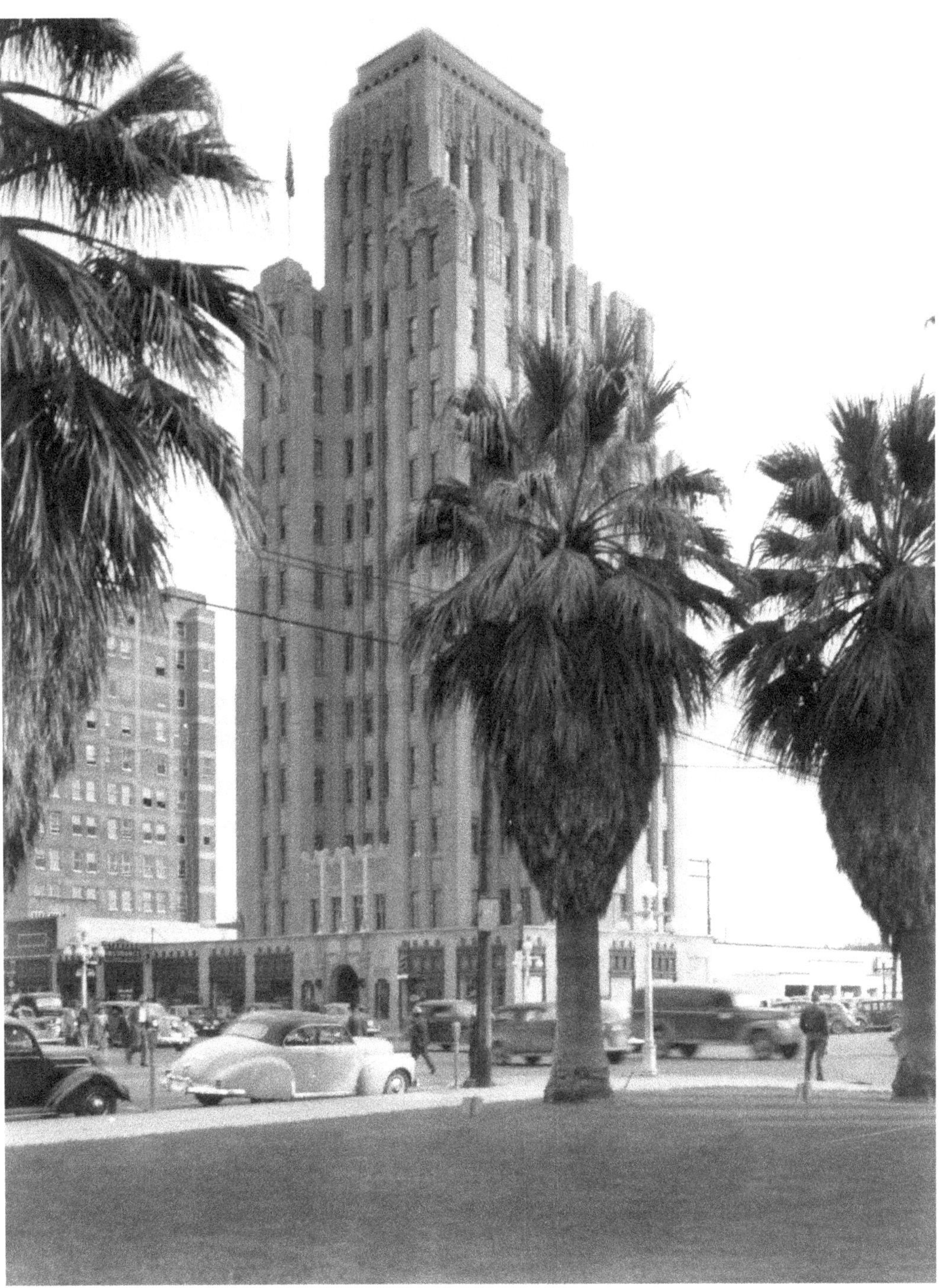

In 1937, three Phoenix businessmen founded the Phoenix Advertising Club to meet weekly over meals at the Hotel Westward Ho to exchange ideas and to listen to invited speakers such as Barry Goldwater and Frank Lloyd Wright. The group continues to meet today. Pictured is a 1946 meeting with Mulford Winsor (at left), Arizona's territorial historian and state archivist.

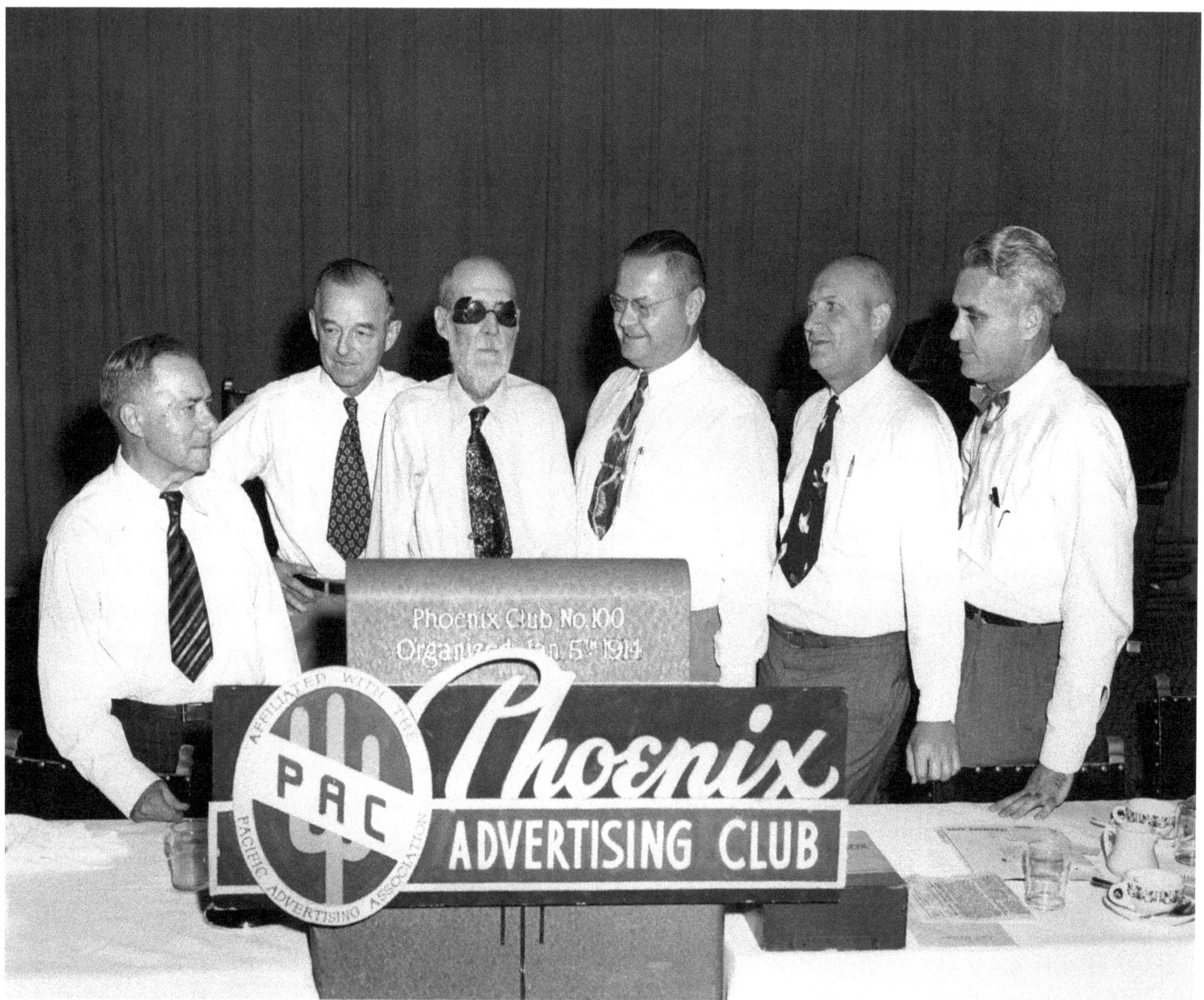

Although the first helicopter powered by an internal combustion engine was successfully flown in 1939, the helicopter had very limited application until late in World War II. It wasn't until 1946 that the Bell 47, pictured here at the Arizona State Capitol in Phoenix, was certified for civilian use. Yale McFate, a member of the Arizona Legislature, debarks at the Capitol.

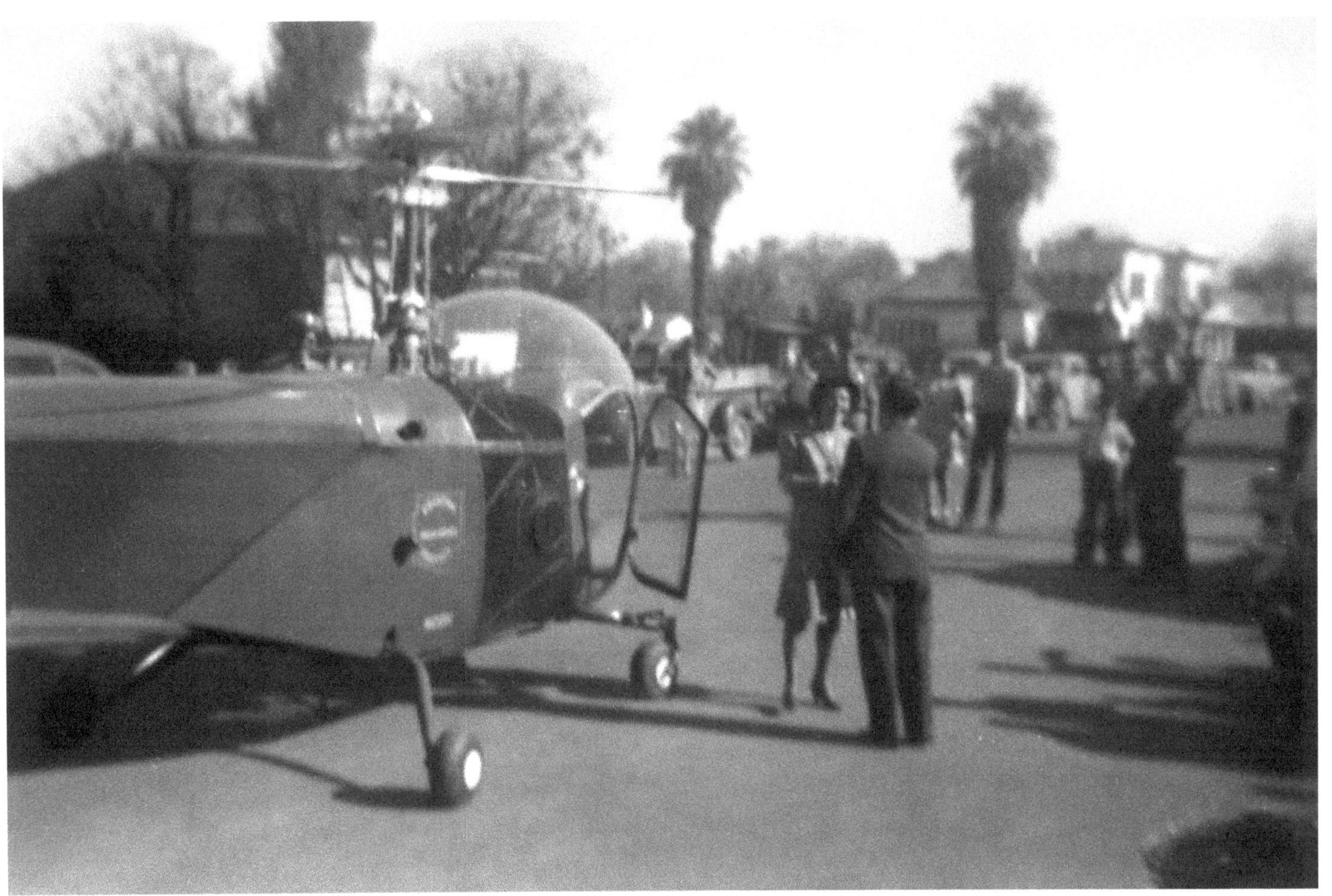

Arizona entrepreneur Rocky Nelson started Arizona Airways in 1942, using a DC-3 airplane to fly passengers from Sky Harbor Airport to other Arizona destinations. The airline specialized in taking tourists on scenic tours of northern Arizona, particularly the Grand Canyon. Faye Shields Duff stands in front of a newly dedicated DC-3 in 1948.

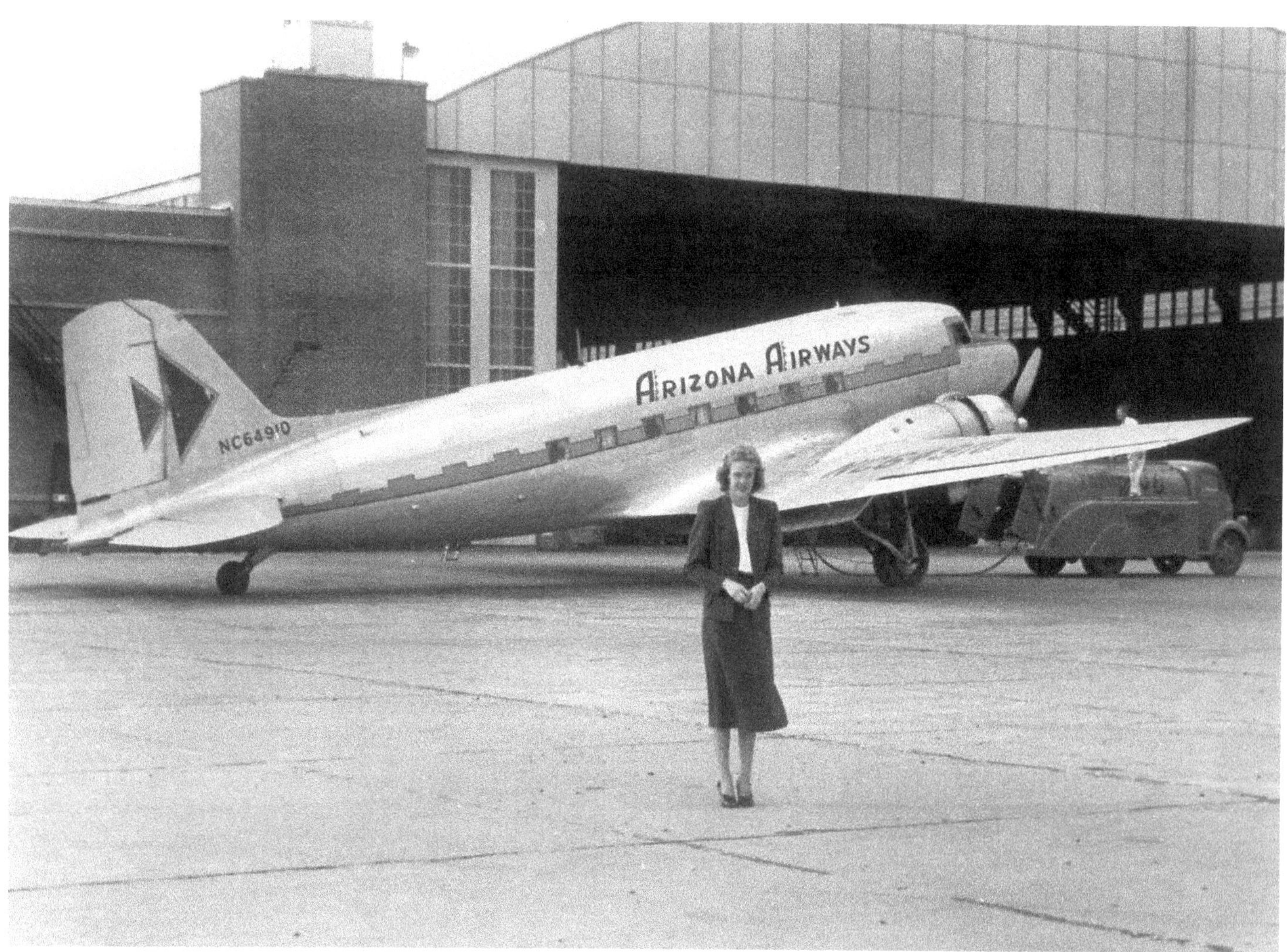

Professional baseball suffered during World War II as many players joined the armed forces and attendance slipped, but after World War II attendance jumped nearly 70 percent. When this 1949 photograph was taken of a baseball game at the Phoenix Municipal Stadium, the color barrier for major league baseball had been broken for two years, with Jackie Robinson's promotion to the Brooklyn Dodgers.

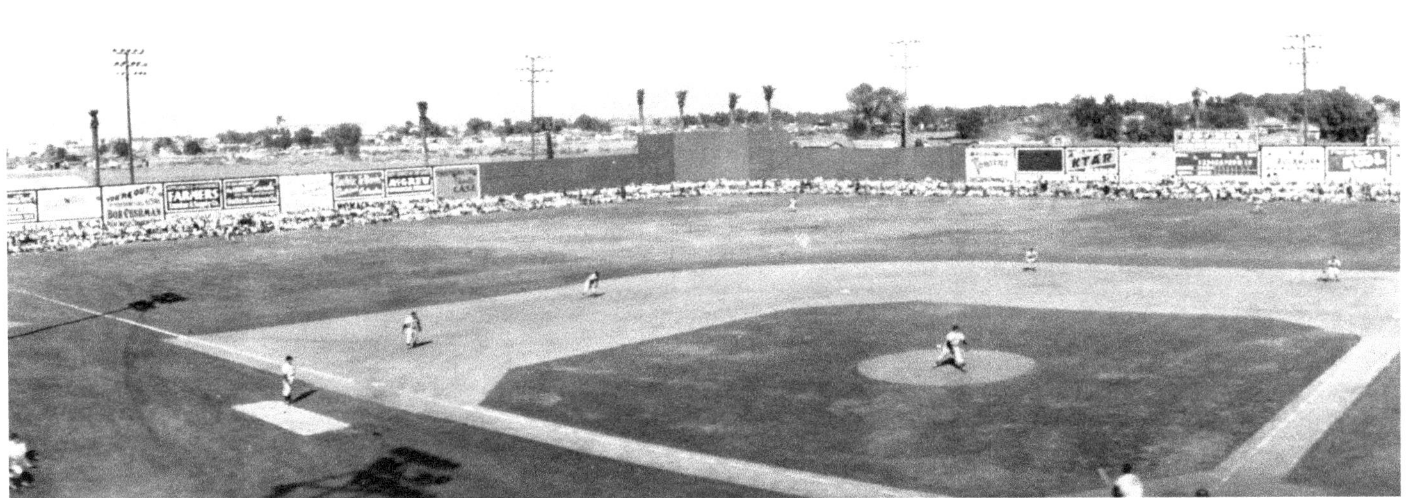

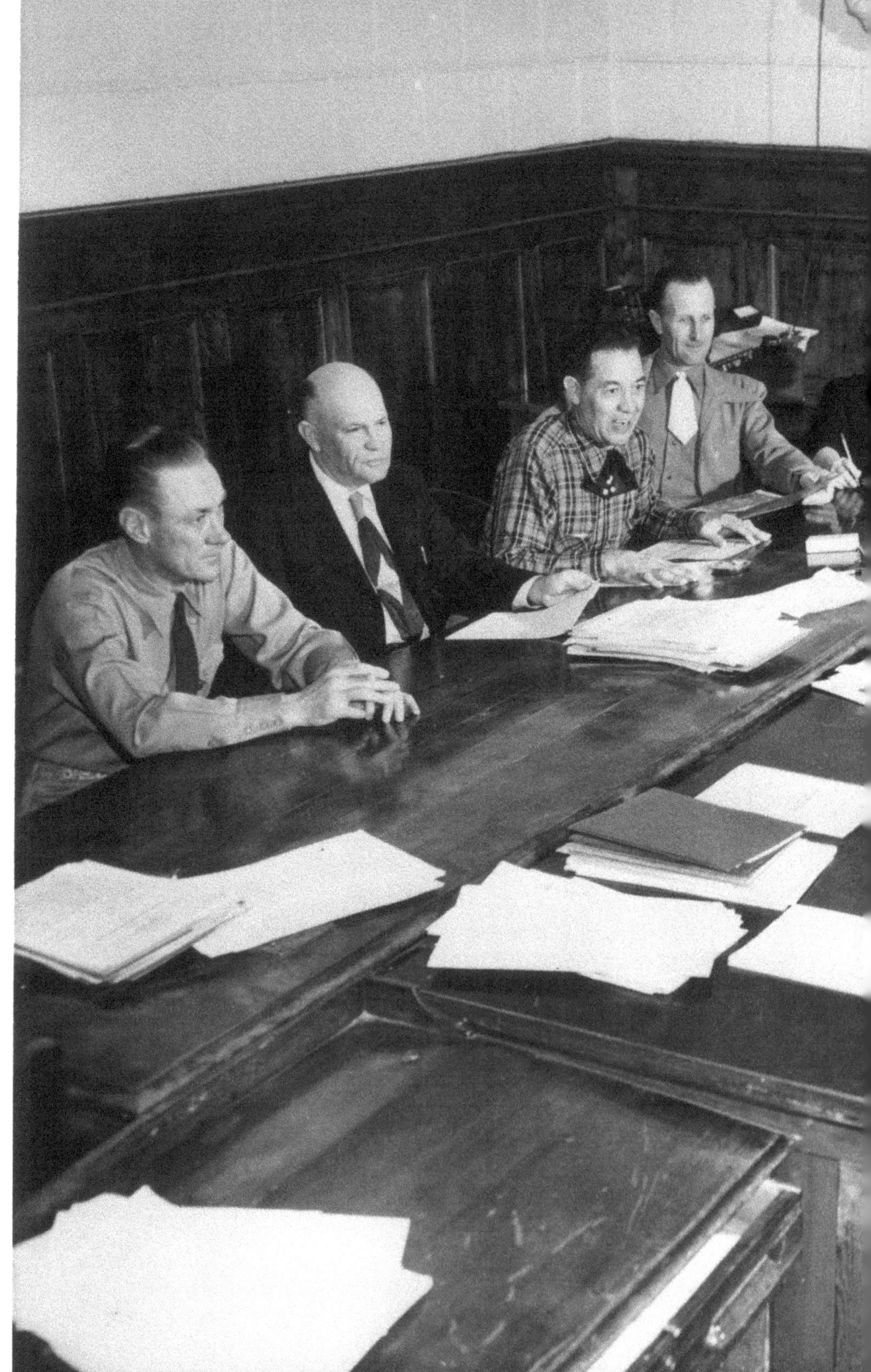

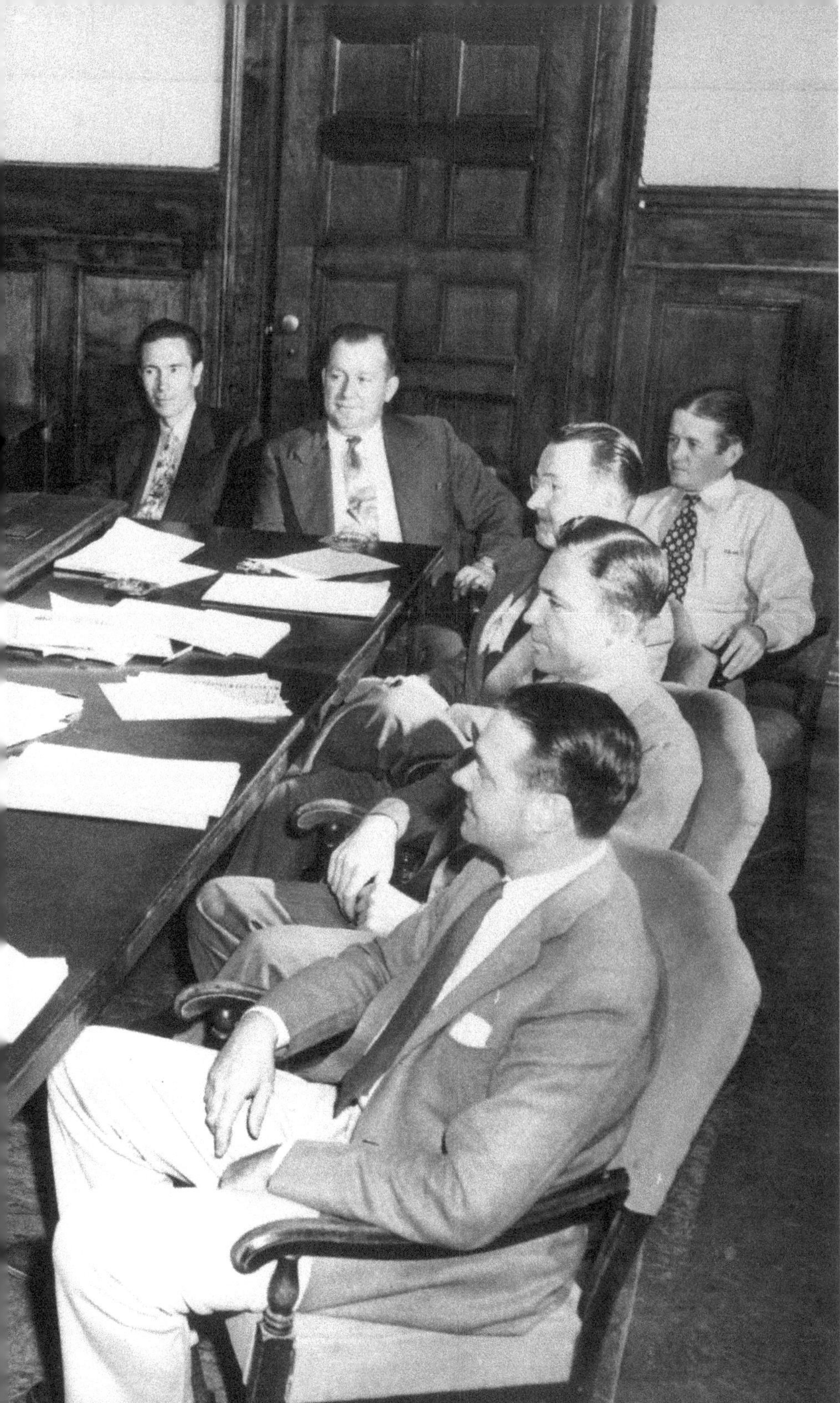

Harry Wimberley and R. H. Wallace meet in a 1949 legislative committee session of the Arizona State Senate.

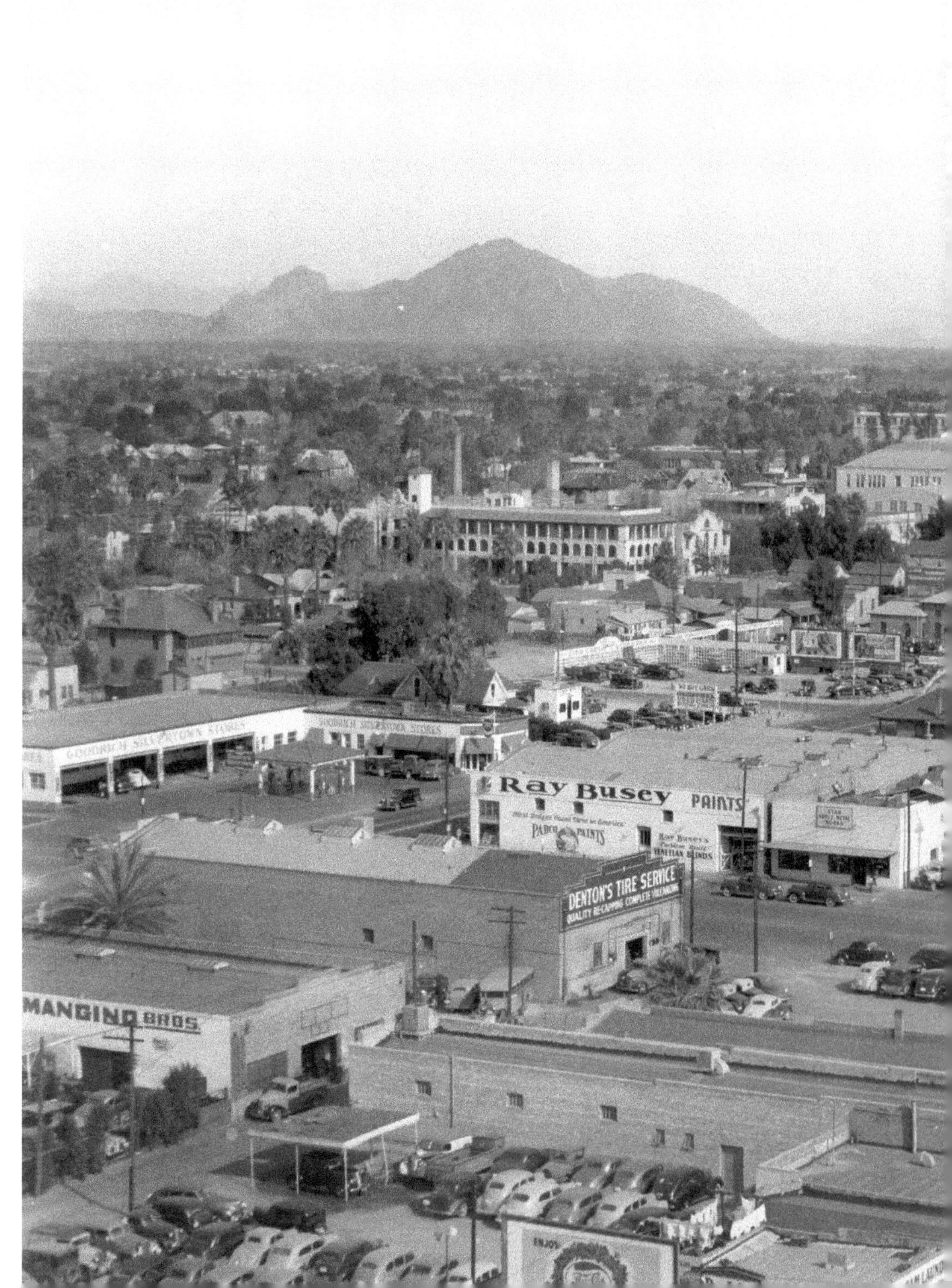
Ray Busey PAINTS
DENTON'S TIRE SERVICE
MANGINO BROS.

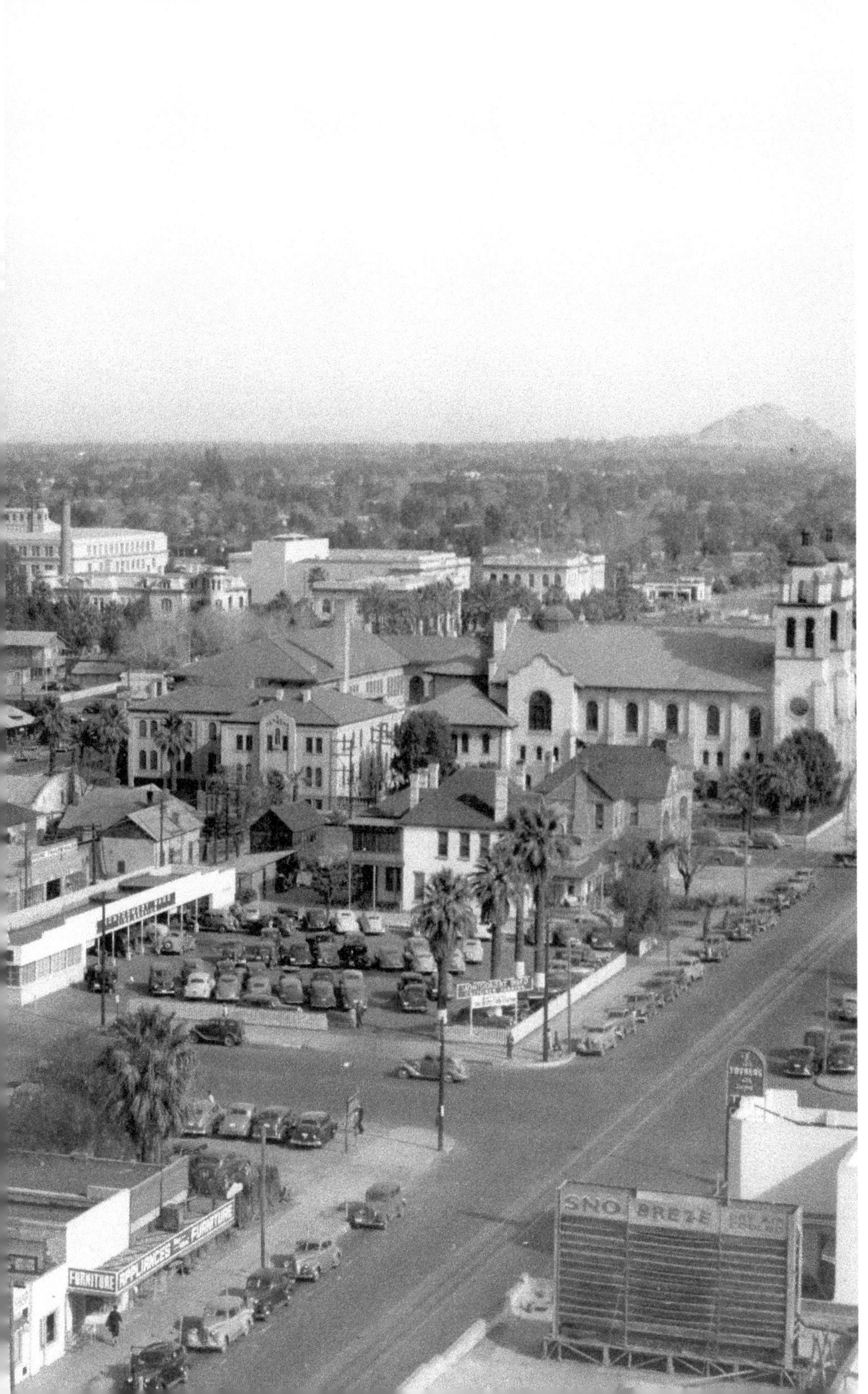

By 1950, the population of Phoenix had nearly doubled over the previous decade as a result of the postwar population boom, surpassing 100,000 for the first time. In view here is the growing suburbanization of Phoenix from the Arcadia area, with Camelback Mountain in the background and the McDowell Mountains in the distance.

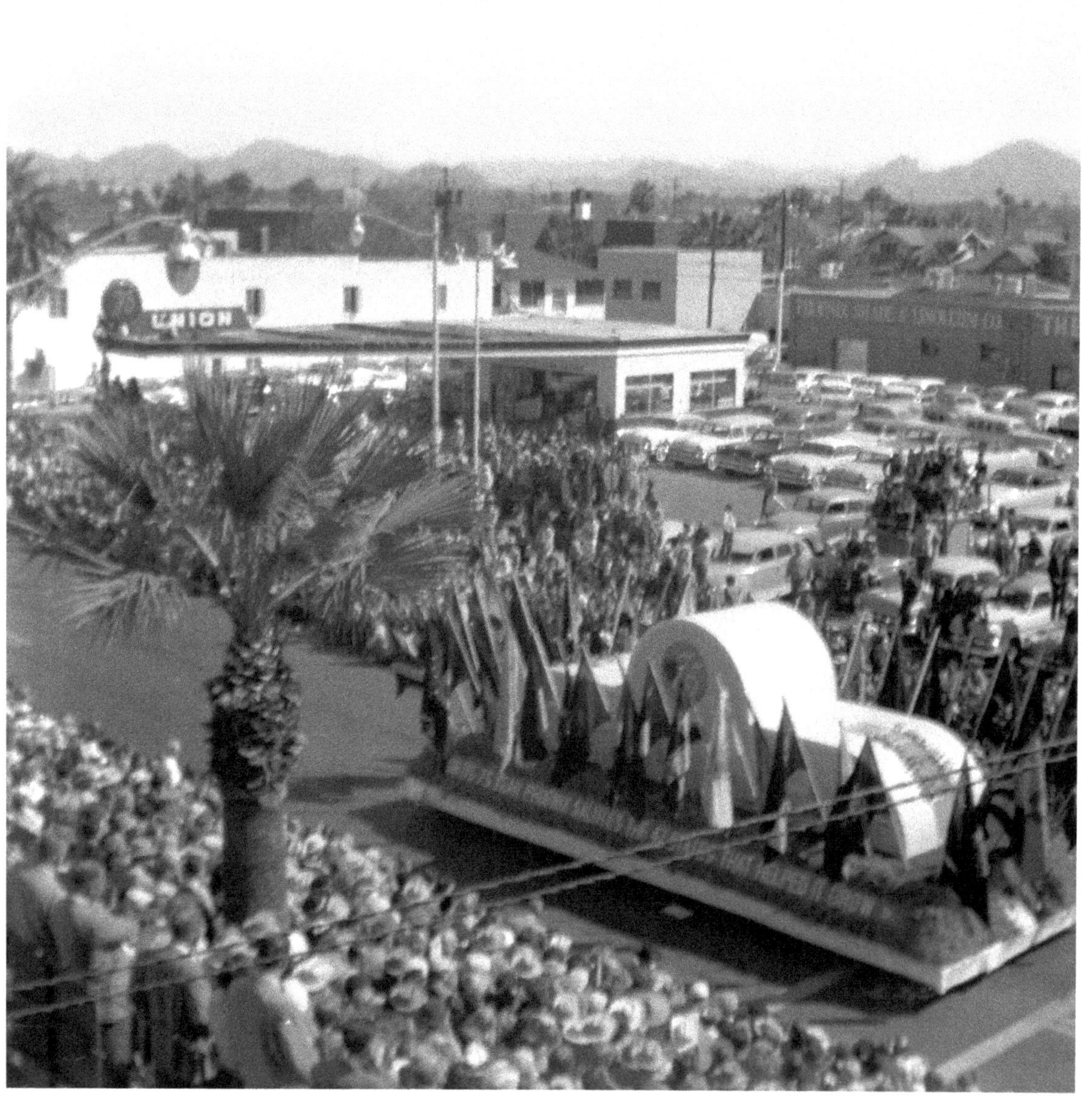

Crowds pack Phoenix streets to watch parade floats in the Fiesta del Sol. On this float are the words "On its 75 year Phoenix salutes the 47 states that helped it grow."

Phoenicians celebrate the Fiesta del Sol—the Feast of the Sun.

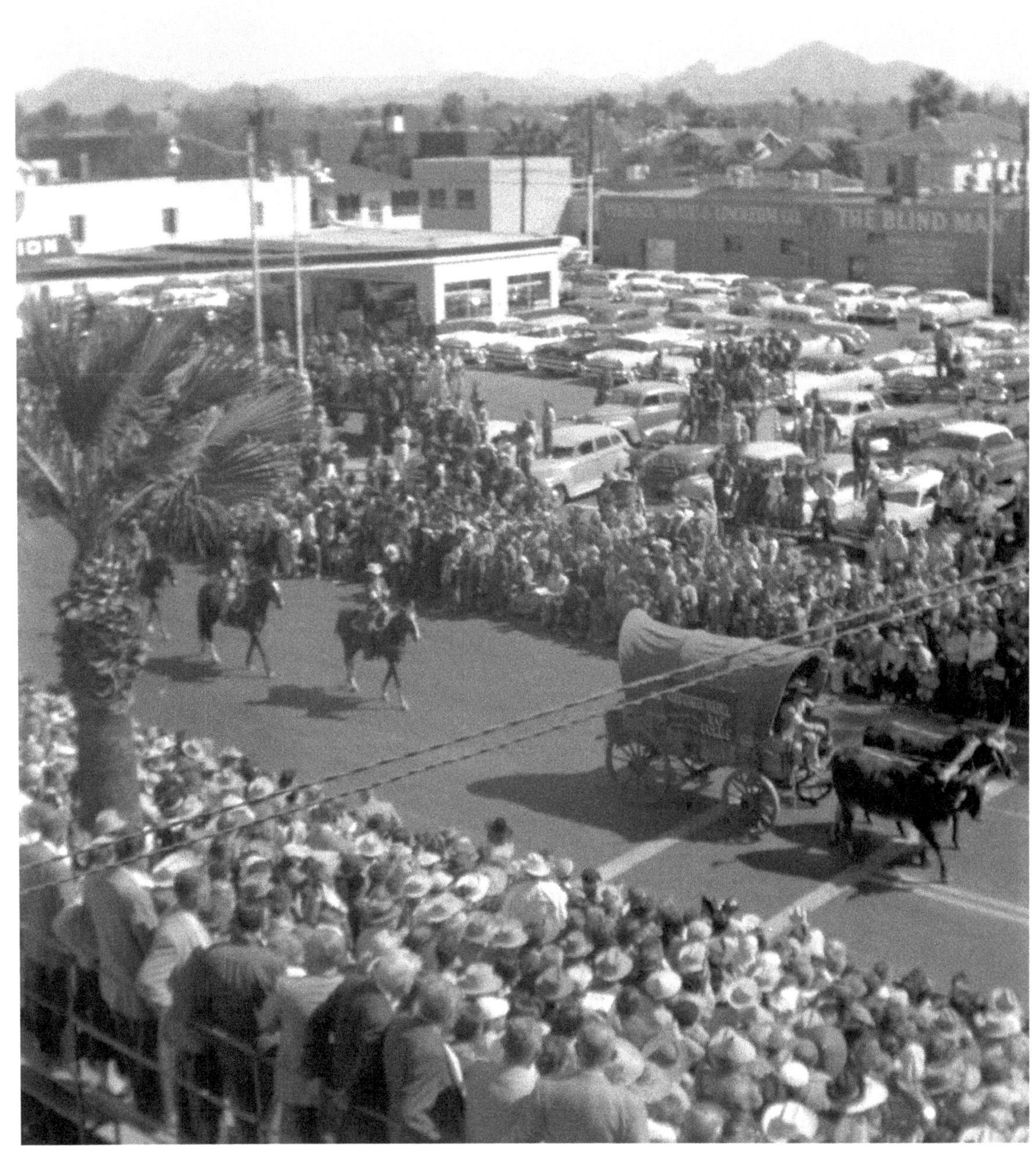

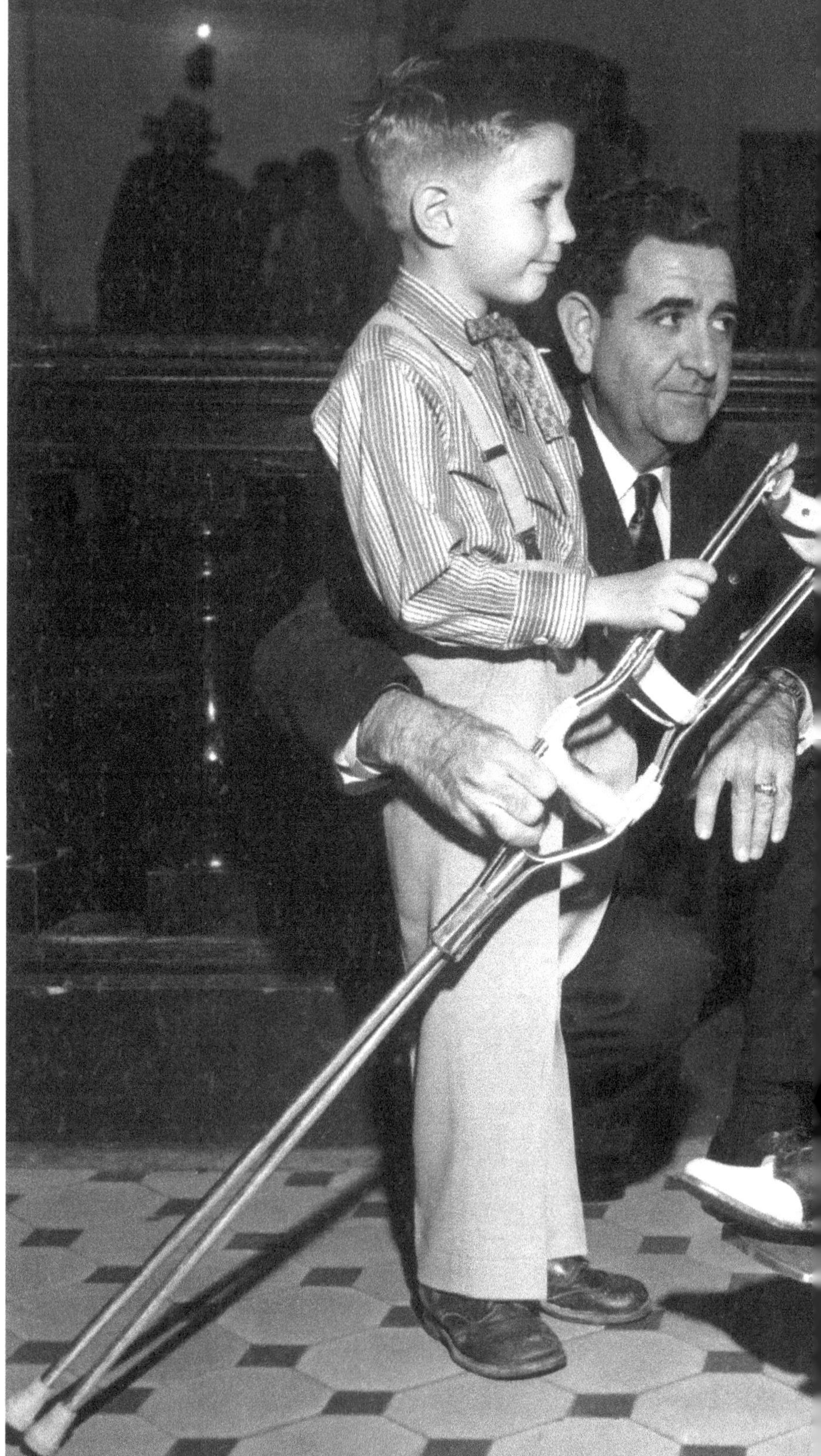

President Franklin Roosevelt founded the March of Dimes in 1938 to raise money to defeat polio, which had killed or paralyzed thousands during the first half of the twentieth century. In April 1955, the March of Dimes announced that Jonas Salk had created a vaccine for polio at the University of Pittsburgh. House speaker Harry S. Ruppelius and senate president Clarence Carpenter of Miami, both native Arizonans, meet with two handicapped children at the Capitol in Phoenix.

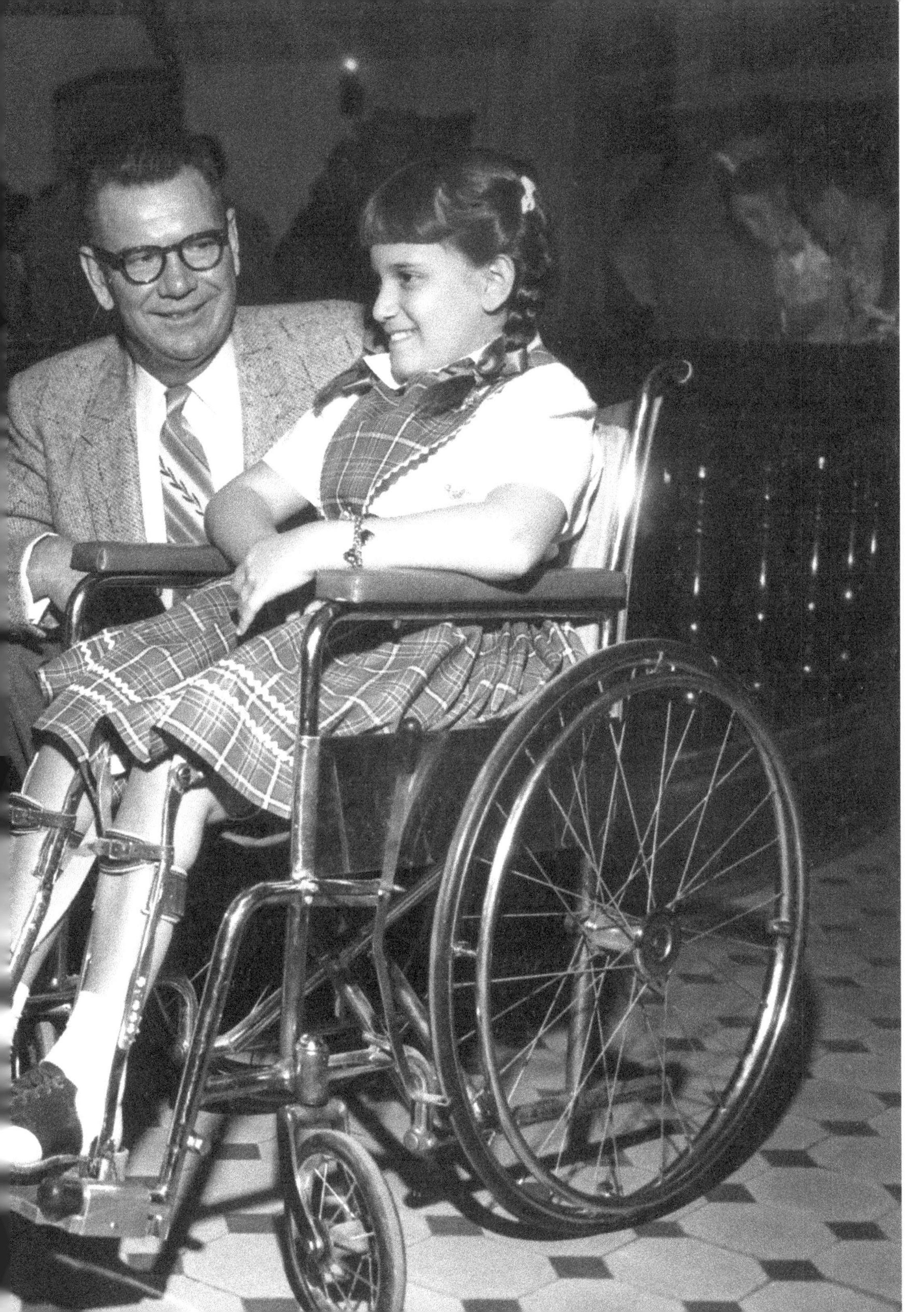

A bird's-eye view of downtown Phoenix in 1950, looking down Central Avenue at the Valley National Bank and Hotel Adams.

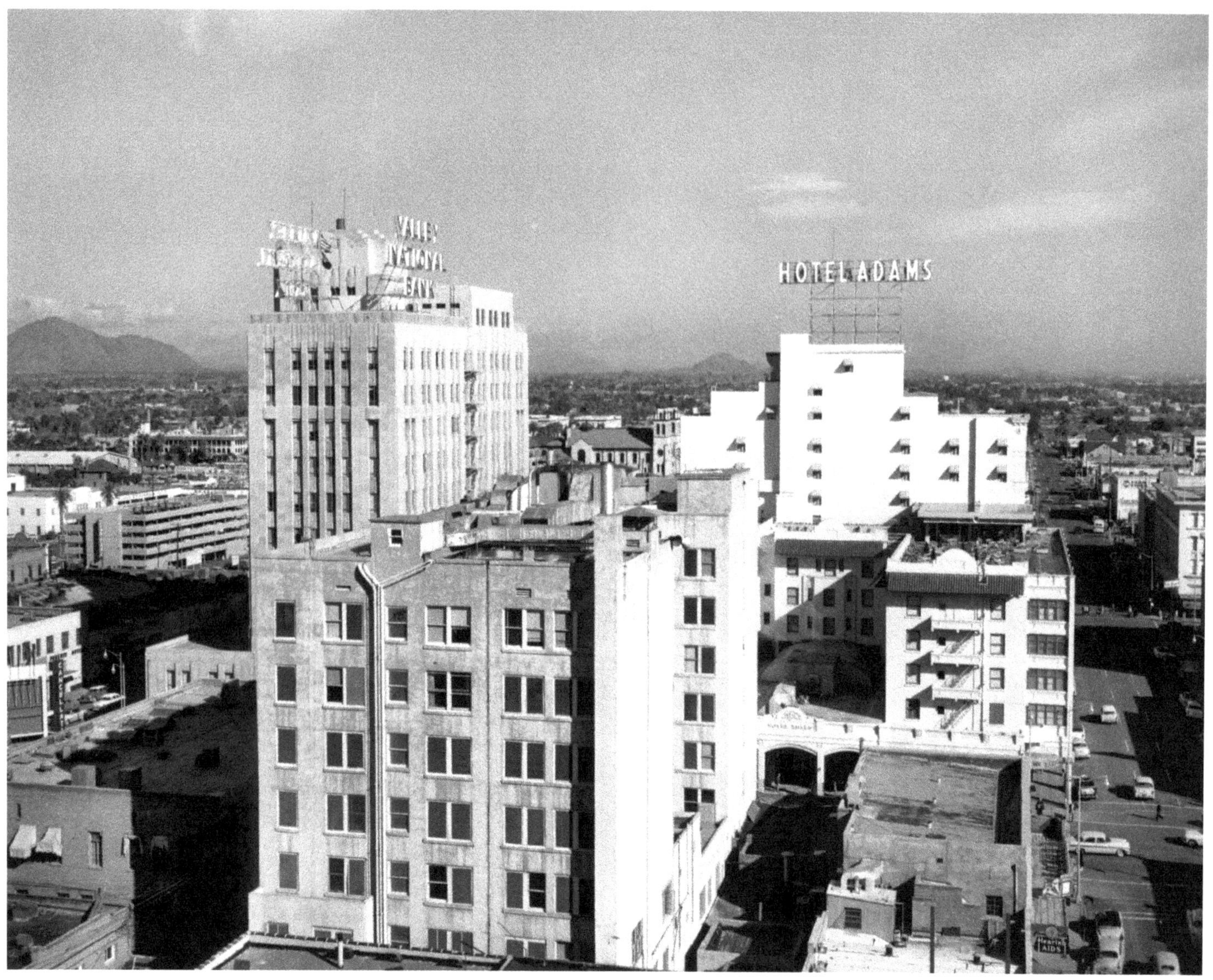

The Phoenix Senators baseball team, a minor league affiliate of the Washington Senators, was coached by noted Phoenix citizen Vic H. Housholder (not pictured). Housholder was a personal friend of Harry Truman from their service together in Battery D of the 129th Field Artillery Regiment during World War I. After the war, Housholder had moved to Arizona to be an engineer for the Gillespie Dam on the Gila River and a flood control dam at Cave Creek, and was very active in promoting sports in Phoenix.

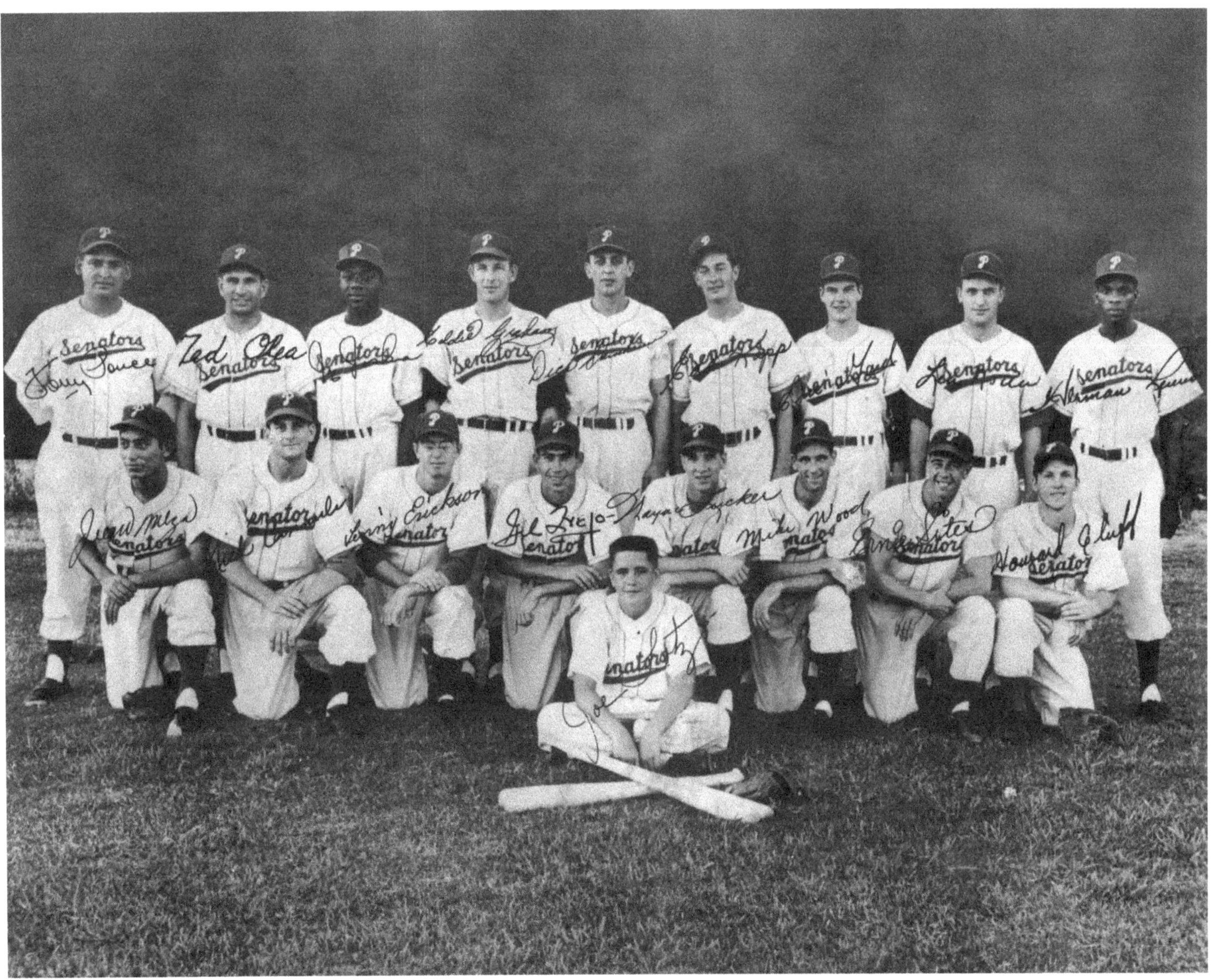

Many of Phoenix's citrus groves and agricultural lands were plowed under to make room for subdivisions in the postwar period. While many farmers profited handsomely from selling their land to developers, homeowners often inherited termites, scorpions, and other desert pests that had burrowed deeply in the fields.

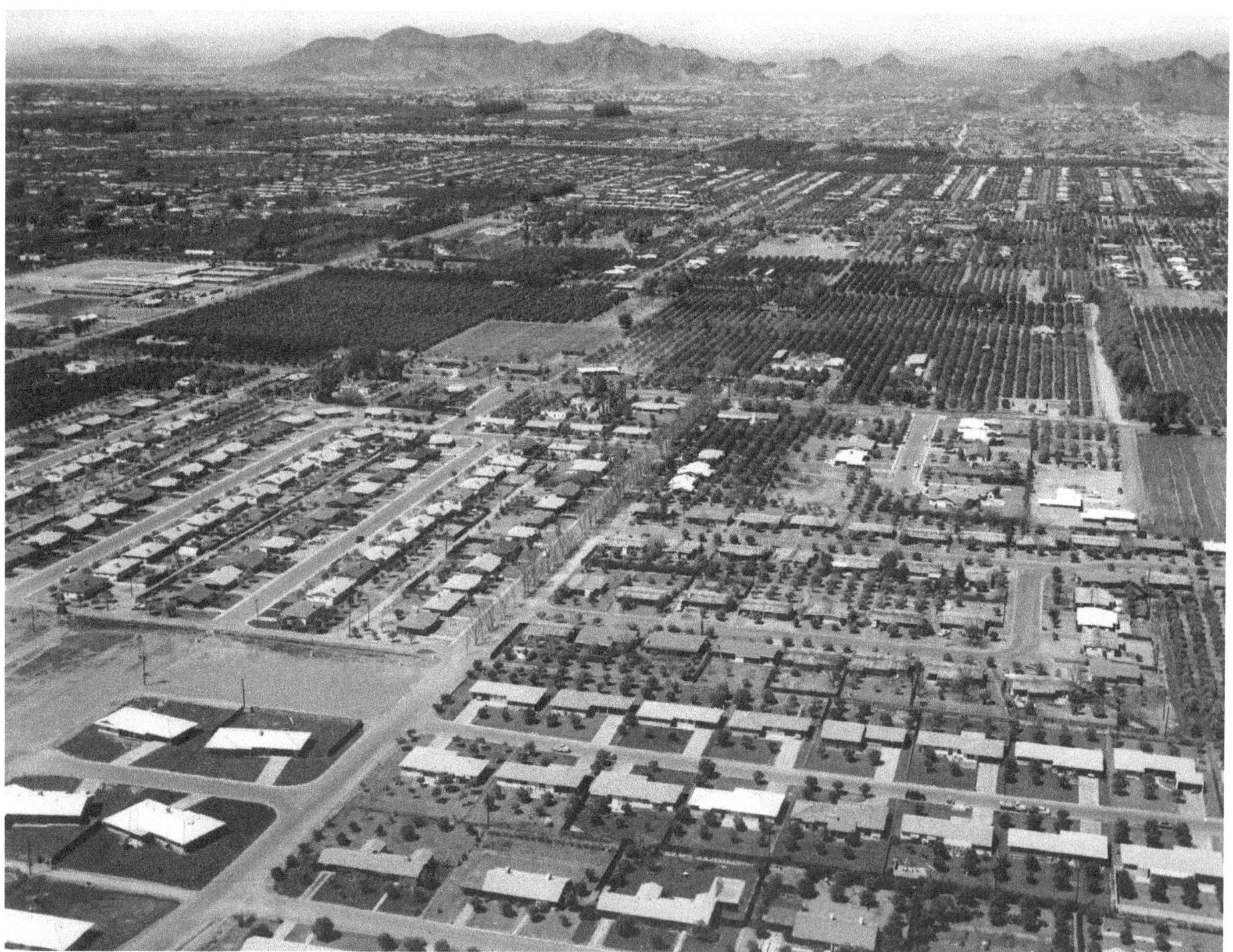

Crowds gather in 1959 for the inauguration of Paul Jones Fannin as the 15th governor of the state. Fannin's family had moved to Phoenix from Ashland, Kentucky, within months of his birth. He attended the University of Arizona but graduated from Stanford University, and became a businessman involved in petroleum and equipment distribution in the Southwest and Mexico. He was reelected governor in 1960 and 1962, and then replaced Barry Goldwater as the U.S. senator from Arizona.

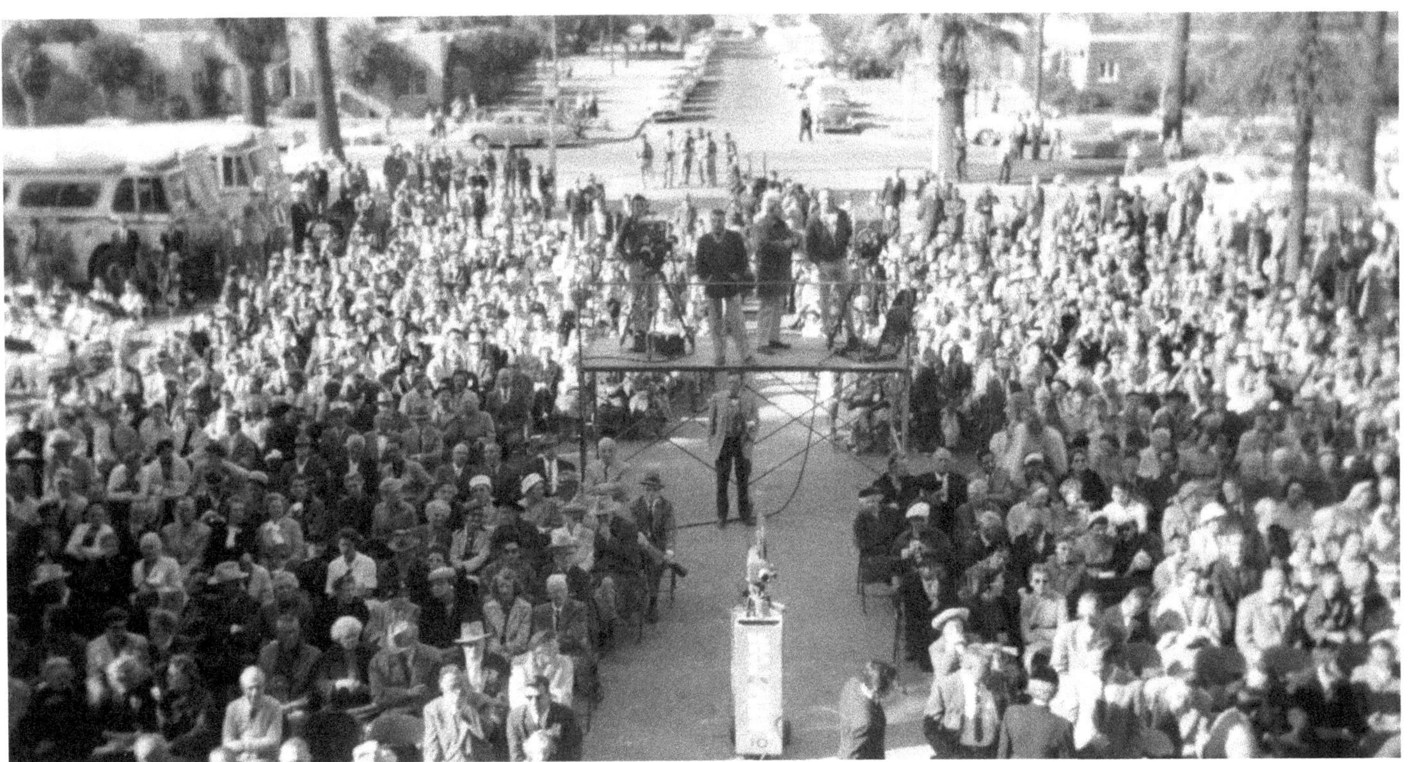

The Phoenix Memorial Hospital was founded in 1934 to care for racial minorities in Phoenix who were denied care in other hospitals. Most Mexican Americans, American Indians, and African Americans were confined to living south of the Salt River.

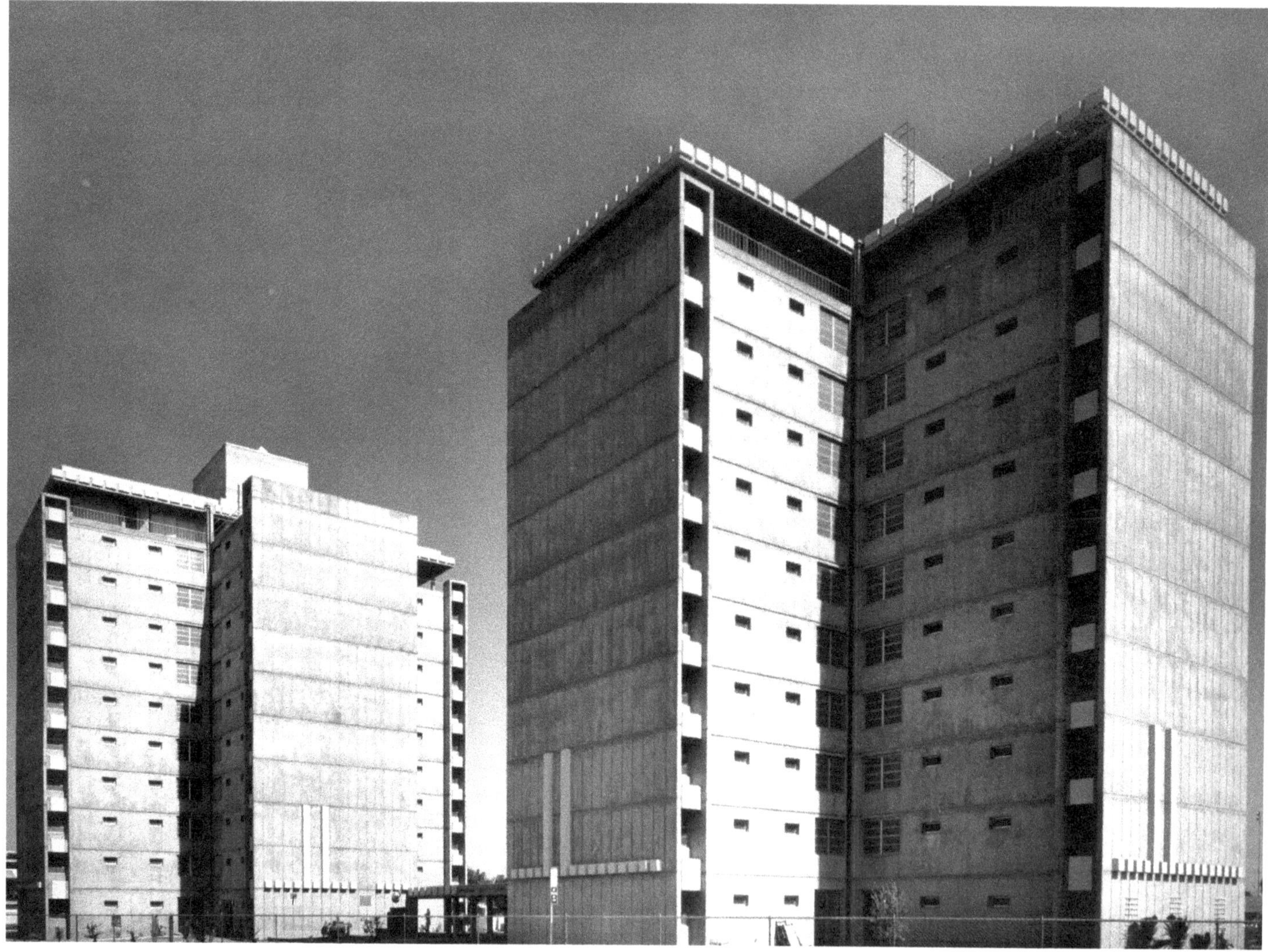

Arizona state legislators pause for this photograph with a group of nurses and other women at the Arizona State Capitol.

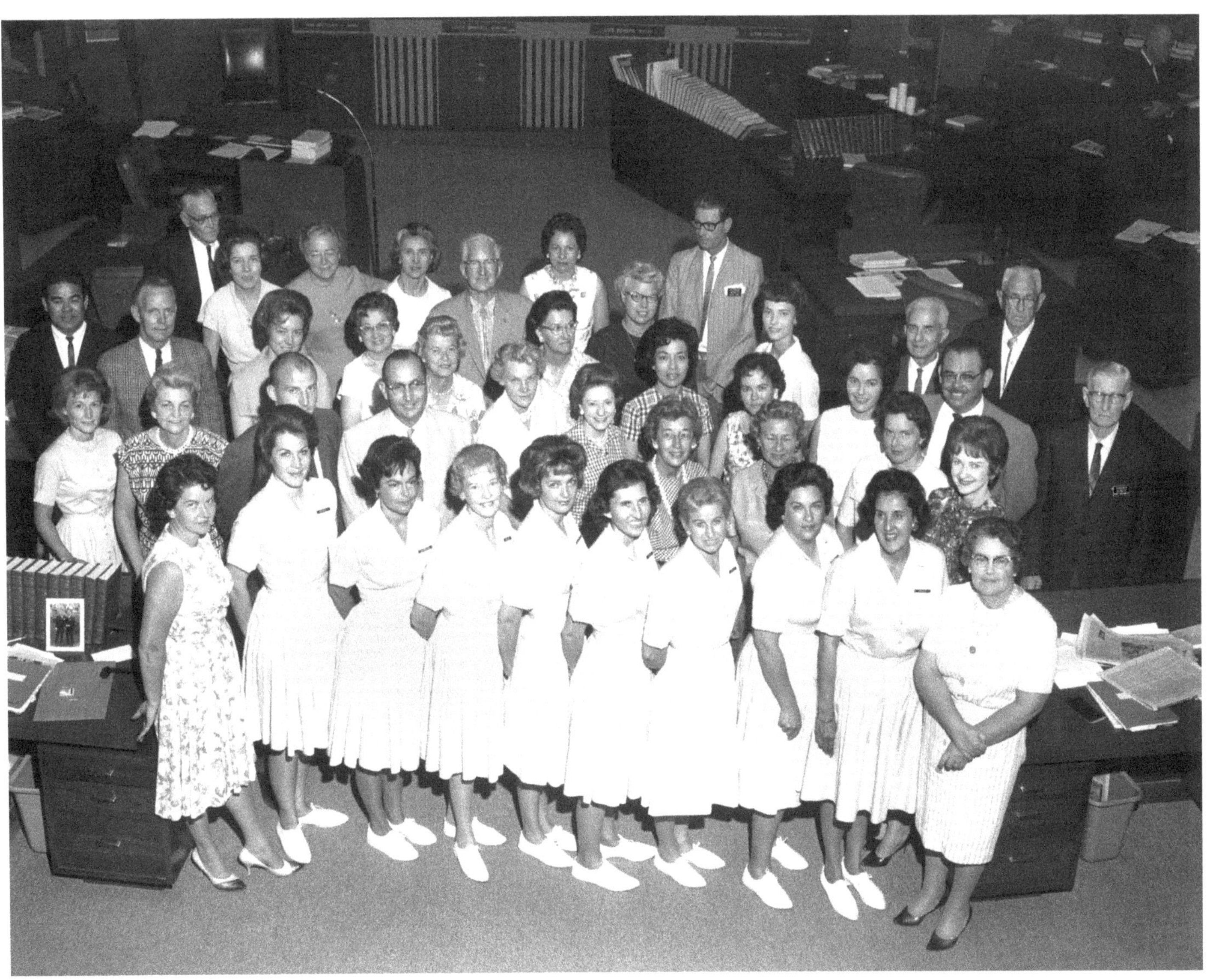

It is believed that the first manually operated electric traffic light was installed in 1882 in Potsdamer Platz in Berlin, Germany. Salt Lake City was the first city to have red-green electric traffic lights in 1912. Five years later Salt Lake City had the first interconnected traffic signal system, connecting several intersections. By the time this 1965 photograph of Van Buren Street at 17th Avenue was taken, traffic lights were common in Phoenix.

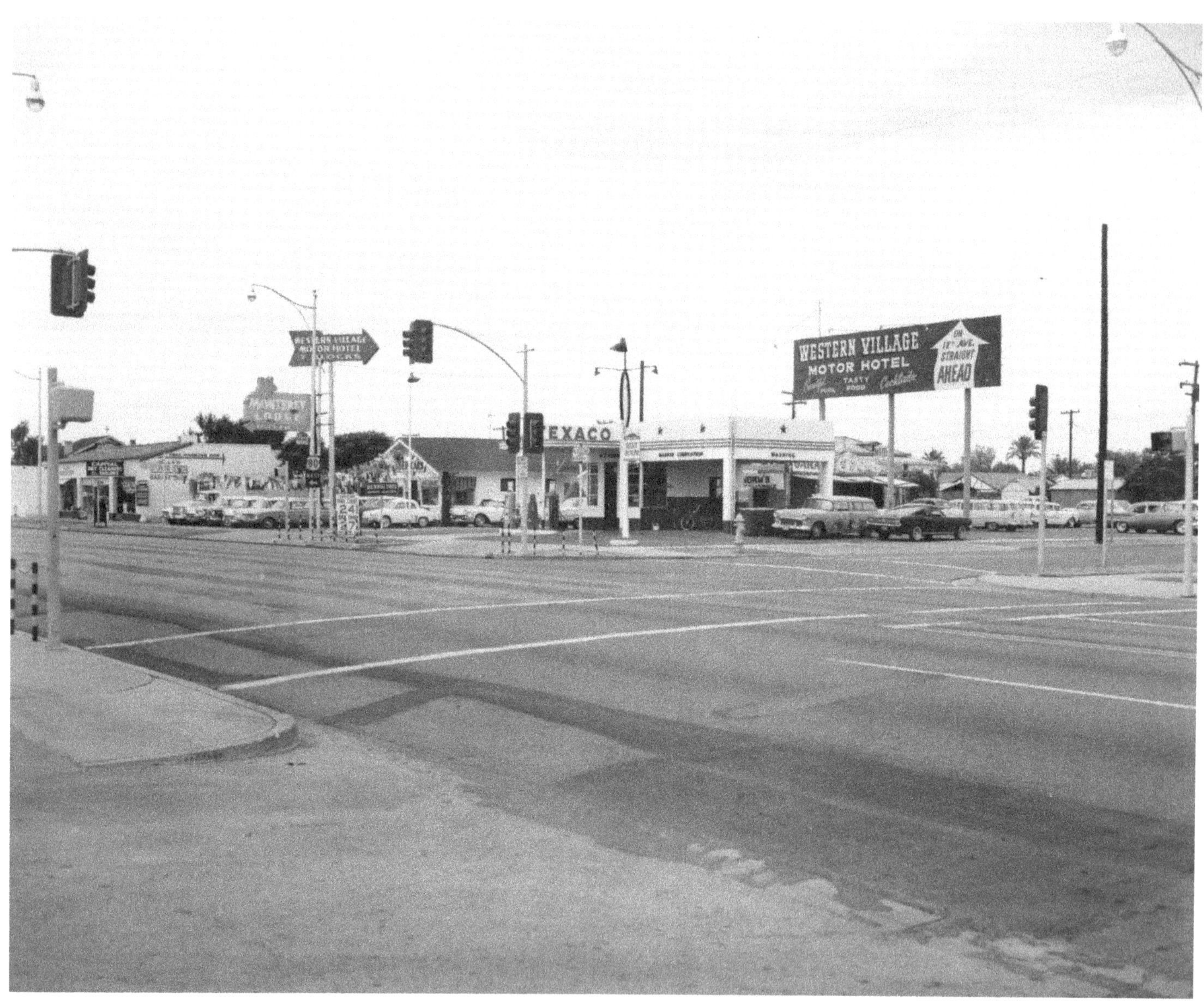

Chefs pause for a photograph of the preparations for a 1963 Christmas party, probably in Phoenix for the Arizona Highway Department.

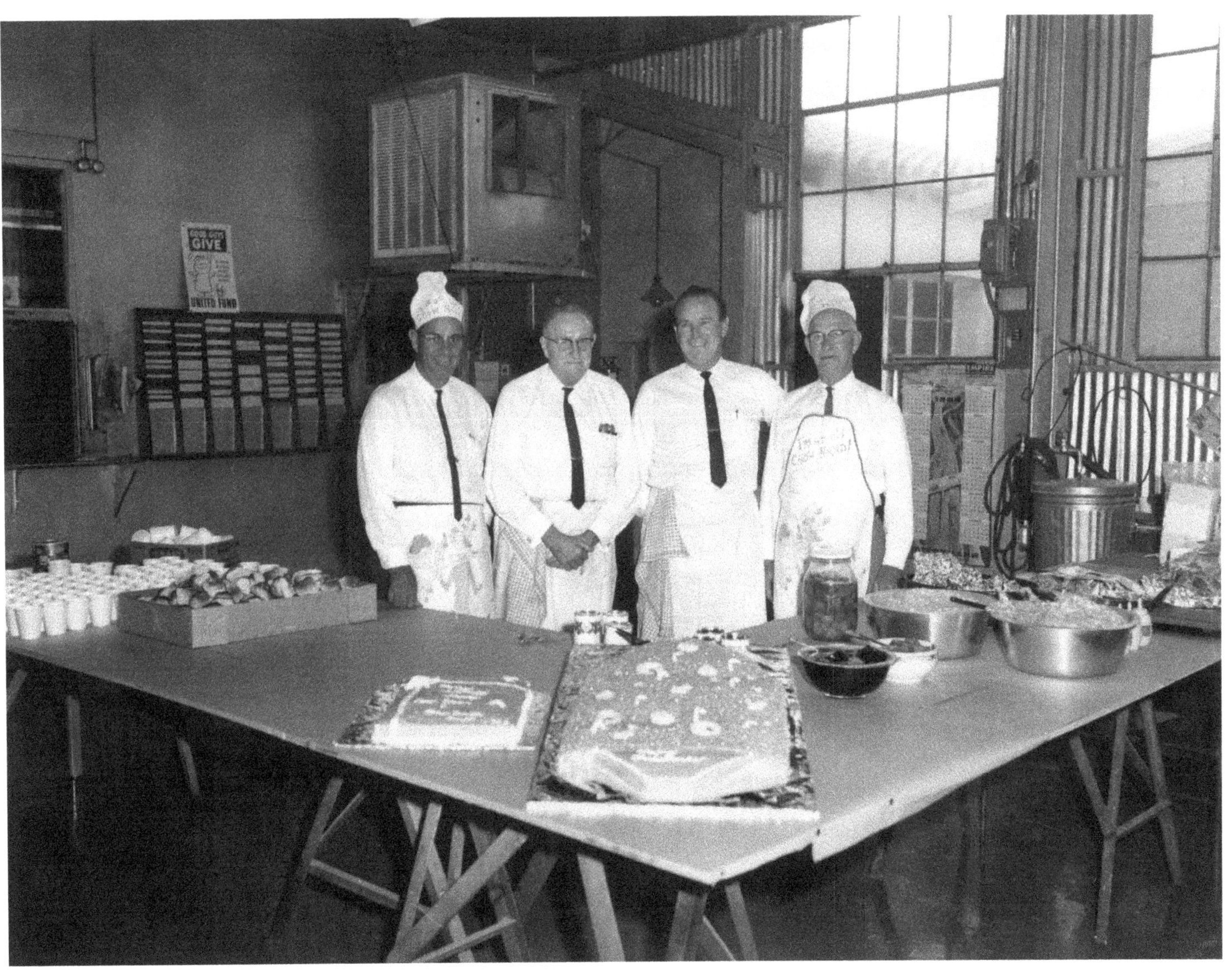

Owing to the rise in highway accidents, the Arizona Highway Department was authorized in 1931 to patrol the highways with one highway patrolman for each of Arizona's 14 counties. Within a year of this 1966 photograph, the governor's crime commission would recommend the creation of the Department of Public Safety to coordinate the work of the highway patrol, the Department of Liquor Licenses and Control, and the Narcotics Division of the Arizona Department of Law.

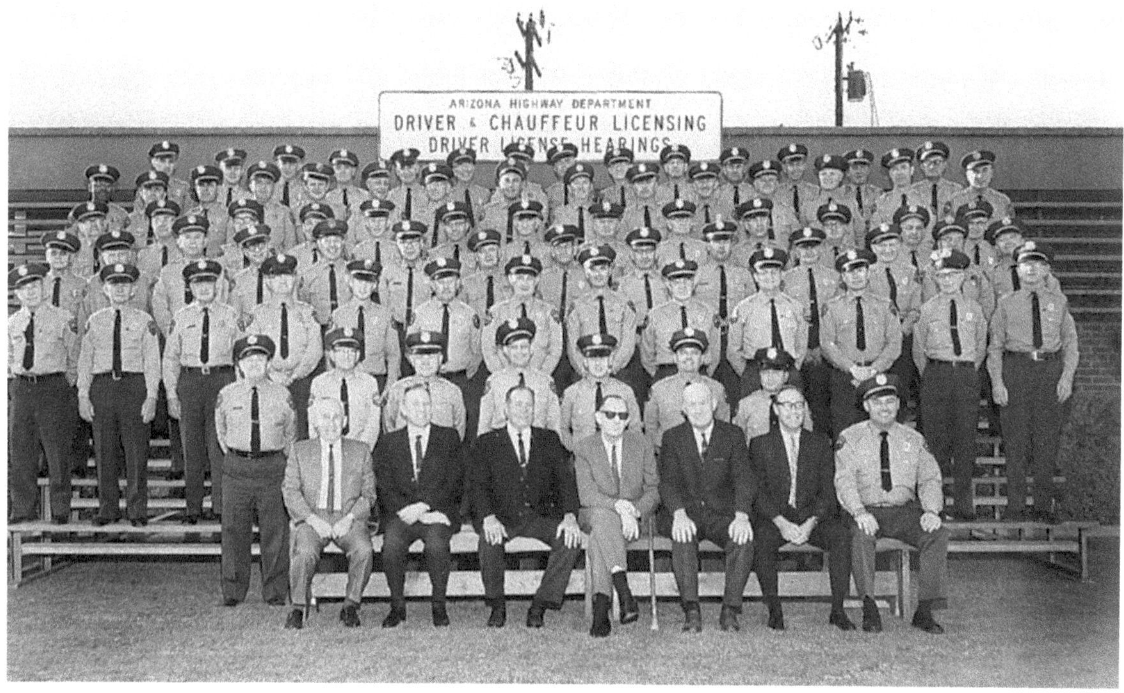

On June 27, 1947, NBC launched the world's first regularly operating television network, serving a few large cities on the East Cost. Within a year the CBS Television Network was formed with 30 affiliate stations. One of them was KPHO, Arizona's oldest television station. By 1955 Arizona had 4 television stations. Shown here, a television cameraman films a report from the governor's meeting held by the Arizona Highway Department in Phoenix in 1966.

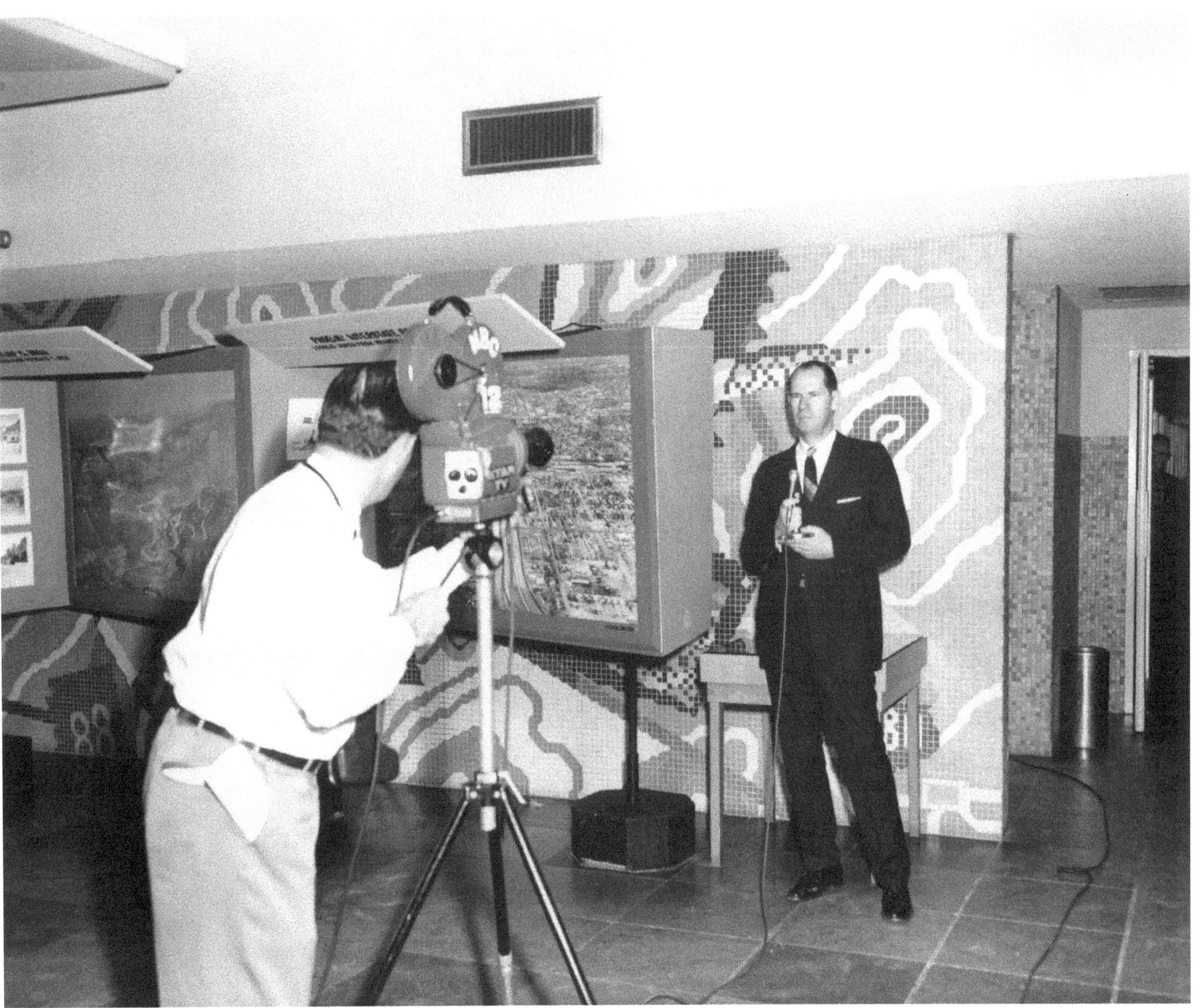

The Phoenix Financial Center was located at Central Avenue and Osborn Avenue, and was home to the Home Savings & Loan Association and the Pioneer Bank of Arizona.

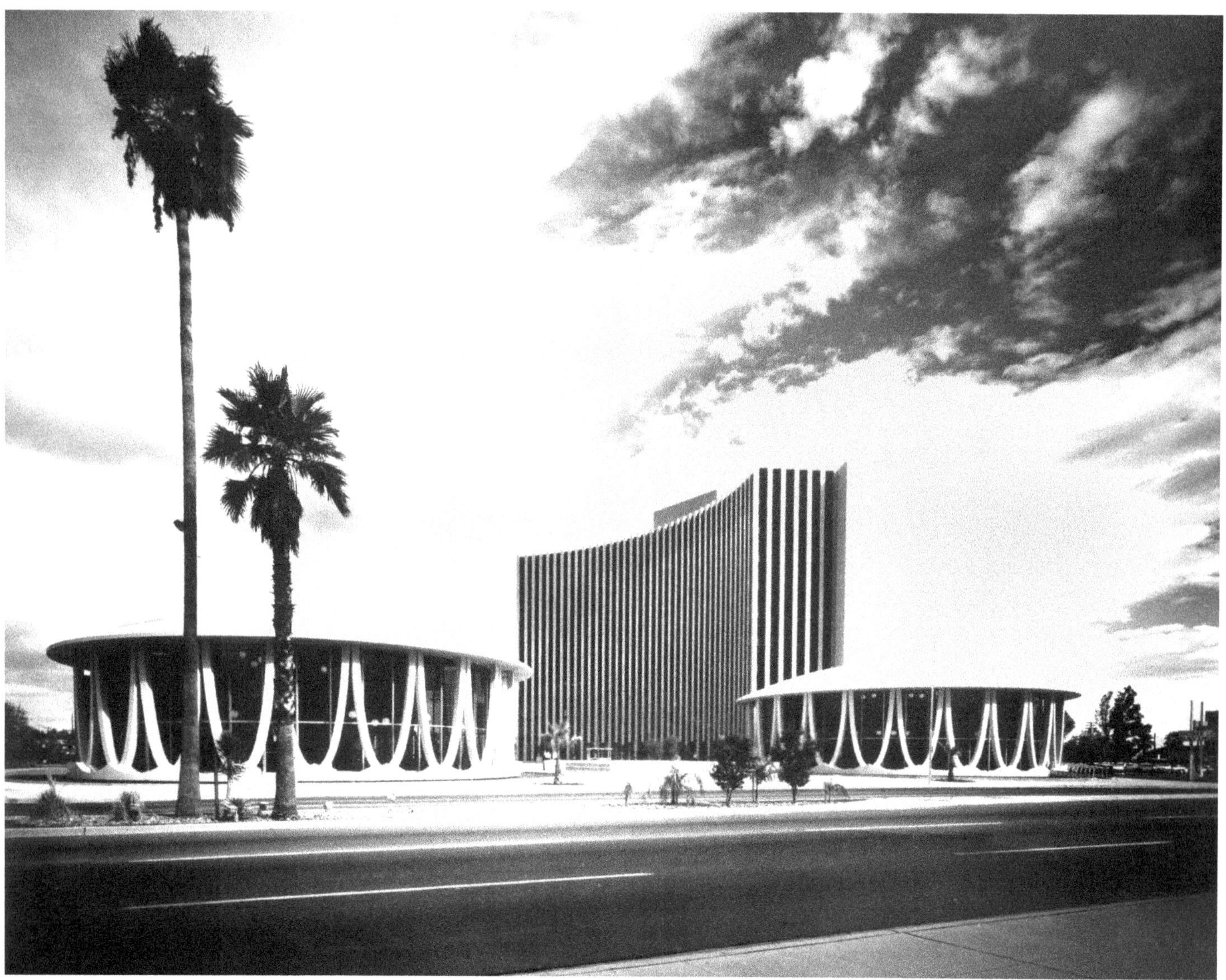

President Eisenhower authorized the construction of the interstate highway system with the 1956 Federal-Aid Highway Act. The southernmost highway, Interstate 10, stretches from California to Florida. The Papago Freeway, the Phoenix leg of I-10, was originally designed to include lanes 100 feet above Central Avenue and "helicoil" ramps that would spiral traffic down to connect with 3rd Avenue, 5th Avenue, and 3rd Street. Opposition to the original design grew as construction started here in 1967.

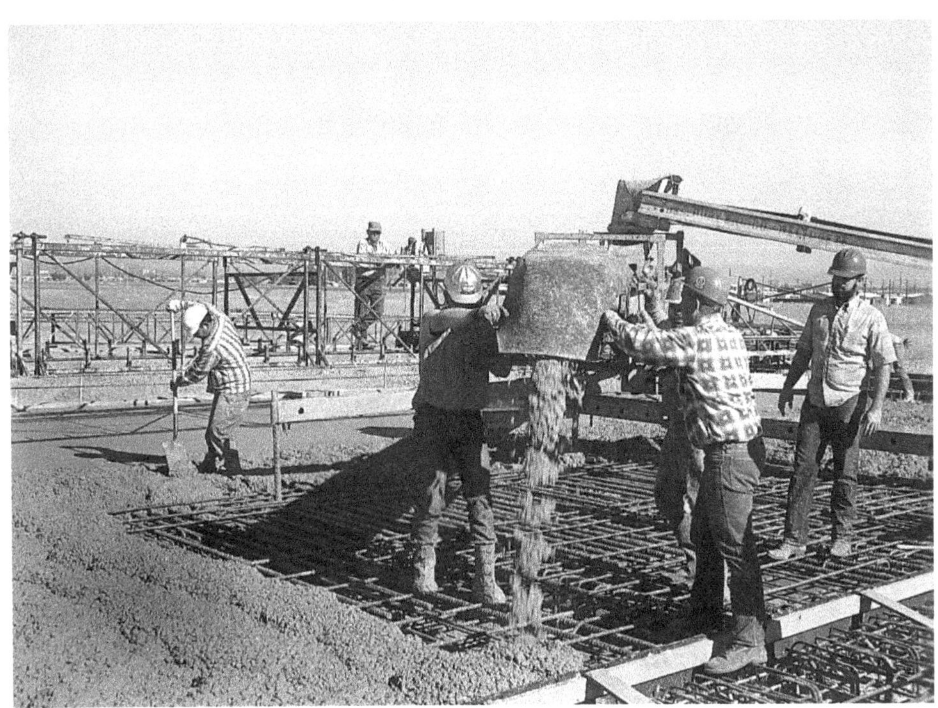

By 1966, the flow of information became so great that managing it became an important role of the Arizona Highway Department. Cutting-edge technology at that time relied on punch cards, magnetic tape, and high-speed line printers for data input and output for mainframe computers.

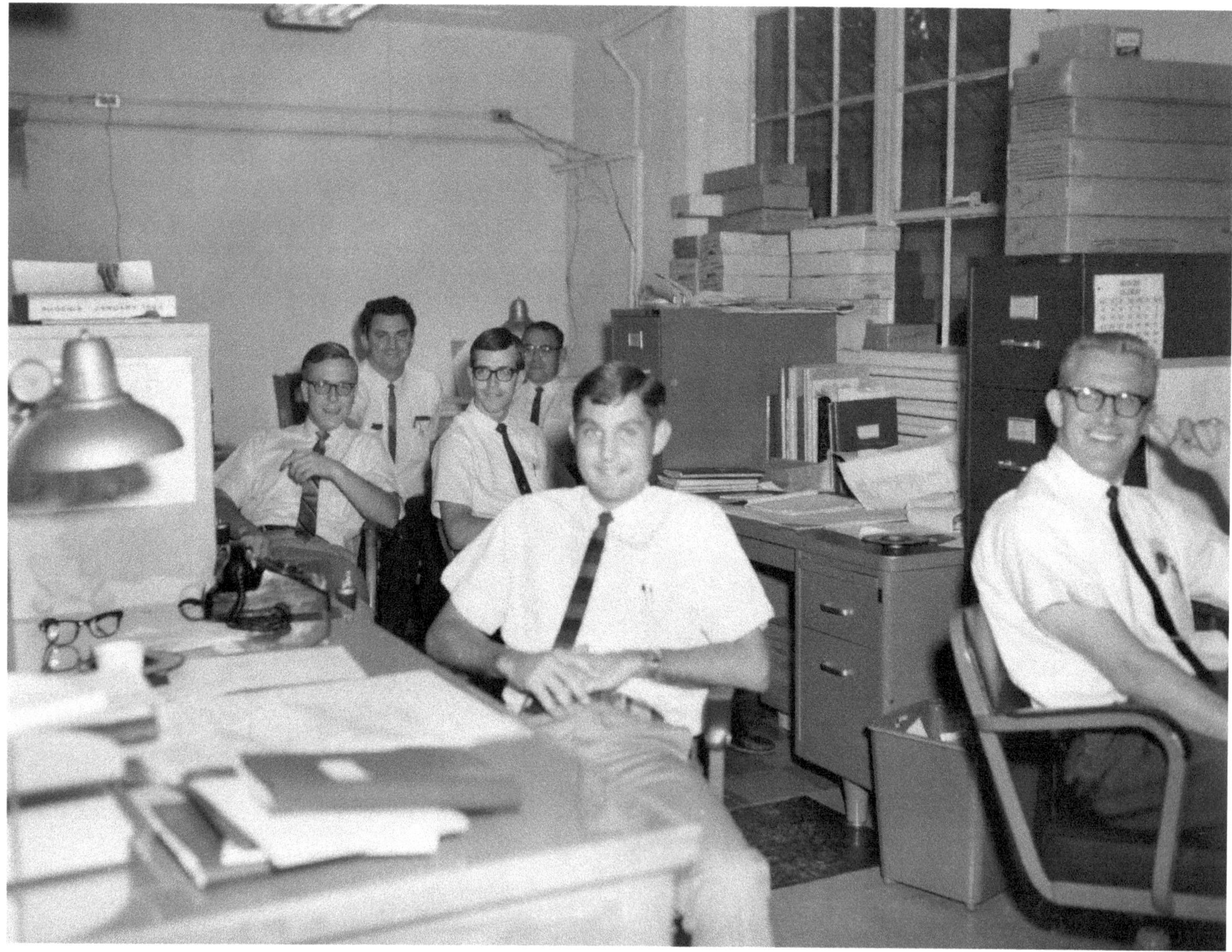

Del Webb's Town House Hotel, pictured at right, was the first hotel to draw customers away from downtown Phoenix, and helped spur the development of uptown Phoenix. Webb is probably best known as the developer of Sun City, Arizona, which was launched January 1, 1960, with five models, a shopping center, recreation center, and golf course. The opening weekend drew 100,000 people and resulted in a *Time* magazine cover story.

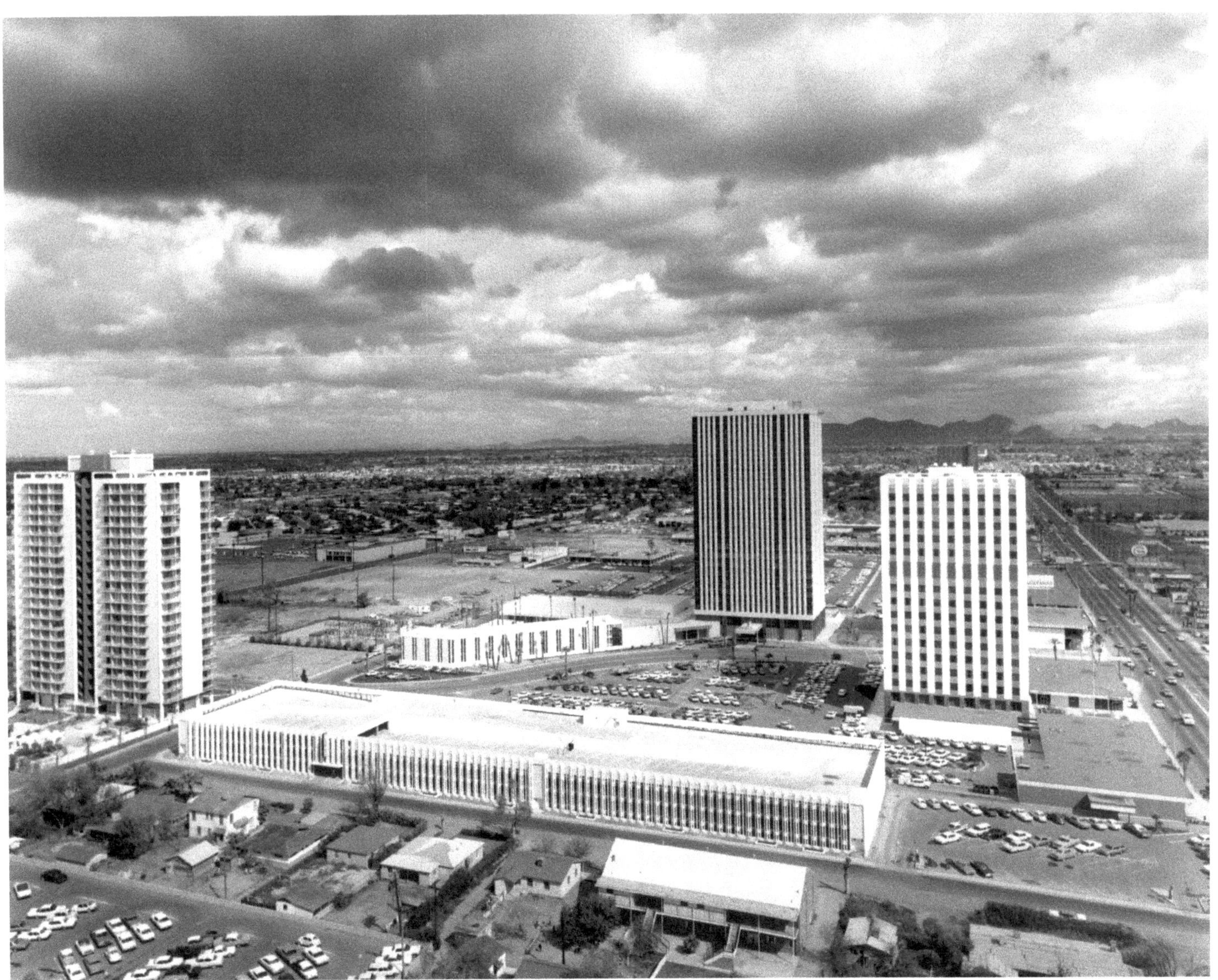

Before the Phoenix Civic Plaza was built, cultural and theatrical events in Phoenix were held in high school auditoriums. In the early 1960s, city developers concluded that the Phoenix metropolitan area would benefit from having an entertainment facility that could accommodate regional and national convention business. The 16.5-acre Civic Plaza was completed in 1972 at a cost of $28 million.

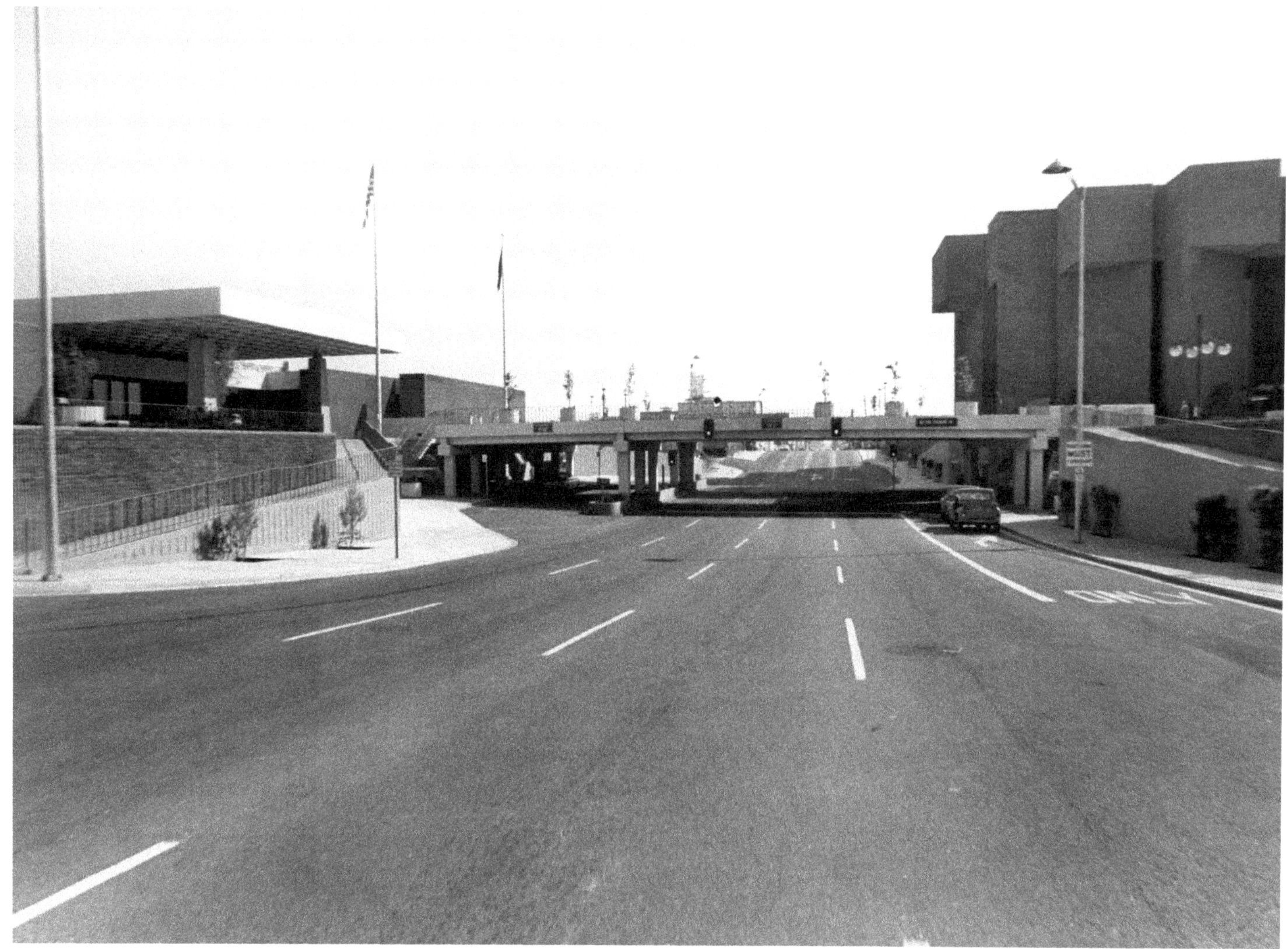

The Phoenix Civic Plaza was host to an automobile trade show in 1974, some seventy years after the first automobile drove into Phoenix as a novelty.

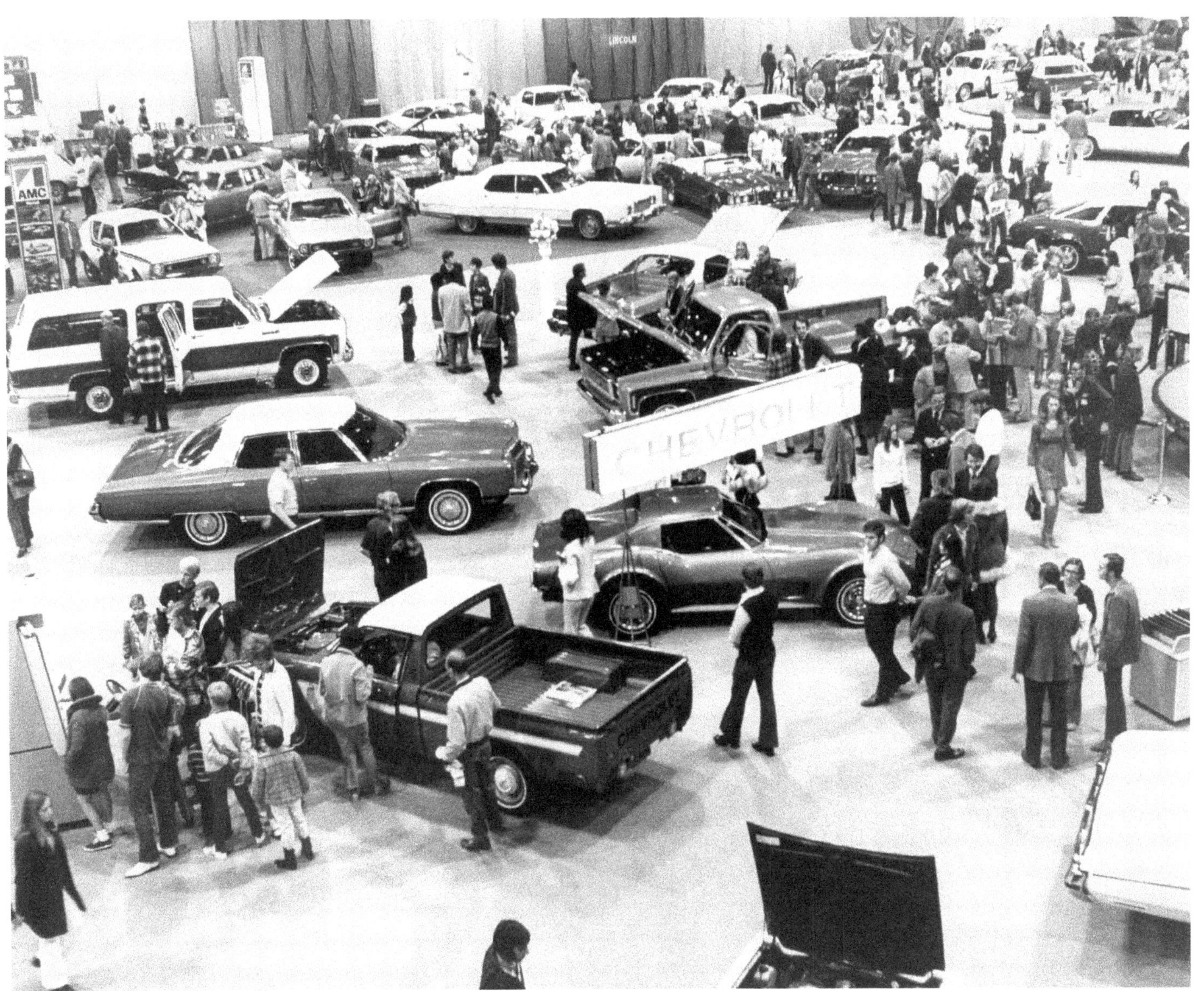

Downtown Phoenix began to be dominated by modern skyscrapers by 1972.

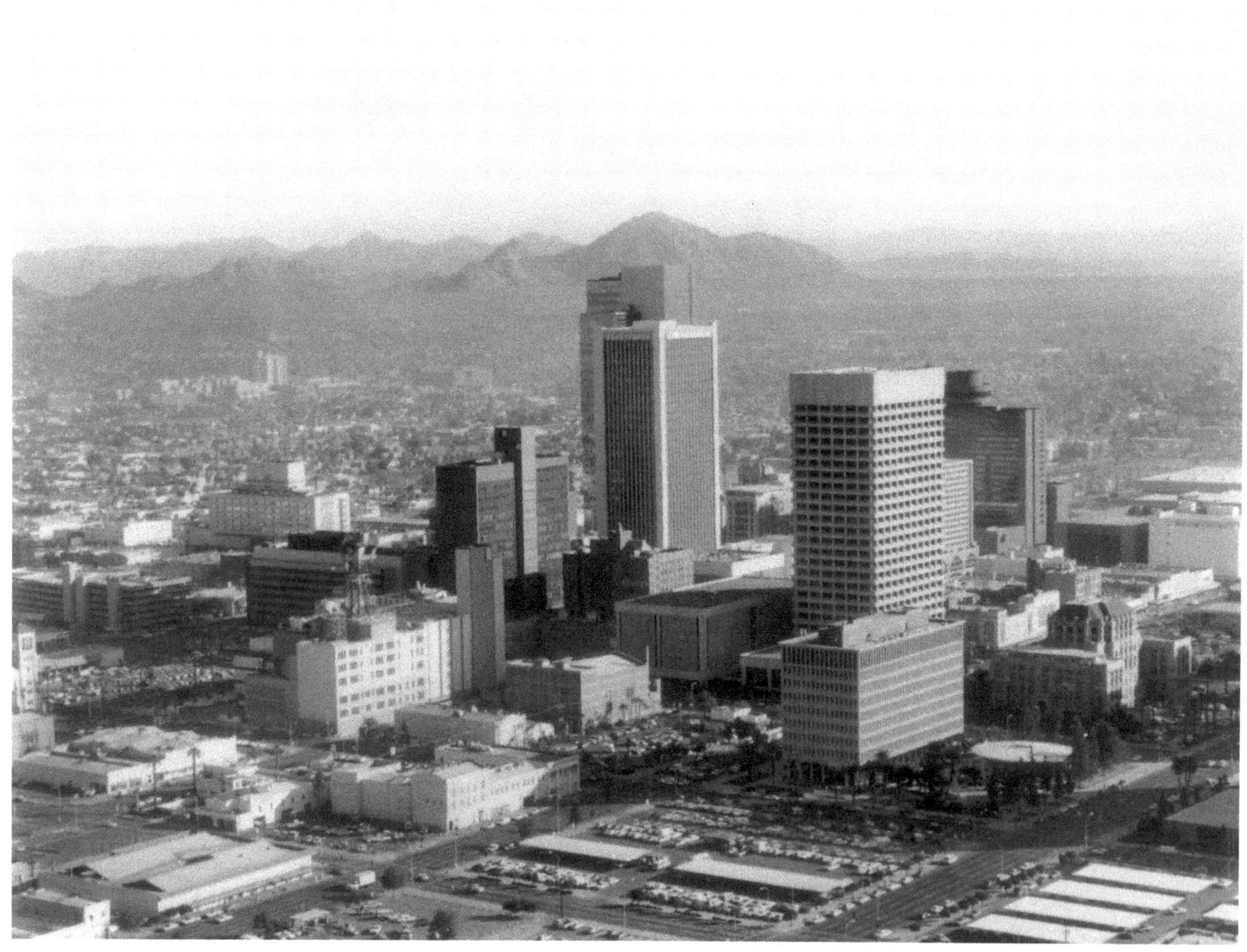

Governor Raúl Castro was the first Mexican American elected governor of Arizona. Born in Mexico, he graduated from the Arizona State Teachers College in Flagstaff. While working for the U.S. State Department, he earned his Juris Doctorate and then practiced law in Tucson. As a Pima County Superior Court Judge, he was known for his compassion and intellect. He served as ambassador to El Salvador, and then to Bolivia, before winning the governorship in 1974.

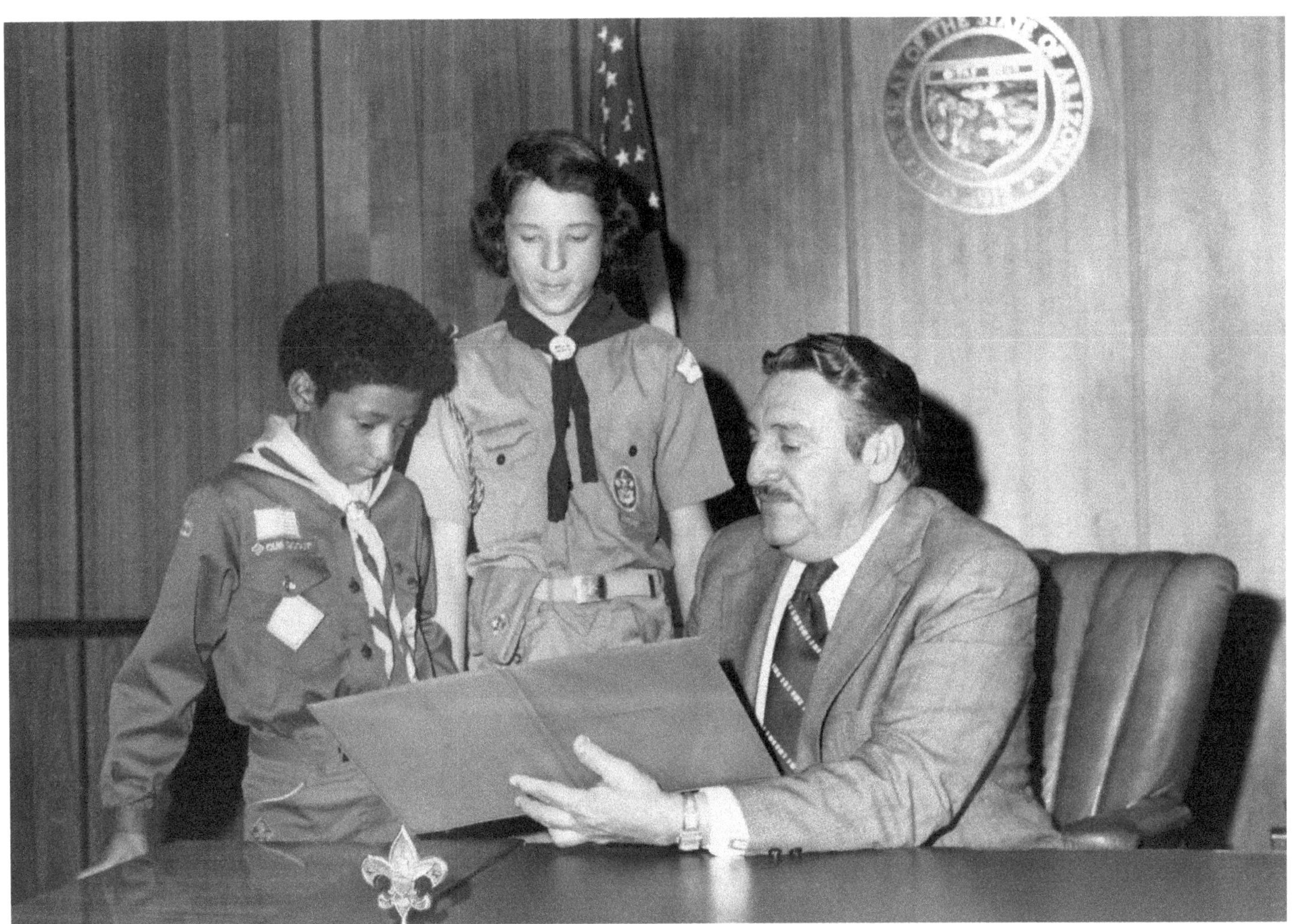

Once the lifeline to the rest of the nation, by 1978, when this photograph of the Santa Fe Railroad Depot in Phoenix was taken, Phoenicians no longer traveled by rail, although railroads continued to be important to Arizona's cattle, citrus, and mining industries.

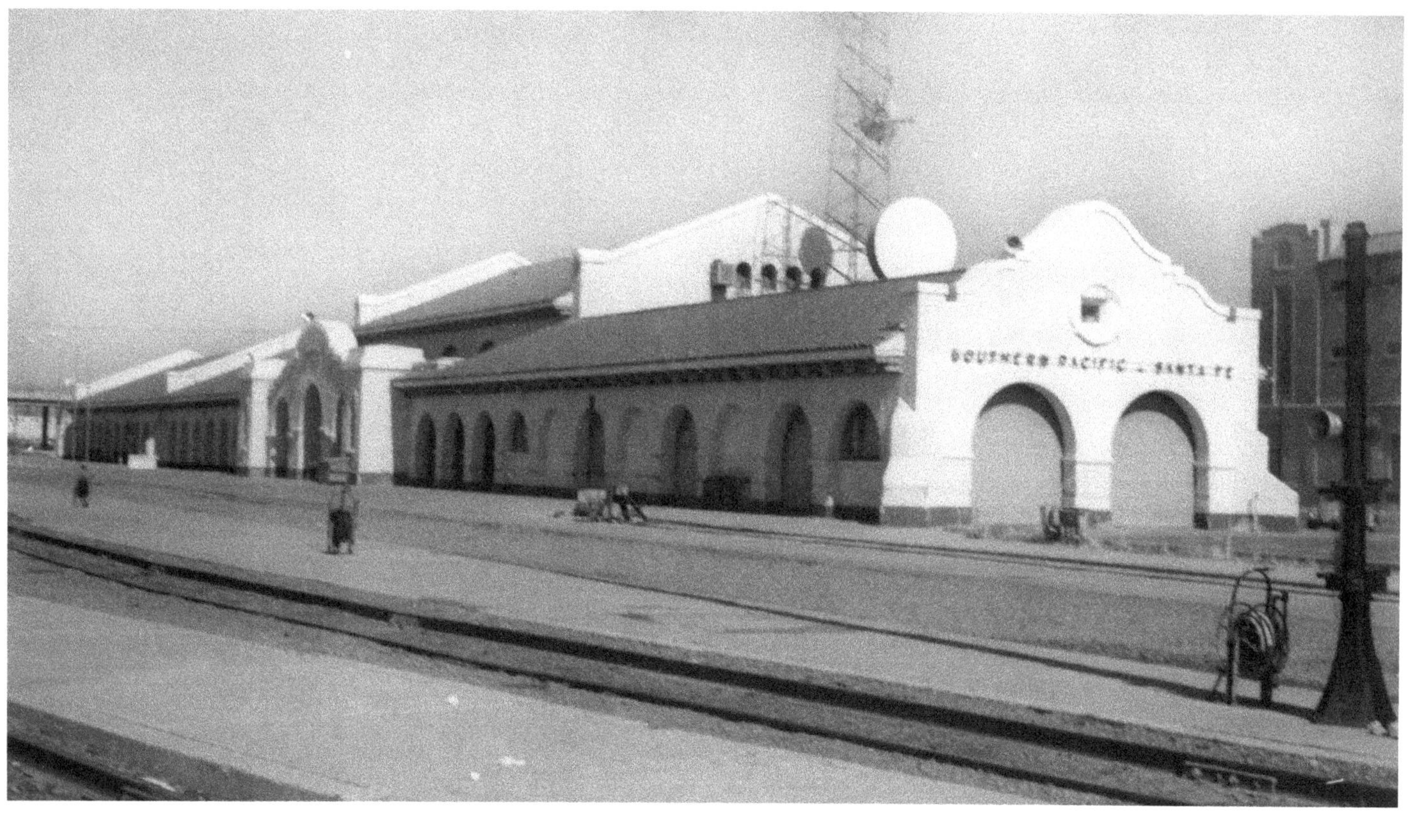

This 1970 photograph shows the addition to the Arizona State Capitol built in 1938, which housed the Supreme Court and the Arizona State Library.

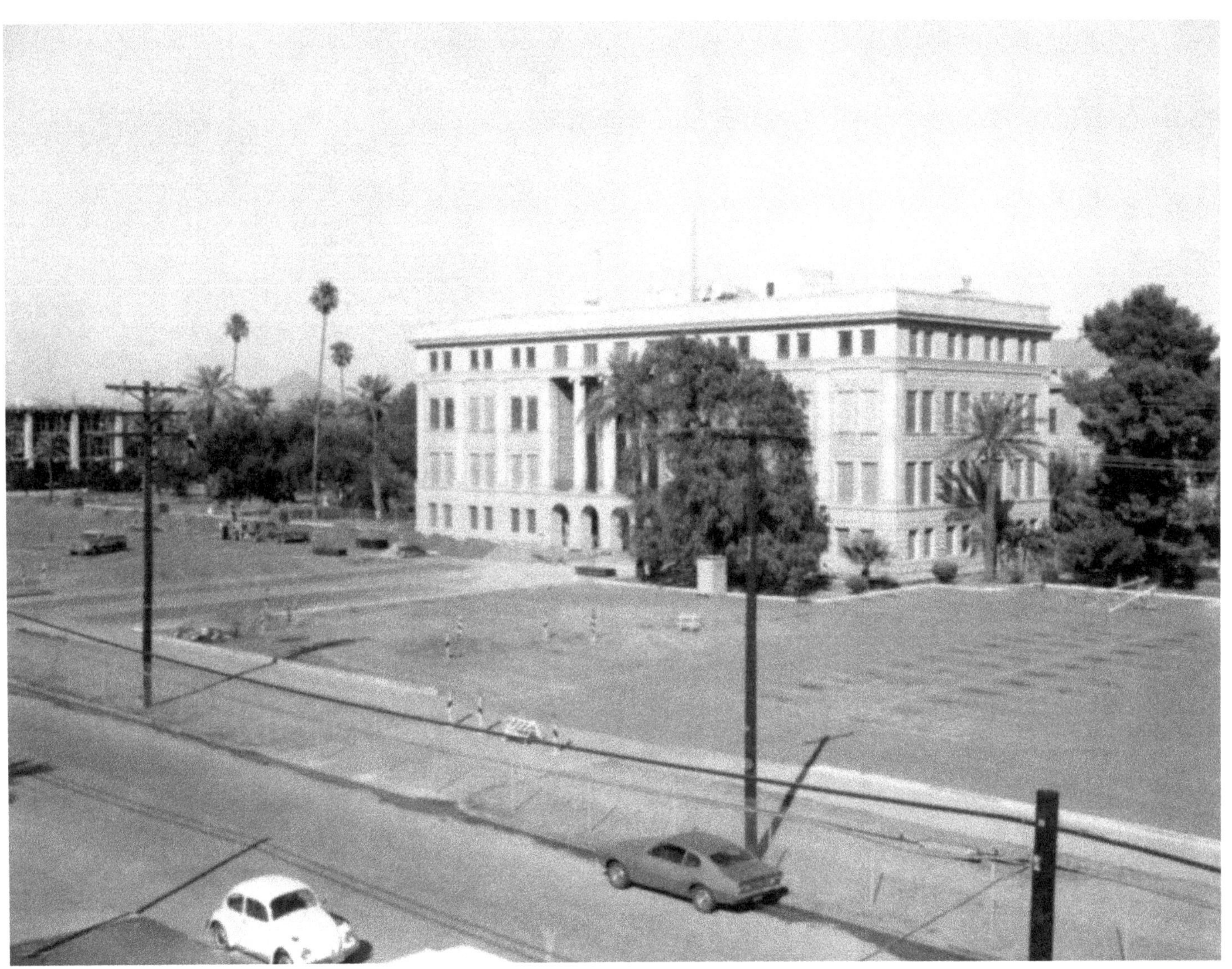

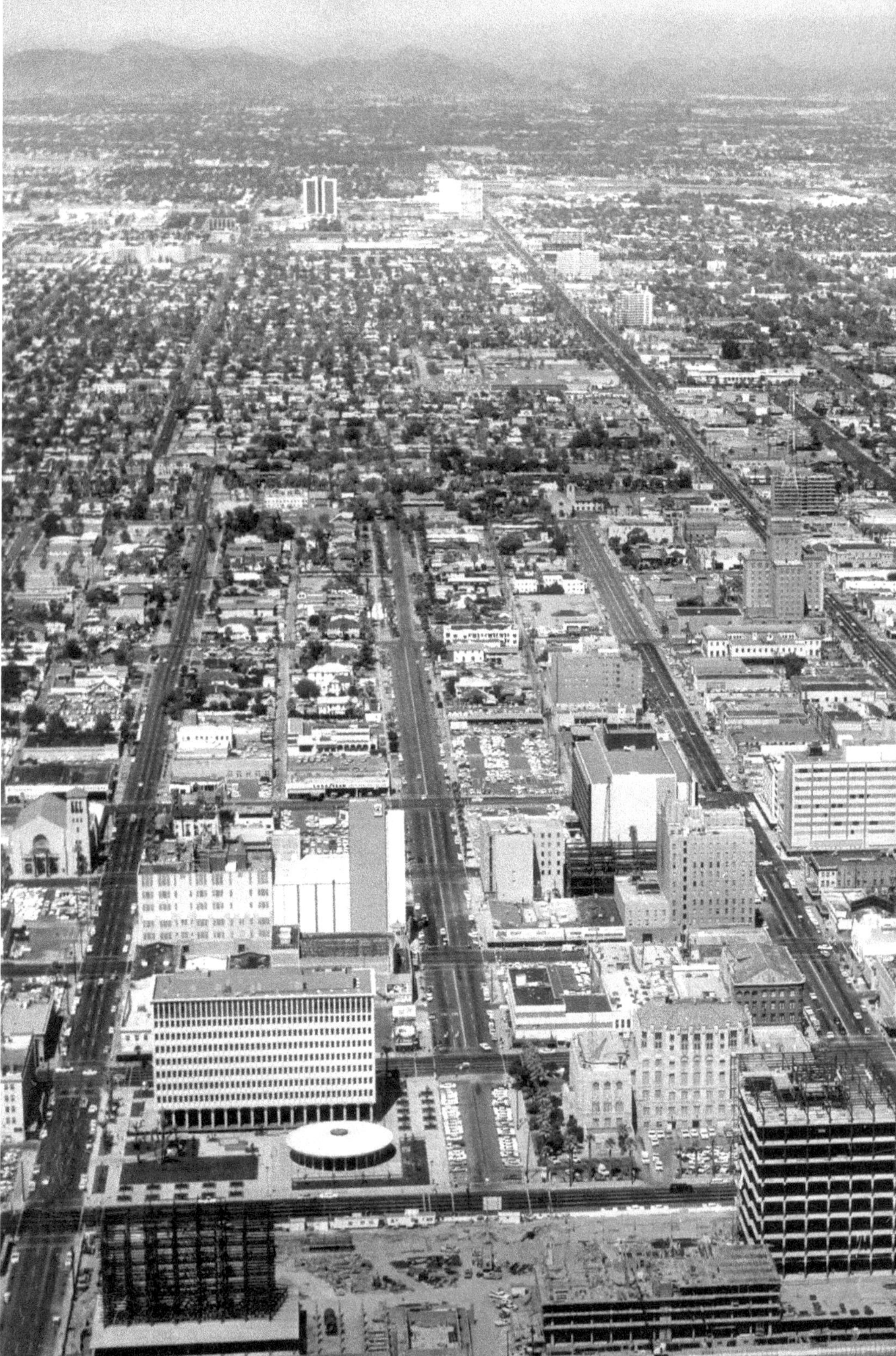

A 1975 aerial view of Phoenix. The city's population had exceeded half a million.

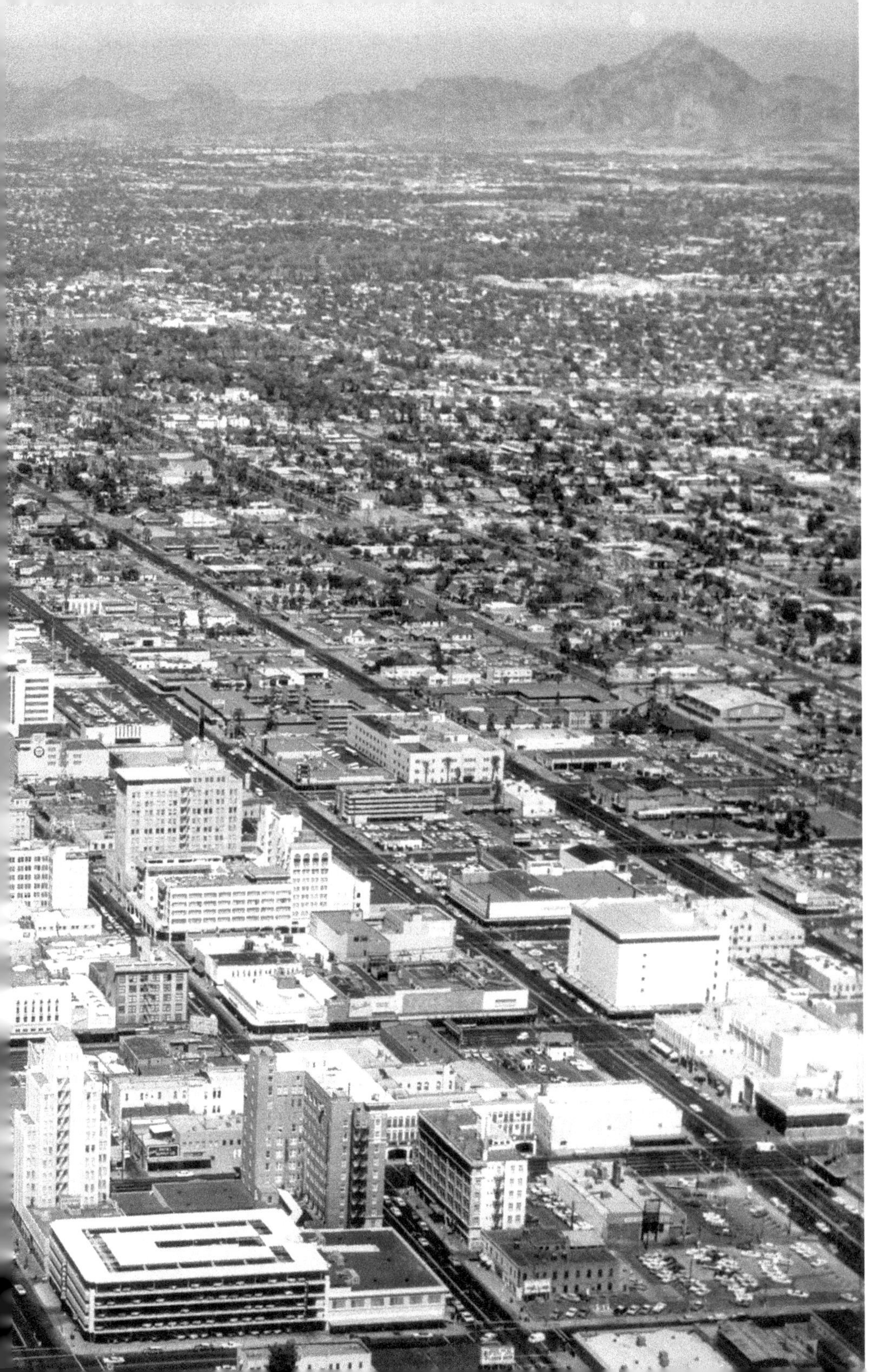

Notes on the Photographs

These notes, listed by page number, attempt to include all aspects known of the photographs. Each of the photographs is identified by the page number, photograph's title or description, photographer and collection, archive, and call or box number when applicable. Although every attempt was made to collect all available data, in some cases complete data was unavailable due to the age and condition of some of the photographs and records.

II **Downtown Phoenix**
Arizona State Library, Archives and Public Records, Archives Division, Phoenix
97-0837

VI **Arizona State Library**
Arizona State Library, Archives and Public Records, Archives Division, Phoenix
95-3858

X **Phoenix Hotel**
Arizona State Library, Archives and Public Records, Archives Division, Phoenix
99-0365a

2 **Dirt Streets**
Arizona State Library, Archives and Public Records, Archives Division, Phoenix
99-0366a

3 **Goldman & Co.**
Arizona State Library, Archives and Public Records, Archives Division, Phoenix
96-1825

4 **Blacksmith Shop**
Arizona State Library, Archives and Public Records, Archives Division, Phoenix
97-7528

5 **Blacksmiths**
Arizona State Library, Archives and Public Records, Archives Division, Phoenix
97-7530

6 **Daily Herald**
Arizona State Library, Archives and Public Records, Archives Division, Phoenix
96-1826

7 **Washington Street**
Arizona State Library, Archives and Public Records, Archives Division, Phoenix
97-0048

8 **Bank Exchange**
Arizona State Library, Archives and Public Records, Archives Division, Phoenix
97-2129

9 **Dressed Up**
Arizona State Library, Archives and Public Records, Archives Division, Phoenix
94-2015

10 **City Hall**
Arizona State Library, Archives and Public Records, Archives Division, Phoenix
98-0463

11 **Centre Street**
Arizona State Library, Archives and Public Records, Archives Division, Phoenix
98-6459

12 **First School**
Arizona State Library, Archives and Public Records, Archives Division, Phoenix
96-3445

13 **Adams Hotel**
Arizona State Library, Archives and Public Records, Archives Division, Phoenix
96-1837

14 **Railroad Depot**
Arizona State Library, Archives and Public Records, Archives Division, Phoenix
96-3315

15 **Churchill Mansion**
Arizona State Library, Archives and Public Records, Archives Division, Phoenix
97-2100

16 **Adams Street**
Arizona State Library, Archives and Public Records, Archives Division, Phoenix
97-2096

18 **Ford Hotel**
Arizona State Library, Archives and Public Records, Archives Division, Phoenix
96-3320

19 **Parade**
Arizona State Library, Archives and Public Records, Archives Division, Phoenix
96-2306

20 Telephone Poles
Arizona State Library, Archives and Public Records, Archives Division, Phoenix
97-2103

21 Centre Street
Arizona State Library, Archives and Public Records, Archives Division, Phoenix
96-1831

22 Lumber Company
Arizona State Library, Archives and Public Records, Archives Division, Phoenix
97-7351

24 Architecture
Arizona State Library, Archives and Public Records, Archives Division, Phoenix
03-1411

25 Goods
Arizona State Library, Archives and Public Records, Archives Division, Phoenix
01-4165

26 Mule-drawn Carriages
Arizona State Library, Archives and Public Records, Archives Division, Phoenix
96-2338

28 Phoenix Hunting Club
Arizona State Library, Archives and Public Records, Archives Division, Phoenix
98-6482

29 Firefighters Parade
Arizona State Library, Archives and Public Records, Archives Division, Phoenix
03-1409

30 Commercial Phones
Arizona State Library, Archives and Public Records, Archives Division, Phoenix
98-6458

32 Thanksgiving Day
Arizona State Library, Archives and Public Records, Archives Division, Phoenix
02-0138

33 Territorial Fair
Arizona State Library, Archives and Public Records, Archives Division, Phoenix
98-6465

34 William Murphy
Arizona State Library, Archives and Public Records, Archives Division, Phoenix
96-4478

36 Insane Asylum
Arizona State Library, Archives and Public Records, Archives Division, Phoenix
97-3453

37 Streetcars
Arizona State Library, Archives and Public Records, Archives Division, Phoenix
97-0013

38 Teachers and Students
Arizona State Library, Archives and Public Records, Archives Division, Phoenix
02-0131

39 Man with Bicycle
Arizona State Library, Archives and Public Records, Archives Division, Phoenix
98-6462

40 City Hall
Arizona State Library, Archives and Public Records, Archives Division, Phoenix
97-1532

42 Ranch-style Home
Arizona State Library, Archives and Public Records, Archives Division, Phoenix
01-2040

43 City Hall
Arizona State Library, Archives and Public Records, Archives Division, Phoenix
96-2303

44 New School
Arizona State Library, Archives and Public Records, Archives Division, Phoenix
97-7096

45 Unpaved Streets
Arizona State Library, Archives and Public Records, Archives Division, Phoenix
97-2108

46 Shirley Christy
Arizona State Library, Archives and Public Records, Archives Division, Phoenix
97-7134

47 State Capitol
Arizona State Library, Archives and Public Records, Archives Division, Phoenix
97-4659

48 John Smith Home
Arizona State Library, Archives and Public Records, Archives Division, Phoenix
97-8482

49 Postmaster
Arizona State Library, Archives and Public Records, Archives Division, Phoenix
97-7043

50 Farmer
Arizona State Library, Archives and Public Records, Archives Division, Phoenix
97-0820

51 County Courthouse
Arizona State Library, Archives and Public Records, Archives Division, Phoenix
95-2854

52 Fire Engine Company
Arizona State Library, Archives and Public Records, Archives Division, Phoenix
96-4427

53 2nd Avenue
Arizona State Library, Archives and Public Records, Archives Division, Phoenix
97-0977

54 Sanatoria
Arizona State Library, Archives and Public Records, Archives Division, Phoenix
96-4033

55 Phoenix Indian School
Arizona State Library, Archives and Public Records, Archives Division, Phoenix
01-8211

56 Sanatorium
Arizona State Library, Archives and Public Records, Archives Division, Phoenix
96-4039

57 Firefighters
Arizona State Library, Archives and Public Records, Archives Division, Phoenix
98-6457

58 Phoenix Bottling
Arizona State Library, Archives and Public Records, Archives Division, Phoenix
98-6479

59 Horseriders
Arizona State Library, Archives and Public Records, Archives Division, Phoenix
03-5814

60 Automobiles
Arizona State Library, Archives and Public Records, Archives Division, Phoenix
96-1829

62 Phoenix Bakery
Arizona State Library, Archives and Public Records, Archives Division, Phoenix
01-4166

63 Flooding
Arizona State Library, Archives and Public Records, Archives Division, Phoenix
97-1581

64 Sisters of Mercy
Arizona State Library, Archives and Public Records, Archives Division, Phoenix
96-4041

65 Flood
Arizona State Library, Archives and Public Records, Archives Division, Phoenix
01-3195

66 Lew Collins
Arizona State Library, Archives and Public Records, Archives Division, Phoenix
97-8048

67 Picnic
Arizona State Library, Archives and Public Records, Archives Division, Phoenix
97-6928

68 School Building
Arizona State Library, Archives and Public Records, Archives Division, Phoenix
01-8202

69 Phoenix Indian School
Arizona State Library, Archives and Public Records, Archives Division, Phoenix
01-8205

70 Territorial Fair
Arizona State Library, Archives and Public Records, Archives Division, Phoenix
97-1760

71 Horse Races
Arizona State Library, Archives and Public Records, Archives Division, Phoenix
97-2524

72 Women's Fashions
Arizona State Library, Archives and Public Records, Archives Division, Phoenix
97-2104

73 President Taft
Arizona State Library, Archives and Public Records, Archives Division, Phoenix
97-0033

74 Postmaster
Arizona State Library, Archives and Public Records, Archives Division, Phoenix
97-7070

75 Adams Hotel
Arizona State Library, Archives and Public Records, Archives Division, Phoenix
97-2154

76 Washington Street
Arizona State Library, Archives and Public Records, Archives Division, Phoenix
97-0006

77 Carnegie Library
Arizona State Library, Archives and Public Records, Archives Division, Phoenix
96-4239

78 Dog Wagon
Arizona State Library, Archives and Public Records, Archives Division, Phoenix
01-3050

79 Westward Ho Hotel
Arizona State Library, Archives and Public Records, Archives Division, Phoenix
97-2137

80 Delivery Boys
Arizona State Library, Archives and Public Records, Archives Division, Phoenix
02-0209

81 First Governor
Arizona State Library, Archives and Public Records, Archives Division, Phoenix
99-1207

82 Governor Hunt
Arizona State Library, Archives and Public Records, Archives Division, Phoenix
01-9034

84 Automobile Racing
Arizona State Library, Archives and Public Records, Archives Division, Phoenix
95-2370

85 State Legislature
Arizona State Library, Archives and Public Records, Archives Division, Phoenix
99-1219

86 High School
Arizona State Library, Archives and Public Records, Archives Division, Phoenix
99-0926

87 Roosevelt Dam
The Library of Congress
LC-USZ62-105191

88 Union Station
Arizona State Library, Archives and Public Records, Archives Division, Phoenix
96-3316

90 Biplane
Arizona State Library, Archives and Public Records, Archives Division, Phoenix
99-9505

91 Hot-air Balloons
Arizona State Library, Archives and Public Records, Archives Division, Phoenix
97-2520

92 Model T
Arizona State Library, Archives and Public Records, Archives Division, Phoenix
96-4452

93 Latest Automobile
Arizona State Library, Archives and Public Records, Archives Division, Phoenix
97-6987

94 Boy on Tricycle
Library of Congress
LC-USF33-013242-M3

96 County Courthouse
Arizona State Library, Archives and Public Records, Archives Division, Phoenix
95-9241

97 Cattle
Arizona State Library, Archives and Public Records, Archives Division, Phoenix
97-1705a

98 Drugstore
Arizona State Library, Archives and Public Records, Archives Division, Phoenix
99-0928

99 Ford Hotel
Arizona State Library, Archives and Public Records, Archives Division, Phoenix
97-2134

100 Boy with Horse
Arizona State Library, Archives and Public Records, Archives Division, Phoenix
98-1397

102 Home Swimming Pool
Arizona State Library, Archives and Public Records, Archives Division, Phoenix
01-3022

103 Arizona Republic
Arizona State Library, Archives and Public Records, Archives Division, Phoenix
98-9903

104 Post Office
Arizona State Library, Archives and Public Records, Archives Division, Phoenix
01-9735

105 Summertime Swim
Arizona State Library, Archives and Public Records, Archives Division, Phoenix
96-2322

106 Women Workers
Arizona State Library, Archives and Public Records, Archives Division, Phoenix
99-9551

107 Phoenix Post Office
Arizona State Library, Archives and Public Records, Archives Division, Phoenix
99-0930

108 Highway Department
Arizona State Library, Archives and Public Records, Archives Division, Phoenix
98-2667

109 Riverside Park
Arizona State Library, Archives and Public Records, Archives Division, Phoenix
99-9533

110 Governor Hunt
Arizona State Library, Archives and Public Records, Archives Division, Phoenix
97-7960

111 Military Airplane
Arizona State Library, Archives and Public Records, Archives Division, Phoenix
01-3488

112 Harry Shea
Arizona State Library, Archives and Public Records, Archives Division, Phoenix
91-2177

113 DH.4A Airmail
Arizona State Library, Archives and Public Records, Archives Division, Phoenix
01-3489

114 Minimum Wage Law
Arizona State Library, Archives and Public Records, Archives Division, Phoenix
00-0200

115 Mowing the Lawn
Arizona State Library, Archives and Public Records, Archives Division, Phoenix
00-0207

116 Phoenix Mountain Park
Arizona State Library, Archives and Public Records, Archives Division, Phoenix
97-0818

117 Dry Movement
Arizona State Library, Archives and Public Records, Archives Division, Phoenix
97-0955

118 Hunt Posing
Arizona State Library, Archives and Public Records, Archives Division, Phoenix
01-2363

119 Hot-air Balloon
Arizona State Library, Archives and Public Records, Archives Division, Phoenix
97-2522

120 Roosevelt Hotel
Arizona State Library, Archives and Public Records, Archives Division, Phoenix
97-2144

121 Governor Hunt
Arizona State Library, Archives and Public Records, Archives Division, Phoenix
01-3524

122 Camelback Mountain
Arizona State Library, Archives and Public Records, Archives Division, Phoenix
97-0810

123 Rough Riders
Arizona State Library, Archives and Public Records, Archives Division, Phoenix
97-7046

124 First Avenue
Arizona State Library, Archives and Public Records, Archives Division, Phoenix
97-0882

125 Water Skiing
Arizona State Library, Archives and Public Records, Archives Division, Phoenix
98-0811

126 New Deal
Arizona State Library, Archives and Public Records, Archives Division, Phoenix
98-0775

127 Go West
Library of Congress
LC-USF34-016615-C

128 First Kindergarten
Arizona State Library, Archives and Public Records, Archives Division, Phoenix
96-1596

130 Chartered Flight
Arizona State Library, Archives and Public Records, Archives Division, Phoenix
01-3637

131 Phoenix Cityscape
Arizona State Library, Archives and Public Records, Archives Division, Phoenix
97-0975

132 Mary Green
Arizona State Library, Archives and Public Records, Archives Division, Phoenix
96-3444

133 Swimming Suits
Arizona State Library, Archives and Public Records, Archives Division, Phoenix
98-0795

134 Children at Trinity
Arizona State Library, Archives and Public Records, Archives Division, Phoenix
98-3349

135 New Swim Suit
Arizona State Library, Archives and Public Records, Archives Division, Phoenix
98-0796

136 Paving Preparation
Arizona State Library, Archives and Public Records, Archives Division, Phoenix
98-3547

137 Paving Streets
Arizona State Library, Archives and Public Records, Archives Division, Phoenix
02-3400

138 Amphitheater
Arizona State Library, Archives and Public Records, Archives Division, Phoenix
98-9830

139 Food Preparation
Arizona State Library, Archives and Public Records, Archives Division, Phoenix
96-1670

140 Meat Cutters
Arizona State Library, Archives and Public Records, Archives Division, Phoenix
98-0577

141 South Mountain Park
Arizona State Library, Archives and Public Records, Archives Division, Phoenix
98-0603

142 Dramatists
Arizona State Library, Archives and Public Records, Archives Division, Phoenix
98-3340

143 Handicrafts
Arizona State Library, Archives and Public Records, Archives Division, Phoenix
98-3346

144 CWA Clerks
Arizona State Library, Archives and Public Records, Archives Division, Phoenix
98-0606

145 Applying Cement
Arizona State Library, Archives and Public Records, Archives Division, Phoenix
98-0588b

146 Baseball
Arizona State Library, Archives and Public Records, Archives Division, Phoenix
98-3452

147 Sprinklers
Arizona State Library, Archives and Public Records, Archives Division, Phoenix
98-1071

148 Baking Bread
Arizona State Library, Archives and Public Records, Archives Division, Phoenix
98-3441

150 Housing Units
Arizona State Library, Archives and Public Records, Archives Division, Phoenix
98-3431

152 Installing Pipes
Arizona State Library, Archives and Public Records, Archives Division, Phoenix
98-2718

153 CWA Working Area
Arizona State Library, Archives and Public Records, Archives Division, Phoenix
98-0616

154 Phoenix Gazette
Arizona State Library, Archives and Public Records, Archives Division, Phoenix
97-7319

155 Carving
Arizona State Library, Archives and Public Records, Archives Division, Phoenix
98-4072

156 Paving East Van Buren
Arizona State Library, Archives and Public Records, Archives Division, Phoenix
98-9984

157 Washington Street
Arizona State Library, Archives and Public Records, Archives Division, Phoenix
97-0853

158 Hospital
Arizona State Library, Archives and Public Records, Archives Division, Phoenix
95-9301

159 Phoenix to Buckeye
Arizona State Library, Archives and Public Records, Archives Division, Phoenix
98-9986

160 State Senators
Arizona State Library, Archives and Public Records, Archives Division, Phoenix
99-0602

162 Cattle
Arizona State Library, Archives and Public Records, Archives Division, Phoenix
97-1718a

163 Streetlamp Posts
Arizona State Library, Archives and Public Records, Archives Division, Phoenix
97-0839

164 Card Catalog
Arizona State Library, Archives and Public Records, Archives Division, Phoenix
95-3857

165 Luhrs Hotel
Arizona State Library, Archives and Public Records, Archives Division, Phoenix
97-0981

166 Advertising Club
Arizona State Library, Archives and Public Records, Archives Division, Phoenix
97-9525

167 Helicopter
Arizona State Library, Archives and Public Records, Archives Division, Phoenix
97-7770

168 Arizona Airways
Arizona State Library, Archives and Public Records, Archives Division, Phoenix
99-0483

169 Baseball Field
Arizona State Library, Archives and Public Records, Archives Division, Phoenix
96-4421

170 Legislative Committee
Arizona State Library, Archives and Public Records, Archives Division, Phoenix
01-2042

172 Bird's-eye Phoenix
Arizona State Library, Archives and Public Records, Archives Division, Phoenix
97-0982

174 Fiesta Del Sol
Arizona State Library, Archives and Public Records, Archives Division, Phoenix
95-9228

175 Covered Wagons
Arizona State Library, Archives and Public Records, Archives Division, Phoenix
95-9223

176 March of Dimes
Arizona State Library, Archives and Public Records, Archives Division, Phoenix
01-9620

178 Valley National Bank
Arizona State Library, Archives and Public Records, Archives Division, Phoenix
97-2153

179 Phoenix Senators
Arizona State Library, Archives and Public Records, Archives Division, Phoenix
96-4423

180 Subdivisions
Arizona State Library, Archives and Public Records, Archives Division, Phoenix
97-0970

181 Fannin Inaugural
Arizona State Library, Archives and Public Records, Archives Division, Phoenix
97-8196

182 Phoenix Memorial
Arizona State Library, Archives and Public Records, Archives Division, Phoenix
98-7100

183 Group of Nurses
Arizona State Library, Archives and Public Records, Archives Division, Phoenix
01-9611

184 Van Buren Street
Arizona State Library, Archives and Public Records, Archives Division, Phoenix
93-0845

185 Christmas Party Chefs
Arizona State Library, Archives and Public Records, Archives Division, Phoenix
02-2501

186 Patrolmen
Arizona State Library, Archives and Public Records, Archives Division, Phoenix
98-6305

187 NBC
Arizona State Library, Archives and Public Records, Archives Division, Phoenix
93-1564

188 Financial Center
Arizona State Library, Archives and Public Records, Archives Division, Phoenix
98-1658

189 Papago Highway
Arizona State Library, Archives and Public Records, Archives Division, Phoenix
98-6338

190 Highway Department
Arizona State Library, Archives and Public Records, Archives Division, Phoenix
93-1713

191 Town House Hotel
Arizona State Library, Archives and Public Records, Archives Division, Phoenix
97-2149

192 Roadway
Arizona State Library, Archives and Public Records, Archives Division, Phoenix
96-4105

193 Phoenix Civic Plaza
Arizona State Library, Archives and Public Records, Archives Division, Phoenix
96-4104

194 Downtown Phoenix
Arizona State Library, Archives and Public Records, Archives Division, Phoenix
97-1656

195 Governor Castro
Arizona State Library, Archives and Public Records, Archives Division, Phoenix
97-7665

196 Railroad Depot
Arizona State Library, Archives and Public Records, Archives Division, Phoenix
97-4014

197 **Arizona State Capitol**
Arizona State Library, Archives and Public Records, Archives Division, Phoenix
97-0943

198 **Aerial View**
Arizona State Library, Archives and Public Records, Archives Division, Phoenix
97-0851

HISTORIC PHOTOS OF PHOENIX

With the coming of the railroad in the late nineteenth century, the town of Phoenix in the Territory of Arizona would experience a rapid inflow of settlers who would call themselves Phoenicians and help to bring about Arizona statehood in 1912.

The images collected in *Historic Photos of Phoenix* offer a remarkable glimpse into the history of this unique desert community. Included among hundreds of photographs are snapshots of the Hotel Adams and Westward Ho, Riverside and South Mountain parks, the Cave Creek Flood of 1905, the Santa Fe Prescott and Phoenix Railway Depot, George Hunt as the first governor of the state of Arizona, the State Capitol, the Phoenix Senators baseball team, Thanksgiving Day 1899, Arizona's Rough Riders, Camelback Mountain, and countless others.

Published in vivid black-and-white, these images communicate the historic events and everyday life of two centuries of people and two centuries of America. *Historic Photos of Phoenix* is sure to captivate anyone curious about the region's past, from the student of history to the local history buff.

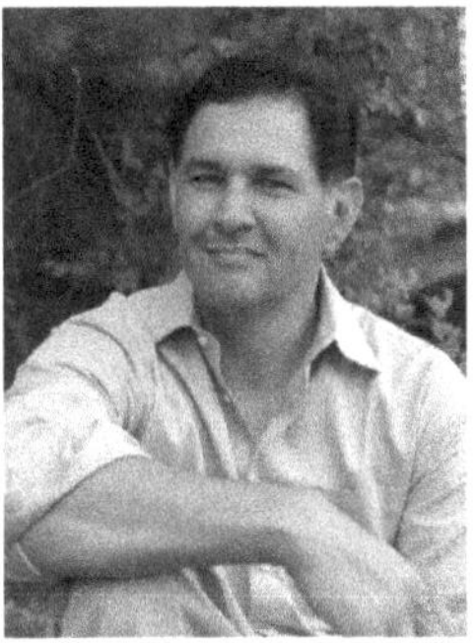

Photo by Carl Vance

Eduardo Obregón Pagán was born and raised in the valley. He received a B.A. from Arizona State University, an M.A. from the University of Arizona, and an A.M. and Ph.D. from Princeton University in U.S. history. Before returning to ASU, Dr. Pagán was a faculty member at Williams College in Massachusetts and a senior program officer at the National Endowment for the Humanities in Washington, D.C.

WWW.TURNERPUBLISHING.COM

www.ingramcontent.com/pod-product-compliance
Lightning Source LLC
LaVergne TN
LVHW060606110826
845154LV00003B/46

9781683369622